Publishing for Libraries

Also by Charles Chadwyck-Healey

Cecil Lubbock: A Short Biography
A Walk along Hadrian's Wall
A Companion to the History of the Book [contributor]
Literature of the Liberation: The French Experience in Print 1944–1946

Publishing for Libraries
At the Dawn of the Digital Age

Charles Chadwyck-Healey

BLOOMSBURY ACADEMIC
LONDON • NEW YORK • OXFORD • NEW DELHI • SYDNEY

BLOOMSBURY ACADEMIC
Bloomsbury Publishing Plc
50 Bedford Square, London, WC1B 3DP, UK
1385 Broadway, New York, NY 10018, USA
29 Earlsfort Terrace, Dublin 2, Ireland

BLOOMSBURY, BLOOMSBURY ACADEMIC and the Diana logo are trademarks
of Bloomsbury Publishing Plc

First published in Great Britain 2020
This paperback edition published in 2021

Copyright © Charles Chadwyck-Healey, 2020

Charles Chadwyck-Healey has asserted his right under the Copyright,
Designs and Patents Act, 1988, to be identified as Author of this work.

Cover design: Eleanor Rose
Cover images © Getty Images

All rights reserved. No part of this publication may be reproduced or transmitted
in any form or by any means, electronic or mechanical, including photocopying,
recording, or any information storage or retrieval system, without prior permission
in writing from the publishers.

Bloomsbury Publishing Plc does not have any control over, or responsibility for,
any third-party websites referred to or in this book. All internet addresses given in this
book were correct at the time of going to press. The author and publisher regret
any inconvenience caused if addresses have changed or sites have ceased to
exist, but can accept no responsibility for any such changes.

A catalogue record for this book is available from the British Library.

A catalog record for this book is available from the Library of Congress.

ISBN: HB: 978-1-3501-2094-5
PB: 978-1-3502-3596-0
ePDF: 978-1-3501-2095-2
eBook: 978-1-3501-2096-9

Typeset by RefineCatch Limited, Bungay, Suffolk

To find out more about our authors and books visit www.bloomsbury.com
and sign up for our newsletters.

In memory of
Hans Fellner

1925–1996

Contents

List of Illustrations ix
Foreword *Peter Fox* x
Preface xiv
List of Acronyms xvii

1   Beginning   1
2   Johnson Reprint Corporation   14
3   Chadwyck-Healey   21
4   Cambridge and Our Own Production   39
5   Official Publications   46
6   Visual Images on Microfilm   73
7   Carving up the Centuries   91
8   The Sanborn Fire Insurance Maps   107
9   Finding the Archives   115
10   The New York Times   125
11   France and Spain   135
12   Black Studies   155
13   The National Security Archive   162
14   The Last Years of Microform   170
15   The Silver Catalyst   185
16   Other Digital Ventures   198
17   *English Poetry*   215
18   *Patrologia Latina*   232

19	*Periodicals Contents Index*	244
20	Publishing Online	256
21	German Literature	268
22	Red Archives	273
23	Towards the End	303
24	The End	322

Appendix 1: History of Microfilm Publishing	331
Appendix 2: Microfilm Technology	341
Notes	349
Index	366

Illustrations

1	Atlantic City, New Jersey. The Cornmarket Press booth at the ALA conference. June 1969.	7
2	London, Carter Lane. Publishers archives in the cellar of the offices of Routledge & Kegan Paul. 1973.	23
3	Teaneck, New Jersey. Peter Kurz in his office at his home. 1977.	26
4	Cambridge. Hans Fellner visits our new office in Bateman Street. 1976.	34
5	Bassingbourn. Mitsuo and Hisaku Nitta at Manor Farm, 1983.	98
6	New York. Bertie Bonnell and Robin Alston at the ALA conference. June 1986.	103
7	Washington, DC, Library of Congress. Presentation of the FSA and HABS microfiche collections. 28 February 1982.	111
8	Paris. Microfilming at the Archives nationales. 1993.	142
9	Alexandria, Virginia. Staff of Chadwyck-Healey Inc. 1989.	183
10	London. Demonstration of the *Guardian* on CD-ROM at the Online Conference. December 1990.	196
11	Munich. IFLA conference, with John Ferguson, Bill Buchanan and Richard Coward. August 1983.	201
12	Cambridge. The editorial office in Cambridge Place. 1994.	221
13	Cambridge. Conference on journals contents pages. December 1990.	246
14	Cambridge. The Quorum. Our new networked office. Spring 1994.	256
15	Manila. Staff at Innodata keying newspapers and books. May 1995.	270
16	Moscow. The official opening of the archives of the Soviet Communist Party. 25 February 1992.	282
17	Moscow. Signing the first agreement for the microfilming of the archives. 17 April 1992.	284
18	New York. Completion of the sale of Chadwyck-Healey to Bell & Howell Information and Learning. 7 October 1999.	328

All photographs taken by the author except for Figure 7, from the Library of Congress, and Figure 17, taken by an unknown person on the author's camera.

Foreword

For many students and academics in the humanities and social sciences in the 1990s and early 2000s, the name Chadwyck-Healey was almost as familiar as that of more mainstream publishers such as Cambridge University Press or Routledge. Although it is now part of the ProQuest family, a Google search for Chadwyck-Healey will produce a list of titles ranging from *Literature Online (LION)* to *Sanborn Fire Insurance Maps* and the *Guardian/Observer Archive*. This book charts the history of the company and Charles Chadwyck-Healey's involvement with publishing from the 1960s until he sold his firm to Bell & Howell in 1999.

My own association with Chadwyck-Healey dates from the mid-1970s when, as a fledgling librarian, I was employed by the fledgling company to examine the catalogues of archives in the faculty and college libraries in Cambridge in the hope of finding some that were of sufficient interest to justify being published on microfilm. This aspect of the project came to naught, but the firm went on to produce the *National Inventory of Documentary Sources* for archives in both the United States and the United Kingdom. Since then I have watched Chadwyck-Healey develop and become a major player on the library scene, and as the director, successively, of two large academic libraries, I have not only been a purchaser of many of its products but have worked with Charles on aspects of national policy for archives and legal deposit. In latter years, Charles has also been a great supporter of Cambridge University Library and not only agreed to my suggestion that he should deposit the archive of the company in the library but also generously paid for an archivist to catalogue it.

Chadwyck-Healey is one of a rare breed of publishers that has largely eschewed publication on paper, a decision made when Charles left the employment of other publishers and branched out on his own. What makes this book so fascinating is its documentation of the progression from an entirely paper-based information environment, through microform and CD-ROM, to the online platforms of today. The company was the brainchild of one man and for much of its history it was he who determined policy. The book describes in detail how decisions came to be made and how some turned out to be hugely successful, but Charles is not afraid to admit how others ended in failure. Far from being a dry company history, the book is enlivened by vignettes of the author's encounters with many of the major figures in libraries and publishing, some of whom became friends, while others were difficult characters to negotiate with, or hard drinkers or, indeed, both.

Charles Chadwyck-Healey was never seriously interested in traditional publishing of monographs or journals. He records how the stupendous vision of the Irish University Press publication of *Nineteenth-Century British Parliamentary Papers* in over 1,000 large-format, beautifully produced volumes in the 1960s aroused his interest in reprint publishing. The IUP project turned out to be vastly over-ambitious, the company went into liquidation and Charles realized that by the 1970s the traditional reprint industry was in decline. On the other hand, the economics of publishing on microfilm were completely different from those of printed books. A book publisher has to print several hundred copies at a considerable cost, and then hope to sell them. With microfilm the break-even point could be as low as the sale of half a dozen sets and, as sales developed, more copies could be produced on demand. Microfilm, however, was – and is – widely disliked by users of libraries and archives, because it is so clumsy to navigate.

The Chadwyck-Healey company was established in 1973 and quickly moved on from microfilm to the more user-friendly microfiche for a project similar to that which had piqued Charles's interest a decade earlier. This was the publication of all 6,000 volumes of nineteenth-century British Parliamentary Papers. The project ran to a staggering 4.2 million pages on 46,000 microfiche, five times the size of the IUP set but occupying a few cabinet drawers rather than the sixty metres of expensive shelf-space required for the IUP set. Once Charles realized that he had a success on his hands, he negotiated to publish the twentieth-century Parliamentary Papers up to 1975, making a combined total of 7.5 million pages on 82,000 microfiche. He then persuaded HMSO to allow him to publish the current Parliamentary Papers on an annual basis. This project continues today under the ProQuest banner as *UK Parliamentary Papers*, an essential online resource for historians.

By the mid-1980s the library world was moving from microform to digital for many of its reference sources, and Charles recognized the opportunities that this new medium offered. In 1989 the company signed an agreement with the Bibliothèque nationale de France to publish the French National Bibliography on CD-ROM. This was followed by other CD-ROM publications such as *English Poetry*, *Palmer's Index to the Times*, and *Periodicals Contents Index*.

But CD-ROMs were a short-lived and interim stage in digital publishing until online access to databases began to take off. They were more popular with users than microforms, but for librarians they were a nightmare. Paper-based library materials are kept on shelves and can be used without any form of technology. Microfilm may not be user friendly, but it is comparatively simple to store and use: the rolls are kept in cabinets and they can be viewed using a reader that employs basic technology that has barely changed for half a century and is easy to maintain. CD-ROMs, on the other hand, were subject to the vagaries of rapidly changing digital technology. I have personal experience of our library buying expensive CD-ROM publications and finding, when a new version of our operating system was released, that the CD-ROMs were no longer compatible and that, having sold its initial print-run, the publisher (not Chadwyck-Healey) was uninterested in producing an updated version for the new platform. This meant either that we had to maintain a computer using the old software or, more realistically, dump the CD-ROM as being no longer usable and accept that we would lose access to its content.

This particular problem was solved with the availability of online databases from the mid-1990s, where libraries pay an annual subscription for access to the content. It is, therefore, incumbent on the publishers to ensure that the databases are compatible with the latest technology. Chadwyck-Healey took advantage of the ability to link databases with, for example, its *Literature Online* (*LION*) publication. This provides full-text access to thousands of literary works with links to a wide range of reference materials, such as the *Oxford English Dictionary*, Oxford Companions series, biographies and works of criticism.

Unlike traditional library materials, where the library owns the material and can decide whether or not to keep it, online resources are subject to a completely different funding model, whereby libraries pay for *access* rather than *ownership*. For those of us in the major research and legal-deposit libraries, this became a source of concern in the 1990s. Library policy was that, once acquired, library materials would for the most part be held indefinitely as a record of the national and international publishing output. A book published in the nineteenth century might be of equal importance to a researcher as one published last year. It did not matter whether or not the publisher still existed, as the book was safely stored in the library. Online databases changed all that. For access to this material, libraries were reliant on the continued existence of the publisher and on that publisher's willingness to continue to provide the service. If the publisher went out of business or found it no longer economical to maintain the database, then potentially all that information could be lost. Libraries and publishers have wrestled with this issue for several decades, and some aspects have now been clarified in most of the major publishing countries by the revision of their legal-deposit regulations to include the deposit of non-print works, as well as by the provision of 'perpetual-access licences' by publishers and the establishment of digital archives in a number of universities and national libraries.

When I first became a librarian in the 1970s, publishing for libraries was simple: books and journals were printed on paper by traditional publishers, they arrived in the library and were catalogued (on cards or in 'guard-books'), they were shelved and made available to readers in the reading rooms and stacks. There were a few microfilms around, but to most of us they were of little significance. Today we take for granted that we will have online access to full-text databases of journal articles, official documents, reference materials and books, not just from within the library building but from wherever we happen to be in the world. The firm of Chadwyck-Healey has played a major role in these developments, and this excellent book records the successes and (rather fewer) failures of its founder in helping to foster that revolution.

Peter Fox
University Librarian Emeritus
University of Cambridge, April 2019

Preface

The purpose of this book is to tell the story of a publisher of reprints, microfilms and CD-ROMs sold to libraries throughout the world, from the 1960s to the end of the century. It also describes how in the final years the physical media were almost entirely replaced by the online delivery of databases to libraries via the Internet.

There are many theoretical books and journal articles, mainly by librarians, about the reprint industry, about microfilms in libraries and about the digital revolution. Much has been written about the conversion of library catalogues, CD-ROMs and the online delivery of databases to libraries. But very little has been written by the publishers themselves. The most notable account is *Edition of One* by Eugene Power, the father of microfilm publishing.[1]

I have been able to write this book that looks back over a period of over fifty years because in 1999 Peter Fox, the Cambridge University Librarian, invited me to deposit the business records of the Chadwyck-Healey group of publishing companies in the university library. He regarded the development of Chadwyck-Healey as mirroring the development of libraries themselves as they embraced each successive publishing medium. He also wanted to preserve the records of a local Cambridge publisher. By this time, I no longer owned the companies and Bell & Howell, the new owner, generously sent over to my home filing cabinets and boxes of papers covering the previous twenty-seven years. It took seven years of organization and indexing before they were ready for deposit in the Department of Manuscripts.

I describe the process of microfilm publishing in some detail in order to demonstrate what a significant publishing medium it once was. It may have appeared to be nothing more than a mechanical copying process that hardly equated with 'real publishing', but I hope that this book will show that finding material to publish on microfilm or microfiche, producing it and selling it was demanding, interesting and enjoyable, and often very profitable. But our branch of publishing was quite separate from trade and academic publishing. Our purpose was to take the publications and archives of the past and republish them in another medium. In the 1950s and 1960s out-of-print material was reprinted in book form. In the 1970s and 1980s much of the same material was republished on microfilm. From the late 1980s we created databases of material of the past by keying or scanning. Newspapers that since the 1950s had been republished on microfilm were now republished on CD-ROM, and then in the 1990s CD-ROMs were replaced by online delivery via the Internet. These new media were regarded by many mainstream book publishers either with disdain or alarm, but for us the coming of each new medium was a licence to start the publishing process all over again. Since then there has been nothing new and it seems that this succession of new media in the last forty years of the last century was a unique occurrence. I was fortunate to be publishing in this sector throughout this exciting period and it is what this book is mainly about.

In the book just over 100 publications are described in varying degrees of detail, but our final catalogue listed 229 print and microform publications and 105 electronic publications. We often called them collections rather than publications because they contained many individually available parts and overall there were thousands of individual titles that libraries could buy. While sales of the older titles fell off after a few years it was this large back catalogue that provided a solid base for our publishing programme.

While 'microform' is the generic word for the two formats we used – microfilm and microfiche – it is still an unfamiliar word and I have used microform and microfilm interchangeably.

Halfway through the book I begin to be addressed as 'Sir Charles Chadwyck-Healey', having previously been Mr. On the death of my father in August 1986 I inherited a baronetcy, which had been awarded in 1919 to my great-grandfather, Charles Chadwyck-Healey, for his founding of the Royal Naval Volunteer Reserve (RNVR), and his membership of the Admiralty Transport Arbitration Board during the First World War. As well as being a successful lawyer, a Queen's Counsel specializing in patent law, he was also an important book collector, an amateur historian and the author of several books.

There are many people to thank, particularly my wife Angela, whose good advice I always relied on and who supported me so faithfully through both the good and the difficult times. She and our three children had to live with a husband and father who was absent for many weeks of each year. With our microfilm production company in a building across the garden I was also someone who, when not away, brought his work home. But I could only publish what we did with the help of many other people and I thank all of them for their remarkable skills and hard work, which enabled us to publish some ground-breaking projects.

I also want to thank Alison Worthington (formerly Moss) who for twenty years played such an important role at Chadwyck-Healey and who, with her husband David, has edited and indexed this book; and Peter Fox, for the reasons given above, and for reading an early draft of part of the book and writing the Foreword.

The book is dedicated to the memory of Hans Fellner, who was an important mentor and friend and without the benefit of whose advice I might not have started my publishing company. Hans died in July 1996. In his affectionate obituary Nicolas Barker writes:

> The survivors of the great diaspora of the Thirties are few now, and Hans Fellner's death has taken one whose special grace and learning were at once typical and unique.[2]

I like to think that Hans's spirit, so grounded in the traditions of European culture and learning, stayed with us in our publishing until the very end.

Charles Chadwyck-Healey
May 2019

Note

The Chadwyck-Healey publishers archive is in the Department of Manuscripts in Cambridge University Library. Any researcher wishing to use it can apply to the library to do so. In the book there are references to both incoming and outgoing letters and internal memos and reports. They can usually be found in the archive under the name of the publication to which they relate. The archive is indexed but at the time of writing the index is not online.

Acronyms

ABELL	*Annual Bibliography of English Language and Literature*
ALA	American Library Association
ARL	Association of Research Libraries
ASLIB	The Association for Information Management
BAN	Russian Academy of Sciences Library
BnF	Bibliothèque nationale de France
CAPP	Central American Papers Project
CAUL	Committee of Australian University Librarians
CHE	Chadwyck-Healey España SL
CHEST	Combined Higher Education Software Team
CHF	Chadwyck-Healey France SA
CHMPS	Chadwyck-Healey Microfilm Publishing Services
CIA	Central Intelligence Agency
CIG	Cambridge Information Group
CIS	Congressional Information Service
COM	computer-output microfiche
CPSU	Communist Party of the Soviet Union
CRL	Center for Research Libraries
CUP	Cambridge University Press
CURL	Consortium of University Research Libraries
DCMS	Department for Culture, Media and Sport; since July 2017, Department for Digital, Culture, Media and Sport
DNH	Department of National Heritage
DTI	Department of Trade and Industry
EDR	Environmental Data Resources
EEBO	*Early English Books Online*
EGPP	Emma Goldman Papers Project
EPA	Environmental Protection Agency
EPO	European Patent Office
ERIC	Environmental Risk Information Center
ERIIS	Environmental Risk Information and Imaging Services
ESTC	*Eighteenth Century Short Title Catalogue*

FOIA	Freedom of Information Act, 1967 (USA)
FSA	Farm Security Administration
HABS	Historic American Buildings Survey
HMSO	Her Majesty's Stationery Office
IDC	Inter-Documentation Company
IFLA	International Federation of Library Associations
II	International Imaging
IRHT	Institut de recherche et d'histoire des textes
ISI	Institute for Scientific Information
IUP	Irish University Press
JISC	Joint Information Systems Committee
LA	Library Association
LIC	Library and Information Commission
LION	*Literature Online*
LISC	Library and Information Services Council
LSE	London School of Economics and Political Science
MARC	MAchine-Readable Cataloging
MCA	Microfilming Corporation of America
MHRA	Modern Humanities Research Association
MIT	Massachusetts Institute of Technology
MLA	Modern Language Association
NCBEL	*New Cambridge Bibliography of English Literature*
NEH	National Endowment for the Humanities
NHPRC	National Historical Publications and Records Commission
NRA	National Register of Archives
NSA	National Security Archive
NSTC	*Nineteenth Century Short Title Catalogue*
NUCMC	*National Union Catalog of Manuscript Collections*
NUKOP	*New Catalogue of UK Official Publications*
NYPL	New York Public Library
OCLC	Ohio College Library Center (now Online Computer Library Center)
OCR	Optical Character Recognition
OUP	Oxford University Press
PA	Publishers Association
PCI	*Periodicals Contents Index*
PLD	*Patrologia Latina Database*
PRO	Public Record Office (now National Archives)

PSM	Primary Source Media
RFE	Radio Free Europe
RL	Radio Liberty
RLG	Research Libraries Group
RSFSR	Russian Soviet Federative Socialist Republic
SAA	Society of American Archivists
SGML	Standard Generalized Markup Language
STR	Space Time Research
TEI	Text Encoding Initiative
THES	*Times Higher Education Supplement*
TLS	*Times Literary Supplement*
TSO	The Stationery Office
UCLA	University of California, Los Angeles
UKOP	*Catalogue of United Kingdom Official Publications*
UMI	University Microfilms International
UPA	University Publications of America
USPTO	US Patent Office
VAT	Value Added Tax
WPA	Works Projects Administration

1

Beginning

In October 1957 the Russians launched Sputnik 1 and I looked for it out of my window at school. As it was only 58 centimetres across, it is unlikely that I saw it. If I saw anything, a mere glint in the night sky, it might have been the much larger last stage of the rocket that propelled it. Short-wave radio hams, on the other hand, easily picked up its haunting signal.

In February 1968 I was summoned to a meeting by Clive Labovitch, the chairman and founder of Cornmarket Press, a publishing company in London for whom I was working. In the 1950s Labovitch and Michael Heseltine, whom he had met at Oxford, had created Cornmarket Press, which published *Man About Town*, the most fashionable men's magazine of its time, and *Management Today*, an entirely new-style glossy business magazine with colour and outstanding design. But the successful partnership ended when Labovitch set off on his own taking with him their very profitable annual, *Directory of Opportunities for Graduates*, which was given free to every student leaving university, with every page paid for by companies advertising for students to apply to them for jobs. This was followed by *Which University?* and several other equally profitable titles. After the parting Heseltine started a new company, Haymarket Press, which grew into the well-known magazine publishing group. Cornmarket Press was making money and the directors wanted to diversify. I had needed a job and I joined the company as a telephone salesman, but I had some management experience and had brought them an idea for making training videos using the new small Sony video cameras that had just come on to the market. Now, Labovitch asked me to look at another new idea, one that had been suggested to his board by the chief librarian of Birmingham Reference Library (since 2013, the Library of Birmingham), one of the largest public libraries in the UK. It was to reprint out-of-print books for libraries. My brother Nicholas had worked for Arnold Fawcus in Paris who published beautiful facsimiles of the books of William Blake, but this kind of reprinting was different. Its utilitarian purpose was to republish for libraries books that were now out of print and could no longer be obtained from antiquarian/second-hand book dealers. The reprints themselves were made by rephotographing the book, with no added introduction and often with the reprint publisher's own name and address overprinted on the original title page. The market for these reprints was libraries, not collectors. They were bound in plain buckram with no jackets because libraries tore them off.

I was given a week to research the idea and report back to the board. I knew immediately that it was what I wanted to do. My family were technical journal publishers, but I had never wanted to work either for the family firm, Morgan Grampian, or in traditional book publishing, which was badly paid and required an ability to understand what people wanted to read that I knew I did not have. I was more interested in finding the books of the past that were needed by libraries, and I also liked the idea of selling to libraries throughout the world, since in the 1960s there were few businesses that sold directly to their overseas customers. Most sold through agents and other intermediaries.

It was years before I understood the connection between the two events. The response in America to the successful launch of Sputnik (which had been within one second of being aborted due to a malfunction in the rocket) was almost one of panic. The USA, the dominant world power in the 1950s, had been overtaken by the Soviet Union, in what came to be known as the 'Space Race'. Mortified, Americans decided that there were several reasons for this, and one of them was the poor state of science education in American schools and colleges. *Life* magazine's cover of 24 March 1958 proclaimed in red letters on a black background, 'Crisis in Education'. Within a year Congress passed the National Defense Education Act, a four-year programme in which billions of dollars were poured into the US education system. It has been described as, 'a telling example of the usefulness of a crisis, real or imagined' and its clever title invoking national security broke down the resistance that there had previously been to the federal funding of higher education.[1] Between 1954 and 1958, following the end of the Korean War, federal funding grew by fifty per cent[2] but in the next two years it quadrupled. In 1960 Clark Kerr, president of the University of California, Berkeley, appeared on the cover of *Time*, facing the challenge of what was described as 'the tidal wave of students'.[3] By 1968 0.25 per cent of US gross domestic product was being spent on research and development in universities and some of this funding went directly into university and college libraries. Many libraries in the USA had suffered from a lack of funding in the Depression and had not been able to buy the books and journals published in that period. While federal funding was intended primarily for the sciences, there was so much money pumped into higher education that, inevitably, some of it overflowed into the humanities and social sciences, and libraries used it to rebuild their collections. In the UK after the Robbins report on higher education in 1963[4] nine new 'plateglass universities'[5] were founded, each with a new library with miles of shelves to be filled with the books and journals of the past. In Germany university libraries were being rebuilt after the destruction of the war and in countries as diverse as Australia and Japan there was new investment in higher education.

Traditionally libraries bought older books and journals from the antiquarian book trade and from backrun specialists who bought and sold runs of journals. Two of the latter were Dawson in the UK and Walter J. Johnson in the USA. But now the demand for these books and journals began to outstrip supply. A backrun journal supplier would find that the run of an important journal was missing some issues. Completeness increased the value of the run and the dealers began to reprint them. They would need permission from the original publisher and would have to pay a royalty and print at least 200 copies, but it was still worth it. This ad hoc reprinting was soon overtaken by the need to reprint the whole run of the journal because there were now no original sets, and gradually there emerged a new kind of publisher that published facsimile reprints of the journals, and later, the books of the past.

Walter J. Johnson, originally an antiquarian bookseller as well as a backrun dealer, had been the founder of one of the world's most important science publishers, Academic Press. He also founded Johnson Reprint Corporation, which reprinted science journals and books, while his rival Hans P. Kraus, one of the greatest antiquarian book dealers of the twentieth century, founded Kraus Reprint Corporation, solely to make money to enable him to buy more antiquarian books. Because Johnson had monopolized most of the science publications Kraus concentrated on the humanities and social sciences. This was an important distinction because in the humanities and social sciences, unlike the sciences where monographs go quickly out of date, the books of the past are as important as the books of the present. Full-size reprints on paper were not the only medium being used to reproduce books and journals. Microfilm, or its more recent alternative, microfiche, were less expensive and more compact. Microfilm were rolls of 35mm film containing miniaturized images of pages. Microfiche were 105 × 148mm sheets of film, each containing a grid of ninety-eight images of pages. Both microforms, to use their generic name, had to be viewed in readers that enlarged the image of each page on a screen. The technology was unsophisticated and while it was liked by librarians for its convenience and compactness, it was disliked by most readers.

A few weeks later I was in the office of Bill Taylor, the chief librarian of the Birmingham Reference Library. Lit only by a table lamp on a winter afternoon, his spacious office was lined with mahogany bookshelves containing some of the treasures of the library. He had explained to the directors of Cornmarket Press that reprint publishing was dominated by American and European firms and he thought that British publishers should also participate. Over tea, he explained to me that the library contained the Shakespeare Library founded in 1864, a collection of thousands of books, many of which were housed in a special Shakespeare Memorial Room. This included a unique collection of acting versions of Shakespeare's plays, editions of the plays published after Shakespeare's death to the end of the nineteenth century, and he proposed that we should reprint them. After Shakespeare's death his plays were considered to be unfashionable and in need of rewriting to conform to current tastes. In 1679 John Dryden wrote of Shakespeare, 'Untaught, unpractis'd in a barbarous age ... the fury of his fancy often transported him beyond the bounds of judgement.'[6] David Garrick, the famous actor and impresario, summed it up in his 'advertisement' at the beginning of his version of *Romeo and Juliet*:

> The Alterations in the following Play are few except in the last act, the Design was to clear the Original as much as possible, from the Jingle and Quibble which were always thought a great Objection to performing it. When this Play was reviv'd two Winters ago, it was generally thought, that the sudden Change of *Romeo's* Love from *Rosaline* to *Juliet* was a Blemish in his Character, and therefore it is to be hop'd that an Alteration in that Particular will be excus'd; the only Merit that is claim'd from it is, that it is done with as little Injury to the Original as possible.[7]

It seems that Shakespeare's profound understanding of human behaviour offended eighteenth-century sensibilities but by the end of the century original texts began to come back into favour and most of the earlier texts were forgotten. They were now red meat for academics looking for a fresh field relating to Shakespeare and the history of English literature and I could see that reprinting them was a good idea. They were also out of copyright so that no permissions were needed or royalties to be paid when we republished them. There was only a fee to be paid to the library that we negotiated with Taylor.

In those visits to the library in 1968 I was experiencing the last few months of the great late nineteenth-century library that the Birmingham city fathers had now decided to pull down. In 1974 it was replaced with a brutalist concrete block on an island surrounded by busy roads, predictably described by Prince Charles as 'a place where books are incinerated not kept'.[8] An unfortunate remark, as an earlier nineteenth-century library had burned down. Even though it was the largest and at times the most visited non-national municipal library in Europe it too was pulled down and replaced with another new library, of glass and steel, which opened in 2013.

Waveney Payne, the librarian responsible for the collection, was friendly and helpful and selected seventy-nine titles published in the period following the Restoration in 1660 to the death of David Garrick in 1779. The books were sent from the library to the printer to be photographed, and no text was added except for the Cornmarket Press name and address, and the publication date. Five hundred copies were printed and bound in a library-quality red buckram with the title blocked in gold on the spine. A few, which we thought might be sold in bookshops, had colourful jackets designed by a friend, Nick Jenkins, at the Royal College of Art. I produced a catalogue, a detailed list of all the books, with an introduction by Payne, and we were soon receiving orders for the complete set at the pre-publication price of £259.

I was now in charge of Cornmarket's reprint division. Our first project was a success and an obvious sequel was a second series. A young academic, H. Neville Davies, chose fifty titles, mainly from the early nineteenth century, enhanced by new introductions written by Davies and his colleagues, and with jackets. Some librarians regarded reprints with disdain because nothing new was added to them and they were expensive. This was because the editions were small, the only buyers being libraries. There were other librarians who preferred reprints to original editions because they were new, were printed on acid-free paper and had strong bindings; original copies often needed rebinding and conservation, both of which were expensive. But in adding introductions and jackets I had misunderstood the market. The introductions were not valued by researchers who simply wanted the original texts and the jackets were torn off as soon as the books arrived in the library.

In June 1968 I had visited the library of the National Maritime Museum in Greenwich. Michael Sanderson, the librarian, agreed to select books on different aspects of naval history and the merchant marine up to the early twentieth century. The fifty books of maritime interest had attractive jackets but no introductions. We had also started work on a collection of books on art history selected by Ronald Lightbown, who at the time was assistant keeper in the metalwork department at the Victoria and Albert Museum and had an encyclopaedic knowledge of the art history books of the past. It included Gustav Friedrich Waagen's descriptions of the contents of English country houses visited during his tours throughout England in the mid-nineteenth century, in eight large volumes, a true forerunner of Pevsner.[9] In our leaflet Roy Strong, director of the National Portrait Gallery at the time, described Waagen's works as 'absolutely essential'. I was beginning to understand the importance of the eminent scholar's 'puff'.

There were now four series of books either already published or in production. I mailed out brochures and received orders ahead of publication. This lay at the heart of the reprint publishing business model. Publishers issued catalogues listing the books that they would reprint, then waited for sufficient orders before going ahead with publication. The delay between announcement and publication could be one or two years and if the response was poor the books would never be reprinted. This was a constant irritation to librarians because once they had placed an order they had to put aside the money to pay for it. It meant that they tied up large sums of money in orders for reprints that never appeared. By 1969 this had become a contention between reprint publishers and librarians. Librarians did not trust publishers and certain reprint publishers were singled out for their unreliability in not publishing the books that they had announced. June was the end of US libraries' budget year and money that they had set aside to pay for reprints could not usually be carried over and so was lost. During the good years of the early and mid-1960s libraries were not so concerned but after 1969 budgets began to tighten and the market for reprints went into a long decline.

June 1969 was also the month of the American Library Association (ALA) conference in Atlantic City and I arranged for Cornmarket Press to take a booth at the accompanying exhibition of publishers and library suppliers. It was a turning point for me. The first library I visited before going to Atlantic City was the University of Massachusetts at Amherst. There I met Siegfried Feller, an old-time bookseller turned bibliographer and acquisition librarian, who immediately recognized my inexperience and patiently explained what libraries like his were looking for and how they chose what books to buy. We stayed in touch until his retirement in the early 1990s. Flying to Atlantic City I sat next to a college librarian who told me that he had a lot of money but not much shelf space, so did I have any small expensive books? I was happy to tell him that the Shakespeare series were slim volumes of around sixty pages and would suit him ideally at $620 a set.

I had been to the USA as a student in 1960 but nothing had prepared me for the Atlantic City Holiday Inn in midsummer. It was an alien place; the food was unappetizing and the metallic sickly smell of the conditioned air in the hotel was unpleasant. In the conference hall, along with several hundred other 'vendors' as the library community called us, I had a 10-foot by 8-foot booth delineated by red nylon drapery hung on a metal frame. It brought home to me that Cornmarket Press was a tiny player in a field that was much larger than I had realized. I found a kindred spirit in a booth

Figure 1 Atlantic City, New Jersey. The Cornmarket Press booth at the ALA conference and exhibition; the Irish University Press booth is next to it. June 1969.

near me. Nico Israel was the young director of a famous Dutch antiquarian bookselling family who had branched out into reprint publishing. Periodically we escaped to have an ice cream, coffee or a meal at an Italian restaurant on the boardwalk, the long promenade by the beach that was the main tourist attraction of pre-casino Atlantic City. Next to my booth was that of the Irish University Press (IUP), which quickly became the reprint publisher that I most wanted to emulate, and which had a significance for my own company's publishing programme ten years later.

In 1962 the Thomson Organisation had bought the Scottish publisher and printer Thomas Nelson for £1.75 million. The heir, Ronnie Nelson, used the money to set up an investment company in Ireland in partnership with an ex-Thomson manager, James McMahon, who had organized the Nelson acquisition. They bought the large Irish printer Cahills and set up a new publishing imprint, IUP. McMahon and a colleague, Martin J. MacManus, knew that there was a rapidly growing demand for reprints from libraries throughout the world, and an academic, T. P. O'Neill, later professor of history at University College, Galway, introduced them to the Fords at the University of Southampton. O'Neill and the Fords suggested that they reprint selected volumes from the nineteenth-century Parliamentary Papers. The fact that the canny reprint publisher, Frank Cass, had already started to reprint individual volumes, encouraged their interest and they bought out his stock and started work on what has been described as, 'one of the most dramatic events in Irish publishing in the twentieth century' and 'the largest and most ambitious reprint publishing project ever undertaken'.[10] The Parliamentary Papers were the single most important source for the history of the United Kingdom and its colonies in the nineteenth century. Known colloquially as Blue Books because of their blue cloth bindings, they are often confused with *Hansard*, which is the daily record of what is said by MPs and lords in the Houses of Parliament. The most important Parliamentary Papers were those of the Royal Commissions set up to enquire into particular subjects, for example slavery, the labour of women and children, gold, the Poor Laws, education, India and the colonies. There were some remarkable contributors to these volumes, which were far from dry and dull. They included Matthew Arnold on education, Anthony Trollope on the Post Office, John Stuart Mill on the East India Company, and scientists and engineers such as Michael Faraday, Charles Babbage, Thomas Telford and Isambard Kingdom Brunel. It is from these voluminous reports with their foldout plans and maps that comes much of what we know about life in the nineteenth century, not only in the UK but throughout the world. Professor Percy Ford and his wife Grace had established the Ford Collection of official publications at the University of Southampton where he was a professor of economics. They had become interested in the Parliamentary Papers as a uniquely important historical source, and at the time there was no one more knowledgeable about the nineteenth-century Parliamentary Papers than the Fords.

It was the sheer ambition of IUP, who approached the publication of this huge series of books on a grand scale, that impressed me most. Originally envisaged as a set of a few hundred volumes, by 1969 it had grown to 1,000 volumes. They had built a £1 million print works in the international business park in the duty-free zone in Shannon on the west coast of Ireland. It was said that they had bought up the world's supply of the very best goatskin to bind the large quarto volumes in quarter leather – the spines and a few inches into the front and back boards were bound in dark green leather, with the rest in dark green buckram. While almost all printers used an artificial gold foil for blocking titles and volume numbers on spines, IUP used real gold. They printed on a beautiful cream antique-laid paper and while few other reprint publishers reprinted anything in colour, IUP was printing coloured foldout maps to provide exact facsimiles of the originals. The publishing team took as much trouble over editorial matters as it did over production. Seamus Cashman, who joined IUP as a young editor, remembers MacManus going through proofs of reprinted volumes page by page.[11] Yet their ambitions led to an unrealistic initial print-run of 2,000 copies when there cannot have been 2,000 libraries in the world who could have bought the set or even one of the eighty subject-based sub-sets. The Irish author Tony Farmar has pointed out that if every copy had been sold, this one series of books would have had sales of £32 million at a time when Penguin's worldwide annual turnover was £7 million.[12] The print-run was later reduced, first to 1,000 and in 1971 to a more realistic 400. Their publicity declared that 'today we are one of the world's major academic presses' and in other advertisements they cited *The Guinness Book of Records*, which called it 'the largest publishing venture ever undertaken'. Yet without such vaulting ambition and the availability of the Nelson money such a project would never have been contemplated.

Launched in 1966 when library budgets were near their peak the IUP initiative caught the imagination of librarians throughout the world. Very few libraries had original sets of the Parliamentary Papers. Many more had the set published by Readex in microprint (see Appendix 1). Librarians were dazzled by the sheer size of the IUP set and were more worried about the shelf-space needed to house 1,000 large volumes than the $60,000 needed to buy them. In the heady days of the 1960s the set was every librarian's dream. Physically imposing, central to the needs of a wide range of scholars in the humanities and social sciences, and hugely expensive at a time when libraries had plenty of money, it was especially desirable. The IUP reprints achieved a public profile unequalled by any other reprint project. When a set was presented to the Librarian of Congress, the Irish ambassador was present but when in 1972 Ronald Reagan, then governor of California, discovered that the publicly funded University of California system had bought seven sets at a total cost of $350,000, it became a political scandal.[13] Almost the only exception on the West Coast was Stanford University Library, which not only had an original set of the Parliamentary Papers but had the foremost expert in the USA on British official publications, W. David Rozkuszka, whom later I got to know well. He knew that in terms of the number of volumes the IUP reprint was only fifteen per cent of the Parliamentary Papers of the nineteenth century and he refused to buy it. The Fords would have maintained that their fifteen per cent included all the most important papers but the other eighty-five per cent was also important for any scholar doing serious research.

I returned from Atlantic City wanting to create an enterprise like IUP. I persuaded Labovitch and the managing director, Peter Cooper, to visit them. The three of us flew to Shannon only to be told that we had arrived a day early and that MacManus, the managing director, could not see us until the next day. I had not made the arrangements, but it was still an embarrassment. For me the visit the next day was a revelation. The industrial scale of the operation was overwhelming. The smell of the leather in the bindery, the beautiful paper, the colour printing of the foldout maps, all suggested a vision entirely at odds with the rest of the utilitarian reprint industry. In the end IUP proved to be a grand enterprise that could only survive while libraries had excessive money, and when library budgets were cut back at the beginning of the 1970s, the money ran out. In December 1971 IUP was bought by William Stern, a property developer who was trying to diversify, but in June 1974 his company, Wilstar Securities, went into voluntary liquidation, taking IUP with it. Farmar writes, 'Like a dandelion seed head, once blown apart IUP was the source of a multitude of successors',[14] and I was one of them because the IUP vision stayed with me for the rest of my publishing career.

I approached Robin Jeffs, an acquaintance from my time at Oxford, who was now a lecturer in the history department at the University of Sheffield. I told him of my dream of a grand publishing project and found that he too wanted to prove himself by undertaking a large-scale scholarly publishing venture. He explained to me that during the English Revolution in the 1640s over 1,000 books and pamphlets had been produced, the majority of which could only be found in the largest libraries. He proposed that we should reprint every book and pamphlet published at this time, grouped by subject, with scholarly introductions. We planned a series of 1,000 volumes entitled *The English Revolution*, and while this was met by a somewhat uncomprehending response from my directors, they gave me permission to proceed.

We established a distinguished editorial board including Gerald Aylmer, professor of history at the University of York, George Potter, recently retired professor of history at the University of Sheffield, Ivan Roots at the University of Exeter, and Pauline Gregg who had written biographies of Charles I and Oliver Cromwell. Christopher Hill, the Master of Balliol College and the leading Marxist historian, was an advisor. We met periodically for weekends at a hotel in Sheffield and Cornmarket Press paid all the expenses. We also paid Jeffs well for his time and expertise. He divided the series into groups of publications, the first being thirty-five volumes of Fast Sermons, which were monthly sermons preached to the Long Parliament from 1642 to 1649. Their importance had been recognized by Hugh Trevor-Roper and others as a vehicle for declaring long-term political aims and shifts in policy. Jenkins designed a distinctive binding style in black and tan buckram, even though using two different coloured cloths added to the production costs. Jeffs commissioned introductions and wrote some himself. We were both excited about the project and confident that it would be successful, and there were frequent visits to Sheffield, staying with Jeffs and his Icelandic wife Maia in their comfortable villa in the middle of the city. At Cornmarket Press I now had an assistant as well as a secretary and we moved quickly, considering our limited resources. Just nine months after first acquaintance with IUP in June 1969 we sent out a prospectus on *The English Revolution* to 600 libraries and historians. Soon after we were ready to send out sales brochures and the first volumes were already in production. I then became ill with infectious hepatitis, and was away from work for six weeks, the longest period of illness that I have ever had. When I came back I found that in my absence Cooper, the managing director, had woken up to the fact that we had embarked on an expensive project with no clear indications of how much revenue it would generate or how long it would take to complete. He asked me to delay our first mailing, which I felt was a mistake as we would miss the end of the summer selling season, so I ignored him and let the mailing go. After a short discussion I was sacked.

If the climate at Cornmarket Press had cooled, so had the US library market. In 1970 the relationship between the federal government and universities began to deteriorate because of the polarity of views on the war in Vietnam. A librarian told me later that in her opinion the Kent State Massacre in May 1970, in which four students were killed and nine injured by Ohio National Guardsmen who opened fire on a peaceful demonstration against the bombing in Cambodia, was the point at which students and their universities lost the support of both government and mainstream America. The largesse of the 1960s had evaporated. Library budgets were cut, and increasingly librarians felt that they had bought enough reprints. Most of the obvious holes in their collections had been filled and they could afford to be much more selective. I had also made some fundamental errors in the conception and operation of *The English Revolution*. It is unwise to run a business that your board of directors do not understand, because they will blame you if anything goes wrong. I had received no guidance from them but nor had I asked for it. We should not have been paying Jeffs and his colleagues generous stipends to do original research, or burdening the project with expensive editorial weekends, but the biggest mistake was to be bewitched by IUP and not recognize the vulnerability of publishing one single, very large project, which covered just ten years of British history.

At Cornmarket my direct boss was Philip Kogan, who was publishing director on a part-time basis since he spent two days a week on his own newly founded publishing company, Kogan Page. He had chosen not to associate himself too closely with my publishing activities, so when the differences between Cooper and me led to my dismissal, Kogan's position was that of a mildly concerned onlooker. But he put me in touch with Roger Farrand, a senior editor at Academic Press in London, which led to me getting my next job.

After I left, Cornmarket Press did publish the Fast Sermons and started to publish a further seven series, but a few years later the whole company went into liquidation when one of the banks who had lent them money recalled their loan. Labovitch went on to start other publishing enterprises but died in 1994 at the age of sixty-two. Jeffs was hit hard by the failure of *The English Revolution*. His marriage had already ended, and he was drinking heavily, beset by demons that prevented him from being the very fine historian that he could have been. The university and his department did everything they could to support him, but he was on a self-destructive journey. The last time I saw him was in the 1980s in the bar of a hotel in Hammersmith where I was attending a conference and he was staying. He died in 1985 at the age of fifty-two.

2

Johnson Reprint Corporation

The origins of Academic Press, one of the world's leading science publishers, and its associated companies, Johnson Reprint Corporation and Walter J. Johnson, lay in Leipzig, the centre of German publishing, in the first years of the twentieth century.[1] In 1906 Leo Jolowicz, who owned Gustav Fock, a large international antiquarian book and periodical dealer, founded Akademische Verlagsgesellschaft. Jolowicz had a son, Walter, and an older son-in-law, Kurt Jacoby, both of whom worked for him, and they had built up the company into a very successful science publisher, only equalled in Germany by Springer. As early as 1933 Walter and Jacoby wanted to move the company to London but the financial loss for Leo, who was by then retired, would have been too great and he refused to do so. In the late 1930s the Nazis seized the publishing company and both the younger men were sent to concentration camps. They were able to buy their way out, and at the beginning of the war travelled in separate, extraordinary journeys round the world – through Russia to Japan, where Maruzen, the local agent, helped them, then to Cuba, finally arriving in New York with their wives and children in 1941. Walter was thirty-three and Kurt sixteen years older. Leo was unable to get an exit visa and died in 1941. Walter changed his surname from Jolowicz to Johnson and together the two men founded Academic Press and, following in the Fock tradition, also founded Walter J. Johnson, a book and journal dealer, and in 1944 Johnson Reprint Corporation. After America entered the war there was a need to acquire both German scientific journals and those from occupied countries such as the Netherlands and France. Single copies were obtained through neutral countries and were photographed, reprinted and distributed to universities in the USA. Academic Press was able to participate in some of this reprinting of both journals and books, and at the end of the war, with so much of the German publishing industry destroyed and with the advances in science and technology resulting from the war, there were huge opportunities for the new publishers. Because of their war work Academic Press also had the advantage of generous paper quotas in the post-war period when paper was rationed, and with Jacoby as editorial director and Johnson handling business and finance the companies grew very quickly.

I was interviewed by Johnson in the palatial offices of Academic Press in Berkeley Square, London. He was heavily built, with a dark complexion, a guttural voice and a strong German accent. With his swept-back silver hair and beetling eyebrows he was intimidating but he seemed to like me and offered me a job as an editor for Johnson Reprint Corporation to work in the Academic Press offices in London. He explained that he wanted my experience in reprinting older out-of-copyright books on which no royalties needed to be paid. He had been paying royalties to publishers for too long because all the early reprint publishers concentrated on reprinting twentieth-century monographs and reference books, which were more important to libraries than earlier, more specialized out-of-copyright books. What he did not say was that most of the important nineteenth- and twentieth-century books had already been republished and he was having to go back to the seventeenth and eighteenth centuries to find books that libraries might want and did not already have. But even the most important of these books would not sell as many copies as the twentieth-century books he had been reprinting for the previous twenty-five years.

Academic Press in London was run by Charles Hutt, one of the leading science publishers of his generation. Johnson had interviewed me when Hutt was on holiday and presented my arrival in his office as a fait accompli. Hutt was not pleased. Barbara Wheeler, his secretary, helped me choose my desk, chair and colour of the curtains and the carpet in my office, and he then sent the bills to New York to demonstrate what an expensive liability I was going to be. Fortunately, Johnson paid no attention.

I joined Johnson Reprint Corporation on 1 September 1970, working on my own and reporting to the editor in New York, Lloyd M. Scott, whom I met when I flew to New York a few weeks later. The company shared offices with Academic Press at 111 Fifth Avenue, near Greenwich Village and New York University. The editorial staff worked in one large room surrounded by shelves of the books that had been reprinted, together with catalogues and bibliographies. A communicating door led to Johnson's office but was locked on his side. If we wanted to visit him we had to go through his secretary's office; if he wanted to visit us he burst through the communicating door, usually in a cloud of rage, waving a competitor's brochure, demanding in his guttural voice, 'Why aren't we publishing this?' Having to respond to this wasted an enormous amount of time.

The main culprit was an enterprising New York reprint publisher called AMS, originally Abraham's Magazine Service, run by Gabriel 'Gabe' Hornstein. He reprinted three-decker novels and other standard works of the nineteenth and early twentieth centuries, books that were not hard to find in the original and had often already been reprinted by someone else. But they were successful, and when I visited Hornstein in New York in 2003 I found that he was still reprinting books in much the same the way as when he had started in 1963.

Johnson Reprint Corporation was run by Fred Rappaport, who had been a secretary at Academic Press and worked his way up to the top job. He was pleasant and efficient but had no editorial knowledge and was very much an administrator. Scott was distinguished principally by his extraordinary good looks. With his neatly trimmed beard he looked like a Pre-Raphaelite depiction of Christ. He was good company but had few new ideas. His predecessor, Albert Henderson, wrote an amusing and affectionate description of working for Johnson at Johnson Reprint Corporation, which mirrored my experience.[2] Johnson was always on the phone, barking instructions while conducting a face-to-face conversation in his office. On one occasion he invited us to lunch at the Four Seasons, one of New York's smartest restaurants. I thought it would give us the opportunity to have a proper conversation with him. But as soon as we were seated and handed menus the waiter brought a phone to the table, and Johnson spent the rest of the meal on the phone while we quietly got on with our lunch.

Back in London I realized that I was a pawn in a battle between Johnson and Hutt that had been going on for years. Hutt despised and resented Johnson, and Johnson went out of his way to needle Hutt by acts such as hiring me and paying me from New York so that I was his agent, not Hutt's employee. This dislike and resentment had grown out of the difficult relationship between Johnson and his older brother-in-law, Jacoby. Jacoby had married into a wealthy family and had always been made aware of where he stood. When he and Johnson founded their publishing companies in New York, Johnson owned ninety-five per cent and Jacoby five per cent. But it was Jacoby who was the brilliant publisher, described as 'the heart and soul of [Academic Press's] presence in the scientific community',[3] while Johnson was seen merely as the financier and businessman. Johnson resented this because he too was well educated and cultured; he had studied at the University of Heidelberg, the Sorbonne and University College, London. But while he could be kind and generous, and was always considerate to me, he often appeared to be brusque, impatient and distant. In spite of their close-knit background and common experience in leaving Germany with their families, Jacoby and Johnson did not get on; their personalities were too different. There would be disagreements at which Johnson would storm out of the room while Jacoby would mutter, 'the bookseller', said disparagingly, as if about a lower form of life.

In 1968 Jacoby died. About that time the companies had got into financial difficulties and Johnson had to factor their receivables to raise cash; the group then went public in the same year. Up to this time, science publishing had seemed too specialized to be of interest to the big trade publishers, but the huge injection of federal money into scientific education and research had made it much more lucrative. In late 1969 the group of companies, excluding Walter J. Johnson, was bought by the publishing conglomerate Harcourt Brace, an old-established house that had been transformed into a major textbook publisher by William Jovanovich, whose own name was added to that of the publisher in 1970. The London branch had been built up by Hutt, who had joined in 1958, into the most successful and fast-growing part of Academic Press. With Jacoby's death Hutt lost a friend and ally and was left with Johnson still in control. For the next two and a quarter years, I was the cuckoo in his nest. Hutt once complained to me that I was being paid more than his most senior science editor, a distinguished scientist. This was simply because I was being paid an 'American' salary of £3,876 per year, and it infuriated him.

A few months before I had left Cornmarket Press I had found a mentor who was able to teach me about reprint publishing and the library market. R. F. L. Bancroft, the superintendent of the Reading Room at the British Museum Library, had suggested that I should seek advice on what to reprint from the antiquarian book dealer Hans Fellner, and I was now sitting in the front room of a house in West Hampstead while a small balding man with a quizzical, slightly owlish face peered at me from behind a desk defended by piles of books, with more books everywhere, in the hall outside and all the way up the stairs. Fellner had been born in Vienna in 1925 and after the Anschluss was sent by his grandmother to London on 'the Children's Train', the 'Kindertransport' that took Jewish children out of Germany and Austria in the late 1930s. The family with whom he was due to stay had moved and he spent most of his school years living in a hostel. He read engineering at the University of Birmingham but after graduating and taking various jobs worked for David Nutt, a West End book dealer. In 1956 he set up on his own near the British Museum selling academic books in the humanities and social sciences in most Western European languages to libraries. His knowledge of these books, why they were important and how much they were worth was extraordinary, and he had close business relationships with two important reprint publishers: Frank Cass, and Augustus M. Kelley in New York, the latter specializing in economic history. At our first meeting he looked through my catalogues, nodded approvingly at the two Shakespeare series, commenting that Shakespeare, Dickens and the Bible always sell (something that I proved later not always to be so). He turned to the maritime history catalogue of which I was so proud and told me that the few titles on the merchant marine would do well because economic and social history was now fashionable but that there would be little interest in the rest, as military and naval history were out of fashion and American libraries were buying much less British history. He also pointed out that the pamphlets by anonymous authors selected by Sanderson would not sell because librarians disliked cataloguing anonymous items. This meeting was the beginning of one of my most important relationships and was fundamental to my own future publishing business.

My other teaching aid was the stacks of concertina paper from the Academic Press mainframe computer recording the sales of every title. For the first time I could see how many copies a large US publisher like Johnson could sell and the results were revealing and somewhat discouraging. While there were many books that sold more than 500 copies, there were others that sold only in the very low hundreds. Sales of titles peaked within three years and then fell off quite sharply. With so many hundreds of titles the back-catalogue sales were still an important revenue stream, but it was clear that the hungry animal had to be fed and that was my job. I was determined to come up with series of books that could hold their own in the Johnson list. I engaged a lively, energetic academic, Peter Davison, at the Shakespeare Institute at the University of Birmingham, to create for us a collection of books about the Stuart theatre around the time of the closing of the theatres in 1642. Called *Theatrum Redivivum*, it contained books ranging from William Prynne's huge *Histrio-Mastix*[4] to Henry Chettle's slight satire *Kind Heart's Dream*,[5] in which the dreamer sits 'near *Finsburie*, in a Taphouse of Antiquity'. Unlike the Shakespeare series where the copies we reprinted came from a single source, for this collection I was able to look at different copies of the same book in libraries on both sides of the Atlantic. I brought together pages from different copies to make what might be regarded as the 'perfect copy' and each book was given a detailed bibliographic collation by Davison. It took two years to complete and could not have been profitable for Johnson.

It was now 1972 and I could see that the reprint industry was in decline. Libraries were more selective in the reprints that they bought, and print-runs were dropping. They were now close to 100 copies, down from the 500 or more of ten years previously and close to the minimum at which printing was economic, even with plastic printing plates.[6] I was now reporting to a new editor at Johnson, Peter Kurz, who had previously worked for the New York publisher of popular reprints, Dover Books. Kurz was a gifted mathematician and musician with an extraordinary general knowledge but even he could not come up with anything that could revive our publishing programme and Rappaport became more and more gloomy. There was not much future for me, isolated in London, only visiting New York a few times a year, and I considered leaving publishing altogether. But I began to look at microfilm as an alternative publishing medium. The economics of microfilm publishing were different from those of book publishing. As described in Appendix 2, a master microfilm is created by photographing pages of the book or journal and then each copy is made to order. There was no economic advantage in making large numbers of copies up-front. This meant that the publisher's only risk was the cost of the creation of the master microfilm, which was not expensive, in contrast to the book publisher, who at the start has to invest in most of the copies that he hopes to sell. The 'break-even' to cover the cost of making the master microfilm was in the range of four to ten copies, while the overall number of copies that might be sold was often less than fifty. The secret was to create very large sets of books or journals to be sold as single collections at a price from at least a few hundred pounds to many thousands of pounds. Only in this way could the total sales revenue be enough to justify the cost of producing and mailing a sales brochure to libraries and academics all over the world.

I had published *Victorian Architecture. A Visual Anthology*,[7] edited by an Oxford friend, Joe Mordaunt Crook, reader in architectural history at the University of London. It was a large-format volume with a jacket and an introduction, reproducing individual plates from nineteenth-century architectural journals such as *The Builder*, and I now proposed to Kurz that we publish *The Builder* on microfilm. He agreed and N. A. Brampton, the director of the oldest microfilm publisher in the UK, Micro Methods, later E. P. Microform, whom Johnson knew well, advised us. He pointed out my errors, which mainly related to the captions and bibliographic information provided on the microfilm, and I realized that I still had much to learn about this apparently simple form of publishing. Kodak microfilmed *The Builder* at their microfilm bureau in Fulham, London, and it sold well because few libraries had the journal in the original and it was an invaluable source for all aspects of Victorian architecture, containing thousands of images and plans of buildings from the period. But Johnson made it clear that at this late stage of his career he was not interested in publishing in the microfilm medium; he was a book man through and through, and I realized that it was time for me to move on.

I was able to do so because in 1971 I had inherited part of a family trust that had a substantial holding in the publishing company Morgan Grampian, which my great-great-grandfather had started when he published *The Engineer* in 1856, the world's first engineering magazine, a weekly that is still being published. My father was chairman of Morgan Grampian and would have liked me to have joined him, but I had decided while still at school that I did not want to work in the family firm. In 1968 the board appointed a new young chief executive, Graham Sherren, an outstanding publisher with a bold vision who came to be regarded as one of the 'whizz kids' of the early 1970s. The Morgan Grampian share price went up strongly and I now had substantial capital, even though it was almost all in shares in the family company. But it was a conversation with Fellner that first made me think about starting my own company. In January 1972 he came down from London to have lunch with us in our house in Essex. Over lunch we talked about the importance of the archive of the publisher John Murray, with its letters to and from Byron and other great writers and poets, and about its saleroom value. It seemed unlikely that Murray would ever consider selling it, but I began to wonder if they might allow it to be microfilmed. I knew that Johnson was not interested and that the only alternative would be to do it myself. I also knew that setting up as a microform publisher would require less capital than setting up as a book publisher, though initially I wanted to do both. I decided that I would only go ahead if Fellner was part of it, and he and I talked about it for months. He hated commitment; he already had his own bookselling business and he liked to stay on the outside, commenting and looking on. But eventually he did agree, and I left Johnson at the end of 1972 to set up my own publishing company.

3

Chadwyck-Healey

In 1973 company names had to be registered and often the chosen name was already in use, so I called my company Chadwyck-Healey because anyone could register their own name. On 3 January 1973 my wife Angela, our accountant David Armitt and I signed the documents incorporating the company. We were living near Great Dunmow in Essex and I found a 1,000-square-foot office suite in our nearest town, Bishops Stortford, in a modern building close to both the railway station, so I could get to London easily, and the main post office, since all our selling would be by direct mail and we would be despatching parcels to customers every day. The office consisted of one small room and two very large rooms, one of which I sublet for the first two years. Most of the office furniture came from a second-hand office equipment supplier in the Holloway Road in London. My first employee was Pat Skyrme who had worked for the *Financial Times* and was typical of the many women who had been in high-powered secretarial or administrative jobs with big companies in London and then came out to the country with their husbands to find that there were few worthwhile jobs. She was a highly efficient secretary and book-keeper and was the first in a long line of well-organized women who took on the task of trying to manage me. I started with three employees: Skyrme, Ann McIlhenny, our production manager who had a first-class degree from Sussex University, and Jean Lodge, our typist, who was a key figure in our publishing programme, as she typed the camera-ready copy for the printed guides and indexes that accompanied our microform publications. Letters were our most important means of communication, as we were dealing with a literate community who put a high value on the written word. I dictated them on a Philips dictating machine while Skyrme and Lodge used the tape transcriber operated with a foot pedal and with headphones. In 1974 I employed my first editorial assistant, Stephen Claughton, who had a degree from Oxford and had worked in a university library. But working for a small company did not suit him and he soon left to pursue a career in the civil service.

It should have been obvious that John Murray would turn down our proposal to microfilm their archive as it would affect its saleroom value. I later discovered that Harvester Press, one of our main rivals, had written to Murray at about the same time, had a similar response and did not take the idea any further. The next most obvious archive was that of William Blackwood, the publisher of *Blackwood's Magazine*, which was in the National Library of Scotland. It was the only archive to already have a substantial printed index. In response to my approach, Alan Bell from the National Library interviewed me in his club in London but the library decided not to grant permission to me or to anyone else.

I thought that there must be other publishers' archives that were neither well known nor valuable and I wrote to three publishers that were already established in the nineteenth century. To my surprise I received positive replies from all three. Rayner Unwin of Allen & Unwin told me that they had in their basement in Museum Street the letter books of George Allen who had been Ruskin's engraver and then his publisher, and of Swan Sonnenschein who had published the first volume of Marx's *Das Kapital*, as well as J. M. Barrie and George Bernard Shaw. Norman Franklin, the chairman of Routledge & Kegan Paul, wanted to know more about me and my company but then offered me the archives of both George Routledge and Kegan Paul, Trench, Trübner & Henry S. King. Most extraordinary of all was the response of Cambridge University Press (CUP) where the Publisher, R. W. David, gave me permission to microfilm their archives, principally those held in the university archives, without even asking for a meeting. This was followed by an agreement from the university archivist and the usually demanding Syndics (the governing body of the press made up of eighteen members of the university). I sent them two copies of our standard publishing agreement, which was modelled on Johnson's, and offered a ten per cent royalty on sales and a copy of the microfilm, the cost of which would be set against royalties. They all signed. Unwin told me that there was a young academic, Brian Maidment, from the University College of Wales at Aberystwyth, working on the George Allen letter books. I made him editor of the first series of publishers' archives and on his recommendation we added the archive of a small but interesting late nineteenth-century publisher, Elkin Mathews, which was at the University of Reading. Our first collection consisted of these six archives. They could

Figure 2 London, Carter Lane, near St Paul's Cathedral. Publishers' archives in the cellar of the offices of Routledge & Kegan Paul. 1973.

be bought separately or together with a pre-publication price of £965 for ninety-seven reels of microfilm, three printed indexes and one printed guide.

In the summer of 1972 I had met three important figures in the world of nineteenth-century literature and publishers' archives: Ian Willison, at the time superintendent of the North Library (the rare book reading room) at the British Museum Library; Simon Nowell-Smith; and an American, W. E. 'Dick' Fredeman, who had a chair in English literature at the University of British Columbia. Willison was a quiet man, with an urbane, emollient manner and a huge network of contacts and friends, and was one of the instigators in the UK of the new, fashionable 'history of the book' that had been pioneered in France by Lucien Febvre and Henri-Jean Martin. Nowell-Smith was a patrician scholar and book collector who after the war had been Librarian of the London Library, the private library in St James's Square founded by Thomas Carlyle in the nineteenth century, and was later editor of the *Times Literary Supplement*. He had private means and had built up an important collection of English poetry. His great friend,

Fredeman, was different from him in every way – an orphan from Arkansas, who had been adopted by a wealthy childless couple, he had discovered the Pre-Raphaelites while at college and then became an academic. In the early 1950s the Pre-Raphaelites were out of fashion and it must have been some strange attraction of opposites that drew this brash Southern boy to the refined world of Dante Gabriel Rossetti and his followers. He and Nowell-Smith, the odd couple of the book collecting world, spent every summer exploring the many second-hand and antiquarian bookshops that existed before the coming of the Internet in search of poetry and the Pre-Raphaelites.

Fredeman had described publishers' archives as, 'the last major untapped reservoir of primary materials available to the scholar of nineteenth-century publishing'[1] and came with me to look at some of them. Nowell-Smith agreed to approach Oxford University Press (OUP) on our behalf, a major omission in our list of publishers, for permission to microfilm their archives but to his surprise was firmly turned down. Further approaches were made over the next few years but always with the same answer. (At the end of the 1980s, OUP asked if we would be interested in microfilming their archives. It was too late; our interests had moved on and now it was our turn to say 'no'.)

Although the series *The Archives of British Publishers* was our largest and most high-profile publication it was not our first. At Fellner's suggestion we published on microfilm *Reports from Committees of the House of Commons 1715–1801 Printed but not Inserted in the Journals of the House* with the index reprinted as a book. Published in 1802–1806, it was itself a reprint of all the important Parliamentary reports of the eighteenth century. In spite of being published almost 170 years ago copies were still available from Her Majesty's Stationery Office (HMSO) and Fellner could see them wrapped in brown paper on the shelves behind their trade counter in London, still at their original price. He tried to buy them but, alerted to what they were, HMSO had them valued and repriced. The microfilm edition on ten reels with a hardbound printed index sold for £95 and orders began to come in immediately. It was ordered by every library in Australia that we mailed, a record that we never achieved again.

On 1 April 1973 we issued our first invoice. It was the day that Value Added Tax (VAT) was introduced in the UK and it became an important source of income for us over the next few years. We paid VAT on everything we bought, and we charged VAT on microforms sold within the UK but not on books. Because most of our sales were overseas, the total VAT we charged was less than the VAT we paid and the difference was refunded to us. Each month we sent in our VAT return as quickly as possible in order to receive our repayment.

In April I received a letter from Hutt terminating my contract to work on a project that I had agreed to continue for Johnson after I left and paying me in lieu of the three months' notice I had given myself since I had written the contract. Johnson had had a serious disagreement with Harcourt Brace Jovanovich over some transactions that had taken place with his private company Walter J. Johnson and he had had to resign from the board. Hutt came out of semi-retirement and took over the running of Academic Press and Johnson Reprint Corporation. It must have given him great satisfaction to settle old scores with his colleagues in New York, and to also close down Johnson Reprint Corporation, firing almost all the staff, including Kurz. In July Johnson and his wife Thekla took me out to lunch in London. This time there was no telephone on the table, and he made light of what must have been a very painful end to his relationship with the companies that he had founded.

My original business plan was to publish collections of books and archives on microfilm and microfiche, to reprint important reference books and bibliographies and to publish translations of academic monographs in European languages. In the autumn of 1973 I asked Johnson if he would consider investing in the publication of the translations of the academic books selected by Joseph Rykwert, professor of the history of art at the University of Essex. He wrote, 'I am definitely interested in carrying out joint projects with you.'[2] I proposed that he should invest fifty per cent and have an interest of thirty per cent in these publications. After another meeting he wrote to me in early 1974 to explain that he did not want to invest in publishing the books although he thought that publishing translations was a good idea. 'You surely know, Charles, that I have experience, in some cases, not very pleasant ones, in running firms abroad. It is very difficult, even impossible, to do so if you are not involved in the day-to-day operations.'[3] I wondered if he was referring to Academic Press in London. For many years I used to see Johnson at the Frankfurt Book Fair, on his own, in a small booth selling backruns of journals and sets of books, and we would chat for a few minutes. After the sale of Academic Press, he was a wealthy man but in his old age he continued to sell books to libraries. He died in 1996, always 'the bookseller'. None of the biographical dictionaries were ever compiled and we only published one translation, *Anamorphic Art* by Jurgis Baltrušaitis. Microfilm publishing seemed much easier and more financially rewarding than the publishing of individual monographs, with the extra overhead of translation costs and the prospect of only modest sales even in the 1970s.

Fellner proposed that we reprint two multi-volume bibliographies of French literature, Avenir Tchemerzine, *Bibliographie d'éditions originales et rares d'auteurs français des XVe, XVIe, XVIIe et XVIIIe siècles*, 1927–34, and Georges Vicaire, *Manuel de l'amateur de livres du XIXe siècle*, 1894–1920. Together there were eighteen volumes and we used a method of reprinting that had been pioneered by Readex (see Appendix 1), in which we printed nine or twelve reduced images of each page of the original on one page of the reprint, with a consequent saving on paper, binding and printing, though there was the extra cost of stripping up the images to make up a page. To make what we called 'reduced reprints' financially viable we had to expect to sell 500 copies – more than most reprints were achieving in the 1970s, so we had to be selective in what we chose to publish. Both these titles were still in copyright – in the UK and Europe. In the USA, to be protected by copyright, a book had to be registered at the Library of Congress and a fee paid.

Figure 3 Teaneck, New Jersey. Peter Kurz in his office at his home, working on an early version of page-making software. 1977.

Twenty-eight years later the book had to be re-registered and copyright was then extended for another twenty-eight years – fifty-six years in all. But many publishers, especially overseas ones, forgot to re-register and, as we expected, we found that neither of these bibliographies was still in copyright in the USA. I established a US company because I knew that the USA would be our largest and most important market. For copyright reasons, I did not want it to be a branch of Chadwyck-Healey, so I named it Somerset House. By this time Kurz, to whom I had reported at Johnson, had set up his own reprint publishing business from his house in Teaneck, New Jersey, and he agreed to manage Somerset House in the USA on our behalf, receiving orders and payments and responding to enquiries from US libraries. Accordingly, the two French bibliographies were published under the Somerset House imprint in single, large quarto volumes.

Another reason for having a US imprint was that the libraries of state-funded colleges and universities were not allowed to buy directly from overseas; they had to order through agents or book dealers such as Blackwell's. The agents expected a discount or commission. We started by offering five or ten per cent, which they reluctantly accepted, but on a microform publication selling for $2,000 this was still $100–$200. We preferred to sell directly to institutions and we eventually reduced our discounts to zero. The dealers complained, but as they had what was often an exclusive agreement with a library to supply all its books and microforms, they had no choice but to fulfil the order – on our terms.

Both the index to *Reports from Committees* and the French bibliographies were printed by Scolar Press in Yorkshire, set up by Robin Alston as both a printing press and a publishing house. Alston was a lecturer in English literature at the University of Leeds and had a special interest in the development of the English language – his life's work was a bibliography of books on the English language to 1800. He wanted to make available good-quality reprints of sixteenth- and seventeenth-century books at prices that individual academics could afford. He was a close friend of Fredeman, who admired him enormously, and when I first met him in 1970, I was impressed by his publishing operation. But it did not survive his idealistic approach, and he went back to academia, his bibliography and, later, to working at the British Library and, ultimately, to working for us on a part-time basis. Scolar's printing continued under new ownership, maintaining the high standards that Alston had set, but with commercial prices. They were our preferred printer for many years.

I knew that my company could only become viable if it had volume – not just volume of orders but volume of material to publish. We needed large, solid series, which might take two or more years to complete. One early, unglamorous but essential series was the English Record Society publications. These were historical documents, painstakingly transcribed by historians, often amateurs, who worked on the documents in their county in England and Wales. Almost every county had a record society and the earliest had started in 1835. Johnson had considered reprinting them but it was too expensive to do so in book form, even in the golden years. Fellner, who bought and sold many sets of record society publications, agreed that microfiche was the ideal medium for a collection of over 1,000 volumes with expected sales of around fifty copies. A bibliography, *Texts and Calendars*, listed the volumes for each of the record societies and this would act as the key to the series.[4] I met the author, a retired colonel, E. L. C. Mullins, in January 1973 and set about getting permission from each of the record societies. This took time and even involved being interviewed by some of their committees. All the important record societies agreed and, after a second series a few years later, only one still refused to give us permission, the Somerset Record Society, of which, ironically, my great-grandfather, a keen amateur historian, had been the editor in the late nineteenth century. The many series that we did republish sold steadily for years.

One of our most important early visitors was Alan Meckler, the publisher of *Microform Review*, the specialist journal for microform publishing which he had only founded in 1972. At the time, he was living in London with his family but later moved back to New York. He ran an annual conference for librarians and microform publishers, which from 1976 I always attended. We became good friends and I would often stay with him and his family when I was in New York. Through him I met Les Sufrin, who became my accountant and financial advisor, and Burt Rubin, who became my lawyer in the USA. Meckler was interested in all new media and his response to them was to publish a journal and books, and to organize conferences. In the 1990s he did this with the Internet, the importance of which he recognized immediately, creating a company that published a wide range of material and ran large conferences on the subject. He sold it very successfully in the late 1990s.

The next year, 1974, did not start well. From January to early March the government imposed the 'Three Day Week' to conserve electricity during strikes by miners. We were supplied with electricity on only three designated working days, and only to 5pm. We had large plate-glass windows in the office and so on the two days without electricity we had enough light to work in until well into the afternoon, but we could not use the electric typewriters that we needed not only for correspondence but also for the in-house typing of indexes to the microfilm editions of the publishers' archives. By then we had hired an American, Sandy Merritt, who managed the indexing of three of the first publishers' archives. Lodge and freelancers typed the indexes on IBM proportional-spacing typewriters, which were the closest we could get to creating text that had the appearance of print. At the time union-dominated printers would not accept non-union camera-ready copy, and I never understood why our typescripts were accepted by the local printers who printed our indexes, which were either hardbound or softbound books. The industrial unrest of the time meant that there were also constant shortages of essentials such as envelopes for mailings. In 1974 I spent too much time driving to Spicers on the outskirts of London to pick up consignments of brown envelopes that I had only been able to obtain with difficulty.

Johnson phoned to tell me that the bound and unbound stock of IUP's *British Parliamentary Papers* was for sale from the receiver. Books in a warehouse are books that no one has wanted to buy, a mantra that I repeated to myself in the 1990s when I was invited by Kraus to their warehouse outside New York when they were looking for a buyer for their reprint business. Frank Cass, Littlefield Adams (a New Jersey publisher and owner of the Barnes & Noble imprint), a UK printer, and Michael Adams, who had been the IUP sales director, set up a new company, Irish Academic Press, and paid around £200,000 for the stock. They probably got their money back within the first two years and may have sold around another fifty 1,000-volume sets by the time we published our microfiche edition of the Parliamentary Papers in the early 1980s. The receiver of Cornmarket Press also offered me the unsold stock of their reprints. Three series from *The English Revolution* had been published, another five series were being planned, and they had had good advance orders for some of the series. Most of the other reprint series I had published were almost sold out, but I was no longer interested in buying unsold stock or future series of *The English Revolution*.

The only capital that I invested in the companies was £20,000, which I borrowed from Coutts bank, secured against my shares. Coutts also provided an overdraft facility of up to £10,000. Our first financial year ran for fifteen months to 1 April 1974, and in the twelve months from when we had issued our first invoice our total sales were £27,000, of which 42 per cent was from the USA. In the second year sales were £54,000, with 34 per cent from the USA – a 100 per cent increase but still not enough to support a viable business. However, to put the figures in context, Skyrme was paid £1,200 per year. In a similar job today she would be earning at least £25,000 per year – a twenty times uplift. If this was applied to our second year's sales total, it would be equivalent to sales revenues of over £1 million.

I was now working on the next publisher's archive. In the typical archive there were rarely incoming letters from authors; they had either been thrown away or taken out of the archive and sold or given to a library. Such letters presented us with problems of copyright because we would have to trace and get permission from every copyright holder, which was difficult to do. Manuscripts remained in copyright indefinitely, but most libraries observed an informal understanding that if a manuscript was over 100 years old the publisher could reproduce it but had to take responsibility for any possible infringement. We liked archives such as that of George Allen, where the surviving material consisted of copies of outgoing letters only. They were contained in 'wet letter books', each of which consisted of up to 1,000 pages of thin paper using a copying technique developed by James Watt in the eighteenth century. The left-hand page in the book would be dampened and the letter to be copied pressed against it, with considerable pressure in a press, and with thin waterproof sheets either side to protect the other pages. An image of the writing on the letter was thus impressed on to the page of the letter book.

I was advised by Nowell-Smith that one of the largest and important archives was that of the nineteenth-century publisher Richard Bentley. With his brother and, later, his son, they had consciously preserved a large archive which was subsequently sold off in three parts. The largest part was in the new British Library, another part was in the library of the University of Illinois in Urbana-Champaign, and the smallest part was in the library of the University of California, Los Angeles (UCLA). We would use the microfilm medium to bring these three parts together again so that researchers could use the archive in its entirety for the first time.

While at Cornmarket and Johnson I had dealt with the British Museum Library and I now had to deal with the new British Library in the first months of its operation. The year that I started Chadwyck-Healey, 1973, was the year in which responsibilities were transferred from the British Museum to the newly formed British Library Board. In February a joint executive committee of British Museum and British Library staff had been set up to deal with day-to-day problems until the two institutions were fully in operation as separate bodies.[5] My letter of August 1973 to Daniel Waley, Keeper of Manuscripts, for permission to microfilm the archives of Richard Bentley was one of those problems. In an undated reply on paper headed 'THE BRITISH MUSEUM', in which 'MUSEUM' had been crossed out and 'LIBRARY' typed in, he observed that, 'it is not very likely that such permission would be granted ... it would be short-sighted of the Board to permit such marketing rather than to undertake it itself'. He ends, 'The Board is such a recent creation that it might be wise to wait at least some weeks [before approaching it].' I waited until October and then sent a proposal to Michael Hoare, who had been appointed director of the Department of Publications at the British Museum but who also had responsibility for the publications of the British Library. He eventually responded in February 1974 on paper headed 'The British Museum Publications' with 'Ltd' typed in, stating, 'I have cleared with Dr Waley in the Department of Manuscripts of the British Library the principle of your publishing on microfilm the British Museum's Bentley Collection. In due course, as you know, the contract will have to be signed with this company.'

Encouraged by this, I obtained permission from the trustees of the estate of Richard Bentley and told both the University of Illinois and UCLA that the British Library had granted us permission to microfilm their part of the Bentley archive. This was followed by a visit to Illinois in April 1974, where I was given a warm welcome by the rare book librarian N. Frederick 'Fred' Nash and his younger colleague from the English department, Scott Bennett. Gordon N. Ray, scholar, author and book collector, while vice-president of the university, had helped it to acquire the correspondence files of Richard Bentley & Son to enable one of their professors, Royal Gettman, to research his book on the Bentley publishing firm, *A Victorian Publisher*.[6] The main purpose of my visit was to meet the principal people in Rare Books and get them on my side, because the detailed page count that would have to be done first and then the microfilming itself would have to be managed by the library staff as I had no one in the USA who could oversee it. Bennett had been released from all teaching duties for a year to put the material in order and establish a catalogue, and I agreed to pay $2,080 for three months' work by a graduate to assist him and carry out the page count. Page counts were a fundamental part of the microfilming process as they told us how many frames there would be and consequently how many rolls of film or numbers of microfiche the whole collection would consist of. We published our sales brochures months ahead of starting production and we needed to state in the brochure the number of reels of film, as our price was based on it. Bennett became a good friend and colleague, and I enjoyed the friendliness and informality at Urbana, which was so typical of the Midwest. While I was in Urbana, I was able to talk to Gettman about the Bentleys and discovered that the library also had the archives of an important twentieth-century British publisher, Grant Richards. It was a particularly comprehensive archive of a publishing house that had opened in 1897 and lasted for fifty years, during which time it had published George Bernard Shaw, A. E. Housman and Arnold Bennett. I warmed to Grant Richards and liked the fact that he had recorded his thoughts in a daybook from the very first day he had opened for business, and we added his archive to our series.

I was then informed by Hugh Cobbe, in the Department of Manuscripts, that the permission that had been promised to us could not be concluded due to some internal difficulties. This was a major setback and I worried about how it would affect my reputation in the USA if I now had to notify the University of Illinois and UCLA that the British Library had withdrawn permission without being able to say why. I turned to my friend and mentor, George Potter, the retired professor of history at the University of Sheffield, for advice. He sent me a masterly draft, which I had typed up under my name. It emphasized the embarrassment that there would be for me if the promise made by the British Library was now rescinded. Within a few days I received a note from Waley with a very different tone: 'I entirely understand and sympathise with your feeling of discontent.... In particular I feel perturbed that there seems at one stage to have been a misunderstanding between Michael Hoare and myself.' This was followed by a longer letter from D. T. 'Don' Richnell, the director general of the Reference Division who had only been appointed in May 1974, setting out the terms of an agreement and suggesting a meeting. We met in early August and I returned the signed agreement in September. It was the British Library's first commercial publishing agreement.

I had to go back to Urbana a year later because microfilming had gone too slowly and I wanted to get it finished. I continued to work with Bennett who was still in Rare Books but had now become a qualified librarian. He went on to have a distinguished career as chief librarian of Northwestern University, one of the finest private universities in the Midwest, and then as Librarian of Yale University Library. The microfilming of the Bentley archive at UCLA was carried out for us by the library at a time when the only communications were by airmail letter.

When I did visit UCLA for the first time in 1976 the whole of the Bentley archive had been published and we were now working on Grant Richards and on Longman. Tim Rix, the chairman of Longman, was deeply interested in its long history (it had been founded by Thomas Longman in 1724), and he readily agreed to the publication on microfilm of the archive, which had been deposited with the University of Reading. Rix had already commissioned the cultural historian Asa Briggs to write a history of Longman. As part of his research Briggs, who was then Provost of Worcester College, Oxford, held seminars in the drawing room of the Provost's Lodgings to discuss general aspects of publishing history together with the publishing history of Longman. I attended several of them with other people interested in the history of the book.

But with each new archive there was a fall in sales. Some seventy-five libraries bought the first series; fifty libraries, the Bentley Papers; thirty libraries, Longman, and the same for the voluminous Macmillan Papers at the British Library. Our final publisher's archive was that of the important American publisher Harper & Brothers. The archive was in Columbia University Library and we reached an agreement with Kenneth Lohf, the rare book librarian. But by 1979 the market had diminished even further, and the greater interest in the USA did not compensate for the lack of interest in American publishers' archives in the UK and Australia – two of our strongest markets. Sales were in the region of twenty copies and I no longer saw publishers' archives as viable for microform publication.

From 1974 to 1980 I visited the USA several times a year. As well as visiting libraries where we were microfilming collections, I was making at least two sales trips a year and was going to conferences where we usually exhibited. I would always stay with Kurz who ran our office from his house in Teaneck and he became a good friend. There were also increasingly frequent trips to Washington, DC to work on projects with our editor Sandy Shaffer Tinkham (see Chapter 6). A significant part of the cost of these trips was the transatlantic airfare, so I welcomed the introduction of Freddie Laker's Skytrain with its return ticket to New York for less than £80, and

Figure 4 Cambridge. Hans Fellner visits our new office in Bateman Street, while under construction. Spring 1976.

travelled on it in its first week of operation in September 1977. Laker only lasted for a few years and by the early 1980s, when we had more money, I had elevated myself to business class on British Airways.

During the first few years while I was in the UK, I would visit Fellner every few weeks at his home in Gascony Avenue, West Hampstead, to discuss our publishing programme, seeking both his advice and his reassurance for what we were publishing. We usually had lunch at Cosmos in Swiss Cottage, an old-fashioned German restaurant, but we also tried out Pierre Koffman's new restaurant, La Tante Claire, when it first opened in Chelsea in 1977. When I proposed a new project that I felt excited about, Fellner's response in his dry Viennese-accented English, was often, 'Does anybody care?' To which there was usually no answer. If I mentioned some professor I had consulted, he would nod approvingly or exclaim, 'That man is the kiss of death!' In 1977, at his suggestion, we started our first and only journal, *Publishing History*. Published twice a year it was intended to cover the history of all aspects of publishing including newspapers and magazines, and its relationship with other media such as film and TV, and though the coverage was never as broad as I had hoped, it had its admirers. The formidable Cambridge historian J. H. Plumb wrote to me, 'May I take this opportunity of saying how much I enjoyed the first two volumes of *Publishing History* ... I intend to become a subscriber.'[7] For the first few years it lost money but we then treated each issue as if it was a book and charged £30 per issue and, while the circulation dropped to around 350, we now made a small profit. It was edited first by Michael Turner at the Bodleian Library and later by Simon Eliot, then a young academic at the University of Bath. After I sold the company to Bell & Howell, I expected *Publishing History* to quietly disappear, but it is still being published – still under the Chadwyck-Healey imprint.

Although publishers' archives were the most prominent publications of our first three years, I was determined that our list should be as broad and varied as possible. We were already publishing in a specialized medium and I did not want to confine us to a limited range of subjects. I was always looking for new opportunities and in 1975 responded to an approach from the London School of Economics (LSE) to publish a microfiche edition of Beatrice Webb's diaries. The Fabians Beatrice and Sidney Webb, two of the most important reformers of the twentieth century, founded the LSE in 1895 and the weekly magazine *The New Statesman* in 1913.

She wrote in her diary, 'We are two second-rate minds, but curiously combined.'[8] Second-rate minds that worked out the system of state education almost exactly followed by the Labour Party in 1944 and conceived the political and social programme of the Labour Party for more than forty years. Beatrice, born Beatrice Potter in 1858, kept a diary from 1873 to her death in 1943,[9] and the fifty-seven exercise books in which she wrote it every day are the most precious documents in the archives of the LSE. Webb did not seem to have intended that her diaries be published but Professor Norman Mackenzie, the editor of the Webbs' letters, has described the diaries as, 'one of the great unpublished literary works of the nineteenth and twentieth centuries ... with as much internal unity of feeling and structure as if it had been deliberately conceived as a large scale literary work.'[10] For years after her death it remained unread as well as unpublished because her handwriting is illegible. Webb herself began to type a transcript, which the LSE completed, and they arranged for it to be indexed. They invited microfilm publishers to bid for the rights to publish the diaries and typed transcript on microfiche and to publish the index as a book. Since the LSE had made a significant investment in the transcript and in the index, I offered them a royalty of thirty-five per cent of sales revenue, which was higher than any royalty that we had previously offered, together with an advance against royalties of £500. P. D. C. Davis, the LSE publications officer, told me that another publisher was also being considered, but in January 1976 wrote that his committee had agreed for us to publish the diaries. Harvester Press had also bid for it, and Alastair Everitt, its managing director, later admonished me for breaking ranks by offering such a high royalty. The redoubtable Roberta Routledge, who advertised her services, 'Archive Arrangement', on the back page of the *Times Literary Supplement* (*TLS*) every week, had been employed by the LSE to compile the index, which was enhanced by contributions by several eminent scholars,[11] but was many months late in delivering it to us. In May 1978 we shared a launch party at the LSE with CUP, who were publishing an edition of the letters of the Webbs.[12] *The Diary of Beatrice Webb* was a prestigious title at a time when we were still trying to establish ourselves. Sales were good as the price of £295 was within reach of most libraries and the Webbs were of sufficient international importance to be of interest to researchers in universities all over the world.

There was one final episode in November 1982 that underlined the cultural gulf between book publishers and microform publishers. Virago, who at the time was making its name by republishing worthwhile books by women that had been unfairly forgotten, had published a four-volume edition of extracts from the diaries of Beatrice Webb. It was widely reviewed in what Davis called, 'all the better dailies and weeklies'.[13] Most of these reviews implied that this was a complete edition of the diaries, the implication being that anything in four volumes must be as good as complete. We responded with an advertisement in the *TLS* in which we described our microfiche edition as 'complete' – the word being underlined. Davis wrote:

> Your recent advertisement in the TLS ... has caused a great deal of anger at Virago. They feel that by using the word complete and underlining it ... you are not merely cashing in on the excellent publicity earned by Virago

(which is reasonable) but that you are implying that the Virago volume [*sic*] is somehow second rate ... the intention is clearly to persuade [the reader] that your edition is superior, that there is something lacking in the Virago edition.

Which indeed there was – many hundreds of entries from Beatrice Webb's diary. I could not believe that Carmen Callil, the tough Australian founder of Virago, could have cared less about our advertisement and I told Davis how hurt I was by the tone of his letter and by 'the appalling quality of current reviewing in so-called serious journals like the TLS and THES' (*Times Higher Education Supplement*). I pointed out that only the *Observer* had mentioned the existence of the microfiche edition and that I had only seen one review that made clear that the Virago edition was not the complete text. A conciliatory reply from Davis ends, 'I hope I may still wish you a happy Christmas and a successful 1983, for I do so most sincerely.'[14]

Selling

Selling was as important a part of successful publishing as the selection of what to publish and its production, and in the first three years I spent more time writing brochures, arranging for their design and printing, and writing sales letters than anything else. Because our publications – reels of microfilm in plain cardboard boxes or microfiche in white envelopes – lacked the presence of a book it was even more important that we produced high-quality brochures with good design, illustrations and printing, as well as accurate and full descriptions of our publications. Some of our publications cost as much as a small car (or, later, a large Mercedes) and the librarian's decision to buy was based solely on the information in the brochure. Fellner had once said to me that the Kraus Reprint catalogue could be used as a reliable bibliography because of the accuracy of the descriptions of their books and I wanted ours to be regarded as equally authoritative. We bought mailing lists from IBIS in the UK and from companies in the USA and we mailed thousands of brochures to both libraries and academics. Every brochure was accompanied by a sales letter. I had learned the importance of personalizing the communication with the recipient at the seminars on direct mail that I regularly went to. In the first two years I also spent much of my time taking boxes of brochures, letters and envelopes out to the people who stuffed the envelopes, and then collecting them and arranging for bulk posting. We spent thousands of pounds on mailings from September to the end of the year. By then we had usually run out of money so only restarted mailings in the early spring, by which time money was coming in from the orders generated by the earlier mailings. In the 1970s UK public libraries had comparatively large acquisition budgets and their year-end at the end of March was important for us as they often had money they needed to spend quickly. The most important date was the end of June when US college and university libraries also needed to spend their 'year-end money'. This was the biggest bonanza of the year as libraries started their wants lists before Christmas and then waited until June to see how much money they had left to spend.

In 1974 I had made my first sales tour in the USA, visiting libraries in Texas and the Midwest. In the early years we did not have much to offer college libraries and it was only the largest, most sophisticated university libraries that were interested in our British- and European-oriented list. I made at least two US sales tours a year, to states such as Mississippi and Alabama, as well as to our most important customers – Harvard, Yale and Princeton on the East Coast where the 'collection development' librarians, who were able to make decisions on what to buy without having to consult faculty, became important allies and advisors. I made fewer sales trips after Bertie Bonnell joined us as sales vice-president in the USA in 1980, as she was on the road for much of the time. She also started to build a team who sold on the phone. We did no phone selling in the UK until Steven Hall joined us as sales director in 1988.

4

Cambridge and Our Own Production

For the first year Kodak carried out microfilming and made copies for us at their bureau in Fulham, London. Large libraries such as the British Library, the university libraries of Oxford and Cambridge, and the Library of Congress also had their own microfilming facilities that we were required to use if we wished to have their books microfilmed, and for which they charged us.

All our US competitors had production facilities but I was reluctant to take on our own because at first I had seen myself more as a generalist publisher of microforms, reprints, original monographs and reference books. In 1974, when I could see that microform was becoming our main publishing medium, Kodak closed their only microfilm bureau in the UK. They recommended a new company, Micromedia, in Bicester near Oxford, set up by two young men, Mike Davies and Peter Ashby, with financial backing from Blackwell's, the Oxford bookselling and publishing group. Ashby had been working for Kodak who passed on their customers to him. They were later joined by Chris Ronaldson, also from Kodak, who was the most experienced manager of the three. By moving to Micromedia, we were putting ourselves entirely in their hands as they held our most important tangible assets, our master negatives and the printing masters that were used to make the microfilm copies (see Appendix 2). As volumes increased, Micromedia struggled, both with quality and delivery. In 1975 on my first visit to Stanford University, California, I was looking forward to meeting the staff of a library that was already one of our best customers. In the room where several librarians were waiting to meet me, I could see on the table in front of me a pile of our microfiche. This was not a good sign. It was a set of *European Official Statistical Serials* in which many of the microfiche were under exposed – the images were too light and some were blurred. What was I going to do about it? I apologized profusely and said that I would replace the entire set. The atmosphere improved and they began to talk about other things that they wanted to buy. But it was humiliating and showed me that we would have to improve our own quality control so that a defective set like that could never be sent out again. We began to make sample checks of microform copies, but it was impossible to check every microfiche that we sold; no book publisher examines every book it sells.

Cambridge

Angela and I wanted to send our children to school in Cambridge and in the summer of 1976 we moved our office from Bishops Stortford to Cambridge, into a terrace house in Bateman Street that we had bought and converted into a flat on the top two floors and an office in the basement and ground floor. At weekends we went back to our house in Essex. It was a disruptive move because only two people of the six who were working in Bishops Stortford could move with us. I had to hire new staff and quickly found that in Cambridge the university and CUP were the dominant employers, offering higher salaries and longer holidays than the two weeks' paid holiday that we provided. But McIlhenny and Merritt continued to work for us in Cambridge and I was able to hire our first experienced editor, David Pratt.

Initially Pratt worked on what proved to be one of our most successful publications at the time, a fourteen-volume set of reprints of articles, pamphlets and parts of books entitled *Literary Taste, Culture and Mass Communication*. Libraries tended not to buy reprinted collections of journal articles, but I had noticed that one of the most innovative new publishers in our sector, Garland Publishing in New York, was now publishing books that contained reprints of articles. It was a section in the *New Cambridge Bibliography of English Literature* (*NCBEL*) that gave us our title and I discovered that it had been compiled by my old friend and colleague Peter Davison, who was now professor of English literature at the University of Kent. We hired as fellow editors Rolf Meyersohn and Edward Shils, two heavyweight American sociologists, and, surprisingly quickly, obtained rights to over 200 articles and extracts from books. The fourteen volumes were published over the next two years, sold out and were later reprinted; Davison indexed the whole set over one Christmas holiday. The American library journal *Choice* wrote, 'A library seeking to build a general collection quickly could do no better than to purchase all the volumes.'[1]

In 1978 we moved our office to larger premises on a corner of the Newmarket Road, a red-brick Victorian building with a curious domed tower. It was owned by the city council who intended to pull it down to provide access to the new, much opposed at the time, Grafton Centre shopping mall. They offered me a one-year lease at £1 per square foot. We were there for the next eight years and although it was not demolished, they refused to sell it to me.

We now had sufficient space, but I had still not resolved two other weaknesses in the company, namely the lack of strong financial controls and the poor handling of orders, invoicing and despatches. One of the many order clerks that came and went in the late 1970s observed that for a company with such a small turnover, by then still less than £1 million, our business was remarkably complicated. At the time far fewer companies were trading directly with clients in countries throughout the world and a large part of our business was in dollars at a time when the transfer of foreign currencies through banks was much more laborious than it is now. It was only in 1979 that currency exchange controls were lifted. They had not affected us because we did not have to send money to our company in the USA; its costs were always covered by its revenues. Les Sufrin, my accountant in the USA, was becoming an important advisor and friend, but in the UK I still only had a part-time financial manager, who was a lecturer at a local college, to look after our finances. Order fulfilment and financial control did not interest me – all that I was interested in were publishing ideas and sales. But in 1980 I was able to hire a commanding, highly experienced woman to manage orders, invoicing and despatches. Mildred Bacon, a true Mancunian who always spoke her mind, quickly imposed order, and stayed with us until she retired in the 1990s. Our part-time financial manager guided our book-keeper and produced monthly accounts, but then a temporary accountant, Peter Miller, joined us for a few weeks while between jobs. He had been running the accounts department, with sixty staff, of an international engineering company and I did not think that we were big enough for him to be interested, or that we could afford him. Bacon encouraged me to ask him and in January 1981 he became our finance director and stayed with us for the next seven years. What attracted him was that we had cash – the advance payments from libraries that had started with the nineteenth-century Parliamentary Papers microfiche edition (see Chapter 5). He explained that having cash makes the finance director's job so much easier. For me, the presence in the company of both Bacon and Miller was transformational. I had two people, both older and more experienced than me, whom I could trust to manage the parts of the business that interested me least and yet were essential to our survival. It was also a comfort to have someone as experienced as Miller to talk to every day.

Chadwyck-Healey Microfilm Publishing Services (CHMPS)

We were struggling to keep up with the production of large series such as *European Official Statistical Serials* (see Chapter 5). We urgently needed to step up our rate of production and I installed two Kodak microfilm cameras in a rented room near our Bateman Street office. We hired Jo Patten, a technician from the university photographic service, to manage the microfilming, but we were still firmly on the 'dry side' because we had to send our camera film to Micromedia for processing. Our first camera operators were two newly graduated students. One of them, Paul Greengrass, went on to have a remarkable career as a film director, making hard-hitting documentaries such as *Bloody Sunday* and the feature films *United 93* and *The Bourne Ultimatum*. But now doing our own filming did not solve our main production problem, which was the need for a faster turnaround of our orders for microform copies.

From time to time Coutts invited me to lunch at their offices in Lombard Street in the City of London. Over one lunch in early 1979 our manager expressed his concern about our dependence on Micromedia who, they could see, was not fulfilling our orders quickly enough, which was affecting our cashflow. While book publishers have many printers to choose from, there was now no other bureau in the UK offering the same range of services as Micromedia. All the copies that Micromedia made for us were on archivally permanent silver halide film, as opposed to diazo film, the film used by industry and commerce where archival permanence is not needed. Coutts offered to lend us money to finance the setting up of our own production unit, for which we would not only need to buy cameras but also processors to develop the film and copiers to make copies. High-quality microfilming involves expensive and sophisticated machinery; it uses chemicals, some of which, like the silver compounds, are highly toxic and difficult to dispose of, and the processes require stringent health and safety practices. I had seen how difficult Micromedia found it to achieve both high volumes and high quality and wondered if we could do any better. But I was impressed that our bank, normally so conservative, wanted us to improve the security of our business and were willing to lend us money to do so. I knew what equipment we needed and realized that I already owned a building that might be suitable for microfilm production.

We had bought an old farmhouse in Bassingbourn, a village fifteen miles west of Cambridge, in late 1977. It had extensive outbuildings, including one of the finest medieval barns in Cambridgeshire and a two-storey brick-built Victorian granary, which could be converted into a microfilm bureau. The farm buildings had been given a Grade 2 listing, which reflected their historical and architectural importance, and we were also in a conservation area, so it seemed unlikely that we would be given permission to use the granary as a factory. But 1979 was a year of crisis with Margaret Thatcher's government having recently come into power; unemployment was rising fast, and bus services to villages like Bassingbourn were being cut, which reduced work opportunities for people who did not have cars. The parish council was already concerned about the number of derelict buildings in the village and a microfilm bureau in the centre of Bassingbourn would create around ten jobs overnight, almost all of which could be filled by people who lived locally and whom we could train. As I expected, our planning application was turned down and I was looking for another site when our architect was approached by the council who asked us to resubmit it. The objection to our first application had come from the local water company, but the council was determined to bring new employment to Bassingbourn. Our second application went through and we started to prepare to convert the granary.

My other concern was to have enough work to keep the bureau fully occupied; I did not want to compete with Micromedia by doing work for other publishers, and we would have to keep the factory supplied with work from our own publishing projects. We needed an exceptionally large project to give us this security and in late 1979 we were able to plan for the microfilming of the 4.2 million pages of the nineteenth-century Parliamentary Papers, already referred to in Chapters 1 and 2 and described more fully in Chapter 5. By early 1980 I was in a hurry to complete the conversion of the granary, as we had twenty-one customers waiting for the microfiche of the Parliamentary Papers. We bought more cameras and once we had begun to install the wet side of the photographic process, we could now process our own camera film. The making of microfiche and microfilm copies, which required a much larger film processor and film duplicators, did not begin until April. I appointed a manager who had previously run a photographic unit for Rhodesian Railways, as I wanted someone who was fully conversant with the processing of silver halide film as used in cameras; most commercial microfilm bureaux only used the very different and much cheaper diazo film.

We hired people who lived locally to work part or full time, initially, on a seven-day-a-week schedule. During the week the manager and Julie Davis, our first employee who stayed with us until I sold the company, managed production, and at the weekend a different manager took over with a weekend team. The weekend manager was an electrician who had a part-time job and needed to earn extra money by working at weekends. We brought back our microfilm master negatives from Micromedia so that now we could make all our microfilm and microfiche copies. We also bought from our neighbours a large corrugated-iron traction-engine repair shed that had been built up against the back wall of the granary and this extended the area of the factory to over 4,000 square feet.

Having our own microfilm production facility transformed the publishing business and gave us a new self-confidence, with solid financial benefits as the volume of microfilm and microfiche increased dramatically. Much of the money that would have been paid to Micromedia was now retained within the group. Chadwyck-Healey Microform Publishing Services (CHMPS) was not a limited company but was me operating as a sole trader. It meant that I had unlimited liability, most of which I could insure against, but there were generous personal tax advantages that had been brought in by the last Labour government only the previous year. The first manager left and was replaced by an entrepreneurial manager, Jim Rawles, who also developed profitable commercial microfilm bureau work. He then successfully sold that part of the business to Microgen, one of our large competitors. The third manager, Dave Chapman, stayed almost until the end in 1997 when I sold CHMPS to the same Chris Ronaldson who was still running Micromedia. Once again, our microform master negatives were being held by Micromedia on our behalf, but it was now part of the US conglomerate Bell & Howell, who also owned UMI and who were to buy Chadwyck-Healey in 1999.

The production of microfilm for the publishing companies divides into three periods:

- 1973–9: Microform production carried out by Kodak and Micromedia.
- 1980–97: Microform production carried out by CHMPS (later renamed International Imaging).
- 1997–9: Microform production carried out by Micromedia.

5

Official Publications

In 1969, a new microform publisher, Congressional Information Service (CIS), had been founded by a New York book publisher, James B. 'Jim' Adler. While doing research for a book on American politics he had difficulty finding the documents he wanted because there was no comprehensive bibliography or index to the 300,000 to 400,000 pages of Congressional material published each year. The Library of Congress was not able to get funding to provide such tools so he and his French wife Esthy created an index which, when brought to market, was a great success. The *CIS Index* was well designed and produced, with attractive sans serif typography and his timing was perfect because in the 1970s, partly through the stimulus of the new index, Government Documents or 'Gov Docs' became one of the best-funded departments in most college libraries. Adler had assumed that the 1,100 to 1,200 depository libraries, which he saw as the main customers for the index, had the original documents that they were supposed to receive from the government for free. But now that there was a comprehensive index, librarians found that their collections were far from complete. Adler responded to this by publishing the documents on microfiche. Dissatisfied with the prevailing standards he built his own production facility and the design and presentation of CIS microfiche were as good as that of the index. I knew immediately that this was the standard we should aim for. CIS had another impressive publication, the *American Statistics Index*, that provided bibliographic information on and indexing to all federal documents containing statistics, which he also republished on microfiche.

I asked Adler if we could represent CIS in the UK and Europe. We eventually agreed terms and he came to London to meet me and prospective customers, including the British Library and some government departments. We mailed a sales brochure produced by CIS with our name and address and I made some sales visits in the UK. Dieter Muller, who had been

Johnson's sales representative in Germany, agreed to represent us there. CIS had not mailed brochures in Europe for three years and only had thirteen subscriptions in the UK and Europe for their Congressional indexes and only three for the *American Statistics Index*. I thought we could sell many more but we made very few sales and at the end of 1974 Adler terminated the agreement. The agency had earned us a little money – in August 1974 CIS paid us $12,528 in commissions – but, more importantly, it broadened my vision. I admired Adler and visited him from time to time when I was in Washington, DC. In the late 1970s he sold CIS very successfully to Elsevier, the Dutch publishing giant.

Official statistical serials

It was his *American Statistics Index* that gave me the idea for republishing on microfilm British government publications containing statistical data. Hywel Jones was the co-author of a book that summarized the statistical data in such publications[1] and he agreed to be the editor of our microfilm collection of British government publications from the nineteenth century to 1977, each of which contained significant amounts of statistical data. The 600,000 pages of material covered every aspect of finance, trade and commerce. There were amongst the thirteen series *Annual Statements of Trade*, *Finance Accounts*, *Agricultural Returns*, *Railway Returns* and *Mineral Statistics*, while the *Registrar-General's Statistical Review of England and Wales* provided demographic statistics. One day in early 1974 I came back from lunch to find an envelope from Australia in the second post containing a sheaf of 5 x 3-inch slips, tiny pieces of paper on which someone had managed to type the entire title, *British Government Publications Containing Statistics, 1801–1977*. This was an order from the University of Sydney for the complete set for £3,675 and it made me realize, almost for the first time, that this was becoming a serious business. Jones had told me that he was about to publish a guide to European official statistical serials. They were much harder to find, and their international spread would make them of greater interest. From the late nineteenth century, or from the date of its founding as a modern state, every country in Europe had had a statistics office which published an annual volume containing interesting and important statistical data. We decided to publish this series on microfiche as opposed to microfilm.

These titles were listed in Winchell. One of Fellner's many aphorisms was that 'anything in Winchell always sells'. Winchell was the *Guide to Reference Books* published by ALA, which in the 1960s Constance Winchell, reference librarian at Columbia University Library, had transformed, making it synonymous with her name.[2] The books themselves came from the library of the Royal Statistical Society in Bentinck Street, London. They were stored in a basement which was damp, dirty and cold, a window pane was broken and many of the books were in poor condition, but by the time we were ready to start microfilming, the society had transferred them to the government statistical office in Newport, Wales. There they were properly stored in a spacious modern library, but it meant a seven-hour round trip to collect a car-load of books to bring back for microfilming, not counting the time taken to sort, load and unload them. Most of the government publishers gave us permission. Only Belgium refused and this was restricted to some recent volumes still in print. If there was no response from a country, we still went ahead. *European Official Statistical Serials, 1841–1984* sold solidly for many years and was followed by *Latin American and Caribbean Statistical Serials, 1821–1982*. These titles were in Winchell too and we hoped that they would be of particular interest to US libraries. Finding original volumes and arranging to borrow them for microfilming was the most difficult part of the publication process. However good the original list, when we came to look for the books there were always anomalies. There were books listed that did not appear to exist; books not listed that did; there might be differences in titles and volume numbers; or the volumes we had found were too tightly bound to be filmable or had uncut pages. We had to find the publications of twenty-seven countries for *Latin American and Caribbean Official Statistical Serials* but holdings in the UK were weak. The British Library would not allow their books to be microfilmed because of their condition. But we finally got their agreement on terms which taught me an important lesson in the realpolitik of large public organizations.

In early 1973 I had been stopped at the entrance to the Reading Room by Julian Roberts, a rare books librarian at the British Library, who had said, 'Do you know of the Burney Collection? You might like to look at it. It would be an excellent collection to be on microfilm.' The Reverend Charles Burney (1757–1817) created the largest single collection of English seventeenth- and eighteenth-century newspapers. It was bound up in 700 volumes, with 1,271 titles in all. It was our second publishing agreement with the British Library but neither Fellner nor I spent enough time on it. A young researcher, Michael Harris, drew up a plan for the microfilming of the collection, but, realizing that it contained very few complete runs of newspapers, I decided that we should try to complete the runs by filming individual issues in other libraries. Once again I was making what should have been a straightforward project, where all the microfilming would have been done for us by the British Library, into an unnecessarily complicated and labour-intensive project – and this by a very small company that lacked the resources to do so much additional editorial work. In 1977 after I had asked the British Library for permission to microfilm their volumes of Latin American statistical serials I was invited to a meeting with Hugh Cobbe and a senior colleague, Andrew Phillips. They pointed out that I had still not started microfilming the Burney Collection and that the conservation department wanted to disbind the volumes to undertake major conservation, which would mean that they would not be available for microfilming. They asked me to agree to cancel the agreement and in compensation they would microfilm the volumes of Latin American statistics that we had requested. I should have realized that the ideal time to microfilm the newspapers was when they were disbound and before they were rebound, but I was so anxious to get on with the statistical serials that I too readily agreed to abandon the Burney Collection. A few months later Research Publications announced that they were publishing the Burney Collection on microfilm and I learned later that it was the British Library that had approached them, explaining that the collection was being disbound and that they wanted it microfilmed before it was rebound. At the time I was upset but later I understood why the British Library had taken this decision. Research Publications had a significant presence in the USA and were in a better position to sell it there than we were, the British Library thought we were too small, and we had done nothing to further the project for several years so deserved to lose it. But it rankled. I had a further experience of the British Library's pragmatism in choosing its publishers when they chose us to publish the *Index of Manuscripts in the British Library* in preference to another much smaller publisher (see Chapter 10).

The Library of Congress microfilmed some of the Latin American statistical volumes while twenty volumes came from the New York Public Library (NYPL). They had drawn up with us and with some of our competitors 'An Agreement for the Use of New York Public Library Materials in Republication Projects', which acted as a blanket agreement for any books we wanted to microfilm. It saved time for both the library and us and I never understood why other libraries did not do the same. I went out to the bureau in Brooklyn where the books were being microfilmed. The staff showed me some of the volumes and I was alarmed to see a deep pile of brown fragments on the floor around each camera. The pages of the volumes were so brittle that after they had been turned and flattened, they disintegrated into flakes of brown paper. I hoped that we would not have to re-microfilm any of the volumes to correct errors and wondered how I was going to explain the destruction of the volumes to John Baker, the librarian responsible for the loan of books who had no great love of publishers. To my surprise nothing happened; I realized later that they knew the condition of the volumes and were happy to get a free set of microfiche to replace them.

The volumes at the British Library were in much better condition than those in NYPL because of the very different climatic conditions in the two cities. In NYPL the books were stored in stacks that were not air-conditioned, heated by fierce radiators in the intensely cold New York winters, and in suffocating humidity and heat in the summer. The highly acidic wood-pulp paper deteriorated at a much faster rate in the USA than in the UK because of the huge variations in temperature and humidity throughout the seasons.

But the coordination of filming different volumes from several libraries in the USA, finding bureaux to do the filming and providing them with the correct title-strips and contents pages was time consuming. We had many orders, but we were slow to fulfil them. Five years of keeping libraries waiting while we carried out the microfilming, together with quality problems, did nothing to enhance our reputation for reliability. Yet the *European Official Statistical Serials* sold exceptionally well, with orders from libraries in Germany and Scandinavia from whom we had never had orders before. *Latin American and Caribbean Official Statistical Serials* did not sell as well as we hoped in the USA. We also published *African Official Statistical Serials, 1867–1982*, and while the books were easy to find in the UK, the series sold even less well, and we decided not to microfilm Asian statistical serials.

The HMSO catalogues

Our first title had been eighteenth-century Parliamentary Papers in *Reports from Committees of the House of Commons* and, inspired by CIS, I continued to explore opportunities for microfilming or reprinting other British official publications. In Winchell I found the catalogues of Her Majesty's Stationery Office (HMSO) from 1894 to the present. The annual sales catalogues were the only complete listings of all British official publications and so were important for all British and most Commonwealth libraries. In the USA, while a few large university libraries bought British government publications, in smaller college libraries they came under the heading of Area Studies and would only be bought if Britain was one of the areas being studied. These catalogues were also used by librarians to check on what had been published and for ordering. As there were no cumulations of the catalogues, if a library missed or lost one, they had no record of British official publications for that year. Complete sets of catalogues from 1894 were almost unknown, while the more recent ones were even more important because in the 1930s HMSO added the publications of museums like the Victoria and Albert Museum and the British Museum, for which they were the distributor, and, after the war, the publications of international organizations like the UN, UNESCO and the EEC, now the EU, or European Union. We wanted to reprint the catalogues and indexes as 'reduced reprints' with four original pages printed on each octavo page of the reprint. HMSO informed me that they had already granted permission to another publisher and that they were currently considering a further application to microfilm the catalogues. In the light of this, did we want to reconsider? I replied that we did not, as we were confident that our reprint would compete with both the printed edition and the microfilm edition, and we reached agreement to reprint the catalogues and indexes that were still in copyright.

The two competing publishers were both American, Oceana Publications for the reprint and Carrollton Press for the microfilm. At the time I did not know that the expert on this esoteric subject was K. A. 'Ken' Mallaber, the Librarian of the Department of Trade and Industry (DTI), who had been planning to publish a reprint of the government sales catalogues from 1836 to 1965 for Oceana Publications and had published an article announcing his reprint in April 1973.[3] I had introduced Adler to Mallaber and he had been helpful in advising us on the launch of the CIS publications in the UK, but now we were in competition. In an angry phone call, he told me he had asked Scolar Press for a quotation for a reprint of the catalogues, as we had done, and did not believe me when I told him that the idea to reprint these catalogues had not come from them. Bill Buchanan's Carrollton Press was planning to microfilm the catalogues as part of the *Controller's Office Library*, in which their grandly named Historical Documents Institute in Inverness would publish everything that HMSO had published from 1922 to 1972, both Parliamentary and non-Parliamentary Papers, 12 million pages on 4,000 reels of microfilm.

At a reduction of four original pages on one reprinted octavo page, we would publish over 112 catalogues and indexes, from 1894 to 1974, totalling 18,000 pages, in seven volumes, bound in maroon buckram. As with our previous reduced reprints (see Chapter 3) we had to print 500 copies to justify the high cost of stripping up the pages. I wanted to test the market and we mailed a typed announcement to libraries in the UK for the five volumes covering 'fifty years of government publications 1920-1970'. By return came the first order, from Essex County Library in Chelmsford. I knew we had a winner. We published the first five volumes in 1974 but took longer to publish the two volumes covering 1894-1919. We were still sourcing original copies of the early catalogues in 1975 and I asked Mallaber if we could borrow the early volumes and some other government publications that we needed for another microfilm collection. He replied that his library was a private collection and that it would take too much staff time to deal with our request; we should use a public collection like that at the British Library. In my response I wrote, 'A senior civil servant in a department whose role is to foster British trade is using delays and evasion knowing that such actions are fully in the interests of an American company with whom at some time he has formed a personal link, and against the interests of a competing British company.'[4] There was no reply but when I wrote to him later to ask him if he would lend us the 1895 volume because the British Library copy was defective it was sent to us in the mail by return. I felt that the public institutions we were now dealing with – the British Library, HMSO and government departments, all funded by the taxpayer at a time when the UK was in a serious economic crisis – showed very little interest in supporting British business and industry, which were always being exhorted to innovate and export. We were trying to do both, but I had been bruised by my experiences with the British Library with the Bentley archive and the Burney Collection. I found HMSO at times difficult and pernickety to deal with and now I was faced with a senior government librarian putting the interests of a US publisher ahead of those of a new UK publisher. This was the climate of the 1970s. In contrast to the USA, small businesses in the UK were regarded with some disdain, the term 'entrepreneur' having slightly negative connotations, and it was not until the Thatcher years that starting your own business and being an entrepreneur were seen as 'a good thing'. But we had some support from the library community. R. G. Surridge wrote, referring to Mallaber's earlier article:[5]

> This mentioned a plan for a reprint of the catalogues by an American publisher, and it is a matter of satisfaction that those catalogues should now have been published by a British publisher, not least because the reprint's sterling price protects British purchasers from the recent weakening of the pound against the dollar.

Sales of the HMSO catalogues were thirty-eight per cent of our total sales for the financial year 1974/5 and were one of the mainstays of the business for several years. Each morning there were new orders for Cherry, our packer. She wrapped the books first in corrugated paper and then in shiny greeny-brown waterproof paper, working on a bench at the end of the large room which was also my office. A set of the catalogues cost £225; we sold all 500 copies of the catalogues and indexes and after the first edition sold out in 1979, we reprinted them. The production cost of the first edition was about £12,000 and the total revenue of the first printing less royalties and discounts to dealers was in the region of £100,000. Neither the Oceana nor Carrollton Press editions were ever published.

Nineteenth-Century Parliamentary Papers

In December 1978 I visited Diana Marshallsay, the Librarian of the Ford Collection of Parliamentary Papers at the University of Southampton, which had been the source of the IUP reprints of the nineteenth-century Parliamentary Papers. As we walked round the library I admired her set of the Parliamentary Papers, which had come from the Carlton Club in London. She said that, far from being an asset, it was an enormous liability. The wood-pulp paper used from about 1850 was now disintegrating because of its acidity, and the cost of conserving several thousand volumes was far beyond the resources of her library. I asked her why they did not buy the microfilm edition produced by UMI. She replied that while they had listed the Parliamentary Papers in their catalogue for many years, they had never produced it.

On my way home, I wondered whether we should not publish a microfilm edition of the nineteenth-century Parliamentary Papers. The 6,000 volumes totalled 4.2 million pages and I knew that I did not have the resources to undertake such a project without the guaranteed sale of enough sets to cover the production cost. My premise was that if the original sets did deteriorate to the point of being unusable the world's single most important body of historical information for the nineteenth century would only be available in the Readex edition (see Appendix 1) and the IUP reprints. The former was in microprint, which by 1979 was regarded as an outdated and unsatisfactory publishing medium used by only one publisher, Readex, and while their edition had been prepared under the aegis of the American Historical Society and had been edited by an eminent historian, Edgar L. Erickson, using the set of Parliamentary Papers in NYPL together with papers from other libraries, it was not complete. The limitation of the IUP set was that, as stated in Chapter 1, it comprised only fifteen to twenty per cent of the whole. But with so many libraries owning either the Readex set or the IUP reprints the acquisition of a new microform edition would not be a priority, especially at a time when budgets were being cut. I decided to approach it differently, as a national preservation project, arguing that original sets were deteriorating and that there was an urgent need for a new archivally permanent edition to be published. In order to carry out this project I would invite libraries in the UK to become our partners by subscribing to it. Their subscriptions would enable us to cover the cost of creating the microfilm masters and in return the subscribers would acquire a microfilm set at cost. As soon as I announced the idea in 1979, stating that we would undertake the production of by far the largest microfilming project ever done in the UK, Micromedia responded with a rival project in direct competition with us. They hired F. W. 'Bill' Torrington who ran Oceana Publications in the UK as their advisor, but their disadvantage was that they were unknown as a publisher and were also requiring libraries to pay in advance, while we were only asking for payment on delivery of the microfilm.

Of the 208 librarians invited to a meeting at the National Book League in London on 26 April 1979 to discuss the project, twenty-seven came but I had lost my voice and was inaudible. Our editor Pratt was also at the meeting and had to talk for me, although I had not told him what I was going to say. Since the main reason for publishing this edition was for preservation I was concerned when A. G. Parker from Cambridge said that their set was in good condition. Fortunately Bernard Naylor, University Librarian at Southampton, who was there with Marshallsay, said that their set required conservation at a cost of £60 per volume or £250,000 (the pre-1850 volumes would not need conservation), and Stephen Richard from the Bodleian and Eve Johansson from the British Library both said that their sets were in poor condition. During the tea break they also told me that we should publish it on microfiche rather than microfilm because it was a more usable and popular medium with readers. We had produced a sample microfiche, which was on show at the meeting, but microfilm had seemed the obvious medium, as we wanted to keep the production cost as low as possible and it costs less to produce a microfilm master reel than the equivalent number of master microfiche. Others told me that they would not expect to pay more than £12,000 for a set. This was a much lower price than I had envisaged and was absurdly low for over 46,000 microfiche, a price of £0.26 per microfiche at a time when we were selling microfiche for £0.75–£1 each. We also proposed that we would offer subscribers a shared five per cent royalty on all future sales, paid annually. It did not sound much but it was there to emphasize the fact that these libraries were our partners and it was their investment that would make it possible to carry out the project. We struck a chord with the royalty offer, one librarian suggesting that it should be on a sliding scale. No one seemed concerned that I, with no voice, could not answer their questions; it was their opportunity to tell me what they wanted. It taught me two lessons: that it is better to listen than to talk, and the importance of tea breaks. We now knew that there was interest among some librarians, what they expected to pay and what format they wanted the edition to be in. We drew up a legally binding agreement and sent it out with a letter and a sample microfiche to all national, university and public libraries in the UK and Eire.

Microfiche master negatives were more expensive to produce than microfilm masters but, per page, microfiche copies were cheaper than microfilm copies because the image area was smaller and most of the cost of a microform copy is in the silver halide film. I found that the saving in making the microfiche copies was greater than the extra expense of making the microfiche master negatives. Having switched to microfiche I calculated that a subscription price of £12,500 would require twenty subscribers for us to break even. When Albert Boni launched his nineteenth-century Parliamentary Papers microprint edition in 1940, he had stated that he would only go ahead when he had received at least twenty-five subscriptions at $5,000 each. In 1979 this price was equivalent to £11,945,[6] a price that was surprisingly close to ours. The cost of making the twenty microfiche sets, a total of 930,000 microfiche, would be £120,000, leaving us £130,000 to cover the cost of making 46,500 master microfiche – £2.80 a microfiche. Our filming cost would have to be £0.05 per frame compared to that being charged at the time by the British Library of £0.09 and by Micromedia of £0.06.

Each subscriber would also share between them a royalty on all future sales, initially five per cent, rising to ten per cent after a number of copies had been sold. It was now the autumn of 1979 and the closing date of the offer was 1 November; a few signed agreements came in quickly, but we were far from the twenty we needed. If we did not get twenty, we would not go ahead. There were several surprises; first, the Bodleian Library in Oxford, which in the person of Stephen Richard had been so interested in the project, said that it could not subscribe because it did not have enough money. Cambridge, on the other hand, was one of the first subscribers. A signed agreement arrived from the library of the University of Liverpool. This was a library that had never bought much from us and had never allowed me to visit it. Now it was one of our first subscribers. I saw the *Nineteenth-Century Parliamentary Papers* as make or break for this small, six-year-old company. A project on this scale, which would take three years to complete, would lift the company on to a different level and I wanted it to succeed more than anything I had ever done. We had to be sure of having £250,000 of sales to cover our production costs and I kept a piece of paper in my pocket with the names of the libraries that might subscribe and those that already had. Each week it changed. Between 20 September and 9 October, I visited sixteen libraries from Edinburgh to Aberystwyth, including Manchester, Sheffield and Hull. As I lay in my hotel room near Swansea with the light of the Mumbles lighthouse flashing across the ceiling, I knew that this was the make or break trip. The next day I visited the University of Bristol and the day after the University of Exeter. Both subscribed – Bristol had to pay for it out of reserves. From that part of the trip I got four subscriptions; the two others were the National Library of Wales at Aberystwyth and the University of Wales at Cardiff. We were nearly there.

I was then invited to a meeting by Douglas J. Foskett, the Librarian of the Senate House Library, the library of the University of London. He explained that the project was an important one and if librarians were going to support the creation of the definitive national set, they needed to be confident that we were capable of producing it. He agreed that we had two knowledgeable advisors, Marshallsay and Kenneth A. C. Parsons, official publications librarian at Cambridge University Library and the author of the only definitive bibliography of the nineteenth-century Parliamentary Papers Bound Set,[7] but Foskett would only support the project if Bill Torrington was also one of our advisors. This could have been difficult because Torrington had been working for Oceana at the time of the HMSO catalogues project and he was now the advisor to Micromedia for their rival project. But Foskett told me that Torrington would be amenable to an approach from me. He also made it clear that he was not only speaking for his library but for other senior librarians. I was relieved: Torrington would join us as an advisor, the Micromedia project would be no more and, most importantly, our project would have a semi-official seal of approval. Torrington joined our editorial board. He was a nice man with an enormous knowledge of British government publications and went on to edit some other Parliamentary publications for us.

Mitsuo Nitta, our agent in Japan, was making his annual trip to London. I had known him since the late 1960s when his company, Yushodo, had imported books from Cornmarket Press for sale in Japan. He was both an important antiquarian bookseller and a large importer of scholarly reprints and microfilms. He was not the only importer in Japan – Maruzen and Kinokuniya were much larger – but Nitta was easier to deal with as he was the owner of the company that had been started by his father before the war, and he could make immediate decisions, which was so untypical of Japanese business at that time. He had been educated at the University of California and his English was good, though spoken with a clipped, guttural accent in which he seemed to shoot out the words with machine-gun rapidity. At our meeting I told him about the project and he said he would order three sets at the price I had quoted him, £15,000 each. Because we had set a price only for British subscribers, I was able to quote him a price of my choosing rather than the normal practice of Japanese agents of taking a forty per cent discount on the publisher's list price and then marking up the price in yen to a far higher level. While it appeared that the importer was making a huge profit, the yen price was just the basis for negotiation with the library and it was impossible to ever know what the library actually paid. Part of our agreement with Yushodo was that we would never send our brochures to Japanese libraries, though occasionally a library in Japan would try to order a collection at its original price through a foreign dealer like Blackwell's. If we suspected that it was an order for Japan, we would refuse to supply it.

At the end of the meeting Nitta said, 'Charles, this must be costing you a lot of money. Would you like to borrow some money from me?' I was surprised and touched. I thanked him and said that I would consider it but that I did not think that I would need to borrow from him. In almost thirty years, he was the only person who ever offered, unprompted, to either lend me money or invest in the business.

The British Library was already a subscriber but also ordered a negative copy, which they wanted to use to make paper copies and individual microfiche copies in their Lending Division at Boston Spa, near York. There was an extra cost in making the negative copy, but it still added to the prospective total. By December 1979 we had nineteen subscriptions including the British Library's two, and there was one free set due to the DTI (see below). Yushodo's three orders at a higher price could be added, so now we had the equivalent of almost twenty-three orders. The final list of libraries who ordered could not have been predicted. There were disappointments: no orders from the Bodleian, Manchester or any library in Scotland other than Edinburgh, and none from libraries in Eire or Northern Ireland. But there were pleasant surprises too: the library of the House of Commons, the Open University, the North East London Polytechnic, Bedfordshire and Nottinghamshire county libraries, the City of Birmingham and, surprisingly, the University of Hull, presumably sanctioned by the librarian and poet Philip Larkin, who would not see salesmen and had a known dislike of microfilm. In 1972 Ashby, one of the founders of Micromedia (see Chapters 3 and 4), was working for Kodak and had been sent to Hull to extol the virtues of microfilm. Larkin took him to the window of his office, pointed to the just completed library extension and exclaimed, 'It has to be filled with books or they'll take it away from me so f**k off with your microfilm!'[8]

Almost all the libraries who ordered had had representatives at the meeting in April. We now had to deliver the complete collection in three years at the rate of 1.4 million pages a year. But to do so we needed two things: a suitable set to microfilm, and production facilities. By January 1980 we had one but not the other. Earlier in 1979, at a library conference, I had chatted to Lewis Foreman who was Librarian of the DTI, and he immediately offered to lend us the Board of Trade set, which he said would be ideal because it was particularly complete, having been made up from other sets including those from the Treasury and Cabinet Office and had been added to by Mallaber, his predecessor,[9] especially for the difficult first decade of the nineteenth century. The bindings were loose with years of use because the volumes had been used for interlibrary loan through the old National Central Library borrowing scheme and they could be opened flat for filming. In return Foreman simply asked for a free microfiche copy. We remained friends and worked together on other projects when he was Librarian at the Foreign and Commonwealth Office.

The end of 1979 and the beginning of 1980 was a difficult time. The second oil crisis had followed the fall of the Shah of Iran in early 1979 and in January 1980 Jimmy Carter issued the Carter Doctrine, which declared that any interference with US oil interests in the Persian Gulf would be considered an attack on the vital interests of the USA. Thatcher had become prime minister in May 1979 and made the universities one of her first targets as state-funded institutions that she considered had grown fat and complacent on taxpayers' money. I was surprised that some of the more conservative academics seemed to agree and even Sir Peter Swinnerton-Dyer, who had been both vice-chancellor of Cambridge University and chief executive of the University Funding Council, said, 'The instinct of a woman is to spring-clean and this country needed spring-cleaning, not least the university sector.'[10] Things were not much better in the USA where there had been a panicky overreaction to the oil crisis with queues at gas stations when world production of petroleum had dropped by only four per cent. But the price of crude oil rose to $39.80 a barrel, a price in real terms that it did not reach again until 2008. I could see that 1980 was going to be a difficult year, just when we had this new production facility and were hiring the staff to man it – though most of them were women. Then, in February, we began to receive cheques for £12,500 from our subscribers – payment in full three years in advance of completion of delivery and before we had delivered a single microfiche. We had expected to invoice the subscribers as the microfiche were delivered but now, in the Thatcher onslaught, library budgets were being cut, even to the extent of clawbacks of unspent money during the financial year. The librarians had signed a legally binding subscription agreement and they wanted to get the money out of their hands before it could be taken away from them. I had also stumbled across a practice that was well known to our large US competitors. If a publication only cost a few thousand pounds, libraries would pay for it only when it was delivered, but if they had placed an order, often to take advantage of an attractive pre-publication discount, for a publication costing £10,000 or more, even if it was to be delivered beyond the end of the current financial year, they preferred to take the money out of the budget at the time of placing the order, and the easiest way to do this was to pay the publisher in advance. They would also only do so if they trusted the publisher and it seemed that in spite of the delays of some of our projects, we had now earned that trust. The impact on our finances was dramatic. We had received over £100,000 and it meant that we would not require a loan from Coutts to convert the granary and buy the processors and duplicators and all the other equipment we needed.

One of the concerns expressed by our subscribers was that we would be overtaken by inflation during the three years of production. In April 1980 the annual inflation rate peaked at 14.76 per cent but during the time that we were trying to get the *Nineteenth-Century Parliamentary Papers* off the ground another international drama was being played out by the Texan Nelson Bunker Hunt and his brother Herbert, which could have done far more damage. In 1979, with their Saudi partners, they tried to corner the silver market by buying 280 million ounces of silver, eighty per cent of the world's production. The price rose from $6 to $48.70 a troy ounce. In January 1980, under pressure from the US government, who saw the hand of the Middle East in the destabilization of the market in an important commodity, exchange rules regarding leveraged positions were changed and the position the Hunts found themselves in became more and more difficult. On 'Silver Thursday', 27 March 1980, the Hunts missed a margin call and the price of silver plunged back to under $11. The implications for our project had been serious: the single largest cost of the whole project was that of the silver halide film from Kodak required to make over a million microfiche. We needed to buy 16,000 square metres of film with a thin coating of silver halide emulsion, an area equivalent to two and a half football pitches. If the price of film had doubled, the project would have had to have been abandoned. As an indication of the price sensitivity of the microfiche copies that we were planning to make, we imported 500,000 microfiche envelopes for $5,000 from a supplier in Louisiana because even with shipping costs and import duty they were each 0.5p cheaper than those sourced in the UK. But during the whole period of the Hunts' adventure Kodak's silver microfilm price hardly moved. I never discovered why not. We had three cameras in Cambridge so could start filming as soon as the first books arrived but our production unit at Bassingbourn did not open until April 1980 and the first deliveries to subscribers were not made until the summer. The Hunts had come and gone before we had produced a single microfiche.

Before we started to microfilm the books, work needed to be done in planning and preparing them for filming, including making layout sheets for each microfiche and creating the text for the eye-legible title-strips. To manage the project Marshallsay suggested a young man who had worked at the Ford Centre but had been made redundant when university budgets were cut. Peter Cockton came to see me, and I immediately employed him. He had to source the volumes and ensure that they were complete. Although we had Parsons' bibliography as our guide, the variation in contents from one set to another reflected the vagaries of publishing the 78,000 separate papers that made up the Bound Set. Cockton had the experience and tenacity to determine exactly what should be in our 'definitive set'. He was also able to examine any set in the UK that he thought might contain variants. He later published his own guide to the microfiche edition, which is itself a work of scholarship.[11] The anomalies that make determination of the 'complete' Bound Set so difficult include papers referred to in indexes that do not exist, and forty-four papers cited in the indexes that are not found in the Bound Set yet were found to have been published and are included in the microfiche edition. There are other anomalies such as variations from one set to another in the contents pages of certain volumes. There was also an index issued in 1884 that was never included in the Bound Set but was then reprinted by HMSO in 1938 and is also in the microfiche edition. Solving these bibliographic problems and ensuring that the volumes delivered for microfilming were complete and correct took up much of Cockton's time. He also realized, as had the Fords and the editors of IUP, that locating documents on a particular subject was difficult and time consuming, and we agreed that he should single-handedly compile a subject catalogue to the nineteenth-century Parliamentary Papers. It was too large a task to index the contents of each paper so instead he took the title of each paper and made an assessment of the subject or subjects that it covered, using a set of subject headings that he had drawn up. For eight years Cockton worked on his own, a diminutive figure surrounded by piles of large quarto volumes. The subject catalogue was published in five volumes in 1988.[12] We entered it for the Library Association reference book of the year award but a bibliography of the literature by and about T. E. Lawrence in one volume was the winner, while ours was 'highly commended'. This seemed to me to say more about the tastes of the judges than the comparative virtues of the two publications. The catalogue was well reviewed, and in 2013 Miles Taylor, then director of the Institute of Historical Research at the University of London and an eminent parliamentary historian, said to me, unprompted, how valuable the Cockton catalogue had been to him. Cockton continued to work for Chadwyck-Healey until he retired several years after I sold the company.

We offered the Parliamentary Papers to overseas libraries at the pre-publication price of £25,000, and while there were few orders in the difficult first nine months of 1980 it sold steadily through the 1980s and then received a surprise fillip after the fall of the Berlin Wall, when libraries in the old East Germany and other Iron Curtain countries began to buy microform collections as well as CD-ROMs, funded by Soros and the European Union. By the mid-1990s each of the original subscribers had received back over £10,000 as their share of the royalty due to the subscribers. It was the best investment most of those libraries ever made and it was a good investment for us too, with total revenues of £2 million. We followed up with a similar subscription offer to UK libraries for the Parliamentary Papers for 1900–21, a further 18,000 microfiche. After 1921, as an economy measure, far fewer Parliamentary Papers were published and the format of the papers themselves was reduced from quarto to octavo, while the number of non-Parliamentary Papers increased. This too was a successful microfiche publication and we continued to microfilm the Parliamentary Papers from 1921 until 1975, which was another 18,000 microfiche. In all, the Parliamentary Papers from 1801 to 1975 totalled around 7.5 million pages on more than 82,000 microfiche. As I had originally envisaged, filming them and making copies for sale were the mainstay of the Bassingbourn production operation throughout much of the 1980s. But now we were also looking at publishing the current Parliamentary Papers as a new publishing service.

Current Parliamentary Papers

Each year the House of Commons generates many hundreds of papers, the Parliamentary or Sessional Papers, including green papers, which are consultative documents, and white papers, which are statements of policy and proposals for changes in the law. These are the record of the policies and initiatives of government that are reported and commented on every day in the press. A large public library or university library should subscribe to these papers but up to 1980, through an archaic practice dating from 1801, most libraries did not receive their set of the Parliamentary Papers until as long as two years after the end of the Parliamentary session. This was because at the end of each session the papers were reorganized into four major categories – Bills, Reports of Committees, Reports of Commissions, and Accounts and Papers – and were further arranged by subject before being bound up into volumes with new contents pages and an index. Within each volume the pages had to be renumbered by hand by the library or its supplier, as it was these page numbers that were referred to in the contents pages and index for each session. While large libraries might have two subscriptions, one for the loose papers as they were published and a second for the Bound Set, this was a duplication that few libraries could afford. Several booksellers including Blackwell's had a profitable business binding up sets and selling them to libraries. The publication and indexing of the Parliamentary Papers had always been the responsibility of the House of Commons Library until 1969 when the Board of Trade Library Services – at the time when they were run by Mallaber – took over. In 1979 they returned to the House of Commons Library, which was in the process of introducing a new computer indexing system, POLIS (Parliamentary Online Indexing System), which bore no relation to the previous index. Papers in the Bound Set were now arranged by the paper number printed on the title page. Libraries could now subscribe to the papers as they were published and have them bound up during or at the end of the session in paper-number order. It made me realize that we could now publish a microfiche edition of the Parliamentary Papers, as the microfiche would not have to be renumbered, and we could send them by airmail so that overseas libraries received them more quickly.

In 1980 I had sensed a change at HMSO. There was a more entrepreneurial spirit amongst some of the new, younger managers and this may have been because of a change in the way that they were financed, which had come in on 1 April. Before then all the printing and publishing that HMSO carried out for Parliament, departments and agencies were paid for by HMSO itself out of its vote or budget agreed by Parliament in advance. Now, while Parliamentary Papers were still produced out of

HMSO's vote, the publishing or printing they did for departments and agencies had to be paid for by the departments and agencies themselves, but the latter were free to go elsewhere for these services. Another important change was that HMSO announced that they would no longer supply free sets to Commonwealth libraries, as they had been doing since 1914.

HMSO agreed to our request to publish a microfiche edition of the current Parliamentary Papers but only for one year, warning me that they expected to publish their own microfiche edition in the future. I assumed that they were just using us to test the market, but it was worth the risk. In June 1980 on a sales trip to Japan, Australia and New Zealand I took a typed sheet describing our new microfiche edition. In Canada the University of British Columbia had been shocked to find that they would now have to pay C$7,000 for a previously free subscription, but then found that our microfiche edition only cost US$1,250, and they would also receive the papers more quickly. In a review Suzanne Dodson, head of government publications and microforms at the University of British Columbia Library, wrote, 'That Chadwyck-Healey was ready and waiting with their excellent set was fortuitous indeed. Were they merely prescient – or did they have a mole in H.M.S.O?'[13] By September orders were coming in from the libraries I had visited and very soon the current Parliamentary Papers became one of our most valuable subscription publications. We charged libraries £750 for a Parliamentary session paid in advance, irrespective of how many microfiche a session contained, although over the next ten years the subscription price rose to £1,500. The annual net revenue varied because some sessions were very short, and when there were two in a year because of an election our income doubled. At other times a session continued for more than a year and the libraries would still only pay for one subscription. HMSO no longer had the expense of printing and mailing hundreds of free copies of Parliamentary Papers but the royalties they earned from the microfiche edition (10 per cent rising to 17.5 per cent) could not have compensated for the paid-for orders for the printed publications that they also lost. Nor were the booksellers pleased to see the income they earned from making up and selling bound sets much diminished. For the next few years the one-year agreement continued to roll over to the next year, but eventually HMSO gave us a longer agreement and never did publish a microfiche edition themselves.

The Non-HMSO Catalogue

In the summer of 1979 I discussed what else we might publish in this area with John Pemberton, the Librarian of the University of Buckingham and one of the UK's most knowledgeable official publications librarians. He told me that what libraries needed most were the many official publications that were not published by HMSO. He explained that government departments found HMSO slow and expensive and were now using new, cheap, fast, short-run printing methods that were increasingly available from both instant-print bureaux and conventional printers. A department would self-publish a report in an edition of a few hundred copies, and the copies would sit in boxes in someone's office without the means of distribution that there would have been if it had been published by HMSO when it would have been listed in their catalogues and properly publicized. It was a bibliographic nightmare for libraries as these documents were not included in the *British National Bibliography* and they had no means of knowing that they even existed or, if they did, from where to obtain them. Pemberton gave as an example a report on a fire at Woolworths in Manchester in 1979, in which eleven people lost their lives, the worst fire disaster in the city since the war. The Home Office had published a report, which was referred to in the newspapers, but few libraries had it or could find out who had published it.[14] Pemberton explained that there were thousands of publications not only from the departments of state but from the hundreds of agencies, organizations and quangos, ranging from the Forestry Commission to the Horserace Betting Levy Board, all of which were publishing books, papers, magazines and reports, none of which were included in HMSO's catalogues. Librarians had already recognized this huge lacuna in the recording of British government publications, but nobody knew what to do about it. Marshallsay had written about it in 1972[15] as had Pemberton himself a year later.[16] Johannsson of the British Library and Richard of the Bodleian had also written about it, but it was only in April 1979 that the Committee of Departmental Librarians set up a sub-committee to consider ways of disseminating bibliographic information about these publications. Although I was preoccupied that summer with the launch of the *Nineteenth-Century Parliamentary Papers*, with the creation of our own production facility and with a very demanding colour microfiche publication at the National Gallery of Art in Washington (see Chapter 6), I knew that we should look at it immediately. We would publish a catalogue of these publications and microfilm the publications themselves. The catalogue would have to be generated out of a computer database – something that would be new for us – while the microfilming of the documents themselves would be the most straightforward part of the project.

Charles Rogers, the chairman of the sub-committee, put our proposal on the agenda of their first meeting in early September 1979. Discussions went on through the spring of 1980 and at a meeting with the sub-committee Alex Allardyce, from the British Library, turned to me and said, 'If we were doing it, it would require considerable resources, I suppose you are doing it with one man and a dog?' 'Not one man, one woman', I replied. Some librarians were disappointed that no national body was taking on the task, but in an article published in June 1980 Rogers wrote that, 'The response so far [to the Chadwyck-Healey proposal] from government departments has been sufficiently encouraging for the firm to indicate that the proposals will be implemented. The firm is expected to announce its plans publicly in September 1980.'[17] By this time we had approached 375 organizations to ask them to send us a copy of each of their publications; 132 had agreed, 12 had refused and 241 had not replied or made a decision. We still had a long way to go. We also had to wait for decisions by the Department of the Environment and the Department of Health and Social Security, since without the agreement of two such important departments, we would not be able to go ahead. Eventually all the departments of state agreed to send us their publications and this enabled us to go ahead with publication of the catalogue. Richard at the Bodleian gave us his unique list of government departments, agencies and quangos that were publishing their own material, which he was also collecting, and our researcher in the Bodleian copied on to cards the bibliographic information about them, which was then all input to our database. This was just before the birth in Cambridge of the BBC Micro, the first popular microcomputer, which as soon as it became available in 1981, we used in the office for inputting data on to floppy disks until a few years later when we replaced it with a PC. The same year we published the first *Catalogue of British Official Publications Not Published by HMSO*, a cloth-bound volume containing the publications of 1980 that we had collected and catalogued. Another mouthful of a title, with a negative in it, it was quickly abbreviated to the 'Non-HMSO Catalogue'.

From 1981 onwards, we published paperbound bi-monthly issues, which were cumulated into an annual catalogue at the end of the year. Libraries could subscribe to either the combination of the bi-monthly issues and the cumulated annual catalogue or just buy the latter. We had already worked with the Cambridge University Computing Centre on a project to publish on computer-output microfiche (COM) (see Appendix 2) the data that Professor Alan Macfarlane and his team had input into the university mainframe computer taken from the medieval records of the Essex village of Earls Colne.[18] We now worked with Dr Robin Anderson at the Computing Centre who wrote the software and processed the data for us, producing camera-ready copy for the printer. The woman whom I had referred to in my meeting with the sub-committee was Hazel Wright who was an excellent editor and established all the processes from scratch, but she and I took time to find a way of working together as she was quite outspoken about my management style. When she left to take an editorial job at CUP, I was about to advertise for a successor when her assistant, Alison Moss, told me that she could edit the catalogue. Moss, who had joined us straight from Cambridge University, was bored with microfilm production and I gave her the job. She did it superbly and made it seem easy. But advances in technology improved the process and over the next ten years, it evolved in the following stages:

1. Entries manually typed and then rekeyed into a mainframe computer by the University Computing Service. Output: camera-ready copy to go to the printer.
2. Entries typed into BBC Micros and later PCs in the office and the floppy disks processed by the University Computing Service. Output as above.
3. Floppy disks processed on a mini-computer owned and managed by Robin Anderson who produced the camera-ready copy.
4. Entries typed into networked PCs and processed in the office. Output: camera-ready copy produced in house.

One of the next editors, David Worthington, married Moss and later became head of technical support until they both left the company in 1998 (see Chapter 23).

HMSO was the clearing house for permissions from the departments and agencies whose publications we were microfilming, and they received royalties from us on their behalf. Organizations could immediately see the advantages of having their publications listed in our catalogue, as we also included the address and even room number from where a publication could be obtained. When in 1981 Frank Hooley's Freedom of Information

Bill had been killed in the House of Commons, the minister for the Civil Service Department, Barney Hayhoe, used our catalogue to defend the government's record on Open Government. In a paper that I gave to an Open Government seminar in May 1982 I suggested that the problem was not secrecy, but the huge amount of published information made available by government, which in practice remained unknown and unused.[19] In the 1980 catalogue there were 3,542 publications. Within two years our coverage had more than doubled. The total peaked in 1991 at 12,056 and thereafter settled down to around 11,000 publications each year – more than were published by HMSO. In spite of the publication of *UKOP* on CD-ROM and later online (see below) we continued to publish the printed catalogue. The microfiche never sold as well as we hoped and unlike CIS, where microfiche sales provided most of the revenue, it was the catalogue that made a profit and provided subscription revenue every year.

In 1980 I also learned about 'online', the provision of bibliographic, numerical and other kinds of data via phone lines from a mainframe computer to the user with a terminal on his desk. It had been in existence for ten years and the dominant company was Dialog based in Mountain View near the Stanford University campus and what later became known as Silicon Valley. I was spellbound by the vision of a researcher having a terminal on his desk in his study at home giving him access to an entire world of knowledge delivered via a phone line. I was in Adler's office in Washington, DC when his financial controller brought in their first royalty statement from Dialog for revenues earned from online access to the CIS databases. It was only a few thousand dollars, but it was another indication of where future revenues would come from. Until then I had only seen computers as backroom resources for the storage and organization of data and for the processing of data for bibliographies like the Non-HMSO Catalogue, but now I began to understand how computers were going to fundamentally change the organization and dissemination of knowledge. For me an exciting new era was unfolding that would culminate in the CD-ROM and, after it, the Internet.

In 1984 we licensed the Non-HMSO Catalogue to Dialog. I met Charles 'Charlie' Bourne, director general of information services, at their office in Mountain View, and our agreement was signed by Roger Summit, the founder of Dialog. The first royalty statement stated that we had had usage so small that it did not earn any royalties. This situation continued until after a few years we terminated the agreement. At the time I thought that the Non-HMSO Catalogue lacked international appeal, though many large US libraries subscribed to the paper edition, but with the coming of the CD-ROM Dialog was revealed as a digital dinosaur, a relic of the prehistory of digital information with structural problems that doomed it to failure, which are explained in Chapter 17.

UKOP

The two printed catalogues of government publications, one from HMSO and the other from us, co-existed comfortably as separate publications until the introduction of the CD-ROM encouraged both of us to consider the creation of a single catalogue of British official publications. Discussions started in July 1987 and an agreement was reached in June 1988. We took HMSO's data, processed it so that it could be merged with ours and produced the CD-ROMs along with their storage boxes and manuals, initially using Online bibliographic software and later our own Caravan software (see Chapter 11). We also provided software maintenance and advice to both our and HMSO's customers. We named it *UKOP* (*Catalogue of United Kingdom Official Publications*) and continued to offer the non-HMSO publications on microfiche. But we and HMSO became complacent, and when by 1996 CD-ROM publications were being replaced by online delivery of data via the Internet, we did nothing about it. In 1997 HMSO was split into HMSO with its statutory responsibilities, and the privatized The Stationery Office (TSO), which was going to take on most of HMSO's responsibilities including commercial activities such as the supply of stationery and office furniture to government departments and agencies. When ASLIB, the association of professional librarians, and the Ford Collection at the University of Southampton together produced a rival catalogue, which they cheekily called *NUKOP* (*New Catalogue of UK Official Publications*), neither of us paid much attention. This changed when in autumn 1997, under the DTI's Information Society Initiative, the publishers of *NUKOP* were given a grant of £50,000 towards its publication. There is nothing more energizing than a well-founded grievance, and we and HMSO stood shoulder to shoulder in our indignation. It was an absurd example of civil servants working in silos as, only a few months before, in February 1997, Peter MacDonald, controller of HMSO, had sent a directive to all departments and agencies to ask them to send their publications to

Chadwyck-Healey more quickly, as we were preparing a catalogue that would be available on the Internet and updated weekly. A director from TSO and I visited Bill McIntyre, head of directorate at the DTI, and got what I reported as 'the nearest we will get to an apology from a civil servant'. But it pushed us into producing our online version of *UKOP*, which was launched at the Online Conference in London in December 1997, on the TSO/HMSO stand, which had been tied up with red ribbon to be cut by David Steel, a previous leader of the Liberal Party. The University of Southampton and ASLIB agreed to stop using the name *NUKOP*, which was a direct infringement of our title, and at a bad-tempered meeting in December 1997 they reluctantly agreed to rename their database *BOPCAS* (*British Official Publications Current Awareness Service*). Launched at the Online Conference in 1998, it was more than just a catalogue of government publications. Under the banner of 'current awareness' they were doing what we and HMSO had unsuccessfully tried to do in 1980 when we had launched two newsletters, *Business and Government* and *Personnel and Government*, which gave brief abstracts of official publications of interest to business and industry. Our newsletters had failed to attract enough subscribers and were terminated after a few months. In February 1999 Mark Barragry, our senior editor, summed up the situation:

> UKOP Online is seen by TSO as a mature product (ie a dead-end from a development point of view) which has performed poorly.... Karen [Brown, of HMSO] does not expect to turn round the poor sales.... TSO shares our view on BOPCAS – that it ... could grow into something much stronger [and] is showing us part of the way in producing current awareness and alerting services.[20]

By then we were preoccupied with the launch of an entirely new online reference publication, *KnowUK* (see Chapter 23), and I was in the early stages of selling the companies (see Chapter 24), and we did little to improve *UKOP Online*.

Hansard

Our penultimate government publication was the *House of Commons Official Report* (*Hansard*) on CD-ROM, published in partnership with HMSO. We were already publishing a microfiche edition of *Hansard* that we included with the current Parliamentary Papers. An easy-to-use digital edition of *Hansard*, the daily record of speeches in the House of Commons, would enable people to go into their library to search the database to see how often their MP had spoken in debates and what he or she had said. All MPs received free printed copies of *Hansard* but were now offered free copies of the CD-ROM edition as an alternative. In December 1990 there had been questions in the House of Commons about *Hansard* being made available on CD-ROM for members, and John MacGregor replied for the government that HMSO and Chadwyck-Healey would publish it during 1991.[21] But production difficulties meant that it was not until October 1992 that we were able to celebrate its publication at a launch party at the House of Lords, with Betty Boothroyd, the Speaker of the House of Commons, as our guest of honour. We took the risk, made the investment and did the work to produce it but the CD-ROM edition remained an 'official publication'. It was produced by Chadwyck-Healey France in Paris using software developed by our French programmers.

A memo from Paul Holroyd, one of our managers (see Chapter 15), to Moss[22] raised an issue that every electronic publisher was faced with at the time – whether to move from the MS-DOS operating system to Windows. Now that there are few computer users who can even remember what a screen before Windows looked like, it seems extraordinary that we were so undecided, but Holroyd wrote:

> I really think that we should be producing programs for Windows now with a DOS interface as a parallel development. Alternatively, we should be doing a DOS version with a Windows version in parallel if you wish to look at it another way. If not, can we convincingly say that we are producing tools for scholarship for the 21st century?

We stayed with MS-DOS even though at the time we were already publishing other CD-ROMs with Windows interfaces.[23] *Hansard* proved to be an awkward database to publish. When 'Mr Adams' spoke in the House of Commons he could have been Gerry Adams, but we knew that Gerry Adams, the Sinn Fein MP, refused on principle to appear in the House of Commons; it had to be Allen Adams, MP for Paisley. Identifying the MPs required our intervention and led us to add biographical information about each MP, which we bought from PMS Publications. We were also faced with long delays in receiving material from HMSO. It was not the electronic data that was held up but proofs of the printed edition that we needed to see to enable us to add column numbers to the electronic edition, which had to exactly match the printed one. Eventually, production settled down and we published four CD-ROMs a year, each being cumulative, so only the latest disk needed to be referred to.

In 1995 we added the House of Lords *Hansard* and in 1997 we asked the House of Commons for permission to publish an online edition. They were not willing to grant this and Carol Tullo, deputy director of HMSO, had to explain to the copyright officer at the House of Commons that, 'The Hansard CD-Rom was an official publication; it was developed, launched and marketed as such. The House was involved in all the proposals.' She went on, 'That the co-operation extended by the House to enable Chadwyck-Healey to produce the official archive should not be extended to another route for electronic transmission of the same data does seem contrary to the aim of increasing access.'[24] Eventually we were able to publish an online version.

6

Visual Images on Microfilm

Drawings of Robert and James Adam

In the 1970s *Playboy* magazine had been published on colour microfilm and in some college libraries readers had cut out single frames, mainly those reproducing the centrefold nude. The images in our first colour microfilm publication were more staid but in their own way just as beautiful; they were the architectural drawings of Robert and James Adam, in Sir John Soane's Museum in London. Mordaunt Crook, through whom I had published my first microfilm publication, *The Builder*, had suggested the Adam Drawings and introduced me to Sir John Summerson, the curator of the Soane Museum and one of the twentieth century's most important architectural historians. More formidable than gentle Sir John was the guardian of the Adam Drawings, Miss Dorothy Stroud, who I was warned would not take kindly to the idea of her precious drawings being microfilmed, a form of publication that would mean little to her. Fortunately, she had known and approved of one of my great-uncles and it seemed that I was approved of too. It was not an easy first colour publication because the colours of many of the drawings, of ceilings and other internal plasterwork, were the most subtle greens and pinks, but the relatively large format of 35mm microfilm, which was used extensively for reproducing engineering and architectural drawings, was able to provide satisfactory reproductions of even such delicate drawings as these. In 1986 we returned to the museum to publish on microfilm all the architectural and ornamental drawings, and the illuminated manuscripts in the Soane Museum. While the *Drawings of Robert and James Adam* were on twelve reels of microfilm, this was a much larger collection of sixty-one reels. By the time it was published we were in the electronic era but in the early 1990s digital scanning was in its infancy and colour microfilm was still the only cost-effective way of making this great collection available to researchers.

English cartoons and satirical prints

Our next visual collection was also from the eighteenth century. These were the satirical prints from the huge collection in the Department of Prints and Drawings in the British Museum. On a visit to Cambridge University Library in the summer of 1975 I had found on the shelves in the main reading room the inventories of the Royal Commission on Ancient and Historical Monuments, which we subsequently published on microfiche (see below), and the twelve-volume catalogue of cartoons and satirical prints in the British Museum.[1] This exhaustive catalogue, the life's work of two great experts, Frederic Stephens and Dorothy George, describes in detail every one of the 17,400 prints together with comments on their origin and historical context. I found it extraordinary that so much effort had gone into describing each print when a reproduction would have transmitted the information to the reader so much more economically and comprehensively. In a letter to Hoare, the director of British Museum Publications, I wrote, 'I have become increasingly interested in the use of microform for reproducing visual material', and I envisaged publishing 'a form of visual catalogue which scholars, using the printed catalogue, would then refer to, to look at the illustrations',[2] to which I received a positive response.

Around 1,300 prints were in books in the British Library, but the Keeper of Prints and Drawings in the British Museum would not allow British Library books to be brought into his department, and the microfilming had to be done by the library's own photographic department. We now had two microfilming series to undertake, one of loose prints in the Department of Prints and Drawings and the other of prints contained in books in the British Library. The two series would then have to be combined into the same sequence as in the printed catalogue. We employed Giulia Bartrum, a young graduate, on the recommendation of the Department of Prints and Drawings, to locate the prints and microfilm them, and paid her £2,708 per annum, the museum's clerical officer grade. As well as carrying out the microfilming she had to locate and identify prints in the British Museum's vast collection, some of which would not have been seen since Stephens had published the first volume of his catalogue over 100 years earlier. She quickly gained a unique knowledge of the holdings in the department and forty years later is still working there as a curator. To find the prints in the books in the British Library we employed a researcher who was given a stack pass to locate the books on the shelves and who then completed cards that identified the plates in the books that were to be microfilmed.

Microfilming in both the British Museum and the British Library started in October 1977 and was completed in spring 1978. The individual frames then had to be put in order, sometimes frame by frame. Mary Levine, our new production manager, spent a week in a room with only a table, a chair, a microfilm splicer and many tins of negative microfilm. She painstakingly spliced together over 1,000 frames using the blank film that had been deliberately left either side of each image or each sequence of images, on which to make the splices. With great trepidation we sent the thirty-two reels of master negatives back to Micromedia to make a duplicate printing negative. Because the film is under tension when it goes through the duplicator it can easily break or split at one or more of the splices and there was the prospect of having to refilm some or even many of the prints. But Levine's splices held firm and Micromedia now had a printing master negative from which they could make copies. Each print on the microfilm had a number that corresponded with the number in the catalogue, and we bought the remaining stock of the Stephens and George catalogue so that we could supply it with the microfilm. British Museum Publications reprinted the catalogue and we bought fifty sets, but it went out of print again and we could now only offer libraries a microfilm copy of the printed index, which was difficult to use with the prints themselves on separate reels of microfilm.

English Cartoons and Satirical Prints, 1320–1832 on thirty-two reels of microfilm with the printed index was originally priced at £875, though by the mid-1980s we had more than doubled the price to £2,100. Microfilm editions were rarely reviewed, usually just noticed in specialist journals, but the historian Harry Dickinson wrote a two-page essay/review in the *Times Higher Education Supplement*, contrasting the difficulty of researching the prints in the British Museum with their availability now through the microfilm edition.[3]

I also decided to publish a series of books reproducing prints, making use of our images on microfilm. Michael Duffy, the series editor, recruited six other talented historians, including Dickinson and John Brewer, to edit individual volumes on subjects such as crime and law, the constitution and religion. But the images on microfilm were too high contrast to make halftones suitable for reproduction, so we had to rephotograph the 900 prints using conventional cameras and film. It also revealed our limitations as a book publisher; the historians took their time delivering their work and we took even longer in the preparation and production of the books. They were published in 1986 and while the edition did sell out, it proved to me how difficult it was to make money out of publishing scholarly books. In July 1988 Miller summarized it as: sales £62,837, costs £71,693, value of unsold stock £18,000. He pointed out that there was no contribution to overheads and added, 'I would look for at least £20,000 so pick your loss figure.'[4] The books were widely reviewed, with good reviews in the *Guardian* and the *Daily Telegraph*, and even a notice in the *Financial Times*. BBC *Timewatch* used examples of the prints in a programme about xenophobia, and Roy Porter in the *London Review of Books* wrote, 'Yet no one beyond the heroic band of cognoscenti who have buried themselves for years in the British Museum has ever seen more than the tiniest fraction of them.... Hence, it's a joy to have ready access to these seven volumes.'[5]

I had lived with the satirical prints for eleven years, from my first approach to the British Museum in 1975 to the publication of the books in 1986. In that time the company had grown and changed and was now on the brink of the electronic era, but for me the microfilm edition of the 17,000 prints was more satisfying than the books; this huge collection, which had probably only ever been looked at in its entirety by the two authors of the catalogue, was now accessible in libraries throughout the world and, far more than the books, was the real raw material of research. Unlike the books, it was also a very profitable publication for Chadwyck-Healey.

Russian Futurism

In 1976 Fellner had introduced me to a fellow book dealer, Harold Landry. Tall, gaunt and bohemian, he lived and worked in his large house in Tanza Road, Hampstead. He had acquired at considerable cost, by borrowing money from his father-in-law, a very important collection of Russian Futurist manifestos, believing that he had a ready customer in Australia. Unfortunately, the institution changed its mind and soon after I met him Landry found himself with a collection that only a few libraries or museums could afford to buy, together with a large debt. He agreed to us publishing a microfiche edition in the hope that it would generate some revenue for him. The collection was on both monochrome and colour microfiche and for the latter we needed to make slides to send to Kodak in the Netherlands, who would rephotograph the slides to make colour microfiche in the COSATI format of sixty frames per microfiche (see below and Appendix 2). I bought a Nikon F2 35mm camera, a copying lens and a copying stand and lights, and hired a young woman to spend two months photographing the books in Landry's house. Susan Compton edited the collection, which also included books held by the Bodleian Library; by St Anthony's College in Oxford; four titles from A. B. Nakov, a prominent collector in Paris; and the colour slides of two books from Elaine Lustig Cohen in New York who owned the book dealer Ex Libris. After we had finished the microfilming, the British Library, on the recommendation of Isaiah Berlin, bought the collection from Landry. It was a superb collection at a time when few scholars in the West had ever seen these manifestos, small, often handmade books by artists and writers, most notably Malevich, Mayakovsky, Goncharova, Kruchenykh and Burliuk. *Russian Futurism: A History* by Vladimir Markov,[6] the first history in any language, had only been published in 1968 and this collection gave scholars their first opportunity to see many books that had been inaccessible since the Russian Revolution. These were poets and artists who had welcomed the revolution but, as Markov writes, 'This colourful, complex and influential movement was systematically denigrated and belittled, considered "a harmful influence" or "a bourgeois error". Markov describes the books in detail because 'most of the books described will remain unavailable or difficult to obtain for a long time'. It was an important acquisition by the British Library and an important microfiche publication at a time when this material was much less known than it is now.[7]

The Index of American Design

In the early 1970s the University of Chicago Press had announced a new publishing initiative by a newly formed division to produce scholarly publications called 'text fiche', where the printed text was accompanied by a set of colour or black and white microfiche providing reproductions of paintings, prints and photographs. Unfortunately, the severe limitations of microfilm technology, especially the poor-quality microfiche readers in most libraries, led to customer dissatisfaction with a new type of publication into which the university press had invested considerable resources. Stuart Levine in a review in 1978 summed up the response of many readers: 'As anyone who has worked with fiche in a library knows, fiche technology is inexcusably crude at present', and because of the deficiencies of standard microfiche readers, even the Bell & Howell SR VIII reader that he had been given to use, he commented, 'paintings projected on it have about the fidelity one would expect in a poorly-printed color publication'.[8]

Inspired by the Chicago University Press initiative, I was looking for other collections of images that we could publish on microfiche in colour. Chicago were publishing collections such as *American Art in the Barbizon Mood* and *Whitney Museum of American Art: Selections from the Permanent Collection*. I was sure that the reproduction of oil paintings or watercolours on colour microfiche with all their subtleties of tone and detail was bound to disappoint and what we wanted was some other category of illustration with clearly delineated lines, and bright, not so subtle colours. In October 1976 I found it, in the café of the National Gallery of Art in Washington. I was due to meet the new librarian Jerome 'Mel' Edelstein with whom I had corresponded about the publishers' archives when he was rare book librarian at UCLA. I had lunch first and as I took my tray to a table, I saw on the walls framed illustrations of costumes, textiles, domestic utensils and architectural objects such as weathervanes. They were magnificent in their clarity and colour and I could see that they would be perfect for reproduction on colour microfiche. When I met Edelstein he explained that this was a Works Projects Administration (WPA) project called the Index of American Design that had employed out-of-work artists in the Depression and that the paintings were called 'renderings', the technical term for painting a faithful, non-interpretive representation of an object.

The WPA had been set up in 1935 as part of Roosevelt's New Deal. Included in it was 'Federal Project No. 1', which employed musicians, artists, actors and directors in ambitious arts, drama, media and literacy projects. One of these was the Index of American Design. In 1918 Van Wyck Brooks had written an article lamenting the poverty of American culture, that the USA did not have a 'usable past', 'no cultural economy, no abiding sense of spiritual values'.[9] Although he was writing specifically about the lack of literary traditions, his article was often cited in the context of American arts and crafts and was used by Ruth Reeves, a textile designer, and Romana Javitz, head of picture collections at NYPL, when they persuaded the WPA to adopt the project they had conceived to create a national survey of American culture. Requiring nationwide organization on a grand scale, over 1,000 artists and illustrators produced the 15,000 renderings of objects that were found in museums, antique shops and private collections between 1935 and 1942.

After our proposal was accepted by the National Gallery of Art but before we had signed an agreement, Kurz and I made further visits and hired a researcher to reorganize the collection into ten subject groups, from costumes to tools, and then within each group by the state in which the object was found when the rendering was made. We signed a publishing agreement in November 1977, but I then began to have doubts about the project, which would be technically complicated and expensive, and I was not sure of the size of the market, though I assumed that all the larger US art libraries would buy it. I talked to Bernard Karpel, librarian of the Library of the Museum of Modern Art in New York, who had guided me towards some of the important post-war modern art galleries in New York, most notably Sidney Janis and Curt Valentin, for our collection of art exhibition catalogues on microfiche. He reassured me that it was a worthwhile project and in January 1978 Angela and I went to Washington. It was a good time to visit the National Gallery because the East Wing, the magnificent new gallery designed by I. M. Pei in an entirely modern angular style clad in golden sandstone, was nearing completion. The Index of American Design was in the main gallery that had been completed in 1941, housed in a large utilitarian workspace behind the public galleries at the west end of the building. The curator of the collection, Lina Steele, a quiet, very pleasant woman, had worked for the National Gallery for sixteen years and was the guardian of the collection. In the mid-1970s the New Deal and the WPA were not yet fashionable areas of study and the Index of American Design was just one of the many creative projects undertaken by the WPA. A two-volume work had been published in 1972 that reproduced the renderings of several hundred objects,[10] the National Gallery had regular small exhibitions of different groups of objects, and in 1949 there had even been an exhibition at the Tate Gallery in London. Renderings were sent out on loan, but the majority had never been exhibited or reproduced, and had only ever been seen by a few people. This was the great benefit of the microform medium, the ability to reproduce in black and white or in full colour collections of images that were too large to be reproduced in print or as slide sets. The disadvantage of colour microfiche was the quality of the images, which was partly due to the limitations of the microfiche readers.

Like Stuart Levine, the critic above, I thought that the colour microfiche images that I had seen were not as sharp and contrasty as they should be and that this was a consequence of the process used by Kodak to produce colour microfiche. In the USA Kodak would not accept slides and insisted that the original material be sent to them for filming. Their bureau in the Netherlands, which had produced colour microfiche for the Russian Futurist manifestos, would accept slides, which they then rephotographed to make the microfiche master negatives. We could not take the Index of American Design renderings to Kodak's bureau in the USA, so we would have to make slides that they would rephotograph in the Netherlands, leading to a discernible loss of sharpness and contrast. If we could make colour microfiche master negatives directly from original camera film, we could then give those to Kodak who would not have to rephotograph the images, which was the cause of the greatest loss of quality. Andy Pibworth, a manager at Kodak in the UK, told me that there was an exceptionally slow but very sharp colour negative film used for making internegatives in the film industry.[11] This was a film that was only used for copying and was never used for photography because it was so slow – about 6ASA, roughly three times as slow as the slowest colour transparency film at that time, Kodachrome 25, which was 25ASA. I convinced myself that by using this film we could produce colour microfiche of a superior quality, which, combined with the clarity and contrast of the originals, would result in an exceptional colour microfiche publication.

There were several problems that had to be solved. The first was format. To microfilm the renderings, almost all of which were larger than A4, we needed special camera heads with a frame size that was larger than the standard 98- or 49-frame formats. Kodak had made camera heads that produced 60- or 30-frame microfiche but no one in the UK had them or knew where to find them. A Kodak manager in the USA heard about this from Pibworth and phoned me to say that they were closing several bureaux and that they had 60- and 30-frame camera heads that they could sell me. They cost $125 each and were soon shipped to the UK. Kodak microfilm cameras had a fixed shutter speed of about 1/25 second and a lens with a relatively small aperture designed to be used with standard microfilm with a speed of about 25ASA, with the subject illuminated by four 150-watt flood lamps. We modified the camera heads so that they had an adjustable shutter speed of up to ten seconds with the renderings illuminated by two Berkey Colortran high-intensity flood lights, normally used in TV studios. Their lamps were 1,250 watts each and at the correct colour temperature for photographing in colour.

When Angela and I visited Washington in January 1978 Steele gave me the CV of Sandy Shaffer Tinkham who had heard about the project, had been assistant curator of textiles at Colonial Williamsburg, and was now working part time at the Library of Congress as a visual information specialist. I immediately hired her at $100 a day to manage not only this project but other microfilming projects that I was planning to do in Washington. I knew that I could not manage it from the UK and, with Tinkham in charge, the whole project became feasible. Microfilming began in October 1978, two years after I had first seen the renderings in the café. We had been lucky to obtain the camera heads and we were lucky again that there was a laboratory that could process this highly specialized film only ten minutes' walk from the National Gallery. The film could be dropped off at the end of the day and the processed film picked up the next evening. The camera operator would examine it by eye to check that the camera was exposing the frames and that there were no long scratches down the film. Any obvious camera faults could be immediately picked up, saving days of wasted filming. In the UK a positive copy was made in order to check the images and then it was sent to Kodak in the Netherlands to be made up into microfiche. A production operation taking place in three countries at a time when there was no fax or email should have been fraught with difficulties, but the process went remarkably smoothly thanks to the efficiency of the women who were doing the work in Washington and in our production department in Cambridge. Steele and the National Gallery were always helpful; for example, we had noticed that the lights dimmed slightly, affecting the colour temperature, every time a nearby elevator started; within twenty-four hours electricians had run a new electric supply to our lights. Steele herself enjoyed having new people with her working on the collection. She remembered that I took the staff out to lunch each time I was over and that I always left in a hurry to catch my plane back to the UK.[12] The microfiche edition made it possible to view the whole of the Index of American Design for the first time, and we also compiled and published a cloth-bound 560-page catalogue of the collection. By this time we had changed the name of Somerset House to Chadwyck-Healey Inc., and *The Index of American Design* was one of the first titles to be published under the new imprint.

Our brochure covering part 1, costumes and textiles, was mailed before microfilming had even begun. It was illustrated in full colour, with an introduction by J. Carter Brown, director of the National Gallery, and was the most lavish brochure we had produced. The orders began to come in but not from where we expected. The art libraries that I had assumed would buy the complete collection for $3,950 were slow to respond. I had not appreciated how little interest fine arts libraries have in the applied arts. But we had also mailed the brochure to academics in an entirely new subject area, Home Economics, or 'Home Ec.', which was a subject taught in almost every college in the USA. This involved cooking and other aspects of domestic science with a library budget that was often underused, especially before the 1980s boom in cookery books. In this subject a research collection with a high price was a welcome novelty and most of our sales were to 'Home Ec.' Because of this *The Index of American Design* was one of our most successful 1970s publications, selling over eighty sets. Microfilming was completed in February 1980 and the catalogue was published in the autumn.

Publication had come at the right time for the National Gallery. The director had received a letter from the vice-president's wife Joan Mondale, nicknamed 'Joan of Art' for her strong interest in the arts. She and the First Lady, Rosalynn Carter, were concerned that this important collection, paid for by federal funds, was not being circulated to the public.[13] The director was able to send her our brochure and tell her that any school might have the microfiche and she could come and see them for herself.

Having put so much effort into producing high-quality colour microfiche I wanted to ensure that they were viewed on microfiche readers with neutral grey screens – rather than on the many readers that had green or blue screens – so we offered to sell microfiche readers to libraries. We also advertised equipment that could project microfiche images for class use. There was some interest amongst librarians in the new processes we were using to produce colour microfiche. Betty Jo Irvine, fine arts librarian at Indiana University, wrote to Tinkham to ask about our techniques, wanting to know more about how we were producing our microfiche and commenting on the poor quality of the University of Chicago Press microfiche.[14]

On a sales trip in October 1982 I visited the public library in Milwaukee and saw a notice advertising the *Index of American Design* in a corner of the reading room, but I was told that it was not much used. In spite of the efforts of the University of Chicago Press, ourselves and a few other small publishers, colour microfiche never became a mainstream publishing medium and we only published one more colour microfiche publication,

Portraits of Americans, the permanent collection of nearly 2,000 portraits in the National Portrait Gallery in Washington. Kodak used the gallery's own slides to make the colour microfiche. I was less concerned about the quality of the reproductions because I saw the importance of the publication as being the likenesses of historical figures rather than the aesthetic quality of the paintings themselves. It was published in 1981 and sold surprisingly well, but in June 1983 Kodak ceased production of colour microfiche.

In January 1978 a young man had stopped by our booth at the annual conference and exhibition of the College Art Association in New York and introduced himself as Ford Peatross, curator of architectural collections at the Library of Congress. He had picked up our brochures on *Historic Buildings in Britain*, the inventories of the Royal Commission on Ancient and Historical Monuments on microfiche, and the *Drawings of Robert and James Adam* and explained that he was responsible for a very large collection called the Historic American Buildings Survey (HABS). He suggested that when I was next in Washington, I should visit him. As Angela and I were already going to Washington to visit the Index of American Design I went to see Peatross at the Library of Congress. He showed me HABS, which had begun in 1933 to document buildings of architectural, historical and sociological significance, and which comprised 45,000 photographs and 20,000 pages of text describing 20,000 buildings. I did not know how well it would sell, but I realized that it was our entry ticket to the Library of Congress, especially to the Prints and Photographs Division, and if I was to have Peatross's support we would have to publish it. At the time we microfilmed the collection there were many thousands of HABS photographs that were not ready for publication, and we returned to HABS in 1988 and published a supplement, which was much larger than our initial publication, confident that the same libraries that had bought the original microfiche publication would buy the supplement.[15] But they did not, and sales were disappointing. Library buying had changed; we were now in the CD-ROM era and librarians may have found that their original microfiche collection had not been used, so chose not to add to it.

The Farm Security Administration photographs

My first visit to the Library of Congress was important because not only was I in one of the greatest libraries in the world but there was another collection of photographs of great interest to me, the Farm Security Administration (FSA) photographs. In 1962, when I was working as a photographer, I had bought a copy of the Swiss magazine *Camera*. The cover photograph, the bleached skull of a steer on bare, cracked earth, by Arthur Rothstein, epitomized the 'Dustbowl' of the 1930s, when climatic conditions and bad farming practices on marginal agricultural land had led to the crisis described in John Steinbeck's *The Grapes of Wrath*.[16] Inside were more photographs by the FSA photographers and they made a strong impression on me. The FSA, originally called the Resettlement Administration, was created in 1935 to combat rural poverty throughout the USA. It bought sub-marginal agricultural land from poor farmers and resettled them in group farms on better land. It was later transformed into a programme to enable poor farmers to buy land and it still continues as the Farmers Home Administration. It would have been an obscure but worthy federal initiative had it not been for a programme of documentary photography that ran from 1935 to 1944, another federal project designed to record life in America, not dissimilar to the Index of American Design in its purpose and in its employment of creative people, in this case photographers.

The Historical Section (Information Division) was part of the Resettlement Administration, and then the FSA. From 1942 to 1944 it was extended as a propaganda project and came under the Office of War Information (OWI). Its head, Roy Stryker, believed strongly in the use of photographs to help the public understand the plight of both the rural and urban poor but also record everyday life in America at all levels. He understood how a good photograph could add an emotional dimension and he employed the most able photographers and demanded from them their best work. Well-known FSA photographers included Dorothea Lange, whose photograph known as 'The Migrant Mother' is one of the most reproduced photographs of all time; Walker Evans, who had the first one-man exhibition of photographs at the Museum of Modern Art in 1938; Ben Shahn, a left-wing artist and photographer; and Gordon Parks, the most important black photographer of the period. But other lesser-known photographers – Arthur Rothstein, John Vachon, Marion Post Wolcott, Carl Mydans and Edwin and Louise Rosskam – also produced outstanding work for the FSA.

They each worked in different regions of the USA, and Stryker made sure that they were well funded and well prepared for each assignment. He also enabled magazines and newspapers to have access to the photographs so that they were constantly in the public eye. Stryker's editor's eye ensured that the photographs in the collection met a uniform standard and he was ruthless in punching holes in negatives that he did not consider good enough. By the end of the project in 1944 there were 175,000 negatives and over 600 photographs in colour. In 1948, just before the McCarthy era, there was a move by some politicians to have the collection destroyed because it was thought to reveal too much about the state of the USA in the 1930s. Stryker and his supporters fought successfully to protect the collection, which by then had been deposited in the Library of Congress.

Jerald 'Jerry' C. Maddox, curator of photography, had written, 'relatively few individuals ... have taken advantage of this great resource. In part, this has been because of the very size of the collection.... anyone wishing to use the collection extensively must spend time in Washington delving through the Division's files.'[17] He now showed me the 87,000 captioned photographs in filing cabinets in the reading room, all around 10 x 8 inches, mounted on boards and arranged by region. Under federal law the library had to make its collections available for reproduction or publication and with Dana Pratt, the newly appointed director of publications at the Library of Congress, we negotiated agreements to publish on microfiche both HABS and the FSA photographs. The royalties were on a sliding scale, with no royalty payable on the first twenty copies and a maximum royalty of fifteen per cent on seventy-six copies and above. Pratt had been an officer in the US Navy but had then worked with university presses and understood the publishing industry. I always appreciated his relaxed, pragmatic approach to every problem. The microfilming would be done by the Library of Congress's own photographic department at their low filming rate of ten cents a page, and I was worried that they would not achieve the high standards we required. But they agreed to use Kodak Panatomic X camera film in place of standard microfilm so that the full tonal range of the photographs could be properly reproduced, and to produce the microfilm in a format that could be made up into microfiche (see Appendix 2). The Prints and Photographs Division also wanted us to relabel each photograph using a new numbering system, which we did for them at our expense. The Photoduplication Service eventually completed filming, many months late, in 1981.

I published the FSA photographs because of their importance as an inspirational historical archive without knowing who would buy them. In the late 1970s Media Studies was growing and so was the interest in the FSA photographs – in 1976 Saint Martin's Press had published Hank O'Neal's book of FSA photographs, *A Vision Shared. A Classic Portrait of America and its People 1935–1943*. Our publication had to sell well in the USA as there would only be limited interest elsewhere. But *America, 1935–1946*, 87,000 photographs on 1,572 microfiche, at $4,950, sold well, not only in the USA but also in Australia and Canada, and even in the UK. An editor working in our US office in the late 1980s had used the collection on microfiche for his PhD thesis on attitudes to blacks in America, and a young Australian scholar told me that he could not have completed his thesis without the microfiche edition. I appreciated this recognition of the value of the microfiche edition because most academics tended not to cite such media in their lists of sources; they simply cited the original documents or collection as if they had used the originals and not the microfilm copy. Perversely the same did not apply to reprinted books. This was partly due to scholars not knowing how to cite a microfilm edition but also not recognizing its validity as a publication in its own right. It was as if the microfilming process was simply regarded as a reproduction service rather than the production of a formal publication. On the other hand, in the bibliography on the Library of Congress FSA photographs website, the microfiche edition is cited, and in the most scholarly book published on the FSA photographs the authors list individually the microfiche edition, the printed index to the microfiche edition and even the sales brochure.[18]

Collections of images on microfiche had another advantage. They could be seen with the naked eye just by holding the microfiche up to the light. Once in the reader full-size images could be scanned very quickly by moving the platen from side to side and up and down; thus the collection on microfiche was much easier and quicker to use than going through the drawers in the Prints and Photographs Division. In addition we published a handbook, which indexed the photographs by place and by subject, giving a level of access to the collection that it had never had before. In the 1990s the Library of Congress scanned the negatives and now the collection is being rescanned to achieve better-quality digital images.

We also marketed the microfilm edition of the *Roy Stryker Papers, 1912–1972*, reproducing his archive at the University of Louisville, Kentucky, including his personal selection of nearly 2,000 FSA photographs.

The Vandamm Collection

The *American Library Directory*, which listed special collections held by libraries, was one of my best sources for new publishing ideas, and in the rich collections of NYPL I found the Vandamm Collection of theatre photographs.

Florence Vandamm was the sister of Vivian Van Damm who owned the Windmill Theatre in Soho, London, which staged decorous nude shows and boasted that 'it never closed' during the wartime Blitz. She had trained as an artist at the Royal Academy and in 1908 had opened a photographic studio in London but, in 1923, after she had married an American engineer, George R. Thomas, they moved to New York. At the time Francis Bruguière, a friend of Alfred Steiglitz and an important avant-garde photographer, was also the contract photographer for the New York Theatre Guild. But he became more and more unreliable as he immersed himself in his own dark, moody, abstract photography, and Thomas and Vandamm, who had set up a studio in New York, became the back-up who gradually supplanted him. Through their professionalism they established themselves as the leading theatre photographers and after George died in 1944 Florence continued on her own and was the dominant theatre photographer in the heyday of the Broadway musicals. Her photographs were set pieces taken with a large-format camera on a tripod but the technical quality of the photographs and their coverage of every aspect of the theatre in New York – serious classical theatre, popular shows and musicals, from the 1920s to the 1950s – make the collection one of exceptional importance. It was said that a Vandamm photocall became a New York theatre tradition and she would see each play several times in rehearsal before photographing it. After a performance, actors would walk over in their costumes to her studio on West 57th Street to be photographed. Still photography cannot reproduce the movement, sound and atmosphere of a production but it can freeze a single moment, and the best photographs capture the quality of the actors, most of whom knew how to respond to the camera – Henry Fonda in 1934 in a beautifully choreographed fight scene in *The Farmer Takes a Wife*, Leslie Howard in 1936 as Hamlet, Katharine Cornell and Raymond Massey in 1941 in *The Doctor's Dilemma*, and the young Marlon Brando in 1944 in *I Remember Mama*.

When Vandamm retired in 1961 NYPL bought her collection of negatives and prints for the high price at the time of $73,000, equivalent now to $600,000, and with remarkable foresight also bought the copyright of the photographs. Collections of photographs, manuscripts or letters are often deposited in archives without the copyright being transferred, which means that the repository bears the cost of storing and conserving the material but requires permission from the original copyright holder to reproduce any part of the archive, which may also require paying a fee. The collection also includes the negatives and prints of Bruguière, which are probably more valuable than Vandamm's, but as a record of New York theatre hers and Thomas's are unsurpassed.

A capable library science student, Vanessa Piala, who went on to become a conservator at the Smithsonian Institution, was already microfilming for us the archives of Harper & Brothers at Columbia University Library (see Chapter 3) and she carried out a Vandamm photograph count in the autumn of 1979. We set up our microfiche camera in the reading room at NYPL's Library and Museum of the Performing Arts in the Lincoln Center near the bottom of Central Park. The atmosphere in the library's reading room was different from that in the great temple of a library on 42nd Street. The readers were either students or theatre buffs enthused with the magic of 'showbiz' and Broadway, and Piala had to work with these readers all round her. The camera with its four floodlights did not go unnoticed as readers asked her to make copies on what they thought was a photocopier. It was an annoying distraction because it was a microfilming project that needed particular concentration, as the filming of each frame required the handling of two photographs. The Vandamm photographs had captions on the back, which we also filmed. To achieve this, each photograph was positioned in a specially designed black cardboard mount and the caption on the back appeared in a slot in the mount immediately below the photograph it referred to when the next row was filmed. The camera, which we had bought new from Kodak, had faulty wiring, which resulted in some wasted filming, and we found that processing labs in New York constantly scratched the film. But Piala made very few mistakes and in spite of these technical problems filming was completed by the end of 1980. Thor Wood, the curator at the library, wrote to me in October 1981: 'It is very impressive, and a source of satisfaction to know that this important archive is not only preserved but can be available at other institutions as well as ours.' *New York Theater, 1919–1961* on 877 microfiche with a printed handlist of productions cost $2,950, and we sold many copies, not only in the USA but also in Europe, and in Australia, where we sold six copies.

From early 1978, when I made my first visit to the Library of Congress, to the opening of our first office in the USA in 1984, was a golden period that I later looked back on with nostalgia. Tinkham not only got me into every library, museum and gallery in Washington that she thought I should visit but handled all editorial and production with great efficiency from the back bedroom of her house in 'old' Alexandria, Virginia, one of the most attractive suburbs of Washington, DC. The projects she worked on included all the image projects in Washington and New York described above. At the same time, orders, payments and answers to enquiries were managed by Linda Fox, who had been Kurz's assistant, working from the basement of her house in Teaneck. I appointed Bertie Bonnell as vice-president, sales, in January 1980. She had been trained in the world of New York trade book publishing at Harry Abrams, the art book publisher. She had moved to UMI, and it was a courageous decision to leave the security of UMI to join a small UK-based publisher that didn't even have an office in the USA. When she was not travelling, she worked from her spacious house with its beautiful garden, which she had created in Ann Arbor, Michigan. Bonnell had a soft-spoken manner that belied the tough, highly experienced sales person that she was. Managing people in three different states from another country 3,500 miles away when communications were limited to letter, phone and visit, was not a sensible way to build a business in the USA. Now the concept of a decentralized business with people working at home or hot desking is much more accepted because communications have been transformed through email and the ability to share digital data, but at that time most people would have predicted that it would fail. It worked because the three women had such integrity and were so good at their jobs. We were able to use the facilities offered to us by institutions like the Library of Congress and National Gallery of Art, who either allowed us to microfilm on their premises or did the microfilming for us so that there was no need to have a production facility in the USA. Our US competitors took the opposite view and avoided setting up cameras on location or having their microfilming done for them, in the belief that it would not meet their own quality standards or the efficiency of their own production operations.

There were no more image publications, other than the Sanborn Maps and the Artists and Print files from NYPL described in Chapters 8 and 10. In response to the oil crisis in 1980 with its impact on library budgets I had decided that we would now concentrate on microfilming printed material in mainstream subject areas like history and literature. I thought that publishers' archives, and most art and media publications, such as several that we had published in microform with the BBC, were too specialized. Yet all our visual publications continued to sell well through the early 1980s.

7

Carving up the Centuries

The twentieth century saw various attempts to catalogue all English books from the birth of printing onwards. The first systematic attempt was *A Short Title Catalogue of Books Printed in England, Scotland and Ireland and of English Books Printed Abroad, 1475 to 1640* by A. W. Pollard and Gilbert R. Redgrave. Published in 1926, the catalogue's own title was too long for easy citation and it soon became known as *STC* or, simply, 'Pollard and Redgrave'.[1] It was followed in 1945 by Donald Wing's bibliography of books published from 1641 to 1700.[2] But the most innovative period in the development of library catalogues was from the 1960s to the late 1980s. Although the card catalogue, introduced at the end of the eighteenth century, had been a major step forward, and cataloguing halls with their banks of oak drawers housing millions of 5 x 3-inch cards, secured in the drawers by copper rods, were a familiar feature of almost all large libraries, older libraries such as the British Library, the Bodleian Library and Cambridge University Library were still using guard-book catalogues well into the 1980s. Typed, printed or handwritten slips were pasted into the guard-books, spaces being left on every page for the books that were yet to be added. From time to time there were printed editions of the catalogues of the largest, most important libraries in which either the guard-book pages or the catalogue cards were photographed and printed in facsimile in multi-volume editions by specialist publishers such as G. K. Hall in Boston. Chadwyck-Healey published nineteen library catalogues on microfiche, including the catalogues of the national libraries of France and Spain. But reprinted catalogues, whether in book form or microform, were unsatisfactory because by the time they were published they were out of date – more books had been added and corrections to existing entries had been made. The outstanding example of such obsolescence was the printed catalogue of the Bibliothèque nationale in Paris, which had taken eighty-seven years to complete (see Chapter 11).

In the 1960s librarians recognized the potential of computers more quickly than publishers. They could see that the computerized database, which could be continuously updated, was the perfect medium for the dynamic entity that is the library catalogue. In 1963 the Jones Report on the use of computers in the Library of Congress led to the birth of the MARC (MAchine-Readable Cataloging) format in 1968.[3] Three years before, Thomas J. Watson Jr had bet the future of IBM on the System/360 computers with random-access disks, cathode-ray tubes, terminals and the ability to send information to other computers or 'remote consoles' by phone line, though the initial distribution of cataloguing records was on magnetic tapes. It was also in 1965 that Ralph Parker, director of libraries at the University of Missouri, and Frederick G. Kilgour, then associate director of the Yale University Library, submitted a proposal of extraordinary vision for a computerized network of libraries in Ohio to provide a shared cataloguing programme based on a central computer store. A book would only be catalogued once and there would be a union catalogue recording the location of the books in libraries throughout the state. Kilgour took the Ohio College Library Center (OCLC) from a one-man operation in 1967 to a not-for-profit institution serving more than 1,600 libraries ten years later. He retired in 1995 and today OCLC is an international cataloguing behemoth accessed online by over 50,000 libraries with a catalogue that contains over 50 million items, still located in Dublin, Ohio. The pioneering work by Kilgour and other librarians laid the foundations for the next great international cataloguing enterprise, the *Eighteenth Century Short Title Catalogue (ESTC)*.

After Wing's catalogue in 1945 nothing much had happened in the listing of early English books until 1962 when the Bibliographical Society set up a committee to explore the possibility of an STC of eighteenth-century books. But the initiative came from the USA in the person of Paul Korshin, who was executive secretary of the American Society of Eighteenth-Century Studies and who had already set up a committee to look at ways in which a comprehensive catalogue of eighteenth-century books could be compiled. Undaunted by the magnitude of the project and the huge sums of money it would cost, he put forward a proposal to the National Endowment for the Humanities (NEH) for funding. The NEH had been set up by President Johnson in 1965 when the government was already giving money to the sciences (see Chapter 1) and had approached the American Council of Learned Societies to ask for help to find humanities projects on which they could spend their money. Korshin turned to the council for funding but believed that the project had to emanate from the UK where most of the eighteenth-century books were, and that this was a good time to approach the British Library, which was only three years old. The chairman of the British Library, David Eccles, and the director, Harry Hookway, saw *ESTC* as the British Library's flagship project. Richnell, who had resolved the Bentley archive difficulty for me (see Chapter 3), had written in the library's first annual report, 'The object of the Board of the British Library ... is in meeting the multiple needs of today's users and satisfying new needs by creating new services.'[4] It was an accident of history that there were powerful institutions on both sides of the Atlantic looking for projects on which to spend money.[5] But Richnell knew that it was not just a question of money; they needed someone in London with Korshin's ambition and energy to drive it forward and in November 1975 Alston, who had left Scolar Press (see Chapter 3), accepted Willison's invitation to come to London to lead the project.[6] It soon became clear even to Alston, who initially was resistant to the idea of a computerized catalogue, that its creation involving several hundreds of thousands of books, pamphlets and broadsides could only be done by using a computer to create a database. There were also two potential rival projects. One was by UMI to undertake a 'Checklist of 18th century books' as a stepping-stone towards an STC, and the other by Dawson, the reprint and book publisher, for a checklist of eighteenth-century books to be compiled by Peter Wallis at the University of Newcastle-upon-Tyne. Neither came to anything but added confusion at a time when the principals were trying to draw up a plan that would be coherent enough to attract substantial funding. In September 1978 Richnell and Alston invited Henry L. Snyder, an American academic, to lead the project in the USA. Snyder had the same forceful spirit as Alston and was the ideal man to push the project forward. He was a tall, lean, fifty-year-old professor of history who soon after went to the University of Louisiana at Baton Rouge as dean. When I made a sales visit to the library in the early 1980s the acquisition librarian told me that Snyder had visited his friend Hans Fellner in London and had ordered hundreds of books that had been shipped back to the library, which then had to pay for them. He complained to me about this high-handed use of the library budget, and it did not help when I had to admit that Fellner was also a good friend and colleague of mine. In 1986 Snyder moved to the University of California, Riverside, where, as a Californian, he was more at home, and continued as co-director of *ESTC* until 2009. I met him several times and always found him stimulating company. But there could only be one leader, and Alston gave way to Snyder and left the project in the early 1980s. In 1987, with Snyder still in charge, *ESTC* was renamed the *English Short Title Catalogue* and was extended retrospectively to include all books in English from the beginning of printing to 1800. It now includes 480,000 books. The contribution that both he and Snyder had made in bringing off this huge project was recognized when Alston was awarded an OBE in 1992 and Snyder who had received a National Humanities Medal in 2007 was awarded an honorary OBE in 2009.

I had had lunch with Korshin on one of his early visits to London to talk to the British Library, and had been impressed by the breadth and ambition of the *ESTC* project, but it had no connection with what I was doing at the time. This changed when I was phoned in late 1980 and asked if I would be interested in bidding for the microfilm publishing rights to the books in *ESTC* that were in the British Library. The other two contenders were UMI and Research Publications and I was told that there was some concern that the only candidates for this potentially lucrative contract were American; it would help the British Library if there were a British participant. We were the only British micropublisher to be seen as a possible contender. The project was yet another iteration of the familiar model, a microform collection based on an established bibliography, in this case *ESTC*. Fellner and I were cautious about taking on such a huge project and were worried that it could become very demanding and might overshadow the other things we were doing. Our nineteenth-century Parliamentary Papers project and the *Catalogue of British Official Publications Not Published by HMSO* were both well under way and I did not want to take on anything else that would burden me with overhead and start-up costs just when we were becoming more profitable, aided by our new production facility. Alston had to appraise the three candidates and met with Fellner and me in London. He told us that the British Library preferred microfilm to microfiche and that he would be happy to be offered the job of running the microfilm project when it came into being. We thought that microfiche was the better format for the many thousands of individual books and pamphlets, particularly as the cost of making copies was lower than for microfilm. We indicated to Alston that we would like him to head the project if we were successful, but we put nothing in writing because we were afraid that it would be considered as an inducement that could put both of us in a difficult position when he came to advise the British Library on which bid to accept. I spoke on the phone to Snyder in the USA but otherwise did no lobbying and made no effort to find influential supporters to press our case. We submitted our proposal to the British Library and waited. I received a letter from Cobbe on 28 July 1981 informing me that the contract had been awarded to Research Publications. The reasons were understandable; they had offered more money than the other two bidders and the British Library wanted microfilm not microfiche as the master film. I was both disappointed and somewhat relieved that this big, complicated project, so full of unknowns, was not going to be ours.

The next day was a public holiday, the wedding day of Prince Charles and Diana. Sitting at home, I felt the full implications of what we had missed begin to sink in. Although library budgets had suffered in 1979 and 1980 there had been no microfilm project on this scale for some years and the large research libraries were still able to find the money to acquire such a project, which was only equalled in importance by *Early English Books*[7] that UMI had restarted after the war (see Appendix 1). There was no more lucrative contract offered to any microfilm publisher in the 1970s and 1980s and it was a contract that Research Publications deserved to win. They had chosen the format the British Library preferred; they had offered to employ Alston if they won the contract, thereby getting him firmly on their side; they had wheeled in the Thomson big guns to personally engage with the British Library to put their case; and they had offered more money than either of the other contenders. UMI might have won but like us were rather limp in their approach and had made themselves unpopular with the *ESTC* team at a much earlier stage by proposing a rival catalogue of eighteenth-century books. Research Publications now had the Burney Collection of seventeenth-century newspapers and the *Eighteenth Century* to sell, both from the British Library – two highly profitable streams of revenue that lasted them for years.

Korshin summed up the importance of having a machine-readable catalogue of eighteenth-century texts at a conference in 1998 in which he said:

> The best that any of us envisaged, in the formative years of 1975–78, was that scholars would use the ESTC as earlier generations had used the first STCs: to locate copies. As the richness of the computer fields developed under Robin Alston's guidance, there was no sense that scholars might one day be able to search every word, indeed, every punctuation mark, in each of these fields.[8]

He was referring to the extent of the information that Alston was including in the MARC catalogue records, describing the books and pamphlets in far more detail than had ever been done before in traditional library catalogues, and all of it fully searchable. What he had not foreseen was that within a few years the texts that Research Publications were microfilming would begin to be scanned from the microfilm and would themselves become fully searchable online, creating a resource of even greater richness. But none of this would have happened if Korshin had not taken the initiative to create such a catalogue thirty years earlier.

Our bid for the *ESTC* microfilm contract was the last project that Fellner and I worked on together. By then he was fully occupied cataloguing major collections in the book department at Christie's, the auctioneers, and I was now confident in my own judgement of what we should publish. In the early 1980s I bought back his twenty per cent interest in Chadwyck-Healey Ltd at an agreed price. We continued to meet to discuss books and projects, often over lunch or dinner, and in 1991 he came with me on a trip to the USSR (see Chapter 22).

Nineteenth Century Short Title Catalogue

In spite of everything else we were doing in the UK and USA I still brooded over the loss of the eighteenth century, concerned that there was only one century left, as the twentieth century could not be considered because most of the books were still in copyright. But the number of books published in the nineteenth century was huge and there was no catalogue to act as a blueprint for the project. In 1983 Julian Roberts, now Keeper of Printed Books at the Bodleian Library, once again gave me good advice. He told me that I should talk to Frank Robinson at the University of Newcastle-upon-Tyne, who was compiling a catalogue of the nineteenth-century books in eight libraries in the UK, Eire and the USA.[9] Like *ESTC* it was a huge undertaking at a time when creating a database of any kind required access to a mainframe computer. I looked forward to meeting Robinson over lunch and was disconcerted to find that he had chosen an old-fashioned drinking pub in Cambridge, where the only concession to food was crisps and peanuts. I soon found out that Robinson did not eat, he drank. His daily consumption of alcohol was remarkable but so was his ability to think and work. The *Nineteenth Century Short Title Catalogue* (*NSTC*) had been the brainchild of Wallis and Robinson, but he had now set up his own company, Avero Publications, with a colleague, Dr Gwen Averley, a very bright young academic from the University of Newcastle, to create the *NSTC*. He was able to use the University of Newcastle mainframe computer, but while the public-funded *ESTC* was being made available through online library networks and, later, on microfiche and on CD-ROM, *NSTC* would be published in printed form in over sixty volumes because Robinson needed a product that he could sell at a high price to recoup his compilation costs. Computer-output microfiche (COM) would have been the most cost-effective publishing medium but Avero would not have been able to charge enough for a publication in this form. We were still in the era of expensive multi-volume library catalogues, and there were many librarians who put a high value on the printed book. But it would have to be actively sold to libraries and we had an international sales and marketing force that could take this on. I also explained to him that we would like to use the catalogue as a basis for a project to microfilm nineteenth-century books.

I visited Robinson in his office in Newcastle, the city in the North East that had been so afflicted by all that was wrong with Britain after the dismal decade of the 1970s. Factories and mines had closed down, unemployment was high and there was real poverty. But I found it to be a proud city that was far from down and out. Avero was in three rooms in a shabby Georgian building near the centre of the city. There were several women typing entries into terminals. Robinson, Averley and other researchers read through the catalogues of the eight libraries on which the catalogue was based and transferred the records of all their nineteenth-century books onto slips, which were then keyed into the database by the women. On my next visit, he invited me to meet his business partner and backer Dr George Miller. I was met off the train by a chauffeur in a grey uniform and peaked cap, who drove me in a dove-grey Mercedes to the office. This was a promising start. There I met Miller, a cheerful, ebullient, middle-aged businessman, who liked the good life and had an eye for the girls, but who I later discovered was unmarried and still lived at home with his mother. Miller was investing in Avero through his company Ladylaw. He set out a number of conditions that we would have to agree to if we were to be granted exclusive sales rights to the catalogue and also be able to use it for our microfiche project. The most onerous was the number of copies we would be required to buy to retain an exclusive sales agreement. Before committing ourselves, I wanted to talk to Nitta, as a large order from his

Figure 5 Bassingbourn. Our agent in Japan, Mitsuo Nitta, and his wife Hisaku cooking tempura on the Aga stove at our home, Manor Farm. This was the first time they had stayed in an English home. 1983.

company, Yushodo, for the Japanese library market would be essential if we were to achieve the numbers Avero were demanding. Nitta was on a short visit to New York and to fit in with his schedule and mine I flew on Concorde to meet him. He agreed to take fifty sets of the catalogue and was also interested in the prospect of a microfiche collection. There were to be three series, 1801–15, 1816–70, 1871–1918, but only the first two were published in book form. Under our marketing agreement we received a twenty-five per cent discount on the first 250 copies that we bought, thirty per cent on the next 150 and thirty-five per cent on all thereafter. Normally a distributor would expect to get at least fifty per cent but we would be invoicing libraries annually in advance and would be receiving their money many months before we were required to buy each volume from Avero. Once we had made a sale, we would continue to receive subscription revenue for the life of the project, ten or more years (it was almost unknown for a library to cancel a subscription to a multi-volume work). Avero could only terminate the agreement if we had sold fewer than 120 copies of each volume by the end of the first year, 240 by the end of the second year and similar increases over the next two years.

We launched *NSTC* in January 1984 at the ALA Midwinter conference in Washington, DC. Both Robinson and George Miller came to it and Bonnell had arranged a launch party at the prestigious Metropolitan Club in Washington, which had a connection with a London club of which I was a member. About 200 people crowded into a large room with original prints from Audubon's *Birds of America* round the walls. A senior librarian from the Library of Congress murmured to me that he had lived in Washington all his life and had never set foot in the club before. Miller had offended Bonnell almost as soon as they met. He was now quite drunk and went up to Robert Warner, who was an imposing man, and asked him what he did. He replied, 'I am Archivist of the United States', to which Miller, not believing him, made some inappropriate retort. Fortunately, Warner did not seem to hold it against us. A third visitor who came over with Robinson was his close friend John Jolliffe, who was Bodley's Librarian and whose mission had been to convert the pre-1920 records of the Bodleian Library catalogue into machine-readable form. In the following year, Jolliffe again came to ALA Midwinter with Robinson, but it was a much more subdued visit as he was ill with cancer and in great pain.

The *Nineteenth Century* microfiche programme

In December 1983, shortly before the launch of *NSTC*, Robinson, George Miller and I met with Alex Wilson, the director general of the British Library, to discuss a microfiche project based on *NSTC* using British Library books. He emphasized that he was only interested in such a project if we were going to microfilm a large number of books. Miller was present at another meeting with the British Library in August 1984 to discuss the details of the project, profitability, security and the number of volumes we expected to film each week. But soon after came the revelation that he was not the successful business man that he had made himself out to be and in

1985 he was declared bankrupt. When in 1986 he appeared in the County Court in an unsuccessful attempt to discharge his bankruptcy, the Registrar commented 'that he was no stranger to the County Court'.[10] Now that Avero had no money in spite of us buying 150 copies of each volume in the first year and 240 in the second year, we were in a difficult position because it was our reputation, not that of the relatively unknown Avero, that would be damaged if libraries were left with a partially completed set of books. Initially we guaranteed a bank overdraft of £80,000, but in 1989 Avero was once again insolvent and we terminated the original sales agreement, and now only bought enough copies to fulfil existing subscriptions, which were about 215. We loaned Avero £140,000 and took forty-nine per cent of the equity with two seats on the board. The completion of series 2, to 1870, in 1995 was the end of our relationship with Avero. Robinson produced the third series to 1918, which was published on CD-ROM and was sold by Avero itself. He had some sets of the catalogue bound in quarter-leather, one of which he gave to me but by then the whole catalogue was on CD-ROM and later became available on the Internet. The sixty-one bound volumes were now an excessively large 'white elephant'. My last meeting with Robinson was at a dinner in 2007, along with his wife Jennifer and Averley, in a pub near the village outside Newcastle where they now lived. In spite of all the arguments Robinson and I had always got on well; each of us wanted *NSTC* to succeed and, against all odds but with a lot of help from Chadwyck-Healey, he and Averley achieved it. We had met in a pub and we parted in a pub. Frank Robinson died in 2010.

Alston had heard that we were in discussions with Robinson and approached me as he was now looking for a job. After Research Publications had signed an agreement with the British Library for the microfilming of *ESTC* titles, they told Alston that they were going to manage the project with their own staff. Not surprisingly he was furious, but he was still working part time at the British Library on the *ESTC* and had other roles in the library, which had given him an office and access to the stacks (where the books are shelved). Now he was ready to throw himself into the creation of a rival project. The number of books published in the nineteenth century was several magnitudes greater than in the eighteenth, and we had to find a way of being selective in the books that we microfilmed. It had been our intention to use *NSTC* as the basis of our selection and it was this that had led me to meet Robinson and then offer to distribute the catalogue for him even though we knew that the *NSTC* was an author/title catalogue and had no subject classifications. In spite of this important limitation, in 1985 we entered into agreements with Avero to use the *NSTC* as the basis for selection and with the British Library to microfilm books from its collection.

There was a growing concern about the poor state of many nineteenth-century books because of their wood-pulp paper, which did not apply to eighteenth-century books, and in 1983 the British Library had invited David H. Stam, the research director of NYPL, to write a report on how they should approach large-scale conservation.[11] Later that year Cambridge University Library hosted a British Library conservation project seminar, which I attended.[12] The British Library and its predecessor had never allowed books to be taken out of the library but it had now allowed Research Publications to microfilm eighteenth-century books in their facility in Reading, so a precedent had been set. It was now in the library's interest to have us microfilm their nineteenth-century books, both for preservation and to generate some royalty income. But we had still not worked out how we would select the titles. Alston then realized that the British Museum Library's classification systems had been subject based after he found in a drawer 'placing guides' from the nineteenth century used to shelve and retrieve the books. He went on to find that all nineteenth-century books on a particular subject were shelved together. He wrote an essay about it and compiled an index, which we and the British Library published.[13] We were now able to choose the subjects of interest to researchers and each year select books from each of these subjects for microfilming in order to deliver to subscribers a balanced selection of books. We did not need *NSTC* and could plan the microfiche publishing programme without the direct involvement of Avero. In a letter of 12 May 1986 from Jane Carr, publishing director of the British Library, it was agreed that selection would no longer be made from *NSTC* but from what were known as British Library 'fourth-copy files'.

Alston conceived the very broad General Collection, which contained books in many subject areas ranging from agriculture and the sciences to psychology, philosophy and jurisprudence. There were also five specialist collections, each with its own editor: Visual Arts and Architecture by Trevor Fawcett; Linguistics by Alston; Publishing, the Book Trade and the Diffusion of Knowledge by Fellner and Alston; and, later, Women Writers by John Sutherland and Alston; and Children's Literature by John Barr. Visual Arts and Architecture required us to enter into a separate publishing agreement with the National Art Library at the Victoria and Albert Museum, which also allowed books to be taken to Bassingbourn for filming. The specialist collections could be bought by smaller libraries or libraries with special subject interests, but most of the sales were to libraries who bought either the General Collection on its own or bought everything. The wide range of titles in the General Collection reflected the rich diversity of British culture in the nineteenth century. Among the first books that we published were Robert Mallett, *The Great Neapolitan Earthquake*, 1862 (Science); Matthew Marmaduke Milburn, *Prize Essay on Guano*, 1845 (Agriculture); Thomas Frost, *The Lives of Conjurors*, 1874 (Recreation); and Charles Forjett, *Facts and Fictions of Mr Gladstone's Policy*, 1881 (Politics). The books arrived in Bassingbourn in a locked trolley, which we unlocked with a second key. On their return to the library the books would be unpacked, checked and reshelved. Library staff also visited Bassingbourn to inspect the premises, both for the security of the books, which had to be kept locked in a safe, and for the quality of the microfilm that we were producing. We paid the British Library a ten per cent royalty and gave them both a microfiche copy and a microfilm copy – we had chosen to publish the books on microfiche but the British Library still insisted on having a microfilm copy. This required us to convert our microfiche images by rephotographing them on a special camera that was purpose built. While microfiche was the better format for publication because the copies were less expensive and they were preferred by readers, microfilm, with its larger images, was the accepted format for conservation microfilming.

We also had to produce machine-readable MARC cataloguing for the microfiche edition of each title. It was another significant cost but we had no choice. Libraries would no longer buy large microform collections if the only access to them was through a printed catalogue. Without the cataloguing of the individual titles, a reader searching the library's catalogue for a particular book would not find it. In the 1980s the Association of Research Libraries (ARL) in the USA started a cooperative project to provide a MARC catalogue record for each of the books in two very large collections published by UMI and Research Publications.[14] Neither of the publishers had to contribute to the cost of the cataloguing and Research Publications were now able to use the *ESTC* records for the individual books in their microfilm publication. For us, creating MARC records for each of the books we microfilmed was a very significant cost, and Alston's small team had to battle with the technical difficulties of cataloguing on the British Library's online system, which was still in its infancy. In 1992 there was a further disruption when the British Library began to move its books to the new library at St Pancras and our staff had to move into a new, smaller office.

Richnell was chairman of the editorial board, having retired from the British Library in 1979. The editorial board was there to reassure the academic community and included M. R. D. Foot, who was both a nineteenth-century historian and the authority on the Resistance in the Second World War; Harry Dickinson, a professor of history at the University of Edinburgh; and Michael Bentley, a historian from Oxford. Averley was also a member in recognition of our relationship with Avero and *NSTC*. The board met annually, on the first Thursday of the year, at the Institute of Directors in London, which had previously been the premises of the United Services Club. Large portraits of bygone generals and admirals looked down on us as we listened to our board's suggestions. The morning's meeting was followed by a convivial lunch. It was a good start to the New Year, but not much of substance came out of it.

The *Nineteenth Century* microfiche programme was well received when it was finally launched in late 1986. John Wardroper wrote in *The Times*:

Figure 6 New York City. Bertie Bonnell and Robin Alston discussing the launch of the *Nineteenth Century* microfiche programme at the ALA conference and exhibition. June 1986.

> Once a fortnight, for many years to come, a van-load of 19th century books will be carried from London to the Cambridgeshire village of Bassingbourn there to be reincarnated by late-20th century technology. In the greatest scholarly project ever undertaken, a quarter of a million books and pamphlets published from 1801 to 1900 are to be filmed, page by page, and put into microfiche form.[15]

But in 1987 the most exciting late twentieth-century technology was the CD-ROM. In comparison microforms were an old-fashioned mid-century analogue technology. H. R. Woudhuysen wrote in the *Times Literary Supplement*:

> It might be said that with *The Nineteenth Century* micropublishing has come of age. The project is about ten times the size of University Microfilms' reproductions of STC books.... The implications for conservation are also important, since much of the material which will be reproduced was printed on poor quality wood-pulp paper.[16]

He also pointed out that the most controversial exclusion was literature, though later we added children's books as a specialist collection.

Sales to libraries were good without being spectacular. We had around twenty-five subscriptions, which gave us some profit. The General Collection with two specialist collections cost £10,000 per annum or £45,000 for the first five years, though a ten per cent discount was offered to early subscribers. One of the most memorable early sales was to Baylor University in Waco, Texas. In January 1987 Angela and I had visited a friend in Houston and we drove through the bleakest, flattest winter landscape to Waco to have lunch as guests of Baylor, the largest Baptist university in the world. It also has the Armstrong-Browning Library, which houses the world's most important collection of the books and papers of the poet Robert Browning, so their interest in British nineteenth-century culture was already strong. At lunch in the presence of about 100 faculty members I was asked to say a few words about the *Nineteenth Century* microfiche programme, and everyone was asked to raise their hands if they thought that the university library should buy it. The decision had, of course already been made and it was their way of responding hospitably to our visit. Sales grew quite quickly and then peaked. In 1988 they were approximately £500,000, and in November I promised Mike Smethurst, who was now the director general of the British Library, royalties for the year of not less than £48,000. But after 1988 there was a disappointing fall-off in the number of new orders and subsequently some cancellations. Hall, our sales director who had an uncanny ability to forecast sales, admitted that he had predicted the sale in 1989 of seven 'possible' general collections and three 'probable', but in the event had only sold one. The director of the Royal Library in Copenhagen had been keen to buy but his subject specialist had not; the National Library of New Zealand had wanted to buy but only if their country's universities made a contribution, which they had refused to do – it was frustrating. At the beginning of 1991 Hall wrote about the consequences of a decline in sales of the *Nineteenth Century* microfiche programme:[17]

> In case anybody has any doubts about this please remember that the 19th century is one of our largest revenue earners, particularly for Inc. [Chadwyck-Healey Inc.] It has high fixed costs so is extremely sensitive to losses of sales. If the fall-off of sales by mid-1992 were to be so great that the project became unviable the effect on both companies would be devastating ... there is no way in which we could replace the 19th Century in the next eighteen months even with such projects as Poetry and Migne.

'Poetry' and 'Migne'[18] were our exciting new full-text electronic databases described in Chapters 17 and 18, selling for £25,000 and £30,000 a copy, while the *Nineteenth Century* microfiche programme was an old-fashioned microfiche project but, unlike the one-time sales of 'Poetry' and 'Migne', it brought in revenue every year and would go on doing so for years. OCLC was uploading our catalogue records as part of their Major Microforms Project so they were available to all their member libraries, and we also published them on CD-ROM. At the January 1994 editorial advisory board meeting I outlined the potential for publishing electronic scanned images, but nothing came of it. At the end of 1998 our new editorial director, Julie Carroll-Davis, disbanded the editorial board and in 1999 produced a well-thought-out plan to scan our microfiche and offer the scanned editions either on subscription or singly on demand. But by then the sale of the companies was well advanced and that did not progress either.

Hall's reference to our high fixed costs was to Alston and his two full-time assistants in an office in the British Library. There were the usual problems of communication and what he saw as insufficient appreciation of him and his small team by what he referred to as 'HQ'. His letters of complaint always started with a flourish: 'I must confess to being disconcerted by the fact that the departure of two members of staff in two weeks seems to be of so little concern at HQ' (22 July 1988). I wrote on the letter, 'He's right to be concerned but is really blowing off steam.' Alston's private life was difficult and his marriage was stormy. Knowing his mercurial nature, brilliant but restless and always looking for new things to do, I thought that he would be good at getting the project off the ground but would then lose interest. I also wondered how easy he would be to work for – he talked endlessly about his feuds with his colleagues in the British Library. I was wrong. Alston proved to be an exemplary manager and remained fully committed to the project even though we paid him modestly. He cared for his staff, was protective of them both in relation to 'HQ' and the British Library, and he in turn had their whole-hearted loyalty. If anyone had lost interest in the project, it was me. We were now in the electronic age with exciting prospects ahead of us. The *Nineteenth Century* microfiche programme ticked over but did not grow. It brought profitable work to the production company in Bassingbourn and some profit for Chadwyck-Healey but there were no more centuries to carve up and, for me, it represented the end of an era, not the beginning of a new one.

There was another benefit for CHMPS, the production company, in that through its close association with the British Library, it was able to win several contracts for the preservation microfilming of British provincial newspapers from the British Library Newspaper Library in Colindale, north London. This provided profitable filming work for almost ten years.

8

The Sanborn Fire Insurance Maps

It was before we even had our own office in the USA that we started work on the largest microfilm project that we ever carried out there, the filming of the 600,000 Sanborn Fire Insurance Maps. In 1981 Tinkham and I made several visits to the Geography and Map Division of the Library of Congress to look for projects. Each time we were given a warm welcome by the chief, Dr John Wolter, who was an anglophile, though his deputy, Ralph Ehrenberg, was more circumspect.[1] The Geography and Map Division is in the James Madison Building, which had only opened in 1980, another huge federal building, clad in pale stone, containing two million square feet of space. Within it is the finest map library in the world, both in terms of its modern, spacious facilities and the extraordinary depth and size of its collections.

Dana Pratt was planning the publication of a volume of early railroad maps[2] and it was a project like this that I was looking for but nothing of interest had emerged. As we were leaving on one of our visits, I noticed some large map volumes piled up in the corridor with Sanborn embossed on their thick board covers. Wolter explained that they were Sanborn Fire Insurance Maps, large-scale plans of American towns and cities that were so detailed that they showed individual buildings and the uses to which they were put. The colours on the maps represented the materials that each building was built from, as insurers needed to know this in order to judge the fire risk. I was immediately interested and asked if they could be microfilmed. Wolter replied that the Microfilming Corporation of America (MCA) was already negotiating with the Sanborn Map Company for microfilm rights. MCA was a subsidiary of the New York Times Company and is described in Chapter 10. On that visit I had a heavy cold and was not only feeling unwell but was also embarrassed by the knowledge that my hosts probably wished that I had not visited them in my infectious state. Being told that MCA was already planning to microfilm these maps that suddenly seemed so interesting made me feel even more wretched.

A few months later Tinkham and I visited again. I asked Wolter about the Sanborn Maps and he told me that MCA had pulled out because the Library of Congress would not allow them to microfilm the Sanborn Maps at their plant in Sanford, North Carolina, and they had also realized how expensive colour microfilming was going to be. He suggested I get in touch with the president of the Sanborn Map Company because the project would first need Sanborn's agreement, and Tinkham and I left feeling more hopeful. I had learned quite a lot about the importance of the maps in providing a highly detailed picture of 13,000 towns and cities during the urbanization of America from the mid-nineteenth century to the 1970s, and I saw it as a huge, extraordinarily exciting project.

In nineteenth-century America fire not only bankrupted insurers but changed the insurance industry. In 1835 a fire in New York cost insurers over $20 million and this led to the disappearance of many small insurers and the formation of large regional insurance companies in Boston, Hartford, New York and Philadelphia. But underwriters still lacked vital information about the buildings they were insuring. They had no way of assessing the fire risk of the other buildings that surrounded an insured property and they had no maps to show them the location of the buildings that they themselves were insuring. When in 1849 another fire in New York destroyed an area of the dry-goods district, the principal insurer in the area, the Jefferson Insurance Company, was at first unaware of how many buildings in the area were insured by them. They had street registers of insured buildings, but these did not show the spatial relationship between them. In 1850 William Perris, an English engineer who had mapped London, walked into the Jefferson office and offered to produce a map of the buildings in New York. Twenty-five subscribers paid $150 each, and between 1852 and 1855 seven volumes of maps were published – the fire insurance mapping industry in the USA was now established.

The success of Perris encouraged other surveyors and publishers to produce town and city maps and in 1867 D. A. Sanborn, a civil engineer, published his first fire insurance atlas, *Insurance Maps of Boston, Volume 1*. By the end of the first year Sanborn had mapped fifty towns and cities and his company grew quickly. He died in 1883 but the company continued to expand. By 1920 almost every underwriter was buying maps from the Sanborn Company, covering over 13,000 towns and cities with maps and atlases priced from $12 to $200. The maps for New York City in thirty-nine volumes cost $10,000 but even at these prices many insurers bought more than one copy. The Sanborn Maps were high-quality lithographs at a scale of 50 feet to an inch on 21 x 25-inch sheets showing not only the materials used in the construction of each building through colour coding but also the use of the building using standard terms ranging from 'bordello' to 'warehouse'. The name of the company that occupied the building was often given and on large industrial sites the buildings and the different manufacturing processes carried out in each of them were identified. The maps were either sold loose or bound into volumes, which contained detailed indexes. The surveyors who gathered the information were called 'striders', 'trotters' or 'pacers' and they not only measured the buildings but interviewed the occupiers to find out what the buildings were used for and what fire hazards they might contain. The greatest challenge was the rate of change of these young towns and cities. In one year, 1921, in Winona, Missouri, the names of twenty-one streets were changed. It was too expensive to constantly republish complete map sheets and in 1876 Sanborn began to use a system of updating maps by pasting printed slips cut to shape onto the areas of the map that had changed. An example of the extent of the 'pasting' was Volume 13 of the maps of Chicago published in 1895. It was updated over the next twenty-six years with 15,000 slips by teams of 'pasters' who serviced their subscribers.

By 1937 Sanborn was the only surviving fire insurance map maker, but during the Second World War map making was curtailed and after the war the traditional business did not recover. There were fewer insurance companies and new systems for recording properties came into use. The profit and share price both declined and at one time the young Warren Buffett owned thirty-five per cent of the company as he realized that the value of the company's portfolio of investments was greater than the value of its equity. He was able to sell on his interest at a large profit. What was left behind was an extraordinary record, building by building, of almost all of urban America, from Reconstruction in the 1860s to 1950 when the last new map was printed, though updates continued to appear until 1977. There might well have been no surviving record because customers were told to destroy their maps when they became outdated or when their subscription had lapsed. Fortunately, many did not, and Sanborn volumes were preserved in libraries and in private collections.

There were also the two copies of each map sheet deposited at the Library of Congress under copyright deposit. But these were not updated with slips so did not provide a continuous record of urban development. In contrast the US Bureau of the Census had maintained a complete set of volumes kept up to date by Sanborn's 'pasters' until 1950. The bureau had acquired the atlases in the 1940s for use in creating census tracts but in 1967 transferred the collection of 1,840 volumes to the Library of Congress. It now had both corrected and uncorrected sheets, and volunteers spent summers sorting and cataloguing the collection while duplicate volumes were offered to universities in return. Finally, in 1981, the Library of Congress published a 700-page carto-bibliography, *Fire Insurance Maps in the Library of Congress*,[3] and it was this that enabled both MCA and us to consider publishing a microfilm edition of the Sanborn Maps.

On 28 February 1982 we had our first formal meeting at the library to discuss the microfilming of the 600,000 maps. The importance of the meeting was marked by the presence of Dr Alan Fern, head of special collections, and Dr Peter Sparks, head of preservation. Ehrenberg, and Norman J. Shaffer, head of photo duplication, were also there. It was made clear to me that the library did not regard the Sanborn Maps as a conservation priority and to have them microfilmed would be a major disruption for the Map Division. Under federal regulations they had to allow us to microfilm the maps, but it would have to be done on their terms. Sparks explained that there was also a conservation issue. Some maps had been bound into volumes and could not be opened flat for microfilming. His department would hire a conservator to advise on how best the maps could be disbound. It was a day of contrasts because although I left the 9.30am meeting somewhat subdued, I met again with Fern later in the day at a meeting to celebrate the publication of the FSA and HABS microfiche collections and, in between, had a meeting with James Moore at the National Archives, which led directly to the birth of the *National Inventory of Documentary Sources* (see Chapter 9).

Linda Blaser, the Library of Congress conservator, advised me that to enable the bound maps to be microfilmed, the most cost-effective method was to guillotine the spines of the Sanborn volumes and after microfilming store the loose maps in specially made solander boxes similar to those that housed the Census Bureau collection. We would have to pay to have them disbound and for the boxes to be made to the Map Division's specification. I also had to decide about the colour washes on the maps representing different building materials such as brick, wood and stone. The need to use colour microfilm had discouraged MCA but I knew that this project was only feasible on black and white microfilm because colour microfilm copies

Figure 7 Washington, DC, Library of Congress. Presentation of the FSA and HABS microfiche collections. Left to right: Dana Pratt, director of publishing; Oliver Jensen, chief, prints and photographs division; Alan Fern, director of special collections and research services; the author. 28 February 1982.

of such a large collection would be too expensive for the library market. Colour film was also unsuitable because it has a lower resolution and we needed the highest possible resolution to make every detail on the map legible. I concluded that the building materials information that would be lost in monochrome reproductions was not as important as the other historical information, which was not dependent on colour, and I informed Wolter that our microfilm edition would be in black and white.

I was also negotiating with the Sanborn Map Company and its president, S. Greeley Wells, a pleasant, old-time easterner who took me to lunch at the New York Yacht Club and asked me to draw up a draft agreement. I included a clause that gave us exclusive rights to make paper copies from the microfilm and in a final clause I also granted to ourselves exclusive electronic publication rights. At the time the only electronic medium on which the maps could have been reproduced was the videodisk – the CD-ROM had not yet been invented – but my intuition was that there would soon be new developments in electronic media and that one day this important collection would be reissued by us in another form. I assumed that my draft would be entirely rewritten by their lawyers – with the electronic rights deleted. But after a few weeks the agreement came back signed and, to my surprise, without a single change. It was clear that no lawyer had even looked at it. At the next meeting at the library, in September 1982, both Wolter and Ehrenberg were present, and I was told that they would require us to:

- Pay for an assistant to prepare maps for microfilming and reshelve them afterwards.
- Pay for the disbinding of tightly bound volumes and for their subsequent re-boxing.
- Pay $5,000 for a microfilm camera to be set up in the Map Division.
- Pay 25 or 30 cents per frame for filming bound or unbound maps respectively, double the normal rate for books.
- Since we had exclusive reproduction rights to the in-copyright maps we were also required to grant the Library of Congress special rights to enable them to make both microfilm and paper copies for their readers subject to restrictions, which we negotiated.

There were 179 bound volumes, and disbinding at $22 a volume and boxes at $90 each added $20,000 to the production cost. The filming rate for these large maps was reasonable and I knew that a self-standing operation, undistracted by other work, had a better chance of meeting its production schedule, and I was happy to agree to all their terms. We signed a 'Cooperative Agreement' on 25 January 1983.

Bonnell and I did some formal market research by talking to map librarians. I guessed that there were few libraries, if any, who would buy the whole of the USA, but that most libraries would buy their own state and perhaps the states near them. Most states are surrounded by three others and I decided to offer libraries an agreement similar to that that I had used successfully for the *Nineteenth-Century Parliamentary Papers* (see Chapter 5), in which they were required to buy a minimum of four states but in return the price would be close to cost and they would share a five per cent royalty on all future sales. The offer was mailed in late 1982 and was met with complete incomprehension. Not a single library responded to the offer, but many wrote to say that all they wanted was to buy their own town or city. I was about to abandon the project, knowing that the Library of Congress was indifferent, and the Sanborn Map Company had already seen one microform publisher walk away. But I found that I could not give up. If we only expected to sell a maximum of four copies of each state, the normal production break-even of between five and ten copies was too high. To make it viable we had to break even at no more than two copies. The 623,000 maps on 1,040 reels of film would cost $312,000 to produce, so if we only had two sales per state, we would have to sell a microfilm reel for $170 compared to the normal price that we and our competitors charged of under $50 per reel. Although it was standard practice to state the number of reels of microfilm in sales brochures, I decided to list only the number of maps together with the price for each state. There were 600 maps on a reel and so a per reel price of $170 was equivalent to 28 cents a map, which I thought librarians should see as good value. The number of maps in each state related to the age and size of its cities and prices ranged from all the maps for Alaska for $100 to New York State for $13,670. Tinkham and I quickly produced a detailed sales brochure, which was mailed out in April 1983. We did not expect to get orders before the libraries' year-end in June, as most college libraries finalize their list of collections and expensive books that they want to buy with year-end money before Christmas. But the response to the mailing of the Sanborn brochure was extraordinary; for the first and only time, librarians telephoned their orders rather than mailing them but found that the Teaneck office phone number printed on the brochure was incorrect. Fortunately, the local Bell Telephone Company rented us the unused 'wrong number' for the next few months. We started production by filming the small state of Delaware and prioritized the microfilming of the states according to the orders we received. Four months after mailing the brochure we had received $274,000 of orders, and towards the end of the next financial year in June 1984 the very much larger total included eight orders for New York, seven for Massachusetts and four for California, three of the most expensive states. In May 1984 Bonnell was able to tell me that for the first time we had achieved $1 million of sales in our financial year, which ran from July to June; the order that achieved it was from Columbia University for the Sanborn Maps of New York State. Later in 1984 we received an order from the Center for Research Libraries (CRL) in Chicago for the complete collection. Set up in 1949 as a resource for Midwest libraries, by the 1980s CRL had become a national resource centre supported by several hundred US libraries who funded it to enable it to buy copies of expensive research collections, which each member could then borrow. Normally we did not want an order from CRL because it meant that its many member libraries would then not need to buy the publication themselves, but in the case of the Sanborn Maps we had already sold the maps of individual states to many libraries and had not expected to sell a complete set to anyone, even at the discounted price of $120,000.

There continued to be a strong demand for the maps of individual towns and cities. Madel Morgan at the State Archives of Mississippi wrote:

> I want to thank you for getting these maps on film as they provide a rich source for information about the communities in our state that was hitherto inaccessible to most people.... A librarian in the Delta called me today to ask if there was any possibility of their acquiring the microfilm copies of maps for their county.[4]

We offered single towns, cities or counties at a minimum price of $100 for up to 200 maps and thereafter 50 cents per map. Over the next five years we received hundreds of orders from US libraries, providing a valuable stream of revenue. We had very few orders from outside the USA, the largest being from the University of Melbourne, which has extensive collections on American history. The next development, which revealed an entirely new use for the Sanborn Maps as a record of historical land use in the USA, is described in Chapter 16.

9

Finding the Archives

National Inventory of Documentary Sources

The first paper that I gave in the USA was at Meckler's second annual Library Microfilm Conference in Atlanta, Georgia, in October 1976. On a platform shared with speakers from Pergamon Press and MCA (see Chapter 10), I stated that we would not be publishing archives on microfilm; we would concentrate on publishing printed works because the number of potential readers for printed material was much larger than for archives. This was in spite of our first important publication being the *Archives of British Publishers*. Even in the largest university there might be only one or two scholars who would use a particular archive, and printed sources were more heavily used by most scholars. What interested me more were the tools that researchers used to find archives – indexes and catalogues and what I later discovered were called 'finding aids'.

In 1972, while still working for Johnson, I had visited the National Register of Archives (NRA) in Quality Court, Chancery Lane, London. It was part of the Historical Manuscripts Commission and its purpose was to collect copies of finding aids to manuscript collections throughout the UK. It had also created a detailed central index, but to use it most researchers had to visit the London office. I immediately thought that this would be an ideal reference collection to publish on microfiche so that copies could be used in libraries throughout the world. The NRA thought otherwise, and I got a firm refusal even though I enlisted the help of George Potter, my friend and mentor, who had been a member of the Historical Manuscripts Commission. While the NRA did make copies for a few large libraries, they were not interested in the dissemination of their material through publication but preferred to simply maintain their collection in central London. Although I went back to them with a publishing proposal every few years for the next twenty years, they were always defensive and always turned me down.

I continued my search for printed catalogues of archives that we might microfilm or reprint and ten years after my first visit to the NRA I was still searching. In February 1982 Tinkham had arranged for me to visit James Moore, a senior archivist at the National Archives in Washington, and he told me that the person I should speak to was Dr Frank Burke, director of the National Historical Publications and Records Commission (NHPRC). A few days later I met with Burke and told him that I was looking for guides, indexes and catalogues to manuscript collections. 'They are called finding aids,' he replied 'and most of them are not published. It is the unpublished ones you should microfilm because they are the ones that no one can get hold of.' He explained that a finding aid is usually a typed description of an archive with an introduction, a detailed listing of the contents of the archive, and an index. For most researchers the only access to an archive is through its finding aid. I asked Burke if he would set out his ideas on paper and offered him a fee. In April 1982 he sent me a five-page letter describing the entire project in detail and correcting my misapprehensions.[1] At the end he explained that as a government employee he could not accept any payment, nor could he be listed as an editor or advisor. He wrote, 'You have piqued my interest and stirred up some old yearnings.' No other publishing idea was ever set out in such detail – by someone who asked for nothing in return. He suggested that we should call the project 'The National Inventory of Documentary Sources in the U.S.' 'The title for this program should be classy. You are dealing with the final remains and fond memories of America's national and local heroes and heroines.... it is national in scope ... and is not just a guide, but in effect, an inventory.' He divided it into four parts:

- Part 1 – Federal Records. The finding aids of the National Archives, the Smithsonian Institution Archives and the seven presidential libraries that were in existence at that time.
- Part 2 – Manuscript Division of the Library of Congress.
- Part 3 – State Archives, State Libraries and State Historical Societies.
- Part 4 – The finding aids of all other repositories including university and college libraries, public libraries and private repositories.

In the 1960s Burke had worked on an early attempt to use computers to index archives called SPINDEX, and he thought we should consult with archivists in four Midwest archives who were developing a joint automated guide using SPINDEX III, but we never did. In our own indexing we used the names and subject headings used by the Library of Congress in their *Index of Personal Names in the National Union Catalog of Manuscript Collections (NUCMC)* (see below), but in response to questions asked at a meeting of the Society of American Archivists (SAA), we stated that the finding aids themselves are the real authority file and we would always index names as they appear in the finding aid.

Part 1 included the presidential libraries that are repositories for the presidents' papers and other historical records. The funds to build the libraries come from private sources, but once completed, the National Archives and Records Administration takes on their running. I had wanted to visit as many as possible but only visited three: the Hoover Presidential Library in West Branch, Iowa, the first presidential library and a modest building compared to the later grandiose memorials to post-war presidents; the Lyndon Baines Johnson Presidential Library on the campus of the University of Texas at Austin; and the magnificent John F. Kennedy Presidential Library on the shore outside Boston. Burke had worked at the Library of Congress and through his influence and our good relationship with the Library of Congress Part 2 was easily achieved.

We compiled a separate index for each part, which was updated every time additional microfiche were sent to subscribers, and the index was published on computer-output microfiche (COM) using diazo film, which was replaced each time a new index was issued. Parts 1 and 2 were finished quite quickly; Part 3 took longer while Part 4 was open ended because there were always new archives and new finding aids to be added. Libraries subscribed to Parts 3 and 4 and received several deliveries of microfiche each year. The index was cumulative so always included all previously issued finding aids.

NIDS was launched in February 1983 and libraries could see that it provided access to archives at an entirely new level. Even the Library of Congress was impressed when they found through *NIDS* that one of their own collections was divided between their library and another repository.[2] Nat Bunker, American history bibliographer at Harvard College Library, wrote:

> We use NIDS all the time – both our staff and users of the library. It's a great tool for helping you locate material you need and for finding out if

specific material is available within a collection. With the difficulty in getting funds to travel these days it's important to maximise preparation time, and if you can read the finding aids before you leave and identify or rule out certain sources, you save time and money. This is one of the best reference works I have seen for years.[3]

In 1984 the powerful US Research Libraries Group (RLG) had just begun to input record-group and collection-level data in a newly developed 'Archives and Manuscript Control' format into their online catalogue RLIN, in which they would also record the existence of a finding aid. It was those finding aids that we were now publishing on microfiche. Roy H. Tryon in the *American Archivist* wrote:

> Both NUCMC and RLIN provide only summary information, and NUCMC excludes National Archives holdings altogether. The NIDS by contrast provides the full text of all significant finding aids submitted and enhances access to them by extensive name and subject indexing.[4]

It was several years before formal reviews began to appear. A review in *American Historical Review* in 1988 stated, 'It has no competition and serves a purpose that has long been identified as needed and important but that no one has undertaken until now.'[5] Kenneth Silverman, a Pulitzer Prize winner and chairman of the English department at New York University, whom I had met at a dinner party, wrote, 'NIDS – which I think is the best news for scholarship since the Xerox machine.'[6] Equally encouraging was the initiative of Mike Unsworth, a young librarian at Michigan State University, who also in 1988 began to organize *NIDS* workshops, teaching researchers how to use the resource alongside other research tools like *NUCMC*.

NIDS was an important turning point, as it not only gave us our first valuable US subscription title that we could invoice in advance every year for the next fifteen years, but it required us, for the first time, to carry out microfilming in the USA on our own premises rather than in a library or gallery. Tinkham also found that there was more work than she wanted, as she now had a young son. This led me to open our first office in Alexandria, Virginia, that had become our de facto base for editorial and production in the USA because Tinkham lived there. Our first office in Prince Street was followed, appropriately, by a larger office in King Street (see Chapter 14). Our first full-time employee was Tony Sloan, our microfilm camera operator, and he was followed by Dr Mark Hamilton who joined in February 1984 as head of editorial and production. Hamilton had an academic background and was an anglophile. He was a good ambassador for the company but had no entrepreneurial experience of developing a publishing business and finding new projects. I knew that I would have to give him a lot of support and advice, but he also had the support of Tinkham, who had worked so closely with me over the previous seven years and was continuing as part-time editor and production manager.

I began to attend the annual conferences of the SAA. The first and most memorable was in Minneapolis in October 1983. At the time the Midwest humorist and radio personality Garrison Keillor was hosting a weekly radio show, *A Prairie Home Companion*, on Minnesota Public Radio, for which he had created the fictional small town in Minnesota, 'Lake Wobegon'. The archivists had a block booking in the theatre in 'downtown St Paul' across the river from Minneapolis, where each week the show was broadcast live on the radio throughout America. The Scandinavian folk choir and Keillor's extraordinary stage presence and ability to create a story out of nothing, intoned in a gravelly, sing-song Midwestern drawl, made it unforgettable. Knowing that he was playing to an audience of archivists he had composed a special song, 'All Archivists Stick Together',[7] in which part of the refrain at the end of each verse was, 'Microfilm those dusty piles!' It is perhaps the only time that the word 'microfilm' has been used in a song broadcast to millions of Americans.

As soon as *NIDSUS* was under way we started work on *NIDSUK*. When I had first visited the NRA in 1972, I had not fully understood the significance of the unpublished finding aids that they collected, and which made up the 'register' that they then indexed. Nor had it occurred to me that there was nothing to stop us publishing British finding aids on microfiche ourselves, independently of the NRA. I needed the advice and encouragement of an expert like Burke to have the confidence to do so and by December 1984 we had published our first unit containing finding aids from these disparate sources: the Bodleian Library, University of Oxford; Royal College of Physicians; Labour Party Archives; and Family Planning Association Archives. The second unit in January 1985 consisted of the finding aids of just one institution, the Imperial War Museum, which included both typed finding aids and a 16,000-card subject index. A year later the museum expressed its surprise when it received a royalty cheque of over £5,000, their ten per cent royalty from the sales of that unit. They also received a free microfiche copy.

The Public Record Office (PRO), renamed the National Archives in 2003, was already microfilming its own class lists and we published the catalogue of manuscripts of the British Library in printed form as described below. What was common to almost all the archivists that we approached was their initial reluctance to allow their finding aids to be published. It was one thing to allow them to be used by researchers but formal publication, even on microfiche, was another, as they were afraid that it would expose them to criticism, especially by peers, particularly of older finding aids, which probably did need updating. My request to David Vaisey, Bodley's Librarian, who was also an archivist, was met with a mixture of concern and incredulity, but once we had talked it over he conceded that there might be some unpublished Bodleian finding aids that were suitable for publication on microfiche, and indeed there were. The response of an archivist in a north London borough was similar. He informed me politely that they had no finding aids that were currently suitable for publication. As I got up to leave, he said, almost wistfully, that there was one that he had been working on which he thought might be suitable, but he realized that we would not want only one. I replied that we would be happy with one, because it was important to have his institution included in *NIDSUK*, and I also knew by then that one would quickly be followed by others.

The reviews of *NIDSUK* were positive. Dr Lamar M. Hill at the University of California, Irvine, described it as, 'An extraordinary research aid that will make the researcher's task immeasurably more effective' and added, 'While the National Register of Archives (NRA) contains valuable finding aids, they generally cannot be consulted outside its reading room and, of equally great importance, NRA does not receive copies of the actual internal indexes, lists and card catalogue entries [finding aids].'[8] From 1993, while the finding aids were on microfiche, the indexes, which had been on computer-output microfiche (COM), were now published on CD-ROM, making the publication a mixture of analogue and digital media at a time of transition. Our main marketing tool was the *NIDS Newsletter*, which was sent to several thousand archivists, librarians and academics. In the 1990s there were few new sales and at an SAA meeting in 1995 an archivist asked if *NIDS* was dead. It was far from dead, and subscribers were still receiving their quarterly deliveries of finding aids on microfiche when I sold the companies in 1999.

Printed indexes to manuscript collections

At the same time that we began to publish *NIDS* we were also preparing to publish four important indexes to manuscript collections as multi-volume printed books. In late 1982 the British Library asked selected publishers to tender for the publication of the *Index to Manuscripts in the British Library*, containing over 1 million personal names and places, and indexing the holdings of the Department of Manuscripts until 1950. This required the photographing of the 380,000 cards in the catalogue. Jim Emmett, an Australian librarian who had his own publishing company, had been the first to propose the publication of this catalogue and he asked us to partner him in what was a substantial undertaking. But Cobbe made clear that the British Library would prefer us or another larger publisher to undertake the work. After my experience with the Burney Collection (see Chapter 5) I understood why; it would have stretched Emmett financially and he did not have a sales and marketing organization capable of selling it throughout the world. The British Library accepted our proposal and we signed the agreement on 29 April 1983, paying the British Library an advance of £10,000. I asked Emmett to manage production in return for an interest in the publication since he had experience in publishing card catalogues in book form. He turned down my offer, judging wrongly, as he later admitted, that it would take up too much of his time.

The tender required us to carry out the photographing of the cards 'a reasonable distance from the library' but we chose Paragon, a printer in Gateshead, across the Tyne from Newcastle, who took on the job at a time when the whole of the North East was still deeply depressed. It was labour-intensive work as the cards had first to be photocopied and then have brackets and abbreviations for the collection to which the entry related added by hand. The entries were then cut up and arranged to make up each page, which was then photographed on a process camera. It had always been intended that the card catalogue would eventually be published in book form, but each card had been encased in a plastic film to protect it. Over the years the plastic had yellowed which made the cards more difficult to copy. After the first page proofs were sent to the library, Waley, the Keeper of Manuscripts, whom I had known since our original negotiation over the Bentley papers in 1973, informed me very firmly that the quality of reproduction was not acceptable. The British Library classmarks, a combination of letters and numbers which enables a manuscript to be located, were not always legible. Letters such as 'e' and 'o' were breaking up so that they looked like 'c's. A wrong letter or number in a classmark would mean that the manuscript requested by a reader could not be found and so staff time would be wasted while they rechecked it. I agreed with him, though I did point out that it was mainly due to the discoloured plastic film on the cards. We hired two women to go through every classmark on every photocopy and fill in every broken number or letter using Rapidograph pens with very fine nibs. Once a routine was established, production went smoothly and the extra work of inking in the letters and numbers did not add significantly to the total production cost.

Even though this was the early 1980s, before the CD-ROM, I thought that this was an opportunity to convert the card catalogue into a database. I had talked to Alex Wilson, the director general of the British Library, at the conservation conference in Cambridge in September 1983[9] and wrote to him, as part of our response to the tender, proposing that the card index be converted into machine-readable form and then be published in print.[10] I listed the obvious advantages of updating, correcting and merging such data in the future but also recognized the disadvantages, the main one being cost. Cobbe replied on Wilson's behalf that the tender panel considered that conversion would be too expensive and too time consuming for the staff. Nor did they want to assign online rights to other parties at this time.[11]

When the first volume was published Waley wrote to say how pleased he was with its appearance, and we were able to publish the last of the ten volumes a month before his retirement in early 1986. But there was one bizarre incident that could have ruined our relationship with the British Library. We used Securicor to collect the heavy oak, four-drawer units from the British Library, deliver them to Gateshead and collect and deliver them back. Travelling through London to return a batch of units to the British Library, the doors of the Securicor van flew open and one set of drawers tumbled onto the street. A car was travelling behind the van and two men got out, picked up the unit and put it in their car, and it was never seen again. The British Library insisted that we replace the cards by reproducing each entry on a 5 x 3-inch card filed in the correct order even though the same cards were about to be published in book form. If this had happened when the drawers of cards were being taken from the library to the printer in Gateshead they could not have been replaced and it would have been a disastrous loss for both of us.

In appearance the large quarto volumes were the finest set of books we ever published. Pavel Buchler, who at the time was the graphic designer for all our brochures, designed a stately title page in Times Roman and the bindings were in dark red buckram with blocking in gold on the spines.

By the time publication of the last volumes of the catalogue had been completed we were already working on an eight-volume *Catalogue of Manuscripts in the Houghton Library, Harvard University*, which we had been invited to publish by an old friend, Ken Carpenter, assistant director of the Houghton Library, Harvard's rare book and manuscripts library. It contained 136,000 entries for a collection of millions of manuscripts. The production of the Houghton Library volumes was also labour intensive because after the cards had been laid out and photocopied onto sheets, information on the back of each card had to be typed underneath the relevant entry. The sheets were then microfilmed for security before they were shipped to the printer in the UK where they were rephotographed. Production went smoothly but, as we found later with the British Library General Catalogue of Printed Books (see Chapter 15), the British Library is one of the world's pre-eminent libraries and its catalogues are more highly valued than those of almost any other library. The *Index of Manuscripts in the British Library* sold well throughout the world, while the *Catalogue of Manuscripts in the Houghton Library* sold respectably in the USA but had far fewer sales elsewhere.

In 1988 the Library of Congress chose us to publish what were our last printed manuscript indexes, the *Index to Personal Names in the National Union Catalog of Manuscript Collections, 1959–1984 (NUCMC)* and its companion, *Index to Subjects and Corporate Names*. The National Union Catalog was a cooperative cataloguing programme in which US repositories reported their manuscript collections and the entries were published annually by the Library of Congress. The two two-volume works were cumulations of names in the previously published annual indexes for the first twenty-five years of the catalogue. We had assumed that merging well-edited indexes already in digital form would be straightforward, but it was not. There were too many anomalies – slight differences that might be errors or might simply be different names. It was important that they were correct because the indexes were used by cataloguers all over the world as the ultimate authority for these names. The strange and wonderful spelling and structure of many of the names were also a reminder of what a racial and cultural melting pot the USA has always been. The difficulties we had with the production of these volumes influenced our thinking when in 1991 we considered merging printed indexes to periodicals but, instead, created an entirely new database, *Periodicals Contents Index*, described in Chapter 19.

10

The New York Times

The largest-selling microfilm publication in the world was the microfilm edition of *The New York Times*. In 1981 it was sold to 4,200 subscribers and this in a medium where a sale of 100 copies of a publication was considered exceptional. MCA published the microfilm edition and was a subsidiary of The New York Times Company. It also published microfilm editions of many other US newspapers and magazines and research collections like ours. But in this latter area it was not as formidable a competitor as Research Publications or UMI. I had met Carl Horwitz, the president of MCA, in 1976 at Meckler's Library Microform conference and two years later he visited us in Cambridge. We discussed the possibility of Chadwyck-Healey selling their publications in the UK and Europe. In 1978 their annual European sales including *The New York Times* had only been $185,000 and I thought we could do better. I visited MCA's 82,000-square-foot office and production facility in a pine forest near Sanford, North Carolina, but we were unable to reach a satisfactory agreement and I was left with the impression that, apart from *The New York Times*, this was a company that had lost its way. I began to wonder why The New York Times wanted to own such a small, specialized company and whether they might be interested in selling it. Meckler had met Sydney Gruson, a senior executive at The New York Times and friend and advisor to Punch Sulzberger, the chairman, whose family owned The New York Times Company, on a transatlantic crossing on the *QEII*. Les Sufrin, my accountant and advisor, seemed confident that we could raise the money to buy the company and in 1982, with Meckler's introduction, I wrote to Gruson to ask if they would consider selling MCA to me. He responded positively, and Meckler and I met him in his executive suite in the New York Times building on 1 October. Also present were William T. 'Bill' Kerr, a vice-president who had joined The New York Times from McKinsey after they had carried out a review for the company in 1978, and Benjamin Handelman, senior vice-president responsible for the affiliated companies. Gruson, an elegant man in his sixties, told Meckler and me that The New York Times had decided to sell MCA because they were buying a newspaper in Florida and wanted to raise some capital in this quarter to offset the purchase cost. As I had been the first to approach them, they would give me first refusal. He said that a prospectus would be made available to us within a few weeks. His parting words were, 'It is going to be expensive. I hope you have got the money.'

While I was in the USA, I was excited; when I got home, I was less so. There would be a huge change in our lives as we would have to move to the USA. If we kept the existing plant and offices near Sanford we would be living in the wilds of North Carolina and our three children would be in local schools, which was not an inviting prospect. But if we did not use the Sanford plant, we would have to find production premises in the USA very much larger than we had in Bassingbourn. The microfilm edition of *The New York Times* was two to three reels of microfilm each month, requiring the monthly production and shipping to the subscribers of over 8,000–12,000 reels, apparently requiring sixty-nine people in production at MCA compared to fifteen at Bassingbourn at that time.

In November we received a package of materials, including a description of MCA and what were described as 'financial exhibits',[1] which made interesting reading, starting with a 'minimum purchase price' of $20 million. Projected sales revenue of the company for 1982 was $10,485,000. The sale of microfilm editions of newspapers and magazines made up most of the revenue, while the sale of research collections was $1.6 million worldwide, compared with Chadwyck-Healey's sales of around $1.8 million in 1981/2. Although this was a company that seemed to have lost its way, the most impressive aspect of the business, thanks to *The New York Times*, was their penetration of the US library market – ninety-eight per cent of the 1,874 universities and colleges, sixty-one per cent of the 3,500 public libraries with budgets of over $10,000, a respectable fifty-seven per cent of 10,000 schools and significant percentages of junior colleges, special libraries and government and military libraries. The operating profit before tax was twenty per cent of sales revenue, which was reasonable, and because more than fifty per cent were subscriptions paid in advance the cash flow was strong. But we were surprised by the number of staff – 145 for a business turning over only $10 million and this had been reduced in recent years from 200. There were twenty-four people in accounts alone, which is a reminder of how labour-intensive billing and accounting work was before the advent of small computer systems. There were also two large costs relating to the flagship *New York Times* microfilm edition, an annual contribution of almost $1.5 million to The New York Times for the compilation of the index, which then had to be printed at the buyer's expense, and a twenty-five per cent royalty on sales. Together this was more than fifty per cent of the revenue we could expect from sales of the microfilm edition. They had prepared a projected income statement for 1982 for a 'Qualified buyer'. This was a buyer that could make extensive savings in management and in production by absorbing the MCA business into an existing business. We did not have such a business in the USA so could not make such savings. In their pro-forma statement, marketing headcount was reduced from twenty-two to four and accounting from twenty-four to three. It was difficult to see how even a 'Qualified buyer' could make such savings in personnel. But it was only with these savings that the asking price could be justified.

After a meeting with Kerr, Mike Ryan, the Times attorney, and Horwitz, Sufrin reported that, 'The New York Times wants out and they want out in the fourth quarter of 1982' and that they would allow us to buy MCA stock, which meant we would also collect the receivables that would bring the effective sales price down from $20 million to $13 million. He and Miller analyzed the figures while I gave them my estimates of future sales. Initially Sufrin had been confident that we could find the money to buy the business and had talked of approaching the large Dutch publishing group that he represented in the USA and, later, floating the company on the stock market. Disturbingly the closer we came to making a decision, the more unclear it was as to where the money was going to come from. Notwithstanding this, Miller and I flew to New York for a meeting on 22 November with Kerr and Ryan. I explained that if we were able to buy the company, we planned to sell the plant near Sanford and move production to our operation in Teaneck, New Jersey, but went on to say that we were having difficulty justifying the asking price. Teaneck, famous for its bagels, is a pleasant residential New Jersey suburb, and during a pause in the discussion Ryan lent over to me and said quietly, 'I didn't think there was an industrial area in Teaneck.' I made some non-committal reply but realized that it was time to beat a dignified retreat. We could not see how the business could be worth more than $10 million to us. We were also aware that The New York Times was only offering us a fifteen-year licence to publish the microfilm edition, which did not seem long enough. Our offer would be too far from what they were asking to be negotiable. The next day I phoned Kerr to tell him that we were withdrawing and followed it with a letter thanking him for giving us the opportunity and regretting that we could not reach an agreement.

We knew that The New York Times would not sell MCA to Research Publications because they published the third most valuable newspaper microfilm publication, the London *Times*, and this was seen as a competitor.[2] Soon after, we read that they had sold the rights to *The New York Times* microfilm edition to UMI, the obvious buyer as they already had a plant large enough to accommodate the extra monthly production and either they or The New York Times itself could dispose of the plant in Sanford. But the ground was shifting technologically; if we had bought MCA we would have been disconcerted by the news, a few months later in May 1983, that The New York Times had granted a licence to the Mead Corporation, publishers of Lexis, the legal online service, and Nexis, the news information online service, giving it rights to sell *New York Times* articles online to customers using desktop computer terminals. This was still mainframe technology with few concessions made to the user, but it was a further indication that electronic media were going to be increasingly used in libraries. I also wondered to what extent my letter had triggered the decision to sell MCA. The New York Times did buy *The Sarasota Herald-Tribune* in the last quarter of 1982, and after the McKinsey review Sulzberger, in July 1979, had appointed his tough, down-to-earth production chief, Walter Mattson, as president of The New York Times Company. Mattson, who before he became president had never visited MCA in Sanford, decided to divest The Times of twenty of its auxiliary businesses, which he described as 'never-no-mind' firms, a term that perfectly described MCA.[3]

MCA could not be sold as a going concern, so MCA titles were disposed of, piecemeal, over the next year and the plant at Sanford remained separately for sale. In June 1983 Horwitz told me that their lawyers had advised them that the rights of many of the research collections that they had published belonged to the institutions who owned the original material. If any of them agreed to let us take over their microfilm collections MCA would sell us the master microfilm and their stock of printed guides in return for what represented a fair residual value of the collection, taking into account how much it had cost them and how much revenue they had already generated from it. I thought this was misguided advice by their lawyers, as I could not see how the institution that owned the original material could have any rights over the microfilm edition providing the publisher continued to pay royalties on sales. He sent me a list of twenty institutions, and we wrote to them all. In the end we only reached agreement with two. One of them, the State Historical Society of Wisconsin, was the source of sixteen separate research collections of mainly manuscript material on different areas and periods of American history. The most important was the *Draper Manuscripts*, 123 reels of microfilm, over 100,000 pages, containing first-hand accounts of the American Revolution and the Westward expansion including Daniel Boone's military account books and his land survey notebooks. Even larger but much more specialized were the papers of five politicians known as the 'Wisconsin Progressives', leaders of the Wisconsin Progressive Party, which was active between 1934 and 1946. I knew that there were few libraries even in the USA who would spend $18,000 on the 350 reels that made up this collection. But we paid MCA and shipped 1,800 reels of master negative film and a large stock of printed guides to Bassingbourn, and in doing so we had added sixteen US history titles to our catalogue. Although we did not expect many sales from the older titles, together they created a potentially lucrative backlist. The other institution was the University of Louisville from which we bought the master microfilm of the *Roy Stryker Papers*, which was a relevant companion to our microfiche publication *America, 1935–1946* described in Chapter 6. Where the owner of the material that had been microfilmed did not choose another publisher, the collection went to UMI,[4] but in 1987 the University of Maryland transferred the MCA microfilm of their important archive, *Samuel Gompers and the American Federation of Labor* records, 149 reels of film, from UMI to Chadwyck-Healey Inc., believing that we would make more effort to sell it.

I did not respond when Howard McGinn, the general manager, wrote to me and to other publishers asking for bids of at least $450,000 for another twenty titles that they owned outright, but in March 1984 Horwitz wanted to know if we would be interested in taking on the publishing agreements for four collections with NYPL. Three of them were very large clippings files that had been created by the library over many years; the fourth was the papers of Norman Thomas, a politician who had been a presidential candidate for the Socialist Party of America from the 1920s onwards, no fewer than six times. The *Norman Thomas Papers, 1904–1967*, totalling almost 100,000 pages, had already been microfilmed by MCA but had not been announced or sold; it was effectively a new title ready for sale.

The three clippings files were the Artists File, the Print File and the Schomburg Clipping File, which was the single most important source for black history in the USA. It had already been microfilmed by NCR as a preservation project for NYPL, funded by the NEH, and comprised 9,500 microfiche. One of the conditions of the grant had been that the microfiche could only be used in the Schomburg Center itself, which was a branch of NYPL in Harlem. That condition had ended, and the library was now allowed to sell microfiche copies.

The Artists File together with the Print File were even larger clippings files started by NYPL in 1911 and closed in the early 1970s for conservation reasons. The Artists File was at the MCA plant in Sanford waiting to be microfilmed. It seemed to be an attractive proposition: two collections already completed and ready for sale and only the two others needing to be microfilmed. Art history was an area in which we specialized, and an important collection from NYPL should sell well. I told Horwitz that we were interested and that I would like to visit Sanford to see the Artists File when I was next in the USA. But I was also concerned about the production cost and wrote to McGinn on 9 April about the Artists File, 'I still do not have a clear idea of the exact nature and arrangement of the material in this project and the kind of editorial and production problems that it will create though I suspect they are considerable.' I did not know how considerable until, in May 1984, Hamilton and I visited the buildings at Sanford, now empty and lifeless. In the corner of a large space was a cluster of fifty-two dark green filing cabinets containing the Artists File. One of the most heavily used collections in NYPL, the Artists File was estimated to contain over 1.5 million pieces of paper on over 100,000 painters, sculptors and architects, as well as craftspeople, jewellers, designers, collectors, connoisseurs, critics and curators. There were newspaper and magazine clippings, auction and exhibition catalogues, letters, invitation cards and even book jackets. In 1942 a typed list from Brentano's, the New York bookstore, advertised original Toulouse-Lautrec posters in 'perfect condition' for as little as $18 each. Now such posters fetch $25,000. The collection had become unmanageable. A folder might contain hundreds of pieces of paper. It was easy to steal items but also to damage them or misfile them in another folder. The library had to close the Artists File and, without the benefit of an NEH grant, find some way of having it microfilmed. In 1982 MCA, attracted as I was to the opportunity of selling the Schomburg Collection microfiche and the Norman Thomas Papers that they had had to microfilm, had entered into an agreement to take on the Artists File and its companion, the Print File, which covered over 15,000 printmakers, illustrators and photographers.

As I looked through the folders, I was still excited about the prospect of publishing this huge collection, though I was worried about how much time it would take to microfilm it as it would require the camera operator to arrange and lay out several items to fill each frame – very different from simply turning over a page. As we were leaving, a young man in the production team took me aside and said, 'I think you ought to know that it is taking us 165 hours per drawer to sort and organize the material before we even get it near a camera.' This was a shock and suddenly the Artists File looked most unpromising. Each filing cabinet had four drawers, which would mean just under 35,000 hours of work before we could even start to microfilm the material. At a UK labour rate of £8 per hour this was £280,000 and a 100 per cent contribution to overheads increased it to £560,000. I also knew that while there were many art libraries in the USA, most of them were medium to small and only a few were large enough to afford such a potentially expensive research collection.

In spite of my new reservations we agreed with Horwitz that we would meet with NYPL the next day. Before the meeting Hamilton and I had lunch with him in a Chinese restaurant near the library. It was only then that he made the situation clear to us. He admitted that NYPL was holding MCA to their contract to complete the microfilming of the Artists and Print files and would take legal action against MCA and The New York Times if necessary. But these two great New York institutions did not engage in disputes in public and he had been told to find a solution. As we walked to the library I realized that we were the 'white knight' for both parties and I should make a proposal that was as much to our advantage as possible. The Schomburg Clipping File would be enormously valuable to us, generating immediate revenue of around $500,000 with no significant up-front costs; the Norman Thomas Papers would also provide some useful immediate income; the production cost of the Artists and Print files was almost certainly going to be greater than the net sales revenues so we would lose money on them, though it was difficult to predict how much. I still wanted to take them on but on my terms, which was to microfilm them in Bassingbourn and give ourselves as much time as possible to do the work.

We met with Ruth Ann Stewart, who had been associate director of the Schomburg Center and was now assistant director of publications, and several of her colleagues. I stated my proposal. We would undertake to publish the Artists File and Print File on microfiche providing that:

- We were given the microform master negatives for the Schomburg Clipping File and the Norman Thomas Papers with exclusive rights to publish them in return for paying the library a royalty.
- The Artists and Print files would be shipped to the UK at our expense to be microfilmed at our premises in Bassingbourn.
- We would have four years in which to undertake the production of the Artists File on microfiche and a further three years to produce the Print File.
- While the library would receive a free copy of the microfiche editions, we would not pay royalties on sales of the Artists and Print files until we had sold fifteen copies of each.
- MCA would complete the typesetting and printing of the guide to the *Norman Thomas Papers, 1904–1967*, and on completion of the microfilming of the Print File we would pay them seventy-five per cent of the sales revenue we had received from the Thomas Papers up to a maximum of $28,000. This meant that we would receive revenues from the sale of the Thomas Papers for several years before we had to pay anything to MCA.

The library and MCA immediately agreed to our conditions, which was extraordinary as no major collection in NYPL had ever been sent abroad. The seven years meant that we could push the production of the Artists and Print files well into the future, but immediately enjoy the revenues from the two other collections.

I had lunch with Stewart in November to discuss details, but we did not sign the three-way Assignment and Assumption Agreement with the library and MCA until 1 March 1985. First, we had to prepare a storage space for the filing cabinets in Bassingbourn. They took up a lot of room because they were oversize and there had to be wide aisles between the rows so that the drawers could be fully opened. We converted another of our farm buildings, our woodshed, into a high-security storage unit by laying a concrete floor and building an inner breeze-block wall with a massive oak outer door. Electrical wiring was protected in steel tubes. An agent of NYPL's insurers visited and found it acceptable to receive the collections. The filing cabinets were shipped from Sanford to Norfolk, Virginia, then to Iceland, transhipped to Liverpool and then brought by truck to Bassingbourn. The door-to-door shipping cost was only $4,255. For CHMPS at Bassingbourn it was a new, very large production project for which they would be paid in full by Chadwyck-Healey, and Chapman, the manager, was keen to start on it. He also wanted to use a new technique for developing the film that enabled standard microfilm to reproduce the full tonal range of illustrations. This process had been recommended to us by Kodak in the UK and is described in Appendix 2. Preparing the material for filming was labour intensive but not to the extent that I had been warned, and at times Chapman used it as 'make work' to keep staff occupied when there were lulls in other production work.

We did not keep a record of how much the production had cost but we sold the 11,000 microfiche for $18,000, the maximum we thought that we could expect a library to pay. We completed microfilming of the Artists File in April 1989, four years and one month after signing the agreement. The Print File, which had remained in the library, was shipped to us in three batches in 1989 because the library had found that it had been difficult to be without the Artists File in its entirety.[5] The 5,800 microfiche were completed in April 1990 and sets sold for $14,850. Sales of the two files were restricted to large libraries in the USA, with a few in Japan, Australia and Europe, including the National Art Library at the Victoria and Albert Museum in London. Under our agreement we were required to send the contents of the Artists and Print files back to the library – without the filing cabinets, which we sold – as some of the items in the files had significant value as collectibles. Donald 'Don' Anderle, associate director for special collections, summed up the library's dilemma: 'While we are eager to have the material back, we face problems in finding a place to store it on its return. My inclination is to suggest that you choose a slow boat for its return and I will in the interim look for a place to put it.'[6] The Artists File was finally returned to the library in May 1990. The Print File followed later.

Thanks to MCA we now had the beginnings of a solid list of research publications in the important area of Black Studies. We already had the *Papers of the Congress of Racial Equality, 1941–1967* from the Wisconsin State Historical Society and now had the *Schomburg Clipping File*, which was the main inducement for taking on these projects, as it was not only an important source for the study of Black history, but also included a large section on African history. It is described further in Chapter 12.

Before the arrival of the filing cabinets the Duke of Gloucester presented to Angela and me the 1984 Rural Employment Award from the Council for

Small Industries in Rural Areas (CoSIRA) for converting the granary at our home in Bassingbourn into a microfilm bureau. The award was to encourage the creation of non-agricultural employment by converting redundant buildings in rural areas. There was an increasing number of unused farm buildings, as modern farming practices required smaller labour forces; there was less livestock on farms in the east of England; and increased contract farming meant that farms no longer needed buildings to store machinery. I was asked to speak about it at a conference near Norwich at which Prince Charles was present. I found that I was in the unenviable position of having to speak immediately before him, to an audience who would be waiting for him and for lunch. The main premise of my paper, knowing that the filing cabinets were being shipped from the USA to Bassingbourn, was that because the cost of transport for high-value materials was low relative to the value of the work done to them, it was possible to set up production operations in remote rural areas with limited transport links and, in doing so, provide local employment. But I recognized that microfilming was low tech and labour intensive and most of the skills could be easily taught on the job to a local work force, which might not be the case in other more high-tech industries. The paper was well received, and Prince Charles referred to it in his speech.

11

France and Spain

France

I was never in love with France but there was a fatal attraction. I saw it as a rich source of material to publish but it was less alluring as a market, as French university libraries were conservative and under funded and bought very little microfilm. Two of our first publications were French, the multi-volume bibliographies by Avenir Tchmerzine and Georges Vicaire, which we reprinted in 1973 (see Chapter 3). When we began to microfilm art exhibition catalogues we wanted to include the catalogues of the national museums and galleries in France, not only the Louvre but all thirteen national museums and galleries in Paris and the fourteen in the provinces, from the Musée Fesch in Ajaccio to the Musée national at Versailles. Fortunately, the publishing rights of all the museums were under the control of Les Éditions des musées nationaux, but I needed someone to negotiate with them, and Fellner put me in touch with Nane Scialom, a charming widow. In May 1976 she became our agent in France, and I agreed to pay her 20 francs (£2.40) an hour, 20 francs a letter and all expenses. She complained that the officials with whom she had to negotiate were often disrespectful to her but she got the permissions we needed, and in October 1976 we mailed a sales brochure listing 324 exhibition catalogues of the national museums of France.

Fellner and I visited Paris in November 1977 to explore the setting up of a new business with his friend Leo Wolf to import copies of sculptures and facsimiles of antiquities that were being sold in the national museums in France. Our plan was to open a shop in London to sell them. Fortunately, the idea came to nothing, since such a distraction would have severely set back the publishing business, now in its fifth precarious year. While in Paris we also visited the Bibliothèque nationale de France (BnF) and looked at the card catalogue of anonymous items, which we thought might be suitable for publication on microfiche. It seems that we were blind to the presence and importance of the main card catalogue, which we must also have seen, but we may have discounted it because at the time it was not complete (see below). We had dinner with Fellner's stepfather, Marc Bernard, Bernard's wife, Jacqueline, and Scialom. Bernard, an old communist, was a well-known author who had won the Prix Goncourt in 1942.[1] Through a chance encounter in the Louvre he had met Fellner's mother, Else Reichman, who had left Vienna after the Anschluss. They had fallen deeply in love and had married but she had died from cancer in 1969. He celebrated their passion for each other in a memoir, *La mort de la bien-aimée*, published in 1972. Scialom commented, 'It was so personal I find it shocking.' Fellner never told me what he thought of it. At dinner Scialom and Bernard also talked about André Gide whom they both knew. Bernard, aged seventy-seven, was a small, red-faced man with a stony stare, wearing a horizontally striped jersey like a convict's. He only spoke French and in the noisy bistro I found him difficult to understand. Jacqueline was more friendly and spoke to me in English. She had been a friend of Albert Camus and had edited *Combat*, the French Resistance newspaper. She told me that she had wanted to ensure that copies of the newspaper, which was published clandestinely, were preserved, and knew that the BnF 'never threw anything away', so she sent a copy of each issue to the library, making sure that it was addressed to a known collaborator in the hope that it would embarrass him.[2] After our visit Scialom approached the BnF and a senior librarian, Janine Roncato (who to me was always 'Madame Roncato'), responded with a list of out-of-print BnF exhibition catalogues that could be made available to us for publication, and this was the beginning of our nineteen-year relationship with the BnF.

In 1980 we stopped microfilming exhibition catalogues and I ended Scialom's employment, which she did not mind as she had become tired of it herself. But I could not forget France and later decided to explore the Archives nationales in Paris, which to me seemed a terra incognita for reprint and microfilm publishers. This was in contrast to the UK Public Record Office where so many other publishers, led by Kraus Reprint, were reprinting or microfilming archives and manuscript collections on a large scale. But in 1987 we did join the others and microfilmed Foreign Office Registers and Indexes of Correspondence 1793–1919 in the PRO as part of *NIDSUK* (see Chapter 9). Once a year I would visit the curators at the Archives nationales and in 1983 they confirmed that they had large numbers of finding aids and slip indexes, but there was still no move towards an agreement.

In January 1985 an American, Donald Goldman, visited me in Cambridge. He was working for MCP Industries,[3] a large French printing group that was interested in developing computer services in libraries and in the retrospective conversion of library catalogues. He had met Bill Buchanan in the USA to find out more about REMARC (see Chapter 16) and Buchanan had advised him to get in touch with me as we were REMARC's European agent. Goldman had been born in Brooklyn and his family had been greetings card publishers. He had moved to France and was now married to a French woman, Monique, and had two small sons. I found him disconcerting; it was impossible to tell what he was thinking, as he showed very little emotion, but he had a dry, throwaway New York sense of humour. Soon after we met, he told me that when he was young his family had sent him to a psychiatrist but after one visit the psychiatrist said there was nothing he could do for him. No New York shrink would give up after only one visit. I explained to Goldman that I wanted to set up a French company in order to get access to the BnF and the Archives nationales. Soon after our first meeting we agreed to establish a publishing company in France, based in Paris, in which Goldman would have an interest and he would run it. We called it Chadwyck-Healey France (CHF).

I discovered that Goldman could walk into almost any institution, however grand, be completely unabashed by the people he met, tell them what he wanted and usually get it. He had immediately asked Roncato if he could discuss with her the microfilming of the BnF card catalogue. A few months later, Goldman sent me a memo that listed all the titles that he expected to publish over the next few years, including the various BnF catalogues, catalogues of the IRHT (see below) and the French National Bibliography on CD-ROM.[4] This was two years before we had distributed or produced any CD-ROM publications. His innate understanding of our publishing impressed me. No one else with whom I had worked had ever produced such a comprehensive and well-thought-out plan.

In 1985 libraries were still willing to pay high prices for the catalogues of the great libraries, even on microfiche, and there was no catalogue more essential than the card catalogue of the BnF. The first volume of the new printed *Catalogue général des livres imprimés* was published in 1896. It continued to be published up to the war and Julien Cain, administrateur général in the late 1930s, had expected to complete publication in 1940, but by then he had been dismissed because he was Jewish. He was imprisoned and later transported to Buchenwald where he survived sixteen terrible months. He took up his post again after the war, remaining until 1964, an immensely energetic and innovative chief. He now made 1959 the end date for the catalogue and started a new catalogue in 1960. But, confusingly, while the supplementary catalogue of books received by the library between 1960 and 1969 was published between 1972 and 1978, the last volume of the 231-volume catalogue started in 1896 was not published until 1982. When Fellner and I visited the library in 1977 we could not have published the card catalogue because it was not yet complete.

There were engaging aspects to the catalogue, which set it apart from other catalogues of national libraries. The first was the authoritative essays on the great writers, such as Voltaire in Volume 214 and Zola in the last volume. The second was the recognition of the contribution of individual cataloguers through the listing in every volume of their names and the range of authors for which each was responsible. The first woman, Mlle Jeanne Odier, appears in Volume 96 in 1929. There was another oddity in the catalogue in that for a handful of important figures, including Sophocles, Cicero, Molière and Shakespeare, the holdings of other major libraries in Paris were also included. This was the remnant of a plan to make the catalogue a union catalogue of all the major libraries in Paris, which had been abandoned early on as being too ambitious.

The BnF was also faced with the difficulty experienced by every library that publishes its catalogue in printed form. No sooner is a volume of the catalogue published than it is out of date because new books have been published. The BnF exacerbated the problem by taking eighty-seven years to complete their catalogue. The volume listing the works of the poet and dramatist Paul Claudel was published in 1907, but he continued to write through the first half of the twentieth century, not dying until 1955. The majority of his works could only be found in the card catalogue, along with 800,000 other 'missing' titles. It was the card catalogue, which could only be accessed by visitors to the BnF, that we wanted to publish on microfiche. The library also advised Goldman that there were many libraries that did not have the printed catalogue and that they had a master copy annotated with 60,000 handwritten corrections and emendations. We signed an agreement in May 1985 to microfilm both, together with the printed catalogue for the books received from 1960 to 1969, which was already out of print. We agreed to pay a 10 per cent royalty, increasing to 12.5 per cent after the sale of fifty copies, and the only unusual terms were their right to have a list of buyers and to buy copies for themselves at a 45 per cent discount.

We announced the forthcoming publication of the catalogues and the establishment of Chadwyck-Healey France SARL in September 1985 and took a full-page advertisement for the catalogues in the *Times Literary Supplement* on 9 May 1986. Together the three catalogues with a printed guide[5] sold for £9,000. There was a strong response and by April 1987 Bonnell in the USA reported that we had had thirteen orders with another twelve to come. There was also a good response in France, though the discounted price of 90,500 FF was a large sum for most French libraries.[6]

Goldman had rented an office in the rue de Marivaux, close to the BnF and across the way from the Opéra Comique, a pleasant if seedy part of central Paris. On my first visit to the rackety building where we had taken the top two floors, I was greeted by a burned-out Mercedes parked in front of our entrance, the result of an altercation by some Albanians in the café next door. Goldman's staff included Josianne Stern, a commanding office manager and mother figure, and later her son Philippe as sales manager. There was also a bookkeeper who reported to both Goldman and, first, to Miller and then to Miller's successor in the UK, Don McCrae (see Chapter 14).

We were soon faced with a major tax problem. When we invoiced libraries in France for the microfiche edition of the catalogues of the BnF we did not charge TVA, similar to VAT in the UK or sales taxes in the USA, as we had been advised that they were publications and therefore not liable for TVA. The French tax authorities thought otherwise and demanded that we pay 33.3 per cent of our sales revenue in France as TVA, even though we had not collected it from our customers. French libraries had bought the catalogues at the advertised price and we could not now go back to them and ask for more. Nor was there any question of CHF being able to pay TVA of over £200,000,[7] and if we were found to be liable, we would have to close down the company. It was another example of the prejudice against microform publications that we were already familiar with. They were not seen as having a similar status to print publications – they were just copies. With the help of Patrice de Maistre, our auditor, we appealed. Shortly before we were due to appear before a tribunal the tax authority announced that, after all, they were deemed to be publications and no TVA was due.

De Maistre may have been helpful on this occasion but he became more and more difficult, and when we tried to replace him, he pointed out that he could not be dismissed until he had signed off our annual accounts, which he might decide not to do. We did eventually part company and he later found a more lucrative client when he became the business manager of Liliane Bettencourt, the elderly heiress of the L'Oréal cosmetics fortune and the richest woman in France. De Maistre was awarded the Légion d'Honneur in 2007 but after the Bettencourt scandal involving President Sarkozy and other French politicians, he was accused of helping her evade taxes by keeping money in anonymous Swiss bank accounts, and in 2012 he spent eighty-eight days behind bars in Bordeaux before raising several million euros for bail.

Microfilming card catalogues is slow work because the cards have to be arranged in a grid by the camera operator to make a single image the size of a page. Goldman had little experience of managing microfilm production; the work had to be done on the premises of the BnF in the rue de Richelieu and it took over a year to complete. The annotated printed catalogue was microfilmed in our Paris office, and Goldman had to personally carry the boxes of books to and from the library, a twelve-minute walk away. The 1960–9 printed catalogue was microfilmed in Bassingbourn.

Goldman soon announced a succession of microfiche editions of other BnF catalogues. These included the *Catalogue de l'histoire de France*, described as the most comprehensive bibliography of French history ever published, consisting of printed volumes and a card catalogue, all of which we published on microfiche. There was the *Catalogue général des périodiques des origines à 1959* and the *Catalogues du département de la musique*, containing over 3 million records. From the Département des Manuscrits there was the *Inventaire des instruments de recherche: manuscrits occidentaux*, in which we microfilmed 200 catalogues, mainly unpublished or out of print, describing over 100,000 manuscripts. We also undertook to complete and publish as printed books, with a subvention from the BnF, the *Catalogue de la Troisième Republique*, but the two volumes did not appear until 1995. In the early 1990s Goldman reported that we had sold worldwide sixty-two copies of the catalogues of printed books, sixty-seven copies of the *Catalogue de l'histoire de France*, forty-seven and forty-nine copies of the catalogues of periodicals and music respectively, and fourteen copies of the collection of manuscript inventories. By microfilm publishing standards the first two sold well, the third and fourth comfortably, and the last was disappointing, though it was expensive at £8,650. The total gross sales revenue of all the BnF titles was approximately

£1.5 million. This was before royalties and commissions to the other companies in the group. It was a promising start for a new company, but much of the revenue was consumed by the overheads of an office and staff in central Paris.

We published on microfiche three catalogues from the Institut de recherche et d'histoire des textes (IRHT). Part of the CNRS, the national centre for scientific research, the IRHT was dedicated to the research of medieval manuscripts and early printed books in all the principal languages of the Mediterranean region. In his memo of December 1985 Goldman had proposed publishing their three card catalogues:

- Répertoire bio-bibliographique des auteurs latins patristiques et médiévaux. The world's most important bibliography of Latin authors.
- Répertoire des fins de textes latins classiques et médiévaux. Enables texts without titles to be identified by the last word or phrase in either the whole work or in individual chapters, sections and poems.
- Répertoire d'incipit de sermons latins antiquité tardive et moyen âge. Enables sermons and religious texts without titles to be identified by the first word or phrase.

A publishing agreement was signed with CNRS on 3 December 1986, and the three catalogues on almost 1,000 microfiche were completed in 1988, selling for £2,500. We received orders from university libraries throughout the world, and after the BnF catalogue they were our most successful French microfiche publications.

Goldman met regularly with Madame Chevalier and her colleagues at the Archives nationales in the beautiful Hôtel de Soubise, an eighteenth-century palace in the Marais, but even though we were now a French publisher, it was still another three years before we signed an agreement. As with the publication of inventories of manuscripts in the BnF, we were only interested in finding aids to manuscript collections, not the manuscripts themselves, and we were told that there were not many suitable for publication. But once our cameras were installed in the archives, curators began to approach the camera operators to ask if a particular unpublished guide or a card catalogue might be of interest. It always was, and by 1988 the list had grown to 740 inventories and unpublished catalogues on 6,500 microfiche, at a price of 215,000 francs (£19,350). The collection was accompanied by a printed catalogue, which for the first time revealed the full extent and nature of the finding aids in the Archives nationales.[8] We expected the same kind of response both in France and abroad that we had had to the catalogue of the BnF, but although over the next few years it sold well enough to be profitable, it did not attract the level of sales we had hoped for. In the UK it was only bought in its entirety by two national libraries, the British Library and the National Library of Scotland. Neither Oxford nor Cambridge chose to buy it. There were probably three reasons for this. First, archives are of much more specialist interest than printed books, so there are far fewer scholars both in France and outside wanting to use them. Second, the price was high, even though libraries could buy selected parts like the inventories of the Ancien Régime (from the Middle Ages to 1789) or the 'Section Contemporaine' (after 1940). Third, and most important, there was a characteristic of the collection that we had seen before. When we had published *Nineteenth-Century Parliamentary Papers* on microfiche in the early 1980s, we had also published three other interesting but virtually unknown series of Parliamentary Papers.[9] While *Nineteenth-Century Parliamentary Papers* sold well, the other series sold very poorly. After talking to historians, it seemed that their mind-set was that they had been able to do their research successfully without using or

Figure 8 Paris, Archives nationales. Kodak MRD microfilm cameras with extension columns for filming microfiche at 24x, with electronic counters (see Appendix 2). The head of one camera has been lowered to take out or load in film. Centre: technician Frederic Lietart looking at a microfiche frame counter. To his right, facing the camera: Donald Goldman. 1993.

even knowing that these series existed and that they therefore could not be of great importance, and they would not recommend them to their libraries to buy. Similarly, the inventories at the Archives nationales were mainly unpublished, so few librarians or researchers knew of their existence. Our experience with *Patrologia Latina* (see Chapter 18) also bore this out. In spite of its very high price, it sold well throughout the world because it was so well known and so heavily used. The success of the *Patrologia* and of the catalogues of the IRHT also suggested that at the end of the twentieth century there was a greater demand for texts in Latin than texts in French in the world's academic libraries.

With two languages and very different cultures, there were misunderstandings between the English and French offices but the French microfiche publications were of good quality, and the only serious quality problem we had was with the BnF catalogue volumes microfilmed in Bassingbourn, which led to a critical review in *Microform Review*[10] and to the refilming of many of them.

Goldman was always more interested in the new electronic media, and in April 1989 he signed an agreement with the BnF to publish on CD-ROM the French National Bibliography. This was the catalogue of all new printed publications in France, but it also included the catalogue records of all books published since 1975. CD-ROM was the ideal medium for a publication that had quarterly cumulated updates. We knew that this would be a publication that almost every library in France would buy and would be central to CHF's future. When it was first launched in 1989, we sold fewer than 100 annual subscriptions at 6,500 francs (£585), but by 1994 this had risen to over 800 subscriptions at 9,000 francs (£1,080). We also found that few French libraries had PCs and CD-ROM drives, and we began to sell these too. Goldman proudly informed me that we were now one of the largest sellers of PCs in Paris, but it did not last for long. Billing subscriptions in advance gave a positive cashflow, but the profitability of the publication was much less than a comparable microform publication in that we were paying a royalty of twenty-five per cent, rising to thirty-three per cent, to the BnF and a royalty of ten per cent to Online Computer Systems, an American company that provided the software. We were employing software engineers to create each quarterly disk, so the cost of production of each quarter's CD-ROM was not insignificant.

Goldman's response, which I entirely supported, was to add more CD-ROM titles – we saw ourselves as pioneers in publishing in a new digital medium that we believed had an unlimited future. We added *Politique et Société, La France des années 80* and *des années Mitterand* from BIPA,[11] and *CD-Actualité*, which provided contents page information to the 450 most heavily used French periodicals. We published *AFP-DOC* from Agence France Presse, one of the world's leading news agencies, which brought together thousands of AFP news reports since 1988 and was fully searchable on CD-ROM. CHF also had all the Chadwyck-Healey titles to sell in France, Belgium and French-speaking Switzerland and became an agent for SilverPlatter (an American CD-ROM publisher, see Chapter 17). But every new title meant new investment, none of the titles except the French National Bibliography were bestsellers, and the company continued to lose money. The losses were financed by Chadwyck-Healey Ltd and by delaying the payment of royalties to the BnF. But in spite of this Goldman was able to maintain a good relationship with senior BnF librarians and in 1989 we sponsored an evening fête at the library to celebrate the 200th anniversary of the French Revolution.

The period of transition, from high-priced microform collections to much lower-priced CD-ROM publications mainly on subscription, is reflected in the pattern of new orders. In the twelve-month period between March 1989 and February 1990 Chadwyck-Healey Ltd and Inc. received fifty per cent more orders in value for CHF titles than CHF itself had received, giving an overall total of new orders of £1,027,964. But from March 1992 to February 1993, while CHF's orders had increased by fifty per cent and Chadwyck-Healey España (see below) provided a useful £139,000 of orders for French titles, orders generated by Chadwyck-Healey Ltd and Inc. were just under £300,000, half of what they had been in 1989/90. More importantly the value of all new orders had only increased by £21,450 in four years, though CHF now had the income from subscription renewals. It was striking that this lack of growth in new orders was in spite of having patent information titles on CD-ROM from our associate company MicroPatent (see Chapter 16) to sell in France since these had opened up entirely new commercial and technical markets. A business built on subscription revenue, which was predictable and was paid in advance, from publications that were sold at lower prices to a larger number of libraries, would seem to be a better business model than a few high-priced titles that were sold only once to relatively few libraries. But for CHF this was not the case, and the CD-ROM publications never generated enough revenue to make the business profitable.

The early 1990s was a time when I was particularly preoccupied with two new companies in the USA, MicroPatent and ERIC (see Chapter 16), and in the investment of millions of pounds in *English Poetry* and the *Patrologia Latina* (see Chapters 17 and 18) but McCrae and I made regular visits to CHF. We took an early flight from Stansted on AirUK in the newly opened, almost empty Norman Foster building. Arriving in Goldman's office mid-morning and fortified by coffee we would have a serious discussion about CHF's financial problems and our solutions for them. We would then go out to lunch, often at a big Lebanese restaurant nearby with plenty of mezze and meat on skewers, washed down with rough Lebanese wine, ending with thick Turkish coffee. Back in the stuffy office I would fight to stay awake until, just before we were due to leave for the airport, Goldman, with the timing of a master, would quietly mention that he was working on an exciting new project that might have great potential. I would wake up and get equally excited about the prospect of working with another French news agency or about some other carrot that he was dangling in front of me, and took the plane home feeling much more optimistic. McCrae would be beside me in a deeply depressed silence, knowing that nothing had changed.

In spite of its lack of profitability CHF expanded in several directions. The team of software engineers were not only producing the French titles but began to produce CD-ROMs for Chadwyck-Healey Ltd.[12] We started a new French company selling MultiLIS computer systems to French libraries, described in Chapter 16, which required more investment and another office in Paris, and which also took up more of Goldman's time. In 1990 we needed more space and Goldman and I spent £220,000 on a property a few doors down from our main office, a bar called the Renardière, a French-Canadian term for a fox farm. We paid for it with a mortgage and money from Chadwyck-Healey Ltd. Advised by Savills, the international real estate agents, we thought we had a bargain, helped by an under-the-table cash payment to the owner, a wily old man from the Auvergne. But the property recession hit Paris two years after the recession in the UK and we eventually sold it at a loss to the bookseller next door. CHF had become a black hole that was swallowing much of the revenue generated by the UK and US companies. But we were still in a dominant position in France and success always seemed to be just around the corner. Even McCrae was sometimes optimistic and in March 1993 wrote:

Although turnover is holding up, the profits are far from spectacular and would indicate that CHF will probably hold its own ... but only just. I do not think that we should get too despondent though. This time last year the company was hopelessly out of control.[13]

Coutts, our bank, told McCrae that they would only continue to lend us money if he promised that none of it went to France. He agreed but then had to juggle the figures to keep France afloat. The other companies sold CHF publications and CHF sold theirs, so there were transfers going on between the companies all the time and McCrae could adjust the timing of these to keep CHF in cash. But by June 1993 even I could no longer tolerate the losses. When I arrived at the Paris office to discuss the business plan for the coming year, which predicted a profit but still required an injection of another £100,000, I told Goldman that I was firing most people in the company including him. He looked both dejected and almost relieved to be at last let off the hook. Nor did he ever remonstrate with me over the abrupt way that he and the company had been treated. The cost to the company of the redundancy payments that we were required to give was extraordinary, and Stern and her son Philippe used the considerable sum of money they received to set up a sales agency to compete with us in selling CD-ROMs to libraries.

I still could not bring myself to close down the company and decided to restructure it as a much smaller entity operating from a less expensive part of Paris. I needed to hire a new PDG[14] and an agency provided some suitable candidates, all of whom had to provide samples of handwriting accompanied by a commentary by a graphologist. This odd practice was a standard part of hiring staff in France. I appointed Jean-Pierre Sakoun, a highly cultured and experienced manager who had worked in Canada for GEAC, one of the largest suppliers of library management systems. His English was perfect and he also spoke Spanish. He had been at the prestigious École normale and had then trained as a librarian. He now wanted to become a publisher. I offered him the job and we met again at the annual IFLA (International Federation of Library Associations) conference in Barcelona in August when I had lunch with him and his wife Aline, who was a senior librarian in the Paris public library system. They were a striking couple and together epitomized French style and elegance. Sakoun started work for us a few weeks later. In 1988 President Mitterand had announced the building of a new Bibliothèque nationale in an industrial area on the left bank of the Seine. Although it did not open until 1996, we no longer felt the need to be near the old library in the rue de Richelieu, and we moved to a small office in the rue de Paradis, amongst the china and pottery wholesalers near the Gare du Nord. The move was well timed for visitors from the UK, as Eurostar trains started to run between Waterloo in London and the Gare du Nord in late 1994.

Sakoun had to sort out the transition with its expensive loose ends, not only the cost of redundancies but extracting us from the lease of the main office, which we had occupied since 1985. Our newly hired accountant found that we had been categorized as a publisher of sound recordings – because we were publishing CD-ROMs – and when our category was changed to 'publisher', it enabled staff to enjoy better and less expensive health plans and retirement benefits. Sakoun drew up a new budget for 1993/4 and predicted that CHF would be profitable. The annual sales did increase to 11,721,194 francs (£1,406,543), a healthy twenty-nine per cent increase on the previous year, but moving to the new office alone cost £50,000 and any profit was eaten up by the costs of the reorganization. We still felt that we were in a strong position in France, as in the last year we had competed against the two leading French publishers, Jouve and Bureau Marcel van Dijk, and against international competitors, Research Publications, K. G. Saur and RTIS (Reed Elsevier), for the publishing rights to five different databases and had won all five. We were also able to replace the Online software with our own software, which we had written in-house and which we called Caravan. This could be an important new product to sell to other publishers. But we were faced with three pressing problems: the extent and age of the royalties that we owed not only to the BnF but also to other publishing partners, the lack of new large 'game-changing' publications, and the fact that under French law we could not trade with a deficit on our balance sheet. This was highlighted in a letter of 16 October 1995 from our auditors, BDA, stating that, 'Your company has had negative shareholders' equity since June 30, 1992; the amount as at 30 June 1995 is FF1.467.927', 'Your company has not fulfilled its legal obligation to recapitalize before June 30 1995', and 'the above facts are sufficient to call into question the ability of the company to continue as a going concern'. This was not resolved until we sold the company just over a year later. The second problem began to be addressed by Sakoun, who had started to pay arrears of royalties at a rate of 161,000 francs (£20,930) a month but, in a letter to Philippe Bélaval, the director general of the BnF, he suggested a six-month moratorium on paying royalties, which would be followed by the payment of the 1995 royalties spread over nine months.[15] The BnF agreed, and a year later in June 1996 at the annual conference of the Association des bibliothécaires de France (the French library association), the BnF announced that for their own CD-ROMs, including the new catalogue of printed books on CD-ROM, they were going to use our Caravan software and that the new catalogue would be distributed by CHF. This was met with interest and approval by the delegates, not least because American software was being replaced by home-grown French software. But by now we were moving to online delivery of our databases and we no longer saw a great future in CD-ROM publications. The BnF's *Catalogue général des imprimés*, containing over three million bibliographic records of books and periodicals up to 1970, was eventually published on six CD-ROMs, at a price of £2,600. This was a far cry from the price of the microfiche edition or the British Library catalogue on CD-ROM, which we had successfully sold for £10,000 a copy (see Chapter 15). The moratorium that Sakoun had negotiated simply delayed the payments but did nothing to solve the underlying problem, which was that in spite of our lower cost base and what we thought was better management, CHF was making an even larger loss than in 1993. In 1994/5 annual sales were 16,729,298 francs (£2,174,808) but the loss was 403,679 francs (£52,478). Even the sales of MicroPatent titles of 1,343,154 francs (£174,610) showed a loss because the thirty-five per cent commission CHF earned from these sales did not cover the salary and expenses or make a contribution to the overheads of the salesman, Fayçal Nagamouchi. We benefitted from these sales in other ways because we owned forty per cent of MicroPatent, but this was of no help to CHF.

In an undated memo Sakoun listed eighteen new projects for publication in 1995/6 including a few for which we had already received orders.[16] He forecast slightly lower sales than the year before and a much greater loss of 3,663,235 francs (£476,220), which was clearly unacceptable. We had to either cut back or invest in a large project, which after the success of *English Poetry* could have been electronic editions of French literature. In May 1995 Sakoun had signed an agreement with a French publisher, La Librairie Honoré Champion, to jointly publish electronic editions of French literature on CD-ROM. Champion was one of the foremost publishers of scholarly editions of French literature and had proposed that we publish with them a collection of editions of books by Montaigne, which we thought was too specialized to sell well outside France. We also had doubts about a collection of French poetry that Champion had suggested to us. It must have been confusing for Sakoun because in June 1995 I had emailed him to say, 'If you want my support now you must accelerate your plans for a French poetry collection so that we can announce it at the end of this year' and ' I don't see how we can afford to wait to fit in with Champion's time scale'.[17] While a few months later, in March 1996, Claude Blum, the editorial director of Champion, complained that we were very slow and hesitant, and that it was difficult to work with an Anglo-Saxon company that refuses to invest in French culture (Sakoun's summary in English of Blum's fax).[18] Sakoun included a French poetry collection in a new business plan in February 1996, which was later described as the largest collection of French poetry ever published on CD-ROM, but it was only published after the company had been sold.

In the autumn of 1996 Sakoun came to Cambridge for a group meeting at which Stephen Rhind-Tutt, the new president of Chadwyck-Healey Inc. (see Chapter 23), was also present. At the end of the afternoon, when we were all tired and frustrated by the intractable financial problems that CHF continued to present, Sakoun announced that he had started a new publishing programme in which he would be publishing electronic editions of French literature at low prices for a more general market by scanning the texts of books, which under French law can be done if the text itself is in the public domain. In-copyright notes and other apparatus would be omitted. He also wanted to sell sub-sets of the databases at low prices to the general public. For another publisher this might have been an attractive idea, but it was entirely at odds with our own policy of publishing large, high-quality, high-priced databases for our traditional university library market. He ended by saying that he would also be interested in buying CHF. He had not previously discussed any of this with me or his colleagues in the UK. Before we all went out to dinner, I warned him that no one likes surprises and that his announcements had not been well received. At breakfast at his hotel the next morning he reiterated that he did want to buy CHF but that it would be difficult to raise the money. Two weeks later he told me that with two old school friends he thought he would be able to buy the company, as he planned to borrow one million francs from Paribas and that they were also hoping for an investment from Caisse des dépôts et consignations, which had an arm that invested in new businesses. Meanwhile CHF's financial situation continued to deteriorate and in

November McCrae warned us that the outstanding royalty liability of almost 7 million francs (£910,000) was worse than had been reported.[19] In spite of CHF's precarious state, the sale went ahead, and in December 1996 we signed an agreement with Sakoun's new company, optimistically named Déjà Là Investissements (Already There Investments). The purchase price was the 3 million francs (£390,000) that Chadwyck-Healey Ltd owed CHF, so no money changed hands. The only works of a major French writer that we published in electronic form were those of Voltaire, through an agreement with the Voltaire Foundation in Oxford, and this was by Chadwyck-Healey Ltd over a year after the sale of the French company.

The sale of CHF was the end of twelve years of fruitless hard work and investment. We never attempted to calculate the total loss and the only tangible benefit I had from my ownership of CHF was a family holiday at a Club Méditerranée in Portugal with Goldman and his family in the 1980s, paid for by CHF. Chadwyck-Healey continued to represent Sakoun's company, now named Bibliopolis, outside France and Bibliopolis sold Chadwyck-Healey publications in France. In June 1998 I was in Paris to speak at a symposium organized by the BnF and NYPL. At the symposium Bélaval, the BnF director general, told me how much they had liked working with CHF when we owned it, which was pleasing but surprising in view of our serious failure to pay royalties on time. But over almost twenty years we had produced high-quality publications for the BnF, we had lost money trying to develop markets in France and abroad for these specialized bibliographic publications, and perhaps they had realized that most of our competitors would have cut their losses long before we did.

On that visit Sakoun told me that his company now had annual sales of 23 million francs (£2.3 million) and had some 3,000 books in electronic media. In the early 2000s Bibliopolis continued to expand into publishing ebooks for a broad market, including schools. The company was doing well but then entered into an agreement with a large French publisher that went disastrously wrong and the company had to be wound up. Electronic publishing in France had proved to be fatal for all of us.

Spain

In the summer of 1986, while Goldman was on vacation in Spain, he walked into the National Library of Spain in Madrid without an appointment and asked to see a senior librarian. He explained that his company was publishing the card catalogue of the Bibliothèque nationale on microfiche and would also like to publish the card catalogue of the National Library of Spain. He was told in response that the library was interested but would prefer to enter into such an agreement with a Spanish publisher. The card catalogue of the National Library of Spain was important because it was unique – there was no published national catalogue of Spanish books and this was the most widely spoken language in the world after English.

Before we could set up a company in Spain or reach a publishing agreement with the national library we had to find a suitable camera because most of the 2 million 5 × 3-inch catalogue cards had information on both sides, which had to appear side by side on the microfiche. We found a specialist microfiche camera in Germany, called a Codufidex, that could microfilm both sides of a catalogue card at a reduction of 48x.[20] Unlike standard microfiche with forty-nine or ninety-eight frames, each microfiche was one large frame containing images of the front and back of 504 catalogue cards. The operator laid out a grid of cards in eighteen columns and twenty-eight rows. The first exposure filmed all the cards but left a blank unexposed column next to every exposed column of cards. The operator then turned over the cards and in a second exposure the images were located in the blank columns so that the back of every card was next to its front. It was CHF, the French company, that entered into a publishing agreement with the National Library of Spain and bought the camera for 80,000 Deutschmarks (approximately £40,000). Goldman also organized the hiring of our first employee, Mercedes Rodriguez, who spoke good English with a strong Spanish accent. She established a small office in the embassy area of Madrid, and I made my first visit to meet her and the filming team in May 1989. Our Spanish company Chadwyck-Healey España SL (CHE) was not set up until 1991.

Frederic Lietart, a technician from the Paris office (see Figure 8 on p. 142), assisted by three young camera operators, ran this complicated microfilming project, and while there were some technical problems with the camera, the project went surprisingly smoothly. The camera used 105 mm-wide film (the width of a microfiche), which was processed by us in a special Codufidex film processor and was then sent to the UK after having been checked. Corrections were laborious, as to refilm a microfiche the same 504 cards had to be retrieved from the drawers to which they had been returned and then both sides of each card had to be filmed in the same order. The *Catálogo de Autores de la Biblioteca Nacional de España* was a huge catalogue consisting of 4 million images on 4,982 microfiche and we sold copies for £12,600. We also published a catalogue of the books acquired up to 1987, and most libraries bought both for £14,500. While it was a large investment for many libraries, it sold well throughout the world. It is now available online and includes almost all the information in the card catalogue, so our microfiche edition is redundant. But it does preserve the images of the cards, which would otherwise have been lost. Until the 1960s they were handwritten, often in a bold cursive hand quite unlike handwriting in northern Europe. They are the evidence of an extraordinary human endeavour that went into the creation of a catalogue of two million entries over almost a century by hundreds of cataloguers. As an example of collective enterprise, it compares with the handwriting of books before the invention of printing.

The first non-bibliographic publication was an idea conceived by Goldman in response to the strong interest there now was in Women's Studies. We employed Dra. Maria del Carmen Simón Palmer, who had extensive bibliographic knowledge of Spanish literature and women's writing, to search through the catalogue of the National Library for books by Spanish women from the beginning of printing to 1900. For the earlier books there was a preponderance of devout texts but by the seventeenth century, novelists such as Maria de Zayas began to emerge, and in the nineteenth century there was a remarkable increase in writing by women. Our reason for publishing it was because we thought it would sell well in the USA. But it proved to be an important initiative because Spanish literature had been regarded as primarily a male domain, and the collection includes many books that until then were completely unknown. *Spanish Women Writers, 1500–1900* (*Literatura Femenina Española*), containing over 600 titles on 2,000 microfiche, was completed in 1993, and at £5,800 sold as well in the USA and elsewhere as we had expected.

We had established a good relationship with the National Library and with its director, Juan Pablo Fusi, a distinguished historian who had signed the first contract with us. His successor, Alicia Girón, was also sympathetic and in 1991 we published our first CD-ROM which, as in France, was the national bibliography, published quarterly and sold to libraries throughout Spain. With a subscription price of £925 it was soon generating more than fifty per cent of the revenue of the company. We were also aware of the large potential market in Latin America and we celebrated the quincentenary of Columbus arriving in the New World by publishing with the Spanish government and the National Library *Bibliotecas sin Fronteras*, a union catalogue of holdings in Spanish libraries of books, articles and theses on Latin America, on CD-ROM. One of our UK sales people, Lynne Marsh, who was a fluent Spanish speaker and also a specialist in selling MicroPatent titles, spent some months working in the office in Madrid and also made a long sales trip through Latin America, but the results were disappointing as Latin American libraries had so little money.

In late 1994 we appointed Alvaro Klasse as chief executive of CHE. He was an ambitious young publisher determined to develop CHE's list of electronic publications and grow the company, while Rodriguez continued as general manager. In February 1996, over dinner in Madrid, he told me that the whole group needed a new vision, that, considering the collective expertise of our directors and our staff, we should be much larger – with a turnover of £30 million rather than what was then a turnover of about £10 million. I understood, but at that time we were having to work hard to even stay still in the face of the move from outright sales on CD-ROM to delivery online (see Chapters 20 and 23). At the end of 1996 Klasse left to run the Spanish equivalent of 'Yellow Pages', for which he was required to hire 200 staff in his first two months, a far cry from the five or six people he was managing at CHE. We parted amicably and Rodriguez continued to run the company with quiet efficiency until 2007.

Klasse was responsible for developing our first electronic full-text database in Spain. The *Teatro Español del Siglo de Oro* included over 800 plays from the Golden Age of Spanish theatre by the great playwrights Cervantes, Calderon and Lope de Vega, as well as many others. A small editorial board of scholars from Spain, Italy, Germany and the USA reflected the international nature of the project, while the production was carried out in Cambridge. The first part became available in September 1997 both on CD-ROM and online. The pre-publication price for the whole collection was £3,000 for an outright sale on CD-ROM and £450 per year for online access for two to four simultaneous users. There was good publicity in Spain with a long article in *El Pais*, 'Calderon y Lope en Internet'.[21] By the end of 1997 we had sold eight copies on CD-ROM and two on the web in Spain, and ten copies on CD-ROM and two on the web outside Spain – with only one in the USA, the majority being in the UK and Europe. It was a very small number, but we were not discouraged because the wide range of libraries that had ordered it indicated that it would do well in the longer term, and we knew that there still was a large potential market in the USA.

Apart from *Siglo de Oro* we struggled to find new, large collections of material in the Spanish language that we could publish successfully either on microform or electronically. The real importance of the Spanish company was through its success in selling British, American and French publications to Spanish libraries, who bought much more foreign material than French libraries. We were fortunate in having an experienced sales manager, Carlos Mascorda, who also spoke Catalan, as the *Patrologia Latina Database* (*PLD*; see Chapter 18), because of its very high price, needed sales people on the spot to sell it effectively. It sold well in Spain with two sets in the Canary Islands alone. At the end of the 1996/7 financial year there were nine university libraries who had *PLD* on trial and we expected to convert most of them. There were also two libraries in Argentina who could not afford outright purchase on CD-ROM but were considering web subscription. There were eleven libraries in Spain trialling *Literature Online* (*LION*; see Chapter 20), while *Periodicals Contents Index* (*PCI*; see Chapter 19) was also selling well. At the time of the sale of the companies we were planning to publish *PCI Español*, containing Spanish-language journals only. In the 1997/8 financial year CHE sales were about £600,000. Each year we either made a small profit or a small loss, of a few thousand pounds. In the early years our cash flow had been helped by the National Library, which took our publications at discounted prices as part of the royalties due to them. What was not reflected in the CHE results was the value of the revenues to the other companies in the group through the sales of their titles in Spain, Portugal and Latin America.

12

Black Studies

The publication of the *Schomburg Clipping File* in the mid-1980s made us one of the most important publishers of research material in the field of Black Studies. The first part to 1974 was on 9,500 microfiche. To it we added a second part covering 1975 to 1988 on 4,500 microfiche. Together the two parts, totalling nearly 1 million pages, sold for $36,000. After our negotiation with NYPL (see Chapter 9) I had spent an afternoon at the Schomburg Center at 135th Street in Harlem looking at the microfiche. While it was mainly a file of newspaper clippings there were also typescripts, broadsides and pamphlets, divided into almost 7,000 subject headings, and some of the subjects, such as lynching, made disturbing reading. We also published a clipping file from Hampton University, whose content came mainly from black newspapers, and the scrapbooks of the boxer Joe Louis from 1935 to 1944 in the National Museum of American History. Most of the 109 volumes recorded the fights of the greatest heavyweight boxer of all time who had remained undefeated from 1937 to 1950.

In 1986 we were approached by a young professor at Cornell, Henry Louis Gates Jr, or 'Skip' Gates to his friends. He was researching the literature and culture of black Americans at a time when the established view was that there was little imaginative writing by blacks before the Harlem Renaissance in the 1920s (which had been a flowering of black writing, mainly in New York). It was assumed that in the nineteenth century slaves and their immediate descendants were either illiterate, or did not have access to pen, ink and paper, or were too exhausted to be able to write in the little free time that they had. There were a few well-known works, most notably the poetry of Phillis Wheatley, the first African-American female poet, published in the late eighteenth century. This and a handful of other works stood out because there were so few of them and this seemed to confirm that there were very few published imaginative works by blacks. The first person to challenge this assumption was John W. Blassingame, professor of Afro-American and

Southern history at Yale, who realized that it was in the many local black newspapers and periodicals, ephemeral material held by very few libraries, that imaginative black literature had been published. With his encouragement, in 1980 Gates, Charles T. Davis (who died in 1981) and Gates's close friend, the philosopher Anthony Appiah, the grandson of the British Labour politician Sir Stafford Cripps, obtained substantial funding from the NEH and embarked on a project that was to continue for more than fifteen years, to identify every piece of black writing in newspapers and periodicals from 1827 to 1919.

By mid-1985 they had completed their bibliography and were ready to talk to publishers. Gates visited us in Alexandria on 17 January 1986 to test our commitment to Black Studies and our ability to both produce and sell his project. He questioned our suitability to be the publisher of such a major project in the field of black culture, but was serious in his request for a royalty of twenty-five per cent of sales revenue and an advance against royalties of $100,000. At the lunch table I quickly worked out the likely cost on either microfilm or microfiche and the selling price and reckoned that we would have to sell thirty-five sets to cover the advance. We had never paid such a large advance, but I saw this as a different, innovative microform publication, one that lay at the heart of the study of American culture and would be of interest to many smaller colleges and public libraries as well as the large research libraries. It would be a major addition to our black history list and I very much wanted to publish it, so I agreed. Gates had told me that Carl D. Brandt, his literary agent in New York, would draw up the agreement and handle the negotiations.

Once I had time to reflect on it, I felt uneasy. I could not understand how the US government, having given a federal grant of many hundreds of thousands of dollars, could allow the recipient to pocket the royalties paid to him by his publisher, and any advance as well. This was only a few years after the Lockheed bribery scandals in which many prominent foreign politicians, including Prince Bernhard of the Netherlands, had received substantial bribes for the sale of Lockheed planes. This had led to the Foreign Corrupt Practices Act in 1977, which made it illegal for Americans to bribe foreign government officials. This was the opposite but was I not a foreigner giving a large sum of money to the principal of this project to secure rights for a publication being funded by the American taxpayer? A day later I was in New York, still thinking about the implications of it, when I noticed that Brandt's office was close to the Algonquin Hotel where I was staying. On impulse I called him and asked if I could talk to him. In his office I explained my concern. He assured me that it was legitimate, and that Gates had the right to demand whatever he wished, as any royalties earned went to him, not back to the NEH. We then discussed the terms of the agreement and I left reassured. The next day a furious Gates phoned me, accusing me of not trusting him because he was black and relying on his agent who was white. I apologized but began to realize that his verbal sparring was his way of dealing with a white English publisher.

Sufrin, my accountant, was also not happy about the agreement. He thought that we would never recoup the advance of $100,000 and I bet him a case of vintage Krug champagne that we would. Neither Sufrin nor I had ever drunk vintage Krug nor had any idea of what a case would cost. But in 1994, eight years later, he called to tell me that as we were now paying royalties to Gates, the advance was used up and I had won the bet. Sufrin arranged for the delivery of a case of Krug but regretted that he had not imposed a time limit.

Gates and I got on well after our difficult beginning and on one occasion I spent a day with him and his wife at his home near Cornell. We were able to publish the first 'Fiction' segment quite quickly because there was material prepared before we signed the publishing agreement and we were now receiving 1,000 pages a week for microfilming. But the project then slowed down and there were further delays when Gates moved from Cornell to Duke University in North Carolina and then, shortly after, he was appointed to revive the ailing W. E. B. Dubois Institute for Afro-American Research at Harvard. Each time he moved, the project had to be set up again with new people. It was labour intensive because every story, poem, essay or review in each newspaper and magazine had to be read and their authors had to be identified, but Gates always had the resources to hire enough people and equipment – photocopiers, and reader printers[1] – to get the project back on schedule. We in our turn were faced with formidable difficulties in the reproduction of the texts. First, the team had to find copies of these publications. In the 1930s and 1940s the Library of Congress, as a WPA project not unlike the Index of American Design and the Farm Security Administration photographs (see Chapter 6), had microfilmed many of these obscure publications and these very early microfilm copies were the only surviving record because the originals had disappeared or had been destroyed. The originals themselves were often badly printed and the photocopies made from the early microfilm were often illegible. In the worst cases researchers had to transcribe the text from the photocopies or even from the microfilm itself, and we then microfilmed the typed transcripts.

In spite of delays, the NEH not only continued to fund the project but offered to fund a second series from 1919 to 1940. In all, 110 black periodicals and newspapers were surveyed. The last was published in 1995 and the final index, with 70,000 bibliographic references, in 1996. Libraries subscribed to fifteen segments of 200 microfiche, initially, at a price of $1,750 per segment. The starting date, 1827, was the year that *Freedom's Journal*, the first black periodical, was published. Black authors had turned to their newspapers and periodicals because they were denied publication by the mainstream institutions. As the project developed, researchers found that many of the authors were either middle class or labourers and domestics who would come home from work and write a poem, a short story, an essay or book review, or even a novel. Large numbers of writers were women who discussed sexual exploitation and the fact that black women had even less freedom than black men. Apart from the social and cultural insights that these writings provided, the sheer number of them was a clear response to the misplaced belief that until recently there had been no imaginative literature written by black Americans.

As I had expected, *Black Literature, 1827–1940* was regarded as a seminal project and was bought by many US libraries. What Gates had described as 'a hermetically sealed library ... after a century of neglect'[2] was now open to everyone. The project had begun in the microfilm era but editions of the index and bibliography, which were such an important part of the project, were published on CD-ROM. It took time to teach Gates's team to format the index entries in a consistent, structured way suitable for digital publishing. His team, led by Cynthia Bond, were dedicated and capable, but in the early 1990s the disciplines of digital as opposed to analogue publishing and indexing were still new to most people.

Gates himself became one of the best-known academics in the USA, being cited by *Time* magazine in 1997 as one of the twenty-five most influential Americans. I had expected him to be interested in the project at the beginning but to lose interest as so many other aspects of his career developed including his many books and *Finding Your Roots*, his high-profile series on PBS television, which had made him a celebrity, but he always ensured that the black literature project was well managed and he regarded it as an important contribution to research in black culture.

Gates and Appiah were already planning another major project to better document the black experience in nineteenth- and twentieth-century America. In 1983 Gates had written a review of a new dictionary of African-American biography, in which he pointed out that there are only 120 blacks in the twenty-four-volume *Dictionary of American Biography* and only forty-one black women in *Notable American Women, 1607–1950*, and that he was planning to index 150 black biographical dictionaries from 1806.[3] Unknown to Gates, two young scholars had been searching out black biographical dictionaries since they were graduate students. Nancy Hall Burkett was associate librarian of the American Antiquarian Society and her husband, Randall K. Burkett, was associate director at the W. E. B. DuBois Institute at Harvard. They had received some funding and had identified nearly 300 titles. But after ten years, working on their project part-time, they had been turned down twice by the NEH for funding and had had to discontinue it. A friend suggested they approach Chadwyck-Healey and when they did Susan Severtson (who was president of Chadwyck-Healey Inc.; see Chapter 14) and I were both excited by the prospect of publishing on microfiche such a large collection of books, which could be enhanced by an index of every person in every book. Gates had not yet moved to the DuBois Institute where Randall Burkett worked and we encouraged them to cooperate on *Black Biographical Dictionaries, 1790–1950*. Gates wrote in the foreword to the index, 'It was Charles Chadwyck-Healey and his staff who first expressed enthusiasm for my project, and who brought me together with Nancy and Randall Burkett, who were pursuing a similar project.'

The Burketts found the books in the libraries of Harvard, the Schomburg Center, the Moorland-Spingarn Collection at Howard University, and in many other libraries and private collections. For one book there was no known copy in the USA[4] and some nineteenth-century dictionaries had been published in the UK and France – the monumental *Tribute for the Negro* by William Armistead (Manchester, 1848) and *An Enquiry Concerning the Intellectual and Moral Faculties, and Literature of Negroes* by Henri Gregoire, first published in France but printed in the USA in 1810. The biographical information in books that spanned 160 years was presented in many different ways and was also accompanied by thousands of portraits. We published the collection in 1989, containing biographies of 30,000 people on over 1,000 microfiche with MARC cataloguing on magnetic tape. It sold for $5,400 and the take-up was immediate. Gates and the

Burketts each received a five per cent royalty and Gates received advances totalling $20,000, which were also treated as a consultancy fee, as he continued to suggest publishing projects to us and always expressed disappointment if we did not take them up.

The large quarto two-volume printed index of almost 1,400 pages followed in 1991. It contained a guide to the dictionaries on microfiche and an index with the name of each person, with birth and death dates, place of birth, occupation and religious affiliation. There were some unusual occupations including thirty 'weather prophets' and twenty-six 'palm readers'. Some indexing was done in the UK where it was not initially understood that 'railway workers' were men and women who had been involved with the 'underground railroad', the network of abolitionists and sympathizers who enabled escaping slaves to hide and travel to the north. The correct term for a railroad worker was 'Expressman'. By the end of the 1990s the *African-American Biographical Database* had been transferred to the web and the dictionaries themselves became fully searchable.

In the 1980s there were plenty of scholars interested in black culture, but few had the sophistication of Gates, who was entirely familiar with mainstream English and American literature, having earned an MA and his PhD at Clare College, Cambridge. He has been the ideal advocate for a better understanding of the rich and enormously important contribution that black Americans have made to American culture as they struggled to free themselves from the stigma of slavery. After the Sanborn Maps, these were the two most important microform publications that we published in the USA. In the late 1980s and early 1990s when we were working on the indexes to Black Literature and to Black Biographical Dictionaries and were also publishing the *Index of Personal Names in the National Union Catalog of Manuscript Collections, 1959–1984* (NUCMC), there was no other publisher as immersed as we were in the names of America's people and its places.

In 1994 we offered to sponsor an annual Chadwyck-Healey lecture at the British Library. There was an informal committee of Michael Smethurst, director general, Henry Heaney, Librarian of the University of Glasgow, David Vaisey, Bodley's Librarian, and me, to select speakers, and I suggested that Gates should be the first. I had heard him speak at an ALA conference. He was a natural orator who spoke movingly about his own childhood, his heritage, and the difficulties that he and his family had had to overcome. In 1994 the lecture could not be held at the new British Library at St Pancras, as the lecture theatre was not yet completed, and it was held elsewhere.

Gates's lecture, 'A Killing Rage', ranged across issues in black, Muslim and Jewish communities in the USA; but the names 'Bensonhurst',[5] Meir Kahane and Louis Farrakhan and issues such as black anti-semitism were unfamiliar to a British audience. He spoke quickly and finished ten minutes early, and at the time I was disappointed. But when I reread the lecture twenty-three years later, I was astonished by its prescience and its passion. He starts with a passage from Ezekiel where the Lord forbids the further use of the proverb 'The parents have eaten sour grapes, and the children's teeth are set on edge.' It is a caveat on the subject of historical guilt, which he states is, 'parasitic on the idea of collective identity' and that, 'cultural identity is so often bound up in memories of who has wronged us, and, less often, whom we have wronged' – a condemnation of the thinking that has led so recently to the 'Rhodes must fall' campaign in Oxford, the renaming of buildings named after men whose wealth came from slavery, and the destruction of statues of Confederate generals in the South. He ends, 'The past must be a wellspring of moral courage; which is to say, we poison its wells if we reduce it to a sump of hatred ... where the sins of the past are visited on the children, and their children, and their children, until, perhaps, there are no children left.' We were left chastened as well as a little bewildered.

After the lecture I lost touch with Gates. He reappeared in the English newspapers in 2009 when it was reported that, on returning home without his keys, he was arrested by the police as he tried to get into his home in Cambridge, Massachusetts, and was charged with disorderly conduct. The arrest generated a national debate on whether or not it could be construed as racial profiling by the police, and even President Obama was drawn into the debate, describing it as 'a teachable moment'. It made me think of the many teachable moments that I had had with Gates during our work together.

13

The National Security Archive

To most Americans NSA stands for the National Security Agency, the secretive US intelligence agency that monitors and collects phone and Internet information from all over the world, but in 1985 another NSA, the National Security Archive, was created with a very different purpose. The origins of this NSA lay in the Central American Papers Project (CAPP), which had been set up in the early 1980s by Jim Moody, a Congressman from Wisconsin, under the aegis of a not-for-profit organization called the Fund for Peace. Moody, who had been inspired by the *New York Times* journalist Raymond Bonner, who shared declassified documents with other researchers, had founded CAPP to investigate the role of the US government in the atrocities being committed by the governments of the tiny central American states of El Salvador and Nicaragua in their fight against supposed communist-inspired rebel groups.

CAPP used FOIA, the US Freedom of Information Act, which had come into effect in 1967 and which gave the public the right to request records from any federal agency, to show the extent to which the US government knew of or was complicit in the human rights outrages that were being committed in these countries in the 1970s and 1980s. Laurence Stern, the assistant managing editor of the *Washington Post*, was also encouraging journalists to use FOIA to uncover documents in investigations carried out by his newspaper, but US officials found plenty of ways of obstructing access. Release of sensitive documents, particularly those relating to the security services and US agencies working outside the USA, was often refused and their existence was often not even admitted to. Parts of the texts of documents that were released were often heavily redacted (blacked out so that they could not be read).

To make a FOIA request the researcher went first to the organization to ask if a document existed and if it was admitted to, ask for its release, or when received ask for an unredacted version. If release continued to be refused the researcher would ultimately have to go to the courts. This could take years and was laborious and expensive. But quite deliberately the federal agency did not keep a public record of a successful or unsuccessful challenge. When another person or organization wanted the same document, they would have to start the whole process again, not knowing whether another researcher had already been successful in obtaining the document.

Stern died in 1979 and his mission was taken up by Scott Armstrong, another investigative journalist at the *Washington Post*. The work of CAPP had made clear to the public, including Congressmen and Senators, that to ever fully understand the extent of the role of US officials and military in war-torn countries such as El Salvador, agencies had to be made to release their most sensitive documents. Armstrong, who was a colleague of Bob Woodward of Watergate fame (they had co-authored a book, *The Brethren*, published in 1979, an inside account of the workings of the US Supreme Court), concluded that what was needed was a central clearing house in which all FOIA requests could be recorded and where there would be copies of the documents themselves so that researchers could go first to Armstrong's NSA to find out if a particular document had already been asked for and delivered – in unredacted form. The Fund for Peace took on the NSA and Armstrong began to raise money to fund it.

It might well have remained a clearing house for documents released under FOIA requests but for Armstrong it was not enough to create a passive database – he wanted to search out documents in areas of public interest and make his own FOIA requests using the skills he and his colleagues had developed as journalists, and publish his own selections of documents. He decided that in view of the volume of material that he wanted to publish, microfiche was the only viable medium. The documents on microfiche would also be described and indexed in printed volumes to a level of detail that went far beyond any other finding aids to government documents. The income from the sale of publications would convince potential funders that the NSA could generate some of its own revenues as it grew. He approached US microform publishers, including Chadwyck-Healey, to co-publish these publications, produce the microfiche, print the guides and indexes, market them throughout the world and pay royalties on sales to the NSA.

I was excited at the prospect of publishing such 'hot' material, so different from the normal academic material we were used to. But I thought that

Armstrong would be likely to choose one of the other Washington-area microform publishers: CIS, which by that time was owned by Elsevier, or University Publications of America (UPA), which was an innovative microform publisher. The NSA had preliminary discussions with both Research Publications and Carrollton Press, who were already microfilming older declassified documents, to find out what the market for them was and we assumed that both these publishers would also be interested. Bonnell and I knew that we would have to make a strong presentation to have any chance of being chosen and we did so on 14 February 1986 at the Brookings Institution where the NSA had rented offices. We had to convince Armstrong that we had the sales and marketing muscle in the USA to sell their publications effectively. At the meeting there was also a consultant to the Ford Foundation, which had provided some initial funding and was considering making a much larger grant. Bonnell thought that the sales estimates that I wanted to propose were far too high, but I was concerned that unless we put forward an ambitious sales target, we would not be able to compete with our larger US rivals. I let Bonnell present her more modest forecast, but when we left the meeting we stood outside on the sidewalk and argued about it, as I was sure that we had no chance of being chosen on the basis of what she had just told them.

We were asked back for another meeting where they explained that the consultant to the Ford Foundation had produced his own estimate of sales and that his figures were close to Bonnell's. This gave our figures an authority that strengthened our case, while my 'unrealistic' figures could have ruled us out. At both meetings the importance of the publishing programme as a source of revenue for the NSA was emphasized and the 'National Security Archive: Development Grant' proposal of 1 March 1986 states that:

> The choice of a microform co-publisher would be heavily influenced by such factors as the quality of services offered to libraries, the quality and pricing of microform product, indexing facilities and experience, the overall degree of access to the major university and research library market, and the degree of access to particular foreign markets.

At the second meeting on 28 February I noted 'expectations totally unrealistic', and in March that we were 'still in the running'. Although the NSA had begun to talk to publishers in 1986, they spent the year engaging with the Ford, MacArthur and Carnegie foundations in order to obtain grants – in the case of Ford, a general support grant of $200,000 and a 'program-related investment' of $1.5 million. It was only in 1988 that we, together with CIS and UPA, made our publishing proposals, and ours was accepted because we offered the most, a fifty per cent royalty on sales revenue. By now Bonnell had left and Severtson (see Chapter 14) signed the agreement on 11 May 1988. It was the longest period from initial discussion to confirmation as publisher that we had ever had.

The NSA had started work in 1986 on *El Salvador: The Making of U.S. Policy, 1977–1984*, but it was not published until 1989. The amount of work that went into these publications is reflected in the extent and quality of the guide and index – two large volumes totalling 1,806 pages – together with 2,142 documents reproduced on microfiche. Each document is fully described in the guide, not only with the date but often the time it was issued – many were cables from the US Embassy in San Salvador; there was also the status of the document – its level of security – and a short abstract. The index included both subjects and names and described a wide range of document types from cables to court records. The publication also made clear the symbiotic relationship between the researchers making FOIA requests and the officials who had to respond to them, requests that were often for thousands of pages of material and involved a huge amount of work for the officials. In the introduction the editor wrote:

> The project would not have been possible without FOIA and the co-operation of dedicated access professionals in Federal agencies. Most important was the staff of the Department of State where many long hours were devoted to this documentation by those searching for documents and declassifiers reviewing them.

But, after the praise, the criticism:

> although the Department has still much to do to improve its performance under the law.... Regrettably there is less to be thankful for from the National Security Council and the Central Intelligence Agency (CIA) since they continue to be unwilling to obey the mandates of the Freedom of Information Act.

In a speech at the National Press Club in Washington in September 1989 Robert McNamara, who had been Secretary of Defense in the Kennedy and Johnson administrations and was on the editorial board for the NSA set of historical documents on the Cuban Missile Crisis, said, 'If you want to read a hair-raising account [of the Cuban Missile Crisis] get the chronology that's published [by the] National Security Archive. It's a public document now ... they've used the Freedom of Information Act.... Get a hold of that. It'll scare the hell out of you.'[1] We published the *Cuban Missile Crisis* in 1990, edited by Laurence Chang. By now it was history, yet few of the 15,000 pages published on microfiche had previously been available to the public.

In 1992 there was a second set of historical documents, *The Berlin Crisis, 1958–1962*, and in 1996 a second set of documents on El Salvador, *El Salvador: War, Peace and Human Rights, 1980–1994*. In this set twenty-seven documents came from the National Security Council and 337 documents came from the CIA.

When the UN Truth Commission published its investigation into human rights abuses in 1993, *From Madness to Hope: The 12 Year War in El Salvador*,[2] Congress asked President Clinton to declassify for public inspection all US government documents relevant to human rights that had been studied by the commission. The NSA brought in 'The Washington Task Force on Salvadoran Death Squads' and other human rights specialists to review the thousands of documents, and the editor selected 1,384 documents for publication. Many of the documents had been excised and/or redacted, particularly those from the Defense Department and the CIA, and because they had not been procured through a FOIA request, excessive deletions could not be appealed against. But some were important, particularly the Woerner Report, which was the blueprint for US military involvement in El Salvador and which had only been obtained by the NSA after years of requests and litigation. Cable traffic between the US Embassy in San Salvador and the State Department revealed the extent of the government's knowledge of many of the worst human rights cases, including the assassination of Archbishop Oscar Romero,[3] the killing of US Marines in San Salvador's 'Zona Rosa' tourist area and the murder of Jesuit priests.

The publication which brought the NSA into the public eye was the collection of key documents for what was the most controversial and bizarre activity by agents of the US government since the Second World War. *The Iran-Contra Affair: The Making of a Scandal, 1983–1988* was published in 1990 and included all the documents released by official investigations, including the Senate Intelligence Committee and the Tower Commission. These investigations had led to the criminal indictments in 1988 of senior figures, Caspar Weinberger and Robert McFarlane, and the less prominent but soon notorious Oliver North, John Poindexter, Richard

Secord and Albert Hakim – all of whom, in the end, had their cases dismissed or received presidential pardons. But the release of Oliver North's diaries through an NSA FOIA request revealed the extent of Vice-President George H. W. Bush's involvement and his acquiescence in the illegal activities of North and his associates, while he himself survived unscathed.[4]

The FOIA came to the UK thirty-three years after it came to the USA. Armstrong visited the UK to talk to foundations and interested individuals about the work of the NSA, and he and I had a drink with Jonathan Aitken at the Savoy Hotel. Aitken at the time was a backbench MP with a strong interest in foreign policy and intelligence and wanted to know how the FOIA was being used to obtain information from reluctant government agencies.

While Armstrong was the successful founder of the NSA, he was less comfortable running it, and there were growing pains in the first few years. In late 1989 eight of twenty-four NSA staff had been laid off. Armstrong also left and neither of the directors who followed him lasted for long. In early 1992 Tom Blanton was appointed executive director, having joined the NSA as director of planning and research in 1986. Blanton, who had previously been a journalist in Central America, was charming, personable and a very effective manager and since then the NSA has flourished under his leadership.

In the early 1990s the NSA had learned that under the Clinton administration the US government planned to purge White House computer messages from the Reagan, Bush and Clinton administrations, and they had filed suit to prevent this. The millions of pages included memoranda dealing with major policies, as well as less high-profile but still important documents. On 13 August 1993 a federal appeals court ruled that the government must save the millions of electronic messages, a decision applauded by journalists and historians. Without the intervention of the NSA it is likely that this material would have been destroyed, setting a disastrous precedent for the future.

Under both Armstrong and Blanton, the NSA was an exemplary partner; they acknowledged us as their publisher by thanking us in the introduction to almost every index, mentioning members of staff by name. They came to many ALA conferences to give papers and also spent time in our booth talking to librarians. They helped us produce well-designed and written brochures, and they put out press releases on every publication. We devoted more sales resources in the USA to NSA titles than to any other series, yet the sales of both the guides and indexes and the microfiche sets never achieved the levels that we and the Ford Foundation had originally envisaged. Sales were patchy: in 1993 only forty per cent of ARL libraries (the large research libraries) had bought at least one set,[5] and libraries would order some titles but not others, when we would have expected them to have placed a standing order for them all. We sold enough copies of both the microfiche sets and the indexes to make each publication worthwhile but our annual royalty payments to the NSA were only around $200,000, and the NSA remained dependent on donations from major foundations. One of Blanton's most important roles was as a fundraiser and over several decades he has raised millions of dollars from foundations like Ford and MacArthur. The NSA has also received many donations from individuals, including Barbra Streisand, a faithful donor almost from the beginning.

In 1994 we published the indexes to the twelve published collections on CD-ROM, transforming access to the 35,000 documents on microfiche. The year before, Blanton and I had discussed other new products, including a new interactive CD-ROM publication listing all CIA documents that had been declassified, with software that enabled the user to generate a standard letter requesting copies of selected documents. We warned that there would be little interest in this overseas. He told me that he had been approached by Research Publications, who were asking the NSA for help in developing their own declassified documents series and had offered an advance of $150,000. We did not think it would be good for the NSA to be associated with the publication of random declassified documents that did not have the editorial control of the NSA sets and in the end it came to nothing.

The NSA was then able to obtain a grant from the John D. and Catherine T. MacArthur Foundation to scan the microfiche in the twelve sets and in late 1998 we launched the *Digital National Security Archive* on the web, in which the scanned images of the documents were accessed through the digital index. We offered a web subscription to all the collections for $8,000 a year with the promise of new collections being added each year, and a sliding price scale based on the budget of the library. It was a time when both we and our customers were tentatively exploring what would be a fair price for online access to collections, which in the microfiche format with the printed indexes would have cost $56,000 to buy outright. With two new collections being added each year, each of which would have sold for $4,500 on microfiche, it represented good value, and online access to the collections meant that libraries no longer had to decide which titles to buy. They now had access to all of them in what the *Christian Science Monitor* had called, 'the largest collection of contemporary declassified national security information outside the United States Government'. This transformed the material that we were publishing, and twenty years after the launch of the online database, with ProQuest as the NSA's publishing partner, royalties have grown enormously and have become the single most important source of revenue for the NSA,[6] as in 1986 we had both hoped they would.

14

The Last Years of Microform

The move to Cambridge Place

After spending eight years in 20 Newmarket Road, a run-down building on which, as a short-term tenant, I was not prepared to spend money, I wanted to move and, if possible, buy our own building. Bacon noticed a small advertisement in the city council newsletter advertising a carpet warehouse for sale. It was in the centre of Cambridge in the grandly named Cambridge Place, in reality a narrow alley leading to lock-up garages, a scrap-metal merchant and an Irish drinking club. The street had not even been adopted by the council and had to be maintained by its users. As the owner of a local business I had no difficulty in getting planning permission for change of use, and I bought the building for £90,000 borrowed from Coutts and we spent £200,000 of the company's cash virtually rebuilding it and turning it into a high-quality office with plenty of walls to hang large pictures by contemporary artists, which I had just begun to collect. The conversion was overseen by Ken Neale, a local architect and friend, and was the most enjoyable building project that I have ever done. We moved in December 1985. Our main method of selling was still direct mail and we received orders by mail, so our address was important to us. It was short and stylish, without a street number: 'Cambridge Place, Cambridge, CB2 1NR'.

The attempted sale to Elsevier

At the time of our move I wanted to take some money out of the company. Sales of Chadwyck-Healey Ltd and Chadwyck-Healey Inc. had grown from £906,313 in 1981/2 to £2,540,341 in 1984/5, and Sufrin suggested that I could realize some of the value by selling a minority stake in the group.

Sufrin knew the Dutch publishing world as his accounting firm audited the Dutch publishing giant VNU in the USA. He introduced me to Rudolph 'Rud' Snoeker, a Dutch consultant, who helped us prepare a formal sales prospectus for the companies in the group, including our new French publishing company (see Chapter 11). CHMPS, the production business, was excluded.

In January 1986 Snoeker, on my behalf, approached Elsevier, the largest of the Dutch journal publishers. They expressed interest and at the first meeting in Amsterdam I found myself facing senior executives from one of the world's most formidable publishing companies. At the end they asked why I wanted to sell only part of the company and they pointed out that with them as a minority shareholder no other company would want to buy the rest. They said that they would prefer to buy the whole company. When I explained that the group was growing fast, that it had a great future and that I did not want to sell all of it now, they suggested that they would buy the company as an 'earn-out' – they would make an initial payment followed by further payments through the next four years, which would depend on the growth and profitability of the company as forecast in our business plan. We all thought it was an attractive proposal and I made several day trips from Stansted to Amsterdam to continue negotiations.

I also approached Tim Rix, the chairman of Longman, whom I knew through our publication of Longman's archive on microfilm, and in February 1986 he replied to say that, while our development was impressive, 'the "fit" between your Company and its activities and Longman is really quite limited and, in our view, an association would almost certainly not be fruitful for either of us'.[1] This simply underlined the gulf that there was between mainstream book and journal publishing, and microform and reprint publishing.

In March Elsevier offered me a down payment of $4.5 million and the prospect of earning at least the same over the next four years. At the time it seemed like a lot of money and I accepted. The net earnings of the group in 1985/6 (year ending 30 June) had to be at least $325,000 for the sale to go ahead. We were confident of that, but the earn-out conditions were onerous. We forecast increased net earnings for three of the next four years and if we had achieved our own forecast, we could have earned another $5 million. The formula was based on a multiple of 8.3 times the increase in profit compared to the year before. If there was no increase from one year to the next, no multiple would be paid in that year. If there were one or two years with no growth the prospective total for the four years would be much reduced.

In the sale of every company, once the owner agrees to sell, the buyer's geniality disappears. A team of hard-faced Dutch accountants, reputed to be the toughest in the world, arrived in Cambridge to carry out their due diligence. There were several things that they did not like. One was the new French company, which was showing a large loss, though this was only because we had not shipped the microfiche edition of the catalogues of the BnF, even though we had sufficient firm orders to give us a substantial profit. Another was that I personally owned the office building in Cambridge and the microfilm production bureau in Bassingbourn. Their concern was that I would either reduce the rent or charge no rent for the next four years and artificially lower our microform production costs, thereby increasing the annual profit of the group on which Elsevier was paying the multiple.

After the sale we would become a subsidiary of CIS in Washington, DC, Adler's old company, which Elsevier had bought a few years before and with which I had had a long relationship (see Chapter 5). On 21 June I was due to fly to Washington to sign the sale documents but Paul Massa, the president of CIS whom I knew and liked, phoned me the day before to tell me that Elsevier had changed its mind and the deal was off. I felt utterly deflated; all I could think of was the amount of time Miller and I had spent preparing for this sale, together with the fees that we would have to pay to our lawyer and accountants in Cambridge, to Snoeker, to Sufrin and to Burt Rubin, our lawyer in New York. Curiously the prospect of not receiving the money worried me least because I had not even decided what I would do with it. All I knew was that, for four years, I would be working so hard to achieve the highest possible earn-out that I would be too busy to spend it. I decided to fly to the USA anyway and to spend the week at our office in Alexandria. As the week went by, I felt an unexpected sense of relief that the sale had not gone through and that I was still my own master, and owner of three publishing companies that I had told Elsevier had so much potential. For the first time I had been made to look at the companies I had started thirteen years earlier objectively and critically. Preparing for a sale is an invaluable discipline. Normally there is no time to step back but now I had learned a lot about the companies that I had not understood before.

I could now see that it was our US company that was the weakest link; it was not growing because I was not spending enough time on it. I was only in the USA about five weeks a year and when I was in the UK, I only spent the equivalent of a day a week exclusively on the US company. I had appointed Hamilton as chief executive, but he did not have the entrepreneurial experience or the skills to grow the company himself, and even though I spoke to him almost every day, the support and advice I gave him was not enough. If I wanted the company to grow, I would have to find someone more experienced to replace him and also spend more time on the company myself. Through working with Buchanan on REMARC, which was based in the Washington, DC area (see Chapter 16), I had got to know one of his colleagues, Susan Severtson, who had been a senior editor at Research Publications. By now it was clear that REMARC would not survive. When I asked Severtson to join me she replied that she would only be interested if I assured her that we would invest in CD-ROM publishing. I told her that I too saw it as the future. In the business plan for Elsevier Snoeker had written, 'Mr Chadwyck-Healey intends to maintain his advantage in technological superiority over his competitors.... He also intends to publish in new formats such as videodisk and digitized optical disks as these new technologies become competitive with more conventional ones.' But the four-year earn-out period would have coincided with the critical early years of the development of publications on CD-ROM. With the need to produce as large a profit as possible each year we could only have made short-term investments and, inevitably, would have stayed with the medium we knew best – microfilm. By the time that CD-ROM publishing became mainstream four years later the companies would no longer be mine. I had been saved from my own bad judgement by Elsevier's abrupt decision not to go through with the acquisition. Although I stayed in touch with Massa (see Chapter 16), I never knew why they changed their mind, and two years later CIS acquired two US microform publishers, UPA and Norman Ross Publishing.

In spite of our expectations of an electronic future, microforms were still our principal publishing medium, and if we were going to have more microfilm production capacity in the USA, we needed a larger office. A very large new office complex occupying a city block in old Alexandria called '1101 King Street' had just been built, with four self-contained three-storey office condominiums. They had extra high ceilings at street level, which was ideal for microfilm cameras. I worked out that the mortgage payments would be close to what we would pay in rent. There was a further advantage in buying, as at that time in the USA companies could write off five per cent of the purchase price of their building against their profits each year. In twenty years, the whole cost of the building would be written off against tax. We bought the condominium for $450,000, a few months before the tax break ended. It was an important gesture that I had made to myself and my colleagues less than a week after the Elsevier sale had fallen through. I needed to prove to myself and to others that we were going to be in business in the USA for the long term. We stayed in the building until I sold the company in 1999, so were able to set 13/20ths of the cost of the building against tax.

There was one other compensation for the time and money lost in the abortive sale. During the due diligence I had got to know Jim Connolly, a senior vice-president at CIS who had been there with Adler from the beginning. He was friendly and helpful and had given me a valuable piece of advice. We invoiced our customers a month before their subscriptions expired. Connolly told me to invoice all subscriptions in the autumn irrespective of when they started. Library systems were set up to pay all journal subscriptions then and we would find that many libraries would pay immediately. At a time when interest rates were around fifteen per cent, bringing forward such payments compensated for some of the costs the failed sale had incurred.

I had to reassure Miller that I no longer wanted to sell the companies. He was not convinced and told me that he thought that I had lost interest in the business. I realized that, although large microform projects like *The Nineteenth Century* were just starting, what he sensed was the beginning of a disengagement from microform as I became more convinced than ever that our future lay in electronic publishing.

On my return to the UK I had visited my father who was ill with cancer and told him that I was pleased that the sale was no longer taking place and that I was now looking to the future. It was our last conversation as a few weeks later he died quite suddenly. I had not realized, or perhaps had not allowed myself to realize, how ill he was, and the end came too quickly. It made the summer of 1986 a time of change at the most profound level.

Management changes

While the early 1980s had been an innovative period with the publication of the Non-HMSO Catalogue, the Sanborn Maps and *NIDS*, the way that

Miller and I ran the companies had hardly changed. One constant was my dependence on my all-important personal assistants (PAs), starting with Skyrme in Bishops Stortford; most of my PAs were good and all of them had to be tough to deal with me, the pressure and the workload, which never seemed to diminish.

The most important management change came in 1987 when Alastair Everitt, managing director of Harvester Press, our major competitor in the UK, asked Fellner, whom he knew well, if there might be a role for him at Chadwyck-Healey Ltd. This would be an important move in our tiny industry, and Everitt and I met to discuss it over a discreet dinner in London. Shortly after, he accepted my offer of the job of managing director. To John Spiers, the owner and chairman of Harvester, to lose Everitt would have been a blow, as he had built up their very successful microform publications list, but, unknown to Everitt, although he may have suspected it, Spiers was in the process of selling Harvester to Research Publications. To Everitt and the outside world Chadwyck-Healey appeared to be an innovative publisher with a company in the USA and now a company in France, and with its own production company. We had even won our first Queen's Award for Export Achievement with a visit to Buckingham Palace to be congratulated by the Queen herself. But the company was run as a two-man band by Miller and me. The former looked after the finances of all four entities and I did the rest. In place of board meetings we reviewed the business at the local pub once or twice a week. Everitt found that there was no sales director or editorial director, as I had assumed both these roles myself. Our sales effort outside the USA consisted of the mailing of sales brochures and my occasional visits to libraries together with an annual visit to Australia and Japan, while one salesman, John Ferguson, who had been head of the British Council libraries in Germany and had worked in Paris, travelled for us in the UK and Europe but with very limited success (see Chapter 16). Everitt quickly convinced me that we needed a sales director and, soon after, we appointed Steven Hall who spoke fluent German, French and Italian and had been working for Information Publications International, a distributor of academic books and journals. Highly intelligent and experienced in selling academic publications, he was an outstanding sales director. Everitt had also turned his attention to the production department where he found that the quality of the microforms being produced by our own production company was uneven. Because production was now in-house the relationship had become too cosy, and he immediately imposed higher standards and started a programme to refilm any microfiche that he considered to be sub-standard. We began to have monthly board meetings, which at the start were awkward and ineffective. The interpersonal dynamics had changed; rather than two people running the UK company, there were now four. Miller decided to leave and his successor Donald McCrae, a young accountant who had been working for a large distributor and publisher of printed music, joined us in June 1989. He had a good understanding of computers and redesigned and upgraded our computerized accounting system. He was also an enthusiastic supporter of our move into electronic publishing.

In July 1987, after she had been working with Hamilton for a few months, I appointed Severtson as president of Chadwyck-Healey Inc. When she took over, both Hamilton and Bonnell left; the latter did not wish to move to Alexandria. The companies began to work together more effectively as a group and in 1989 we had an inter-company meeting in Paris. By then each company produced an annual publication plan and budget, which had to be approved by McCrae and me. Some important US publishing projects, such as *Black Literature* (see Chapter 12) and those from the NSA (see Chapter 13), predated Severtson's arrival, though she was responsible for their development and production. But apart from these and ongoing programmes such as *NIDSUS*, by the late 1980s much of our US publishing programme was mediocre.

In spite of my having stated publicly in 1976 (see Chapter 9) that we would not publish archives, we were tempted by the money that was being given out by Burke's NHPRC to subsidize the publishing on microfilm of manuscript collections of prominent Americans. Academics were being funded by the NHPRC to locate the papers of historical figures, copy and organize them with a written commentary and then have them microfilmed by a commercial microform publisher so that copies would be disseminated to libraries throughout the world. A surprising condition, as we had experienced with Gates (see Chapter 12), was that the royalty on sales paid by the publisher went to the editor of the papers and not back to the NHPRC.

We had first been approached by an academic in 1981 and it had been too tempting to turn down. In each case the editor did all the work and delivered the organized material to us, and all we had to do was microfilm it and print the index. There were the letters of Charles Sumner, the great anti-slavery and civil rights campaigner, edited by Beverly Palmer; the papers of Martin Van Buren, the eighth, rather obscure, president of the United States, edited by Lucy Fisher West; and the papers of John Paul Jones, the American naval hero, privateer and diplomat. The editor of his papers, James C. Bradford at Texas A&M University, in a letter to Hamilton wrote, 'My dean places little value on the microfilm edition and that I have been advised by others to drop it for the immediate future and to put my efforts on a highly select letterpress edition in an effort to further my career. I have rejected this advice.'[2]

The prejudice against microfilm publication and the belief that the only respectable academic edition was an edited selection in book form seemed to be universal. In contrast, in August 1986 the NHPRC announced that it 'took special satisfaction in the recent publication of the *Microform Edition of the John Muir Papers*'.[3] We were the publisher of the papers of this great US environmentalist who had founded the national parks. We thought that we would sell enough copies of all these titles to give us a reasonable profit while providing steady work for our microfilm cameras in Alexandria. But we found dealing with inexperienced editors took more time than we expected, and we only sold eleven copies of the *Papers of Charles Sumner* at a price of $4,950, and fewer than twenty copies of the *Papers of John Paul Jones*, even though the price was only $600. It proved what I had concluded more than ten years before, that libraries did not buy microfilm editions of manuscripts because there were so few scholars that had a sufficiently specialized interest in them to justify their acquisition. It was more cost effective to pay a researcher's travel costs to another library that held the papers of an important historical figure than to buy the microfilm.

There were two exceptions, which came to us through the NHPRC and the NEH. One was *Black Literature, 1827–1940* (see Chapter 12) and the other was the *Emma Goldman Papers*. As a student, Candace Falk had found some love letters of Emma Goldman in a music shop in Chicago. This had inspired her to research the life of Goldman and in 1980 found the Emma Goldman Papers Project (EGPP) under the aegis of the Institute for the Study of Social Change at the University of California, Berkeley.

Jewish and born in Russia, Goldman had emigrated to the USA in 1885. She became involved in the anarchist movement, writing countless articles and pamphlets and lecturing all over the USA. For opposing government she was arrested many times, and for opposing the USA's entry into the First World War she was imprisoned in 1917, and then, with her US citizenship revoked, was deported back to Russia. She and her lover

Alexander Berkman quickly saw through the Bolshevik government, realizing that it was as repressive to the ordinary citizen as any Western government, and she and Berkman left Russia for England, where she acquired British citizenship by marrying a Scottish miner whom she hardly knew. All her life she spoke and wrote on women's rights, on birth control and on the freedom of women to make their own decisions. In 1897 she had written, 'I demand the independence of women, her right to support herself; to live for herself; to love whomsoever she pleases or as many as she pleases.'[4] She was also the first woman and the first American to publicly defend homosexual love, and she publicized, often for the first time, a number of significant social causes including union organization and the eight-hour working day. In 1907, barely more than fifty years since the end of slavery, in the anarchist magazine *Mother Earth*, which she had founded, she wrote, 'Hardly a day passes without a Negro being lynched.... Nowhere in the country does the Negro enjoy equal opportunity with the white man.'[5]

She died in exile in Canada in 1940, her extraordinary life driven by an uncompromising integrity. It also encompassed a passionate love life, principally with Berkman but also with Ben Reitman, a doctor who worked with the poor in Chicago. His belief in 'free love' deeply hurt her and she left him and returned to Berkman, but 450 of their graphic love letters were given by the Reitman family to the University of Illinois at Chicago, while a further thirty were found by Falk. Dover Books republished Goldman's autobiography *Living My Life* in 1970,[6] and in 1972 Alix Kates Shulman, a civil rights activist and feminist, published *Red Emma Speaks*, a selection of Goldman's writings and speeches.[7] Goldman was brought out of obscurity as the women's movement gathered pace and by the 1980s she was recognized as a legendary pioneer in the fight for women's rights.

I had met Ron Zboray, editor of the EGPP, in 1984 and at my suggestion he wrote to Hamilton for advice on how they should publish Goldman's papers on microfilm with an extensive printed guide and index. In February 1985 I visited Falk and her team in Berkeley to present our case as their prospective publisher. At the meeting they told me that they had already had a draft agreement from MCA before it closed down (see Chapter 10), but that we were now high on their list. I had been staying in Palo Alto with my friends Charles and Miriam Palm. He was archivist and librarian of the Hoover Institution on the Stanford University campus (see Chapter 22) and I quickly realized that our association with what was seen by many, particularly in Berkeley, as a right-wing think-tank did not improve our chances of being chosen as the publisher of Goldman's papers. Fortunately, Falk herself was warm, welcoming and immensely enthusiastic; Goldman has been lucky to have such a devoted and energetic disciple. In October 1985 on one of Falk's visits to the International Institute of Social History in Amsterdam, which had a large Goldman archive, she stopped off in London and we had lunch. She had still not chosen a publisher and at the end of the meal I said to her, 'Candace, it was meant that we should publish Emma Goldman's papers because Emma died the day after I was born.'[8] The agreement was signed in January 1986.

Academic interests can be fickle and if we had published the *Emma Goldman Papers* soon after signing the agreement sales would have been much better than they eventually were. But they were still collecting and editing documents from more than twenty-five repositories including archives in Russia, in Beijing, in the House of Lords Record Office in the UK, and, ironically, in the Hoover Institution. Severtson and I visited Berkeley to find out when material would come to us for microfilming, and on behalf of Falk I also visited the institute in Amsterdam and was able to alleviate some of their nervousness in allowing their material to be copied by agreeing to provide them with microfilm copies.

We first announced publication in June 1986, expecting to publish the 40,000 documents on sixty-nine reels of microfilm in 1988, but it was not published until spring 1991 and the guide and index not until 1995. By the early 1990s libraries were spending increasingly large parts of their budgets on CD-ROM publications like those that we were already publishing, and sales were less than we had originally forecast.

Unlike many other NHPRC-sponsored projects, the microfilm edition was not the main objective of the EGPP. For thirty-eight years Falk has worked on the legacy of Emma Goldman, and against all odds has raised money to keep the project going, not only from large funders such as the NEH, the Rockefeller and Ford foundations, and the University of California, Berkeley itself, but also from countless small foundations and private donors. A digitized edition of the papers has replaced the microfilm edition and in recent years Falk and her colleagues have been publishing selected documents in printed volumes entitled *Emma Goldman. A Documentary History of the American Years*.[9] Even in the digital age, printed editions of selected documents remain the most prestigious form of academic publication.

In the UK, Everitt and I were able to publish several successful, high-profile manuscript collections. We had published a series of small books on different aspects of publishing and the book trade edited by Robin Myers, a distinguished and immensely active scholar who was honorary archivist of the Worshipful Company of Stationers and Newspaper Makers,[10] and in 1983 she had approached us and Harvester Press with a proposal to publish on microfilm the records of the Stationers' Company, which she had spent many years researching and organizing. Their records are the single most important source of information on the history of publishing in England. One of the most powerful City of London livery companies, the Stationers' Company had controlled the book trade in England until the end of the nineteenth century, and for 350 years the term 'Entered at Stationers' Hall' appeared in every book until 1911 when copyright became an automatic entitlement. The microfilm edition would be, 'the complete, definitive edition of the Records up to 1920, and occasionally beyond, containing every document in the Stationers' Hall that a researcher might want to see, properly organized and accompanied by a detailed, lucid guide'.[11]

We signed an agreement with the Stationers' Company in March 1984 and published the microfilm edition on 115 reels, selling for £3,950, in 1986. The 'detailed, lucid guide' was published in 1990 by Robert Cross under his imprint, St Paul's Bibliographies. The Stationers' Company is one of the few City of London livery companies that only admits liverymen who are in the related trades, in this case publishing, printing and papermaking, and I was admitted as a liveryman of the company in 1988. The microfilm edition was one of our most solid sellers in the late 1980s.

Everitt was also able to negotiate microfilm publishing rights for the papers of two major figures on our doorstep in Cambridge, Sir Isaac Newton and John Maynard Keynes. It was not until the 1950s that the full extent of Newton's scholarship began to be studied systematically. While many of his papers were in Cambridge, in the university library and in the Wren Library at Trinity College, there were also some in King's College Library that had been donated by Keynes. Others were in repositories in the UK, Europe and Israel. When Newton died, intestate, in 1727, his friend and distant relative John Conduitt claimed his papers but in 1740 passed them to the Portsmouth family. In 1936 Viscount Lymington sold the Portsmouth Papers, as they were now called, at Sotheby's, only achieving a disappointing £9,000. Keynes understood their importance but only heard about the sale after it had taken place. He then bought papers from dealers like Maggs and from the Jewish scholar and collector Abraham Yahuda who was primarily interested in Newton's religious beliefs. Keynes was more interested in Newton's alchemical papers, which had been deliberately overlooked by scholars in earlier centuries who were concerned that his reputation as a mystic might undermine his authority as a scientist. It was Peter Jones, the latest in a long line of distinguished King's College librarians, who edited the microfilm collection and the printed guide, which we published in early 1991.[12] It included papers from twenty-seven repositories including the Yahuda Collection in the Jewish National and University Library, and it was the first time since Newton's death that so many of his writings had been brought together in one coherent whole. The collection on forty-four reels sold for £2,500 to libraries all over the world.

Jones also made it possible for us to publish Keynes's own papers in King's College, Cambridge. This huge collection includes letters to and from more than 4,000 correspondents. Keynes was not only the most influential economist of the first half of the twentieth century but also a member of the Bloomsbury Group, an important author and outstanding editor, an investor for himself and the college, and a collector of books, paintings and manuscripts as we have seen above. His papers range from highly personal letters to and from his parents and to his wife Lydia, to his work on economics and international finance, with articles, speeches and broadcasts. There are thirty-seven albums of newspaper cuttings compiled by his parents and 498 of the letters are to and from Lytton Strachey.

There are few twentieth-century figures of such importance who have left behind such a huge collection of papers and correspondence. The latter was so voluminous that it made us face up to an issue that we had been avoiding for the previous twenty years, the need to clear copyright with many individuals and their descendants in order to republish their incoming letters in the archive. Few of the publishers' archives had incoming letters and if they were from the nineteenth century or earlier, we did not attempt to get permission to reproduce them. Of the NHPRC-sponsored collections we relied on the editor to obtain the necessary permissions but most of those were also nineteenth- or early twentieth-century archives. Keynes was different. He had corresponded with major twentieth-century figures – Freud, Bertrand Russell, E. M. Forster, Virginia Woolf – and formal agreements had to be reached with organizations such as the Strachey Trust at the Society of Authors. It took time but once microfilming started, because the material was well organized, we were able to complete production of 170 reels by the end of 1993. The microfilm publication and its catalogue by Jacqueline Cox, an archivist at King's College, cost £9,700 and, in spite of the high price, sold well.

The 1980s were a decade of change both for publishers in our sector and for libraries. Thomas A. Bourke, chief of the Microforms Division at NYPL, published an article in 1990 entitled, 'Scholarly Micropublishing, Preservation Microfilming, and the National Preservation Effort in the Last Two Decades of the Twentieth Century: History and Prognosis'.[13] He states that in the period after 1983 when the dollar was strong, foreign acquisitions cost US libraries less, and this led to a, 'brief period of recovery in scholarly micropublishing of research collections' but 'was followed in 1987 by a decline in the dollar exchange rate and continuing increases in journal prices which put pressure on library budgets' and, 'This ended the brief period of recovery in scholarly micropublishing of research collections and as a result many executives and sales people were either let go or resigned.' He quotes Alan Meckler's 1983 warning, 'when times get tough retrospective materials tend to lose their allure', and referred to an article I had written, also in 1983, entitled, 'The Future of Microform in an Electronic Age'.[14] I had seen my first CD-ROM in January 1983 (see Chapter 15) but in this article I was writing about the capability of the videodisk to store and display images, and how the academic community found that this new medium's ability to display high-quality images was as limited as that of microforms. I end the article, 'Microforms will continue to be used much as they are at present – until electronic data storage and transmission technology equals or improves on microforms in quality and cost.' From as early as 1983 I could see that electronic media in whatever form they came would, in the end, be dominant.

We too were affected by the ups and downs of library budgets, and in spite of improvements in the way that Chadwyck-Healey Ltd and Chadwyck-Healey Inc. were managed, both companies experienced years in which sales were flat or even declined. In 1986, the year of the attempted sale, they were £3,013,247. At this time our Japanese agent Yushodo was buying almost all our microform publications, including five sets of the *Nineteenth Century* microfiche programme, and we had become unhealthily dependent on their orders, particularly when I discovered on a visit to

Figure 9 Alexandria, Virginia. Some of the Chadwyck-Healey Inc. staff outside the office. Those mentioned in the book are: back row, third from left: Susan Severtson; fourth from left: Cheryl Crosby; far right: Eric Calaluca; in front of him: Sandy Shaffer Tinkham; centre front: Bob Asleson. 1989.

Japan that much of our microfilm was in the Yushodo warehouse, still unsold. In the following year, when Severtson became president, Chadwyck-Healey Inc. sales declined by £400,000, while Chadwyck-Healey Ltd sales only increased by £300,000. In 1989 sales of both companies totalled £4,266,874, but in 1990 there was virtually no growth in the sales of either company even though by then we had successful CD-ROM publications such as the *British Library Catalogue* (see Chapter 15). What set us apart from a normal business was not our sales or our profitability, which also fluctuated, but our ability to generate cash through advance payments by libraries. We paid no tax on these payments because they were only advances, repayable until the publications were delivered. They were equivalent to interest-free loans at a time of exceptionally high interest rates. The interest that the cash earned contributed to the bottom line, while the cash itself gave us the ability to invest as we wished, in particular in electronic publishing. By June 1983 Chadwyck-Healey Ltd's cash had grown in a year from £123,191 to £300,921. By June 1989 it was £398,486, though by then we were having to fund CHF, while in the same year Chadwyck-Healey Inc.'s cash had grown from $496,435 to $1,330,690. In his article, Bourke wrote that, 'the most lucrative sector of commercial micropublishing will continue to be current newspapers, serials and patents'. By 1989 we were beginning to publish British daily newspapers on CD-ROM, and in the same year we invested $400,000 for a forty-nine per cent stake in MicroPatent, a US start-up that published patent information on CD-ROM (see Chapters 15 and 16).

15

The Silver Catalyst

It was in 1980 that we had begun to use computers to compile the *Catalogue of British Official Publications Not Published by HMSO* (see Chapter 5). But by then I had become interested in videodisks. They were electronic but were not digital; the information stored on them in tiny pits on a 12-inch plastic disk was analogue so could not be searched in the way that digital data could. Images stored on videodisks were displayed on TV screens and the number of lines on the screen defined the resolution of the image. They had been adopted by publishers of teaching materials in medicine and in the military, and we embarked on the publication of our only videodisk in 1985 in partnership with Graves Educational Resources in Chelmsford, Essex, who were collecting images to illustrate *The UK National Medical Slide Bank*. It contained almost 13,000 images, the visual manifestations of more diseases than any layman could possibly imagine, and we eventually published it in 1990. It sold for £950 and was not a success because we had no real understanding of the international market for medical publications; it did not fit in with the culture of the company, and we were now in the digital age.

In January 1983 Bill Buchanan (see Chapter 5) and I were both 'vendors' at the ALA Midwinter conference and exhibition in San Antonio, Texas. A 12-inch optical disk player displayed on the Carrollton Press booth contained the Library of Congress shelf list, which he was using for his REMARC retrospective conversion service (see Chapter 16). He pointed to a much smaller machine from which he ejected a disk the size of a music CD. 'This is a CD-ROM,' he said. 'It is like a music CD but it carries text which you can read on the screen of your PC.' Denon, a Japanese manufacturer, had developed the CD-ROM in 1982 but it was not publicly launched by Denon and Sony until 1984. 'ROM' stood for 'Read Only Memory' because one of the advantages of the CD-ROM for publishers was that, unlike the floppy disk, the information embedded on the disk could not be changed, added to or deleted by the user. The CD-ROM was immediately attractive to me as a carrier of huge amounts of digital text – 150,000 pages on a single disk. The market for music CDs, which was still quite new, was growing fast so I could see that it would be possible to make copies of CD-ROMs at a low unit cost. CD-ROM players or drives would also be competitively priced because CD players were already being sold to consumers.

We had been in the microform ghetto for a long time and I now saw the CD-ROM as the way out. So did Moss, who was now our most senior manager and who for some time had found microfilm to be quite limiting as a publishing medium. But ghettos offer security and I was in no hurry to leave for life outside without careful preparation. There was no point in trying to publish on CD-ROM until libraries had CD-ROM readers or drives, an adoption which could take several years. There was also no standard until 1985 when the 'High Sierra Standard' for the formatting of CD-ROMs was established, named after a meeting of twelve computer hardware companies in the High Sierra hotel and casino near Lake Tahoe, Nevada, which later became the internationally recognized ISO 9660.

Cartographic publications

Since we had an international sales team capable of selling to libraries throughout the world and a company in the USA with its own sales team, we started by offering to market the CD-ROMs of other publishers rather than developing our own. The first CD-ROMs for which we were exclusive distributors contained maps rather than text or images. In November 1986, on my annual sales visit to Australia, I spent a day at the Baillieu Library at the University of Melbourne. This was always the most important day of my three-week trip because the University of Melbourne was one of our best customers in the world. I was spending the day with Juliet Flesch, the formidable collection development librarian. Flesch and the University Librarian, Denis Richardson, were on a mission to make the Baillieu Library the pre-eminent research library in Australia and to put it ahead of the more established Fisher Library at the University of Sydney. They were building up their research resources in the humanities and social sciences by buying the large microform collections that were being published by us, Research Publications, Harvester Press and others. They had bought all the publishers' archives and the *Nineteenth-Century Parliamentary Papers* and were the only library outside the USA to buy a significant quantity of Sanborn Maps. Flesch was not only knowledgeable but was rigorous in what she bought, and I knew that I would be closely cross examined in what we had to offer, while she would always explain why she had decided not to buy a particular collection. We talked formally in the morning, mainly about buying *The Nineteenth Century* (see Chapter 7), and continued to discuss how it could be paid for over lunch with Richardson, John Poynter, the deputy vice-chancellor, and Roderick Home, the chairman of the Arts Faculty. After lunch Flesch took me to a room in the library where on a PC was displayed an outline map showing areas blocked in different colours. She explained that I was looking at the population density of districts of Melbourne and that the colours represented numerical values. It is difficult now to understand what a revelation it was to see colour images like this on a computer screen. In an era when computer screens mainly displayed lines of text, white on black, or black on white, here, on a CD-ROM, was a map in colour showing census areas, with a key showing what values the colours represented. (These are called chloropleth maps.)

This took us into an entirely new realm of CD-ROM publishing, and before I left Melbourne I met the inventor Jack Massey who was setting up a new company, Space Time Research (STR), to develop and sell products that used his 'Supermap' software. Massey was a cheerful Australian who was a senior lecturer in geography at the University of Melbourne and also a superb software engineer. He believed that his software was world beating and that he was going to make his fortune. He was also working on a Supermap version of the 1980 US Census and I told him that we wanted to market it for him in the USA as well as elsewhere in the world. This was the beginning of a long negotiation and a difficult relationship, which went on for more than seven years.

My belief in Supermap was shared by others. In 1986 Massey set up his company with A$130,000 funding from the Department of Industry, Technology and Commerce and A$675,000 from Hambro Grantham, an investment bank in Sydney, for thirty per cent of the equity, valuing STR at A$2,250,000,[1] with an ex-government minister, John Miller, as chairman. Massey was visionary, excitable and impetuous, but had an experienced business manager, Ted Hayes, an Englishman originally from Cambridge, to keep him in check. Massey came to London in July 1987 to give demonstrations of his software at Australia House and sent me a discussion document on establishing a commercial relationship between STR and Chadwyck-Healey, in which he suggested that for the Supermap 1980 US Census in the first year we would buy 15,000 units at $500 each ($7.5 million) and sell them for $900 bringing in revenue for us of $13.5 million. In March 1987 Massey, his chairman and his backers thought that they could sell A$9 million of their first product, the 1981 Australian Census on CD-ROM. Neither Severtson nor I thought that this was realistic, but we did think that Supermap could be enormously successful in the USA. I wrote in a memo, 'this could be a tremendously important product for us even though I don't pretend to understand the market for this type of material', and, 'It could all be a waste of time or be the most important new activity for the CH group.'[2] We arrived at an estimate of sales of 450 units in the first year bringing in revenue of around $500,000. In August 1987, while the agreement was still being negotiated, Severtson produced a sales brochure and mailed 40,000 copies before we had even seen the product, which did not arrive until October. To prepare for a product that we had not yet seen Severtson bought two PCs for the sales people, with CD-ROM drives, colour monitors and 40MB hard disks. Our confidence in its likely success was increased by the range of options we could offer. We could sell the census for the whole of the USA at the most detailed level, with time series going back to 1960, for less than $2,000, or sell it at county level for only $990. Customers could also buy one of the three regions offered. When the product arrived, it worked exactly as it was supposed to, and we had very few complaints. But that may have been because we made very few sales. We hired an expensive specialist salesman based on the West Coast who went to businesses and colleges demonstrating Supermap, but he was unsuccessful and soon left. Even though it was described in one review as, 'the best census and mapping system employing CD-ROM technology',[3] we were learning the most fundamental marketing lesson, that the US market, huge though it is, is one of the most inexorable. Americans are pragmatic and surprisingly conservative. If they cannot see an immediate use for something, they don't buy it. Only relatively few potential customers had PCs with colour screens and EGA cards and they did not seem to have a need to display the data of the last US Census in graphic form – by 1988 serious demographers were already waiting for the 1990 US Census.

We did not sign a marketing agreement until January 1988, long after our marketing effort had started. It required us to sell 100 units by the end of March and 3,500 units by the end of 1990, neither of which we achieved.

At first Massey blamed us, which was understandable – the salesman always gets blamed when there are no sales. But gradually he realized that Supermap was not going to be a runaway success and that the contract work STR was doing for the Australian Bureau of Statistics and Statistics New Zealand, who both wanted Supermap versions of their censuses, was going to be essential to their survival.

We did have one unexpected enquiry – from the CIA,[4] who wanted to use Supermap to produce chloroplethed maps of social, economic and political attributes of thirty-one Mexican states and the Federal District. We passed it back to STR.

At the same time as Supermap was being launched in the USA, we were approached by a Cambridge software engineer, Dr John Murray, who was producing *Mundocart*, a digital map of the world on one CD-ROM. Murray, who worked for Petroconsultants, a Geneva-based oil and gas exploration company with an office in Cambridge, had developed a digital map of the world for use by oil companies. It had originally been designed to be used on mainframe computers and the cost to oil companies was over £30,000. Murray thought he could sell a CD-ROM version for £10,000 without affecting mainframe sales and approached us to sell it to libraries. I persuaded him that we should sell it for not more than £5,000 and that this would still not eat into his other sales. We signed a distribution agreement in December 1988 by which we received a fifty per cent sales commission, and hired Paul Holroyd, a digital mapping specialist, to sell *Mundocart* on CD-ROM to commercial and research organizations. Clarinet software was used for the *Mundocart* CD-ROM and predictably it was the Clarinet Systems founder, Stephen Scholefield, who wrote, 'commercially, the most successful CD-ROM mapping application to date is the *Mundocart*'.[5]

Murray also wrote to Steve Jobs, the founder of Apple, who had just launched the revolutionary NeXt personal computer, and in April 1989 he and Severtson visited the NeXt office in Palo Alto, California. Eventually an agreement was made between Petroconsultants and NeXt, and *Mundocart* was listed as one of the NeXt databases. For us *Mundocart* sold steadily but not spectacularly; unlike Supermap products we had no great expectations for it and used it primarily to familiarize ourselves with the selling of an electronic medium that was a great deal more sophisticated than any microform or book. Enquiries came from organizations ranging from *Reader's Digest* to the Swedish Land Survey, but by early 1992 we had only sold thirty-two copies at varying prices, generating £156,800 of revenue, of which half went to Petroconsultants, so it did little more than give us some experience in selling cartographic CD-ROMs.

By this time Holroyd was working with STR to produce the 1981 and 1991 UK censuses on CD-ROM. In spite of the disappointment of the US Census, we had started negotiations with Massey to produce a Supermap version of the 1981 UK Census. We were now becoming STR's partner and one of their main sources of finance. The rest of their business came from producing CD-ROM versions for national census agencies. By early 1991 we had already paid STR advances of £20,000 and were negotiating with the Office of Population Censuses and Surveys (OPCS) and the General Register Office in Scotland to license their 1981 census data, and we licensed Boundary Map Files from Ordnance Survey. The licences were in our name and this made it Chadwyck-Healey's first CD-ROM publication, with STR acting as the production house. On three CD-ROMs with software that ran under Microsoft Windows 3.0 it sold for £1,750. We also produced a schools version on one CD-ROM for £195. There were 750 schools in the UK with CD-ROM drives, but we knew there would be three times as many within a few years (see Newspapers on CD-ROM below). Both versions sold well, and the reviewer in the *Times Educational Supplement* wrote:

> Having worked with this data for over a month or so, it is no exaggeration to say that it is the most exciting and stimulating disk technology I have used. The reason for the hyperbole is simple: the data is rich ... and the software *Supermap* is effective.[6]

Encouraged by this we went ahead with the production of the 1991 UK Census on CD-ROM. The functionality of the Supermap software was constantly improving and the 1991 Census was a much more sophisticated product than its predecessor. It was published in December 1993 on eight CD-ROMs with a price for higher-education institutions and public libraries of £2,500. There was a Local Government version, which allowed consolidation of data at county and regional level, and a Health Service version in which data could be aggregated with health authority districts and regions, and health boards. There was also a schools edition.

Working with Massey was never easy; he constantly changed his mind and we were always having to ward off his demands for more money, but he and his software team were extraordinarily able. At a time when

CD-ROMs, PCs and the software that ran on them were still in their infancy, to create a CD-ROM product as complex as a national census, with data being supplied by several government agencies, and with the work being done by two companies on opposite sides of the world, was a remarkable achievement.

The census sold well, in hundreds of copies, but this was the last STR product that we published. Our final cartographic publication was the *World Climate Disc*, in which climatic data from the Climate Research Unit at the University of East Anglia from 7,000 stations throughout the world could be mapped or displayed in the form of tables or graphs. At £595 this also sold well, with a separate version for schools.

British Library catalogue

In 1988 we were able to announce exclusive worldwide distribution of the CD-ROM edition of one of the world's most important library catalogues, the British Library General Catalogue of Printed Books to 1975. Some months earlier we had been visited by Conrad Lealand, a genial New Zealander who was chief executive of Saztec Europe Ltd. Saztec was a data conversion or keying company that converted texts into machine-readable form by keying them manually, usually in Asia where labour rates were low. Most of their customers were commercial companies including newspaper publishers but, increasingly, libraries were using keying companies to convert their card catalogues into digital form. The British Library was converting their catalogue known as GK III, with supplements. This was a catalogue of books that had been published before 1971 and had been catalogued before the end of 1982, together with books published in 1971–5 that had also been catalogued before a cut-off date.[7] In 1986 Saztec had won the bid for what was a very difficult project. There was also its sheer size – over 5.5 million entries in 360 volumes, estimated to total over two billion keystrokes, with many in the Cyrillic, Hebrew and Greek alphabets. So that British Library staff could keep closely in touch, Saztec set up a new plant in Ardrossan in south-west Scotland and trained staff for this one project. As part of the $3.5 million deal, the British Library had granted Saztec exclusive rights to produce and sell a CD-ROM version of the catalogue, and now they needed a distributor to sell the CD-ROM edition to libraries throughout the world.

Lealand had already visited and had been impressed by OUP. Hall and I realized that this was our only chance to convince him that we were the right partner. Hall explained that we went to libraries all over the world in contrast to a publisher like OUP who did not generally visit libraries, as their books were sold through library suppliers. Lealand then told us that OUP had suggested that the selling price of the catalogue on CD-ROM should be around £300. This was our opportunity. Only the year before, the publisher Clive Bingley and the German publisher K. G. Saur had completed the publication of a 360-volume printed edition of the British Library General Catalogue, which they were selling successfully for £18,000 a copy. We recommended a selling price of £10,000 for an edition that would dramatically undercut the printed edition and would be far more valuable. Hall assured him that we would sell almost as many copies at £10,000 as at £300. This was a high price for a bibliographic CD-ROM set and I could see Lealand struggling to adjust to this new proposal, mentally calculating the revenue Saztec could expect and savouring the thought of a revenue far higher than he had ever envisaged. After we agreed the terms of an exclusive worldwide sales agreement, Saztec announced that, 'They were chosen principally because they were right in the market place and have unrivalled experience in selling high-value one-time items to the major academic and institutional libraries of the world.'[8]

Saztec paid us a commission of twenty-five per cent on the first £4 million of sales and thirty per cent above, and we worked closely with them in preparing the CD-ROM edition for sale. We helped to write the manual and design the packaging, and we did extensive testing of the software and the CD-ROMs. Online Computer Systems, a US company that specialized in bibliographic software, had been chosen by Saztec to provide the software and create the master CD-ROMs from which copies would be made. Initially there were serious problems with the slowness of searches. Searching for titles between, say, 1900 and 1920 could take as long as thirty minutes, but Online was able to reduce this to one and a half minutes. A Boolean search combining a date range such as '1900–1960' and 'Cambridge' could take six minutes, and a search for a prolific author like Dickens twelve seconds. But eventually, following several redesigns by Online, response times were just about acceptable, and the first disk was issued in November 1989 and the last in 1991.

We began to receive orders as soon as the project was announced. I was surprised by the number of orders received from public libraries in the

UK, particularly from Scotland. Every head librarian had been taught at library school that the British Museum catalogue, now called the British Library catalogue, was the finest in the world and I wondered if they were buying it as much as a talisman as for its value to their library. I was told of at least one instance where the catalogue was a very expensive desk ornament as it sat in its box in the chief librarian's office. The importance of a fully searchable catalogue to one of the most important book collections in the world was immediately recognized. There was a review article in the *TLS* by Eric Korn, described variously as polymath, bookseller and brain-box, who had spent 'a delightful day toying, by courtesy of Chadwyck-Healey – notably tolerant hosts – with their *BLC on CD-Rom:* the universe in the palm of your hand'.[9] He gave it a favourable review and pointed out that the catalogue also enabled readers to identify the erotic books in the British Library designated as the Private Case, which until now had been scattered throughout the catalogue but could now be brought together by inputting the letters 'PC'. There was also a book that I wanted to find. *The Secrets of Potsdam* had been in the library (which consisted of three shelves) of the small boarding school that I had been sent to in 1948, and it had stayed in my mind for almost forty years as I had wondered what those secrets were. As so few libraries had title catalogues, I had never been able to find it and thought that it might just have been a figment of a schoolboy's imagination. Now I could search for it and there it was, a First World War anti-German propaganda book, laying bare the secrets of the Kaiser and his family.[10] The transformation of this body of data from the rigidity of print, where the only entry point was usually the author's name, to the freedom of being able to search for every book by its author, title, date, publisher or place of publication, or even any word in the catalogue record, including the class mark, was so profound that it took us all time to understand the potential of what was stored on those three CD-ROMs. I demonstrated the British Library catalogue on CD-ROM on Yushodo's stand at a Japanese library conference, but this was the only CD-ROM publication Yushodo made any real attempt to sell. Nitta was not interested in electronic publishing and we soon found that we were selling our CD-ROMs to the other library suppliers, Kinokuniya and Maruzen.

In January 1992 Lealand and I were standing in a breakfast line at another ALA Midwinter conference in San Antonio, chatting to a young woman who ran one of the US library cataloguing networks. We proudly told her that we had just published the British Library catalogue on

CD-ROM. Her polite but uncomprehending response made me realize that there was a new generation of librarians to whom the British Library catalogue meant little. Digitization was democratizing the library catalogue. No longer were the catalogues of the great libraries the dominant resources; far more potent were the union catalogues, the merged catalogues of many libraries that had been pioneered by OCLC, an opportunity that the Library of Congress had missed. The constantly growing catalogue of OCLC was now dominant and when a few years later national libraries such as the British Library and the BnF allowed their catalogues to be included in OCLC, the transformation was complete. No longer was it possible to charge for access to the catalogues of most libraries. The British Library catalogue was the only major catalogue on CD-ROM sold at a high price. The Bodleian Library pre-1920 catalogue was also published on CD-ROM at the end of 1993 by OUP, but the price was only a few hundred pounds and I was told that they did not sell many copies.

Newspapers on CD-ROM

We knew that eventually we would have to have our own production expertise. But writing software and managing digital data are far more demanding than filming books and documents. There was also a difference in expectations. From the beginning, users of computers expected them to work seamlessly – even though, frequently, they did not. Users of microforms had much lower expectations of the medium, and the occasional underexposed or out-of-focus page was tolerated. We approached the hiring of programmers cautiously because they would be doing work that the rest of us could not understand, and we had heard stories of how difficult it was to communicate with them. When hiring her team of developers, Moss decided not to hire any programmer who could not explain to us in plain English what they were doing. Our first in-house-produced CD-ROM publication was *UKOP*, which combined HMSO's own catalogue of British official publications with our *Catalogue of British Official Publications Not Published by HMSO*, described in Chapter 5.

Samuel 'Sam' Freedman, the founder of Research Publications, had started to microfilm newspapers in the 1940s (see Appendix 1), and microfilm publishing rights for all the British national dailies had been granted to our American competitors long before we started in 1973. Now there was an opportunity to publish newspapers on CD-ROM, and in 1989 I wrote to all the national dailies in the UK to ask for the rights to publish a CD-ROM edition from their digital tapes. The Guardian was the first to respond and they agreed to let us publish an exclusive CD-ROM edition of the *Guardian* and their Sunday newspaper, the *Observer*.

News International invited me to the launch of their CD-ROM edition of *The Times* and there I discovered that the market they were aiming for was UK schools. As publishers of the *Times Educational Supplement* they knew that the Department of Education was giving PCs and CD-ROM drives to every school in the country and that there was an urgent need for content for this new hardware. We quickly set a schools' price for the *Guardian* on CD-ROM of £195 (or £275 for the first two years), while the price for academic and public libraries, which had started at £1,925 for 1990 and 1991 together, was reduced to £545. By March 1991 we had seventy-six orders totalling £41,000. Later we offered CD-ROM editions of the *Telegraph*, the *Independent* and the *Daily Mail*, and in March 1991 we became one of three authorized distributors of *The Times* on CD-ROM, concentrating on the library markets in the UK and Eire but also including schools. Our advantage over the other distributors was that we could offer libraries and schools discounted packages of several newspapers on CD-ROM.

When we had first launched the *Guardian* on CD-ROM we expected to get good publicity for the first UK national to be available in this exciting new format. We were therefore dismayed by an article in the *Guardian* in February 1991 on the subject of 'how the educational message of CD-ROM is getting across', which mentioned that 'most of the broadsheet newspapers are making a year's issues available on one CD-ROM' but had only one passing mention of the *Guardian* in its new format.[11] We asked Gerald Knight, our contact at the Guardian, why the newspaper had given no publicity to its new product and were told that their contributors would never be allowed to promote the Guardian's commercial activities.

In 1991 we were also beginning to sell patent information on CD-ROM published by MicroPatent, a US publisher that we partly owned and for which we had exclusive sales rights outside the Americas (see Chapter 16). We were now selling to business libraries all over the UK and Europe and we wanted to also sell them the *Financial Times* on CD-ROM. We eventually signed a marketing and distribution agreement with FT Information Online Ltd in June 1991 for both the *Financial Times* and *The Economist* on

CD-ROM, both of which sold well until the end of the decade. We had worldwide rights except for the USA and Canada and paid royalties of fifty-five per cent of new sales and sixty-five per cent of existing subscriptions to the publisher. In 1997, as part of a larger deal (see Chapter 23), we were granted exclusive rights to both produce and sell *The Times* and *Sunday Times* on CD-ROM, but by then we were near the end of the CD-ROM era.

We had not taken a conventional route into CD-ROM publishing. Most publishers in our sector started with bibliographic databases, and the companies that came to dominate the library market, SilverPlatter and Ovid, only published bibliographic CD-ROMs. In contrast, we had started with cartographic CD-ROMs, which required entirely different, more complex software, and while *UKOP* was bibliographic we were now publishing on CD-ROM the digital files of a daily newspaper, which proved to be more difficult to make into a usable digital publication than we expected. The data the Guardian sent us was full of glitches and omissions, which had to be cleaned up. Unlike a bibliographic database where a single name can be a search term, in a newspaper, a search on a single word will not be selective enough to find the relevant article. We

Figure 10 London. Duncan Christelow demonstrates the *Guardian* on CD-ROM at its launch at the Online Conference, December 1990.

had to use proximity searching, which recognized the significance of the position of words in relation to each other to enable the most relevant article to be found. 'New England' and 'John Major' were examples of names that could only be isolated through the proximity of the relevant words. In order to achieve acceptable search times, we had to build indexes, which were not normally necessary for bibliographic CD-ROMs with their short fixed-length fields. To do this we licensed Clearview software tools from Clarinet Systems. We included an image of the front page of each issue, which was surprisingly readable on small computer screens, and created links between the front page and the relevant ASCII text.[12]

In December 1990 the *Guardian*, *The Times* and the *Independent* CD-ROMs were all on show for the first time at the annual Online Conference in London. Hall reported that *The Times* was easy to use but only allowed very simple searches, though we were told that other searches would be added. The *Independent* required a familiarity with Windows, which in 1990 was far from universal. It was the most sophisticated interface but also the most difficult to use. Hall thought that, to compete, we should add relevancy searching so that searches were ranked according to the number of times a keyword appeared in an article and that we should add the ability to 'cut and paste'. A review in late 1991 by a senior consultant at ASLIB confirmed Hall's analysis and described the *Guardian*'s search system as occupying the middle ground.[13] Advice that 'A mouse attachment is useful but not essential' is a reminder that software was at an awkward cross-over from keyboard-operated MS-DOS to mouse-operated Windows 3.0, which had been launched in May 1990. It would be several more years before DOS was entirely superseded.

By 1999 we had 4,000 subscriptions to British newspapers on CD-ROM with an annual revenue of around £2.1 million. We also began to acquire online rights, the first being the *Guardian* and the *Observer*.

By 1989 we were not only selling CD-ROM publications but had become a fully-fledged electronic publisher. In 1989 I had invested in two new companies in the USA, MicroPatent, which sold patent information on CD-ROM, mentioned above, and ERIC, which was a database of historical land-use in the USA, both described in the next chapter. For the first half of the 1990s patent information on CD-ROM became one of our most profitable new areas of publishing. Chapter 17 describes the start of our move into full-text publishing on CD-ROM, which was even more fundamental to the future of the companies.

16

Other Digital Ventures

In 1981 we embarked on the first of four digital ventures in the UK, USA and France that consumed considerable time and investment yet stood outside our mainstream publishing activities. Two were failures and two were successes.

REMARC

At a conference in the USA in 1981 there was an entirely new product on the Carrollton Press booth called REMARC. It was so far outside my understanding that several times I had to ask Buchanan to explain it to me. He was converting into digital form by manual keying the shelf list of the Library of Congress, the five million catalogue cards that represented the books and journals on the shelves of this great library. He was converting it, not only to sell it as a database to libraries, but as an aid to 'retrospective conversion'. Every library that wanted to computerize its catalogue was faced with the expense of having to convert all its existing records, which were either on catalogue cards or in guard-books, into machine-readable form. A format called MARC (MAchine-Readable Cataloging) had been developed by Henriette Avram at the Library of Congress in the 1960s, and the library had been cataloguing books and journals in computerized form to this standard since 1971. Libraries had many of the same books and journals, so there was an enormous redundancy in each library carrying out the retrospective conversion of its own catalogue records. It also meant that the inevitable errors and omissions in their records would be carried over into their machine-readable copies. REMARC enabled libraries to match their records of publications before 1971 to the Library of Congress catalogue and to replace them with machine-readable records of the highest quality.

To do so, the customer had to key in the first twenty-nine characters of the record into either its own computer system or on to an Apple IIe personal computer. The twenty-nine-character keys were copied on to diskettes and mailed to REMARC. Matches were either made to REMARC records or to (post-1970) MARC records. Carrollton Press charged the library for the number of catalogue records it downloaded from REMARC at £0.30 per record and for MARC records £0.12 each. If a library had 500,000 books and REMARC matching achieved an eighty per cent hit rate this would generate £120,000 for Carrollton Press.

I had very little understanding of the world of library automation, still in its infancy, or the conversion of existing library catalogues, but it sounded exciting and in late 1981 I suggested to Buchanan that we should be the exclusive sales agent for REMARC in the UK and Europe. Buchanan agreed, with one important condition: that we employed as a consultant Richard Coward, the retired director of bibliographic services at the British Library. Coward, who had also been a director of planning and development at OCLC, was now spending much of his time with his wife at their house on the Greek island of Paxos, but he was intrigued and agreed to help us by using his authority and specialist knowledge to promote REMARC to libraries in the UK and Europe. We paid him $200 a day plus expenses for thirty days of work a year.

Before we signed the agreement with Carrollton in April 1982, Coward and I had already visited the National Library of Wales in Aberystwyth and the Deutsche Bibliothek in Bonn, and attended a seminar held by SCOLCAP, a cataloguing network of Scottish and northern university libraries. I also hired John Ferguson, who travelled for us throughout Europe and the UK for the next few years, selling both REMARC and our own publications.

By the end of the year we were in advanced discussions with Brenda Moon, the diminutive but formidable Librarian of Edinburgh University, for a five-year retrospective conversion project using REMARC. They expected to input one million REMARC search keys and achieve a sixty per cent hit rate and 500,000 MARC search keys and achieve an eighty per cent hit rate. At 1983 prices this would cost them £246,000. We would earn from this £50,000 but the up-front payment based on an estimate of the hit rate would be small, and the bulk of the payment would only come in as the 'hits' were delivered, which would mean that payments would trickle in over five years.

In February 1983 I visited Fred Ratcliffe who had come from Manchester to be the Cambridge University Librarian. Cambridge were considering how they might automate their catalogue, either by buying a system from one of the library automation suppliers or creating their own bespoke system. The library was our 'local', but it was the first time that I had met Ratcliffe. He and Reg Carr, his deputy who later became the first director of the Oxford University libraries, agreed to see me but then spelled out all the reasons why they would not use REMARC. I wrote in my sales report, 'faced with such a barrage of half-truths, misconceptions and generalisations it was difficult to give succinct answers and keep my temper'. Ratcliffe commented as I left, 'We aren't against REMARC. If we ever joined such a network [i.e. London, Edinburgh etc] it would be with outside money and then we would be glad to use REMARC because we would not be paying for it!'

Roy Welbourn, the Cambridge chief cataloguer, told me that Douglas Foskett, Librarian of the University of London, was trying to organize a consortium of the largest libraries with a source of outside finance simply referred to as 'the Foundation'. Derek Law, who was our main contact for the conversion scheme at Edinburgh University Library, told us that this new organization of major libraries was called CURL (Consortium of University Research Libraries) and that it was going to be based at Leeds but that it was too early to discuss REMARC with them. Coward then told me that it was intended to be a 'mini-RLG' and that the 'secret funders' were the Mellon and Wolfson foundations. (RLG, Research Libraries Group, was an established association of the largest research libraries in the USA.) He pointed out that, unfortunately, the gatekeeper to these sources of funds was Sir Fred Dainton, chairman of the British Library Board, who would not endorse any plans that diminished the dominance of the British Library. After our inauspicious start, Ratcliffe and I became friends and I often went to him for advice on library matters.

We regarded the University of Edinburgh as our 'shop window' for REMARC. Susan Severtson, who at the time was working for Carrollton, came over in April 1983 to instruct the library on how to plan for the making of the search keys, and Edinburgh was soon producing these at a rate of 10,000 a week. She also gave a talk to twelve institutions at a seminar at Manchester Polytechnic, and she and Ferguson went to France and Switzerland to talk to libraries there. In August we were at the IFLA annual conference in Munich, where we took a suite in a hotel. Coward, Ferguson and I were all there, together with Buchanan, and we made some useful contacts.

The time that I spent visiting libraries in 1982 and 1983 on behalf of REMARC was excessive. It is difficult to understand why I did not spend the same amount of time and effort trying to sell our own publications to libraries in the UK, rather than relying almost entirely on direct mail. On each visit I did try to discuss our publications with the acquisition librarians, but the main focus was on REMARC. Yet discussions that stretched over years with early contacts like the University of Southampton did not result in a sale. Ferguson and I had many meetings with the departmental libraries at Oxford University, which at that time operated independently of the Bodleian Library (see Chapter 17), but they could never make a decision. The BnF, again through Madame Roncato (see Chapter 11), wanted to buy all French records from 1850 to 1950 but never did, and the Deutsche Bibliothek was interested but was relying on receiving at least 600,000 Deutschmarks from German publishers who then refused to pay up.

Figure 11 Munich, IFLA conference. Left to right: John Ferguson, Bill Buchanan and Richard Coward relaxing in a beer garden. August 1983.

By late 1983 Edinburgh was receiving its first tapes while the University of St Andrews had also signed up and had sent its first diskette to Berkeley. In June 1984 the National Library of Wales, whom we had first visited in April 1982, wanted to immediately negotiate an agreement with REMARC – they had £100,000 to spend by March 1985. We charged them £0.45 a record, a fifty per cent increase since 1982, and £1.15 per thousand characters for inputting search keys. But now we were hearing that libraries were choosing OCLC rather than REMARC as their source of records.

The new libraries that were using REMARC to convert their catalogues were the National Library of Wales, National Library of Singapore, University of Kent Library and the US Army in Europe. Despite Ferguson's many visits to European libraries, not a single one bought REMARC. Including the university libraries of Edinburgh and St Andrews we had only six customers, and by the end of 1984 I must have realized that REMARC was not going to succeed. Although Carrollton had made some notable sales, such as the University of California system, it had the same problems in the USA – lack of money, low hit rates, technical problems, competition from OCLC, and general inertia as libraries began to grapple with the cost and complexity of buying their first automation system and of converting their catalogues into machine-readable form. Yet, in January 1985 I described the Library Association's Retrospective Catalogue Conversion Conference in London as, 'one of the best conferences I have been to for a long time'. Derek Law, now Librarian of King's College, London, spoke positively about REMARC, comparing it favourably to OCLC and pointing out that the records were cheap. He said that REMARC was simple, fast and inexpensive but required more expert editing of the records than was desirable. The turn-round time for the records to be delivered was also too long. OCLC, on the other hand, was liked by staff because the records themselves could be seen immediately and they were achieving an extraordinarily high hit rate of ninety per cent plus. Law suggested that libraries should start with REMARC and then go to OCLC and other sources for the records not in REMARC.

The International Thomson Organisation had been the investor in REMARC and there was an irony for me in working for a company so closely allied to our rival, Research Publications. In December 1984 Thomson had bought UTLAS Inc., the Canadian equivalent of OCLC, from the University of Toronto, and in July 1985 the REMARC database was merged into UTLAS. In April 1986 UTLAS offered us a continuation of our existing agreement and a new agreement for 1987 but there seemed little point in pursuing it further. The commissions from sales over four years cannot have been much over £100,000 and did not cover the time and expenses of Coward, Ferguson and myself. But I learned a lot from it and was able to get to know some of the chief librarians in the UK and Europe and begin to understand the politics of academic libraries in the 1980s.

REMARC was not only one of Buchanan's many innovative ideas but was also the result of the failure of the Library of Congress to enable libraries to carry out retrospective conversion through a RECON project that Avram had conceived at the end of the 1960s. Her RECON pilot project was never completed and the Library of Congress, in effect, allowed Buchanan to do the work that it should have done itself.

After REMARC Buchanan did some consultancy for Chadwyck-Healey Inc. Together with Severtson, we worked on another of his ideas, which he called 'IDIOM' (In-Depth Indexing of Monographs) in which we were going to create a database of indexes of books so that the user could search the indexes of thousands of books at one time. We went as far as producing a sales brochure and a list of the first 5,000 books whose indexes we were going to include but there was not enough interest to take it further. Buchanan also advised the Mellon Foundation on JSTOR (see Chapter 19). With a buccaneering approach that may have stemmed from his previous career in the CIA, he was one of the most engaging and imaginative publishers in our sector.

MultiLIS

After our REMARC experience we should have steered clear of library automation projects but in 1989 Goldman proposed that Chadwyck-Healey France should set up a new company to sell a French-Canadian automation system to libraries in France, Belgium and French-speaking Switzerland. MultiLIS was produced by Sobeco in Montreal and ran on UNIX-based computers, which included computers made by BULL, a manufacturer that was dominant in France. It also had the advantage that the MultiLIS manuals were in French. By 1990 our microfilm publishing in France was diminishing (see Chapter 11), and while our CD-ROM list was growing this was an opportunity for the French company to broaden its scope. I was preoccupied with the two new companies in the USA that I had just started, and I left Goldman and McCrae to set up the new business. I also thought that the company would only fail if it made no sales, in which case we could quickly close it down.

At the first meeting in Montreal in May 1990, in spite of the Sobeco directors seeming to dislike the English, an agreement was reached. At about this time the automation industry was going through a structural change. Up to then companies made most of their money from the comfortable margins they enjoyed on hardware – the reselling of expensive computer equipment – while they had much smaller margins on their own software, in which they were always having to invest to meet the expectations of their customers. Now there was a greater range of hardware available, prices were falling and so were margins. Companies could only make money by selling their own software. We were in the same position. Margins on hardware for the reseller were slim and we had to depend on the forty per cent commission we earned from selling the MultiLIS software, which could range in value from £50,000 for one library to £150,000 for a small network. We charged for writing software to adapt the system to the library's requirements, but sometimes this had to be done for free in order to secure a sale. We also charged for training, which we were required to provide.

Goldman set up a separate office in Paris and hired some experienced people to run it, and at the end of the next two years we had sold over forty systems to a mixture of university and public libraries, including the libraries of the European Union in Brussels, the OECD in Paris and the Court of Justice in Luxembourg. Special libraries ranged from INSEAD, the prestigious business school, to the library of the French corporate giant Air Liquide. We extended ourselves further by opening an office in Toulouse to sell systems to a group of ten public libraries in the south west of France that operated a network called NADAL. MultiLIS had been sold to many public library networks in Quebec and was designed to handle low phone-line transmission speeds, which made it particularly suitable for NADAL, the first public library network in France to operate in rural rather than urban areas. It was an important step in the development of MultiLIS, and Coutts bank lent Chadwyck-Healey Ltd £350,000 as working capital for the NADAL deal alone.

Sales grew fast but we were not making money and we began to realize that we were in a very exposed position. MultiLIS seemed unable or unwilling to re-engineer the parts of the software package that did not perform satisfactorily. We were so concerned that Goldman and I flew to Montreal in September 1992 to meet Jean-Louis Gauvin, the senior vice-president of Sobeco, and remind him that we were entirely dependent on them to make their system meet the requirements that we as their sales representatives had promised our customers. We proposed that either they should buy us or enter into a different, closer financial relationship with us. In response Sobeco agreed to pay 100,000 francs per month to cover the cost of two of their personnel to work with us in France and install software and new modules for our customers. Our concerns were underlined in January 1993 when Eric Gaskell, the head of the EU Library, told me that there was great dissatisfaction amongst MultiLIS users with the inadequacies of some aspects of the system.

In February I tried to sell the company to Jouve. In May Goldman left the company (see Chapter 11) and his departure created even more disquiet amongst customers, whose 'Club of Users' wrote to me immediately to state its hope that in view of the 'uncertain future' of the company their contracts would be honoured.[1] A month later Sobeco sent over a senior manager to run MultiLIS Europe, paying his salary and expenses. By then the cumulative losses of the company were 3,688,374 francs (around £370,000). In September our auditor BDA warned that we were no longer 'a going concern' and that under French law we had to either refinance the company or declare it insolvent. This had to be avoided as we would be in negotiations with the French state for years and it would also be the end for the main shareholder, Chadwyck-Healey France, whose own finances were almost as precarious. We urgently needed Sobeco to take over the ailing company. Fortunately, in 1992 Sobeco, which was a management consultancy that had bought MultiLIS as a diversification, had merged with Ernst & Young, one of the 'big five' international accounting firms. Ernst & Young realized that their good name was going to be associated with the failure of our company and the impact it would have on clients as important as the EU and the OECD, and in late October Gauvin agreed to buy MultiLIS Europe for a nominal sum. The sale was completed on 28 November 1993. Both Sobeco and Chadwyck-Healey had to write off the large sums that the company owed them.

Before joining Chadwyck-Healey France as PDG in September 1993, Sakoun had been a senior manager at GEAC, another Canadian-based library automation company, considerably larger than MultiLIS. I asked him why we had been so unsuccessful. He replied that it was simple: we had taken on the customers that our competitors would not touch because they were so demanding and so slow to pay. That may have been the case with the public library network, but it was also the inability of MultiLIS to deliver a product that worked that contributed to our failure. Sobeco had bought MultiLIS from the University of Quebec because, as reported by McCrae, 'it seemed a good idea at the time',[2] which was very much our reason for taking on the sales agency. With more research we would have found that most library automation businesses were financially precarious and few survived for more than a few years without being sold or refinanced, and that alone should have made us much more cautious.

MicroPatent

In 1989 Peter Tracy, the owner of a small microform publishing company, Opus Publications, approached Severtson as he was looking for investors for a new company that would publish US patent information on CD-ROM. I was immediately interested because I wanted to expand the scope of our CD-ROM publishing beyond the humanities and social sciences. I also liked his plan to offer to subscribers a monthly CD-ROM with data on the latest US patents for less than $1,000 a year. It meant that he recognized what most other publishers had not yet understood, that CD-ROMs were remarkably inexpensive to produce. I agreed to invest $400,000 in return for a forty-nine per cent share in MicroPatent, and we established a partnership in September 1989. I wanted Severtson and Bob Asleson, who was working with us as a consultant, to oversee our investment since I was so involved with other projects and companies, and I made them partners. Asleson had been president of University Microfilms in 1967 before I had even started to publish reprints, and I thought that he would be able to help Tracy build his business. But the closest working relationship that Tracy had with any of his partners was with me.

Tracy took office space in a business park in New Haven, Connecticut, the home of Yale University, but a city that has always struggled with its social and economic problems. The business park was in old industrial buildings, and as an early tenant we paid a very low rent. He bought patent information from the US Patent Office (USPTO) and, using Jouve software, produced the CD-ROMs in house with the distribution copies made elsewhere. While sales grew quickly, we found that many of the engineers and researchers that we were trying to sell to did not have PCs and CD-ROM drives, so we sold those for the next two years. The first product, *Automated Patent Searching* (*APS*), a database of information about US patents without the text or the drawings of the patents themselves, became the market leader. It initially sold for $950 a year for twelve monthly disks, and backfiles to 1975 were also available. It was followed by *PatentImages*, which were scanned images of entire patents, text and drawings. The USPTO had scanned all their patents but a copy of the images on magnetic tape cost over $100,000. Tracy was able to borrow a copy from AT&T's Bell Laboratories, as there are no copying restrictions on US government publications, and gave them in return a set of CD-ROMs. All the CD-ROMs for this huge collection (mechanical and electrical patents alone, from 1976 to 1990, were on 780 disks), were produced in house. Chadwyck-Healey Ltd had exclusive sales rights and received a fifty per cent commission on all sales throughout the world outside the Americas of all MicroPatent products. There was a large market outside North America for MicroPatent's products and Hall hired an outstanding professional, Elizabeth Hearle, to develop it. MicroPatent's total sales revenue in the first eighteen months was $854,000. A year later (to 30 June 1992) it had grown to $1.7 million and the year after that to over $3 million. Of this more than fifty per cent were sales made by Chadwyck-Healey Ltd. We were also faced with competition from two formidable publishers, both owned by the Thomson Organisation, Derwent Publications and our old adversary Research Publications, who for many years had been publishing microfilm copies of US patents. In response to our initiative they also began to publish US patent information on CD-ROM.

MicroPatent was also an agent for the European Patent Office (EPO), which published titles on CD-ROM such as *European Patent Searching* (*EPS*) and *Espace*, which were European patent applications with drawings. We bought their CD-ROMs and resold them. The EPO and MicroPatent had exclusive use of Jouve specialist software, and this gave MicroPatent a significant advantage over competitors such as Research Publications. The EPO in Vienna and Munich was a highly political organization, and Tracy and I made regular visits to their offices to maintain good relationships with Gérard Giroud, principal director of patent information, and with his colleagues.

I had a difficult relationship with Tracy almost from the start. In 1991 we had a serious dispute over the interpretation of a badly drafted clause in the partnership agreement, which could have led to us losing our entire interest. We both hired lawyers to prepare for litigation but in March 1992, as the St Patrick's Day parades passed the hotel in New York in which he was staying, Tracy and I hand-wrote and signed a new agreement. One positive outcome was that Chadwyck-Healey Ltd's sales agreement was extended by another two years. The underlying difficulty in our relationship was that, to Tracy, 'Chadwyck-Healey' seemed to be the main beneficiary of MicroPatent's success. Chadwyck-Healey Ltd retained fifty per cent of the revenue of its sales, which were more than fifty per cent of MicroPatent's total sales, and we also owned forty per cent of the business.

When the sales agency ended in 1995, Tracy set up his own sales office in London and, with our agreement, Hearle moved there to run it for him. After 1995 I wanted Tracy to sell the company, as we were no longer receiving any revenue from it. Fortunately, there were two events that made a sale more likely. First, Tracy hired a financial controller who had previously worked for Mason Slaine, a well-known financier and investor in business information companies. We thought that information about MicroPatent was being fed back to Slaine, and I hoped it would increase the chances of a sale. Second, by 1997 the dotcom boom was under way and some of Tracy's software engineers and technical staff began to ask for more money. This concerned him, as did the realization that online delivery via the Internet was now making the future increasingly uncertain. He began discussions with Slaine who eventually offered us $7.9 million for the business, which we both accepted, and the sale was completed on 1 July 1997. After deductions including escrow Chadwyck-Healey received $2,355,771. It came at an opportune time as the Chadwyck-Healey group was experiencing a severe lack of cash (see Chapter 20).

We were also paid $323,000 for our share of a company called Neato, which Tracy had founded in 1996. MicroPatent made all the distribution copies for *PatentImages* in house. One of the most difficult parts of the process of making CD-ROMs is positioning the label in the centre of the disk – it cannot be done by eye. One of Tracy's staff designed a device consisting of a cylinder and a spring-loaded circular plate, which centered the adhesive label and then pressed it down on to the disk. Tracy patented the device, naming it 'Neato', and began to sell it. He generously gave his partners in MicroPatent their same interest in Neato. I had no wish to continue as a minority partner so was glad to sell out to him but a few years later Tracy sold the company very successfully to a large Chicago paper goods company.

ERIC

In the spring of 1989, the same year we started MultiLIS and MicroPatent, David Slutzky, a businessman from Chicago, called the office in Alexandria to buy a complete set of the Sanborn Maps (see Chapter 8). He explained to Severtson that his company provided reports on historical land use to clients concerned about pollution and that the Sanborn Maps were an outstanding record of the past uses of buildings and land that could have caused pollution.

In 1980 the Environmental Protection Agency (EPA) had been given draconian powers by Congress through the enactment of a federal law known as CERCLA[3] to compel landowners to clean up their land and, if they went bankrupt in the process, the banks or lenders who had financed them, and who now had title to the property, became liable for the costs of the clean-up, which could run to millions of dollars. Even without title they also found that the environmental clean-up lender's lien over the property took precedence over the bank's lien. In 1986 a new law, SARA,[4] was introduced, which established an 'innocent landowner defense' that eliminated liability, providing certain due diligence was performed before a piece of real estate was bought. This included the searching of government records and other historical sources for evidence of past activities that could have resulted in the pollution of the land. Companies sprang up that researched the records of the past such as the Sanborn Maps and the many state and federal databases in which chemical spills and other events were recorded. The document searches came first because they could quickly determine if there was any likelihood of pollution from previous activities, which would enable a buyer to decide if he wished to go any further or warn the seller that he needed to pay for an expensive environmental audit. Slutzky had set up Environmental Risk Consultants (ERC) to provide environmental audits in the Chicago area and had discovered the Sanborn Maps in the Chicago Public Library. He realized that they were the single most important record of historical land use in cities in the USA, and such was their detail that, on a large industrial site like a steel works, the maps showed individual buildings and recorded their use. This enabled his surveyors to know where to drill bore-holes.

He paid $150,000 for the Sanborn Maps on microfilm and, out of curiosity, in late June 1989 I visited him in Chicago on my way to the ALA Summer conference in Dallas. He was a small, excitable man, highly intelligent and full of energy and ideas, but from what he told me it seemed that the 'phase 1' document searches were potentially more profitable than the on-the-ground surveys by the expensive consultants that he had to employ, and I wondered if this was a new business we could diversify into using the Sanborn Maps together with digital media.

After further discussions, in December 1989 Slutzky and I set up a company called the Environmental Risk Information Center (ERIC). We planned to build a database from state and federal sources and use his set of the Sanborn Maps to make paper copies. For the 1990 US Census the Census Bureau had created a digital street map called the Tiger Files containing every addressable site in the USA. We bought a copy on computer tape for just under $10,000, and then bought all the federal and state databases, which we merged so that when a customer gave us the address of a site we could pinpoint the address and ask them if they wanted information on historical land use for the area within a one-, five- or ten-mile radius. Our first employee was an experienced ex-UMI sales executive, Peter Jamieson, who rented an office in Alexandria, Virginia, near Chadwyck-Healey Inc. so that Severtson could keep an eye on him. Building the database was done in Cambridge by John Murray who had brought us *Mundocart* (see Chapter 15). Neither Slutzky, Murray nor I were properly realistic about the technical difficulty of taking a very large mapping database containing millions of addresses, which had been produced by the US government for a particular purpose and had not been refined or debugged, and marrying it with many federal and state databases, which themselves contained millions of addresses formatted in different ways. In our office in Alexandria we installed the databases on several optical disk drives run by VAX workstations. We ran into plenty of unexpected problems, such as the drives overheating when the air conditioning was turned off in the evening.

I could see that the business had potential because of the growing recognition of the effect that the ownership of polluted land could have on a company's value. In June 1990 the share value of PPG Industries in Pittsburgh had fallen in two days from $49.25 to $3 on reports of the company's potential liability for the clean-up of chromium-tainted land in Jersey City.[5] We were also able to sell paper copies of the Sanborn Maps made from the set of microfilm that Slutzky had transferred to ERIC. In the fourth quarter of 1990, sales were $16,000 and in the first two months of 1991 $21,000, but we were still spending heavily on databases and data processing together with the usual overheads of sales and administration, and we had now invested over $500,000 in the company. I began to look for other investors, and through Sufrin discovered that Rubin, who was our lawyer but with whom I had not been in touch for some time, was looking for a historical land-use database company on behalf of a wealthy client, J. Bruce Llewellyn. A prominent investor, he had been the first black businessman to acquire a majority share in a Coca-Cola bottling plant (in Philadelphia). Just before Easter 1991 Rubin sent Alec 'Al' Berger, an entrepreneur who was highly experienced in building database companies, to visit us in Cambridge. He spent the morning telling me that database companies were very different from publishing companies and that most of what I was doing was wrong. In the afternoon he told Murray that if he didn't deliver the next version of the database on time, 'he would come over on Concorde with a baseball bat'. He was a huge man so there was real substance to his threat, but it made me realize that he must be interested in us. The following week Rubin offered to invest $1 million in ERIC in return for a fifty per cent interest for Llewellyn, and I persuaded Slutzky to reduce his interest to eight per cent since I had put up the money, done all the work and found the new investor. But Rubin had one condition – that the Sanborn Maps agreement, which I had written myself in 1982 (see Chapter 8), had to be renegotiated. He explained that it was our major asset but the agreement that I had written could be challenged and leave us tied up in court for years. For a few tense months I waited while Rubin negotiated with TRW REDI Property Data, jointly owned by Elsevier and by TRW, a large US manufacturer. In mid-August we finally signed both the new Sanborn Maps agreement and an agreement with Rubin and his client.

Berger came down to Alexandria to run the company but after only a few months he died suddenly while at home at the weekend. It was a tremendous shock and I was sad that this remarkable man would no longer be there for me, not only to work with but to learn from. I was also concerned about the future of ERIC without Berger. Who was going to lead it? Rubin shared this concern and felt a great personal responsibility for persuading his most important client to invest in this start-up company. At Berger's funeral a young man came up to Rubin and introduced himself as Dan Prickett. He talked about the business and some work that was due to be finished shortly. Rubin asked him how he knew. Prickett explained that Berger had wanted him to join ERIC. Both Rubin and I were impressed by Prickett, liked him and immediately appointed him as chief executive. He had extensive experience of database companies, having spent eight years building the NEXIS database for Mead Data Central. He once said to me, 'Al flunked charm school and I never went.' On the contrary, he was an outstanding people manager. Prickett only met Slutzky once. The three of us had dinner in Alexandria on the night that Clinton was inaugurated as president.[6] I was struck by the difference between them. Prickett was deeply suspicious of Clinton while Slutzky, a Democrat, was completely committed to the new president. By early 1993 Slutzky's business had got into financial difficulties and he sold me his eight per cent interest to raise money. His business closed soon after and, later, he made a new career for himself in Washington, at one time being a White House advisor on environmental issues.[7] I now had a fifty per cent interest in what was renamed ERIIS (Environmental Risk Information and Imaging Services).[8]

Under Rubin's watchful eye and with Prickett's effective management, ERIC grew quickly. In 1991, the year Rubin bought into the company, sales were only $247,000 with a loss of over $400,000, but in 1992 they grew to $1.35 million but still with a loss of $305,000. In 1993 with sales of $3 million we made a profit before tax of $188,000 and in 1994 sales of $4.75 million produced a profit of $1,168,000, a respectable 24.5 per cent of sales revenue. My role was that of a non-executive director, visiting Prickett whenever I was in Alexandria and having lunch with Rubin in New York, always in the Starlight restaurant above his office in the Rockefeller Center, a relic of the 1950s in both cuisine and décor. Soon after Prickett arrived he was able to replace the Tiger Files with a commercial database of all addressable sites in the USA, which was easier to use and more reliable, and the federal and state databases also became more consistent as more commercial entities began to use them. The advantage that we had over our competitors was that we could offer paper copies of the Sanborn Maps by return.

Elsevier and TRW now wanted to sell the Sanborn Map Company and I found myself dealing with the same Paul Massa who had nearly bought Chadwyck-Healey in 1986. Rubin's friend Tommy Unterberg, the senior partner of Unterberg Towbin, a New York investment firm, agreed to provide the finance for us to buy Sanborn and then float ERIIS for $40 million. The firm also arranged for twenty-seven of their investors to buy sixteen per cent of the company from me for $1 million. I had made a profit on my original investment and still owned thirty-four per cent of ERIIS, but we were in the middle of negotiating a new borrowing agreement for the group with Coutts bank in London and one of the conditions of their loan was that the proceeds of this sale were reinvested in Chadwyck-Healey. We never did buy the Sanborn Map Company, which was still pasting pieces of paper onto maps in what was now the Geographic Information Systems (GIS) era. It was later bought by one of our competitors, Environmental Data Resources (EDR), which was one of the three companies that by 1997 dominated the market. The other two were ERIIS, which had now changed its name again, to Geosure, and VISTA Information Solutions, a West Coast company quoted on NASDAQ, led by its president Tom Gay, an aggressive market promoter. After twenty years of regulation every commercial property had been surveyed at least once, many twice, and there was no longer such an urgent demand for historical land-use information. The commercial market was finite, about 200,000 transactions a year, and the three largest companies could only increase their market share by price cutting. This was reflected in our results. In 1996 sales were $6.9 million but our net income was only $564,000. Our costs had also gone up as we now had offices in California and in Austin, Texas, and we had borrowed $1.5 million for working capital and to buy a small competitor. We then diversified by buying the National Research Center and NRC Insurance Services, two companies that specialized in providing banks with flood surveys for home loans and homeowners with insurance against flooding. They were situated in Burnside, a small town in the mountains of North Carolina. We borrowed a further $3.5 million and paid the NRC founders $2 million and continued to employ them. Prickett also had ambitious plans for selling environmental reports and flood and hazard insurance to homeowners, but knew that if there was no residential market, we would have to sell Geosure, as the commercial market was no longer large enough to support three competitors.

Rubin had been approached by both EDR and by VISTA and discussions carried on for over a year until, on 14 January 1999, VISTA bought us in an exchange of shares valuing Geosure at $16,990,400. We as principals were unable to sell our shares for nine months. In August 1999 VISTA announced results that were worse than had been expected by the market. The share price, which had been $6.56 when we sold, collapsed and by October when we were allowed to sell our shares the price was $3.03, falling to $0.81 by

January 2000. VISTA was then bought by EDR, which was now owned by the British Daily Mail and General Trust. In 2003 they sold it to Fidelity National Information Solutions, which was buying up companies that provided back-office services to banks and mortgage companies, and as the housing boom of the 2000s began to accelerate, their share price climbed steadily. Eventually any Geosure shareholder that still had Fidelity shares found that they had now achieved almost the same value as at the time of the original sale. Unfortunately, most of us did not wait that long. For Llewellyn it was a small investment, while I was preoccupied with the imminent sale of Chadwyck-Healey, but for Prickett, who had spent eight years building up the business and now had a large tax bill, the collapse of the VISTA share price was a personal disaster.

Although Geosure itself never digitized the Sanborn Maps, EDR digitized the maps in the Sanborn Map Company collection after they bought the company, and Chadwyck-Healey Inc. had digitized its 600,000 monochrome maps by 1999. By 2017 the Library of Congress had digitized 18,000 of their maps in colour but expects to digitize more by 2020.

17

English Poetry

Origins

In the spring of 1990 Severtson organized an away-day conference at a hotel in Chantilly, Virginia, for our senior US managers, while my family, who were with me for a two-week vacation in Washington, DC, made a trip to New York. In the UK morale was high as we were excited about the success of our new CD-ROM publications while we continued to generate substantial revenues from our traditional microform and print ones, but in the USA the mood was subdued as microfilm sales had declined and we had no US-generated CD-ROM publications that could be called significant.

There was intense competition in the USA from established companies like UMI, CIS and H. W. Wilson for rights to machine-readable databases and there were also new entrants who, unencumbered by the past, had a fresh approach to CD-ROM publishing. The most important were SilverPlatter and Ovid. Libraries subscribed to hundreds of bibliographic databases published in print, and online through hosts such as Dialog. 'Online' was a product of the 1970s mainframe age in the pre-Windows era when accessing or searching for data had to be done by entering a series of complex commands, which in their abbreviated form were like a code and were difficult to remember unless they were being used all the time. Libraries were charged by the hosts for time spent online, so it was expensive for a library if an inexperienced user was not familiar with the commands or did not have a well-thought-out search strategy. Most libraries had trained members of staff who would design search strategies for their users. This helped maintain a mystique, which was a legacy of the early days of mainframe computing, but CD-ROM changed all that. Although the software at the beginning was DOS and required typed commands rather than clicking on icons it seemed that the nature of the medium itself, those familiar silver disks (because we all had music CDs), encouraged the publishers to think in terms of user-friendliness, openness and accessibility – terms that were foreign to the online industry.

Ron Rietdyk was the president and founder of SilverPlatter, but it was one of his partners, Bela Hatvany, whom I met most often at conferences. He was from an aristocratic Hungarian family, had been educated in England and had great charisma. He and his partners had created SilverPlatter to be the provider of bibliographic databases on CD-ROM using SilverPlatter software, which they hoped, through its wide use, would become the software standard for library users. It was a brilliantly simple concept and they had the marketing acumen to put it into practice on a global scale. We saw ourselves as publishers and as publishers we 'created' unique products by microfilming material that could only be bought from us. In CD-ROM publishing we applied the same principles in creating unique products, though our first CD-ROM publications were all databases owned by others. But while exclusive licences were as important to SilverPlatter and Ovid as they were to us, their software was their important selling point. If libraries standardized on it this would give them an exclusivity even for databases that were also available from other publishers. Although their largest markets were in the sciences and medicine, SilverPlatter and Ovid were equally active in the humanities and social sciences and were competing with us for bibliographic databases such as the *Philosopher's Index*. We had been trying to get CD-ROM publication rights to this title for months. We were now offering a royalty of forty per cent and would have to sell more than fifty subscriptions just to break even. Yet the publisher had still not agreed to grant us rights – and never did.[1]

On our away-day we knew that things were not right but none of us could see why or what to do about it. Asleson, who brought to the discussions knowledge and experience beyond that of Severtson and myself, observed that we had moved a long way from our roots, pointing out that the material that we microfilmed became exclusive to us because no one else would then microfilm it. We usually paid little or no royalties, and we sold our microform publications for high prices even though we might only sell relatively few copies. But now we were chasing small publications, which sold at low prices with high royalties, where we had to sell many copies to break even and where there might be other publishers selling the same titles. His observation made us see where we were going wrong but did not offer a solution. Severtson was disappointed with the meeting but I told her that, on the contrary, it had been a turning point because for the first time we had recognized how adrift we were.

A month later I was in London and stopped at the British Library on my way home. I was conscious of what we had discussed, and I did what I often did when seeking inspiration – walked round the shelves in the Reading Room looking at the reference books. One of the books I pulled off a shelf was the *Columbia Granger's Index to Poetry*, a well-known dictionary of first lines of poetry published by Columbia University Press. I could see that it was a natural for a CD-ROM publication, but there were two disadvantages: the book was too small to be worth publishing on its own as a CD-ROM since CD-ROMs, like microfilms, had to have a minimum price to make them worth selling to the library market; and, if the idea had merit, Columbia University Press would publish the CD-ROM edition themselves. On the train home I began to think, 'Why first lines? Why not the whole thing? Why not create a database of all of English poetry?' If we were to create our own database, I could see that poetry was the ideal genre because most of the cost of creation would be the manual keying of the data which is charged for by the character. On the pages of most books of poetry there are relatively few words, relatively few characters and plenty of white space.

But what constitutes the corpus called 'English poetry'? We needed a bibliography and I knew that in each volume of the *New Cambridge Bibliography of English Literature* (*NCBEL*)[2] there is a list of poets and their works. This would serve as the blueprint for the project since it would be trusted by every library. We could start with the earliest poetry in the English language, from 600 CE, and stop at 1900 in order to be almost entirely outside the copyright period and not have to clear copyright or pay royalties.

My new ideas when presented to my colleagues were often met with a very cautious response. In this case, Everitt, Hall and Moss all had questions but embraced it enthusiastically. It was the same throughout the company; people were intrigued, and while they may have questioned its feasibility, they found the sheer scale of it exciting. We were to turn all of English poetry into one huge, fully searchable database, and we all agreed that the *English Poetry Full-Text Database* should be a database of poems, not a digital reprint of books of poetry. We were faced with many unknowns. We would be the first academic publisher to attempt to create a database of such a size. Since the 1970s database publishers like the Mead Corporation had been creating large legal databases by the manual keying of the texts of law books for the legal profession. They and other publishers had also created databases of newspaper and magazine texts. There was a not-for-profit foundation, the Thesaurus Linguae Graecae, at the University of California, Irvine, that had created a database of classical Greek texts, but no academic publisher had ever tried to publish a large database created by manually keying the texts as a commercially profitable publication. To paraphrase Donald Rumsfeld (Secretary of State for Defense under President George W. Bush), there were the known unknowns as well as the unknown unknowns – the things that we did not know we did not know. The known unknowns were fourfold. We did not know which books or how many books we would be handling because it would take several years for an editorial board to work through the lists of poetry in *NCBEL* and decide which editions to use. We did not know the size of the corpus in terms of the number of characters to be keyed. Yet this would be our single largest production cost. We would use a relatively new standard for marking up the text called SGML (Standard Generalized Markup Language) but until now no one had attempted to use it for such a large and varied body of text. We also needed a publishing tool designed to work with digital text with SGML tagging, but it was only that year that DynaText, the only software that could meet our requirements, had come onto the market.

We would not know if the project was feasible until we had made an accurate estimate of the number of characters. If it was too large it would make the production cost too high and hence the selling price too high for the library market, and we would not be able to go ahead. Moss carried out a large sampling exercise in the summer of 1990, employing four students to compile a bibliography and nine students to count pages and characters on many of the pages in books in Cambridge University Library. By the end of September, they had completed a twenty-five per cent sample of every period and had estimated that 'English poetry' was just under one billion characters. Meanwhile Moss was talking to keying companies in Asia and was able to estimate the price range for this work. When the exercise was completed, she reported to the board that the production cost of *English Poetry* would be £1 million.

Everitt and Hall thought that the database could not be sold for more than £10,000 but this would mean a break-even of 100 copies on production costs alone, which did not include marketing or other costs. The price had to be twice as much. I wanted a break-even of fifty copies on production cost and we decided that we would offer *English Poetry* at a list price of £25,000 and a pre-publication price of £20,000.

The sampling exercise cost £20,000 and was the only money at risk. If it had not worked out, we would have abandoned the project and written off the cost. Finding a keying company who could retype the texts to a high enough standard of accuracy at a cost within our estimate was our first and most important objective. Apart from that, we were confident that all other requirements could be successfully addressed, even though we must have realized that if any one of them failed so too would the whole project. They were:

- The selection of books to be included in the database. If the selection was found to be unreliable or inconsistent the project would be strongly criticized and perhaps rejected by the academic community.
- The SGML markup. It had to be properly designed and executed so that the different elements of a poem – e.g. title, first lines and verses – were correctly identified and presented on the screen.
- The software. It had to recognize SGML tags and be capable of managing a very large text database. It should also provide an attractive user interface. We would need experienced software engineers to adapt the software and make it work.

Everitt and I started to put together an editorial board that would meet every month for several years in order to choose the works that would be included in the database. Derek Brewer, whom I knew and who at the time was Master of Emmanuel College, Cambridge, agreed to join. He was a distinguished Anglo-Saxon scholar and had been one of the founders of the publisher Boydell & Brewer. Other members were another distinguished Cambridge academic, Howard Erskine-Hill; Daniel 'Danny' Karlin from University College, London; John Barnard from the University of Leeds; Lou Burnard, who ran the Oxford Text Archive, an archive of electronic academic texts within the Oxford University Computing Service; and Michael Sperberg-McQueen from the University of Illinois at Chicago. We knew he would not be able to come to meetings but wanted his support as he and Burnard had developed the 'Text Encoding Initiative' (TEI),[3] which provided the guidelines for the SGML encoding of electronic texts and which we would use as a guide in drawing up our coding rules.

The board preferred collected editions to individual separate publications, and for nineteenth-century poets chose the last complete edition overseen by the poet in his or her lifetime. For earlier periods, when piracy and unauthorized reprintings were common, earlier printings of the poet's works were more reliable. Only the notes and prefaces that had been written by the poets themselves were included; all others were excluded. The most reliable editions of works between 600 and the beginning of printing in the late fifteenth century were mainly post-war and we had to obtain rights from their publishers to include them. There were many editorial decisions to be made. For example, most verse drama was excluded because we were already planning a separate English verse drama database, while Byron's verse drama is included. Emily Brontë is not listed in *NCBEL* as a poet, but her poetry is included in *English Poetry*. We also included some important anthologies, such as Thomas Percy's *Reliques of Ancient English Poetry* (1765–75). Decisions also had to be made about exclusions, such as street ballads and hymns after 1800. Some academics questioned the basis on which editorial decisions were being made. Professor Malcolm Kelsall from the University of Wales regretted the use of earlier editions in preference to the latest scholarly edition, giving as an example Jerome J. McGann's not yet completed edition of Byron. But Karlin pointed out that by the time McGann's edition was completed, even if permission to include it were given, there would be some other new edition in preparation, which we would also have to wait for. He summed it up, 'If there is to be an English poetry database at all, on the scale proposed, it must be accepted that certain limitations will apply to the choice of texts.'[4]

Production

Once the editorial board had chosen the editions, we had to find copies of them. It should have been straightforward as we had been borrowing books for microfilming for eighteen years, but it turned out to be more difficult than we expected. We started with nineteenth-century poets because the books should be easier to find and the print would be more legible for the keyers. Our best source was the London Library, of which I had recently been on the committee and had been a member since 1966. Other important sources were the University of Leeds through Barnard, the Birmingham Reference Library, where my reprint publishing career had begun, and some of the Scottish universities, including St Andrews. We also used Research Publication's *ESTC* microfilms of eighteenth-century books (see Chapter 7) to make photocopies from the microfilm. Because the poems were being rekeyed and we were not including everything in the books, we were not infringing their copyright. But there were frustrations: books that libraries could not find, books listed in *NCBEL* that did not exist, and books that were unavailable because they were away for binding or conservation.

SGML had been developed for the US Military to standardize equipment manuals and is the precursor of XML and a close cousin to early versions of HTML, with which website content is encoded. The particular rules for our coding system were written by our senior editor Stephen Pocock, who had previously worked on the long-running edition of Charles Darwin's correspondence at Cambridge University Library. They had to be broad enough to accommodate the many different conventions used in presenting poetry over many centuries and yet specific enough to enable the text on each page to be laid out correctly and be fully searchable. Each book was photocopied at our microform production company in Bassingbourn. Editors then marked up the photocopies with SGML tags. They were young graduates, often in their first job after leaving university with a good degree, some of them from Cambridge. In the early 1990s we paid around £12,000 a year as a starting salary, which was low compared to what a graduate might earn in London. The work was demanding, requiring a

Figure 12 Cambridge. The editorial office in Cambridge Place. Most of the paper is *English Poetry* photocopies. By 1994 it was time to move.

complete understanding of the complex rules of encoding text and the discipline and concentration to ensure that it was done consistently. Yet it was monotonous, and it was daunting to be faced with the prospect of thousands of pages to be marked up and checked for a project that would continue for years. We assumed that the editors would stay for a year or two and, with some experience on their CV, find a better-paid, more stimulating job, but most of them stayed for several years and seemed content to be in the collegiate atmosphere of an office that was almost an extension of the university world from which they had just come.

The marked-up sheets were photocopied again, with one copy being sent to the keying company in Asia and another retained in the office. Keying the texts was the most important part of production. Every book was keyed twice, a process known as 'double keying'. The keying company ran the tapes together and where there were differences corrections were made. The texts, sent back to us on floppy disks, were printed out in the UK and a sample (initially twenty-five per cent, later ten per cent) were proofread to ensure that the accuracy met our requirement of 99.95 per cent or better, equivalent to one error in every 2,000 keystrokes. Moss had first approached Saztec, whom we knew well through working with them on the British Library catalogue (see Chapter 15), but they were too expensive. She then chose Computership, which had its keying done in mainland China but had a sales office in Colchester, Essex. They keyed nineteenth-century texts to the required standard but their keyers found the long 'S's of the earlier centuries confusing as they looked like 'f's. They also found ligatures such as 'ae' and 'ff' difficult to recognize. Moss turned to Innodata in Manila in the Philippines, a small company owned and run by a young American, Todd Solomon, which offered us two advantages. Their keyers could read pre-nineteenth-century English typography and, because of their Catholic tradition, were familiar with Latin and Greek. Many of the keyers, in their late twenties or early thirties, had chosen to study for second degrees in science and technology at colleges in the Philippines. They then found that their degrees were not recognized outside the Philippines and, having spent their money, had to find whatever work they could get. Their misfortune was to our benefit because they were sophisticated enough to interpret the vagaries of the spelling and typography of the earlier centuries of published poetry. Another advantage was Solomon himself who had had a colourful career but was the son of a college professor in the USA and the grandson of a chief rabbi in a central European city. For him it was not just another commercial keying project, and his support became even more important when we were struggling with the *Patrologia Latina*, as described in Chapter 18.

Mike Sperberg-McQueen recommended DynaText from Electronic Book Technologies, in Providence, Rhode Island, as the best software for handling SGML texts. We bought it from its European distributor, Berger-Levrault, a large French printing and computer services company. We designed the user interface, drawing up a full specification of the appearance of the opening screens, the presentation of the text and the layout and function of commands. The software allowed the user to make a range of searches which at the time were unique to *English Poetry*. The SGML markup enabled searches on separate elements of the text such as titles, first lines, notes and epigraphs. It was possible to search for phrases and words close together, and for any two words in a single poem. It took thousands of hours of work by our software engineers, and DynaText itself was constantly debugging and improving its software. In 1992 we were faced with a particular problem. Microsoft were just upgrading Windows 3.0 to Windows 3.1. We knew that most of our customers would have 3.0 and we were trying to make the software work with both versions. Windows 3.0 had some well-known memory handling problems and François Chahuneau, the Berger-Levrault representative, persuaded us to drop 3.0 and make the software solely compatible with Windows 3.1, which proved to be the right decision. There was a never-ending succession of glitches that came up during testing – Windows would crash for no apparent reason and too many simple actions were initially too slow. Every problem needed painstaking work to sort out and would then need further testing by several people using different PCs until we were sure that it was cured.

Sales

The complete *English Poetry* was on five CD-ROMs with software on floppy disks. There was a user manual, a coding handbook and a hardbound printed bibliography.[5] We supplied MARC cataloguing so that libraries had a record of each individual title in their online catalogue. Each customer received three sets of the CD-ROMs, in recognition of the limitation of the CD-ROM medium, which could not be easily networked and therefore, like a book or a microfilm, could usually only be used by one person at a time. We also offered *English Poetry* on magnetic tape for libraries to network to their users on their own systems, but only a few libraries took this up. The price of the CD-ROM edition was, as stated above, £25,000 with a pre-publication price of £20,000.

The first order came in 1991 from the State Library of New South Wales in Australia. They bought it to help them answer the many questions from the general public about who wrote a particular poem and where a particular line of poetry came from. Orders were often followed by payment in full and by 1992 many customers who had already paid were waiting impatiently for the first disk. Amongst some librarians and academics there was also a latent disbelief that this project would be successful, and we needed to complete the first disk to prove that it was. Everitt and Hall had set a date for the first release that Moss, Pocock and the software team had to work hard to meet. The pressure continued right through to the final delivery of disks in the summer of 1994. In March 1992 Moss had set out 'a normal month's production': 12,000 sheets, which had to be marked up, checked, corrected and parsed, and which would require four people to work 561 hours. In November 1993 Pocock was forecasting 80,000 sheets to be processed in the next four months. There were also targets for printing the disks, compiling and printing the manual, and designing and manufacturing the packaging, all of which had equally tight deadlines.

Because of the poor response to Supermap two years before (see Chapter 15), I visited three libraries as part of my own market research in North America. At NYPL I met with senior librarians Rodney Phillips and Elizabeth Diefendorf. She said that, 'it was of exceptional interest and importance and that everyone would buy it'.[6] The library of the University of Toronto, which had a digital text unit, did not think that we could produce it at that price, the implication being that the project would fail because the price was too low. But if we successfully produced it, they would buy it. Richard Ring, head of collection development at the library of the University of Kansas, was a friend, and a subscriber to *The Nineteenth Century* (see Chapter 7). He was enthusiastic about *English Poetry* and I was confident that his library would buy it. The exercise confirmed our decision to go ahead but only NYPL placed an order during the production period and it was several years before either Toronto or Kansas ordered it.

Sales in all our traditional markets were strong. The Librarian of the University of Wollongong, a small university south of Sydney, Australia, asked how else would he be able to buy so many books so cheaply? We were only charging just over £5 a volume and the collection required no shelf space and came with cataloguing for every title. In 1992 Hall negotiated an agreement with the Committee of Australian University Librarians (CAUL) to acquire the database on behalf of thirteen libraries in nine cities from Perth to Sydney, including Wollongong. It was the world's first national library consortium agreement, and was also remarkable in a country of only sixteen million people with fewer than forty university-level institutions.

The Bodleian Library at Oxford, which at first was doubtful about the usefulness of *English Poetry*, ordered it after seeing that it was being ordered by much smaller universities. Their order was followed by another from the library of the English department. If Oxford had approached us and asked for six copies of the CD-ROMs, we would have charged them very little more. As it was, each order was at the full price. This was symptomatic of the independence enjoyed by the departmental libraries, over which the Bodleian Library had no control. The expenditure of £40,000 on two orders for *English Poetry* was one of the catalysts that led to a comprehensive reform of the libraries in Oxford, whereby Bodley's Librarian was given the title of University Librarian and by the early 2000s controlled all the departmental libraries in Oxford. The college libraries remained independent. Similarly, the University of London made no attempt to negotiate a deal on behalf of Senate House, the main library, and all the college libraries. The Senate House Library and University College, London, were amongst the first to order and were followed by most of the other colleges, each of them paying the full price.

In April 1993, before the release of the second disk in June, Hall had reported that we had received fifty-three orders totalling £1,020,024, more than our estimated production cost. But in the UK our sales were confined to the larger universities, as few polytechnics could justify such a large capital sum. In 1995, a year after completion of publication, we were approached by Derek Law, who was now library director of King's College, London, and a member of JISC, the Joint Information Systems Committee, which was providing information services to British universities and polytechnics. One of their new services was to provide what they described as a 'distributed national electronic collection', which was to make available a large set of digital resources free at the point of use managed by an organization called CHEST (Combined Higher Education Software Team).

Law was deeply interested in the new digital media, and Hall had been talking to him since March 1992 about the acquisition of some of our databases (described in more detail in Chapter 19). But now, three years later, he asked us to grant them a national licence and a requisite number of CD-ROM copies to provide a collection of our electronic titles to every higher-education institution in the UK. This included *English Poetry*, *Palmer's Index to the Times* and *Periodicals Contents Index*.[7] Law explained to Hall that while they would give a free copy of *English Poetry* to any library that did not already have it, they did not have enough money to compensate the libraries who had already bought it. I was concerned about this and I asked Fred Ratcliffe, the Cambridge University Librarian, for his advice. Ratcliffe, with his characteristic northern bluntness, told me that we could not afford not to accept it. Hall, who was better at handling long, drawn-out negotiations than I was, spent months negotiating terms with JISC, who eventually agreed to pay us over £1 million, of which approximately £600,000 was for *English Poetry*. A few libraries who had just placed orders were upset but it was a boost to our sales, which were now to over 200 libraries. It did create an unfortunate precedent in that each time we announced a new English literature database on CD-ROM we had to convince UK libraries that a JISC deal was not about to happen again. This only ended when online delivery took the place of CD-ROM (see Chapters 20 and 23).

Reception

Erskine-Hill had written, 'The great proportion of the material in *English Poetry* will never have had the attention of a critical editor',[8] and Brewer had said to me how surprised he was by the number of poets in *NCBEL* and therefore in *English Poetry* who were completely unknown and unstudied. Philip Howard in *The Times*,[9] in the first article written about *English Poetry*, months before the first disk had even been published, made the same point. In his article, 'A Literary Database Will Show Whether More Means Verse', he states, 'It will be the largest and most accessible full-text database yet in the humanities', and, 'For many of the poets, it will be the first time they have ever been republished.' This was a recurring theme, while there were few reviewers who could resist the temptation of looking for and quoting the worst verse they could find. Tim Radford, science editor of the *Guardian*, in a news piece,[10] not a review, noted that the first disk contained the works of Charles Mackay (1814–89), declared by Karlin to be the worst poet he had come across so far:

> Thou art old, Grandfather,
>   old and blind
> Be ever cheerful, good and
>   Kind.

The reviews divided into two categories: the ones that wrote wistfully about the highs and lows of English poetry, and the more business-like reviews that analyzed the database and critiqued its various elements, from content to performance of the software. The normally staid *Times Higher Education Supplement* (*THES*), in which book reviews only occupy a few pages, devoted two whole pages to *English Poetry* and managed to cover both categories.[11] The right-hand page contained a long review headed 'Ode to a CD-Rom' by Michael Leslie, an English professor at Rhodes College, Memphis, Tennessee. He is full of praise at the start: 'With a single, albeit very substantial purchase a library can transform its holdings of English literature.' But he is then quite critical of aspects of the database in the hope that his comments will help improve it as further disks are published. He questions some of the exclusions, particularly preliminary texts, and what he calls 'our striking fidelity to the text' – to the extent of repeating a particular typesetter's practice of setting two 'v's side by side when he had run out of 'w's. He points out that such misspellings and typographical oddities make it difficult for the inexperienced user, who will put in a search word but will not get all the matches he should. He criticizes our choice of DynaText and finds searches too slow – four minutes for some simple searches. This was a common criticism at the outset. Fortunately, the power of PCs increased exponentially in the 1990s and quite soon search times were no longer an issue. The *THES* also commissioned Robert Druce, a novelist and poet, to write what was described as 'A Baroque Eclogue for a Database and Three Voices entitled "Of Imagination All Compact"'. Occupying the facing page, it was surrounded by an illustrated border in colour with Adam presenting Eve with a CD-ROM and both standing on a PC held up by a god. There was also a prize of a bottle of champagne and a volume of poetry to the reader who could identify the greatest number of the forty-eight quotations that Druce had used.

In the *Times Literary Supplement* (*TLS*), Robert Potts reviewed *English Poetry* together with *The Columbia Granger's World of Poetry*, which included the book that I had foreseen would be published on CD-ROM, and 90,000 poems, which the reviewer did not consider to be very many.[12] He also reviewed and approved of an edition of the works of Coleridge published by OUP on floppy disk with very sophisticated tagging and software, which only cost £60. He found *World of Poetry* disappointing at $749 but thought that *English Poetry* at £30,000[13] 'should become a resource of enormous value to scholars and readers'. But he wondered 'if the database could be improved on and whether there will be a cheaper deal in the future'. Kevin V. Trickey in *New Library World* wrote, 'Given its lineage from the Chadwyck-Healey stable it had to be good! Given the ambitious nature of its content it had to be good. I certainly was not disappointed.' On the two disks he found the display of text excellent, especially Greek and Anglo-Saxon. Although he considers it a database for scholars only, he still ends, 'Congratulations to all involved – when does the English drama database appear?'[14]

English Poetry was widely reviewed in the USA. In March 1993 the *Wall Street Journal* declared, 'There isn't a library in the world that will be able to match it ... now libraries everywhere want to own the closest thing yet to the platonic ideal of a poetry library.'[15] The most important article was by the journalist and film critic Anthony Lane, published in two issues of *The New Yorker*.[16] Like most *New Yorker* articles, it was long, and like others Lane enjoys himself searching for the worst – Tom Freeman, an epigrammist of the seventeenth century:

> Whoop, whoop, me thinkes I heare
> >   My Reader cry
> Here is rime doggrell: I confess it I.

It is a light-hearted exploration of what the reader can do with this new configuration of centuries of poetry. Unlike Trickey he thinks it is for students who can use the database, 'to dig up some delicately comparative flower imagery in Campion and Blake and still have time to sneak out for an all-day screening of the complete Porky's cycle'. He wonders at 'a demur young Filipino typist scrutinising the lyrics of Rochester.... Manila could be just his kind of town'. He also finds he has to '*de*modernise like crazy' because of our 'admirable pedantry' in keeping to the spelling of the original poems. It has to be 'seeke' and 'chambre' if you want to search on 'seek' and 'chamber' in the poetry of Sir Thomas Wyatt. He ends:

> The principal pay-off of this database, as far removed from technology as you could wish, is to humanize the creative act.... The joys of 'English Poetry' should be open to all, which makes it slightly unfortunate that the complete set of disks will set you back fifty-one thousand dollars. Whoop, whoop.

There was a much longer essay called 'Lumber' by the American novelist and essayist Nicholson Baker.[17] All 148 pages are about the words 'lumber' and 'lumber room', the fruits of a year of reading and thinking about these words, which together with *English Poetry*[18] are his companions on a discursive but highly imaginative journey through Western literature. Authors range from Virginia Woolf and Conan Doyle to Dr Johnson, George Eliot and Goethe. He finds many of his poets in what he describes as

> four silver discs the size of Skilsaw blades by the prodigious Eel of Science[19] himself, Sir Charles Chadwyck-Healey.... nothing can remotely compare, in range and depth and tantric power with their *English Poetry Database*.... Chadwyck-Healey's demiurgic project comes so much closer than anything else in paper and plastic to the unattainable *om* of total inclusion.

But then he points out the exclusions: Emily Brontë's poetry is included (see above) but Charlotte's and Anne's are not. No poems by Dr Johnson except for two of his best-known poems in one of the anthologies; Baker puzzles over the inclusion of the poems by Goldsmith in *The Vicar of Wakefield* but the exclusion of poems by Dickens in *The Pickwick Papers*. There are eighty poems by Francis William Newman but none by his brother Cardinal Newman, whose poems such as 'Lead kindly light' are, in his opinion, both better and better known. But he quotes Professor John Sutherland, who called the database, 'the most significant development in literary scholarship since xerography'.[20]

I met Baker when he was in London in 1999 giving a lecture about the British Library's destruction of some of their original runs of important American newspapers in the belief that the existing microfilm editions would be adequate substitutes. Baker was the first to realize that they were not, and, single handed, rescued as many titles as he could and wrote a book about it.[21]

In contrast to Baker's essay an antagonism towards *English Poetry* was revealed in a review of Baker's book in the *TLS*.[22] Eric Korn, who had so favourably reviewed the British Library catalogue on CD-ROM (see Chapter 15), in reviewing Baker's book also reviewed *English Poetry* and took issue with 'fundamental omissions' in the selection of poems, apparently blaming it on the technology. In a letter published in the *TLS* I replied that it was not the technology that was to blame for our selection, to which Korn responded, agreeing that he had spoken of, 'the technology which threatens what it claims to preserve', but that he was writing for a 'relatively sophisticated audience'. Another letter in the same issue responding to mine, came from Ian Jackson, an antiquarian bookseller in Berkeley, California, who stated that I had 'the effrontery to attribute the grotesque inadequacies of his [my] English Poetry Full-Text Database' to the 'academic vision of another era'. This was a reference to my comments on the limitations of *CBEL* published in the 1960s. I had also pointed out that poems that we had missed could easily be added to future releases of *English Poetry*, on which he observed, 'Such are the loose morals of the electronic publisher: if there is, essentially, no final product, he fancies that there can be no last judgement.' Brewer advised us not to respond but it was a reminder that *English Poetry* was not welcomed everywhere. For some it was an intrusion, disrupting the well-ordered world of printed books. There were still many who thought that only print was synonymous with scholarship. On the other hand, the greatest accolade bestowed on *English Poetry* was by Duke University in North Carolina, who made it their four-millionth-and-first 'book' added to the library. Its addition and that of the four-millionth, an edition of the poems of John Donne, were celebrated in a ceremony in the chapel on 10 April 1992 (the first disk was available by then). It was accompanied by a handsomely produced programme describing the additions and the event.

James Gleick in *The Information. A History. A Theory. A Flood*[23] describes how, in 1990, the American philosopher and cognitive scientist Daniel Dennett imagined, just before the Internet made this dream possible, that electronic networks could upend the economics of publishing poetry. 'Instead of slim books ... what if poets could publish online, instantly reaching not hundreds but millions of readers?' Quoting from Anthony Lane's review in *The New Yorker* he goes on to describe the conception of the *English Poetry Full-Text Database* in the same year, starting with my visit to the British Library, and its production over the next four years. He ends, 'The CD-ROMs are already obsolete. All English poetry is in the network now ... and if not now, then soon.' It seems that he did not know that it had been there in a database since 1998, still in the Chadwyck-Healey name, accessed twenty-four hours a day by thousands of readers all over the world. The bringing together of all our databases into one English and American literature website described in Chapter 20 seemed to us to be as significant as the publication of *English Poetry*. But neither it nor any other digital publication we produced ever achieved the interest aroused by *English Poetry*. As Philip Howard had said in that first article, '[Poetry] is always the most important and the most enduring way of writing.'[24]

English Poetry contained 165,000 poems published in 4,500 books. After completion McCrae worked out that the cost of production had been £995,000. Miraculously this venture into the unknown had not only been cash positive almost from the beginning but had come in half a per cent under Moss's original estimate of £1 million.

18

Patrologia Latina

Origins

There was a friendly rivalry between Chadwyck-Healey Ltd and Chadwyck-Healey Inc., which I did nothing to discourage. Severtson and, later, Stephen Rhind-Tutt, reported to the owner of the company, though they had to recognize that they were part of a group and that they had to work closely with the directors in the UK, especially with McCrae who controlled the finances of all the companies.

Severtson was happy to have *English Poetry* to sell because it was an entirely new publication with a substantial price tag, unlike anything that was being sold by our competitors. We assumed that other publishers would follow our lead and we were anxious to consolidate our position in the creation of large full-text databases as quickly as possible. Chadwyck-Healey Inc. wanted their own digital publication, and Eric Calaluca, the sales manager, put a proposal to Severtson that she then put to me. Behind Calaluca's fast talking and breezy self-confidence was a more thoughtful and academically inclined young man, which stood him in good stead when selling to librarians. He had graduated from the University of Notre Dame, a prestigious Catholic university in Indiana, and had attended lectures on medieval studies given by Professor Mark Jordan. He learned that all scholars working with the Latin texts of the medieval period used the Abbé Migne's *Patrologia Latina*, a collection of 221 volumes containing the texts of thousands of documents by Latin authors from the end of the second century CE to the death of Pope Innocent III in 1216.[1] I only knew of it as a set of volumes bound in drab black buckram on the open shelves in the Reading Room of the British Library. I must have checked it in the past and found that it had been microfilmed by our Dutch competitor the Inter Documentation Company (IDC) and thought no more about it. But

Calaluca explained to me why it was so important, and his enthusiasm made me consider it seriously for digital publication.

The *Patrologia* was not, as its name suggests, a collection of patristics, the studies of the writings of the early Christian writers in the 500 years after completion of the New Testament. It was a collection of medieval texts on a wide range of subjects, not only theology. The volumes also included an enormous range of textual supplements, essays, commentaries, notes, analyses and doctrinal defences, the work of scholars from the sixteenth to the nineteenth centuries, which were themselves primary sources for many scholars. Migne, the creator of the *Patrologia*, far from being a saintly scholar, was an innovative entrepreneur who realized that he could use the new communications of the mid-nineteenth century, the new railway network and the mail service, to sell part-works to impoverished priests throughout France.[2] Having arrived, penniless, in Paris in the 1830s he became a newspaper publisher and later used the proceeds of the sale of his newspapers to establish the Ateliers catholiques in Montrouge.[3] By 1848 there were 47,000 Catholic priests in France, a strong recovery from the reduction in numbers after the revolution, and Migne marketed his series directly to them, bypassing the bookshops, using direct mail and being known as the 'Napoléon du prospectus'. He developed many of the marketing methods that have been used in the twentieth century to sell part-works and subscriptions to magazines. His sales material contained 'puffs', quotations from eminent cardinals and bishops praising his series, many of which are curiously similar and probably written by Migne himself. His motto was 'du bon à bon marché' (the good at a good price) and he reminded his buyers that the 469 volumes of both the Latin and Greek patrologies would cost over 100,000 francs if they bought each volume separately, but they could buy the whole of the Latin series for only 1,200 francs and a little more for the Greek. There was also free home delivery, an important inducement for priests in isolated parishes. He offered subscribers further discounts and free copies of books if they brought in other subscribers – a form of pyramid selling – and, in contrast to the extended payment terms that he offered, there were discounts for payment for the entire series in advance. His approach to the choice of texts to be published was equally commercial. Most of the texts in the series were taken from other printed series, both contemporary and from previous centuries, sometimes with permission but often without. Only very few texts in the *Patrologia* were taken from original manuscripts.

Migne was proud of the fact that he used steam presses at a time when they were only just being introduced in France, and Bloch, his biographer, has described the Ateliers as, 'a bibliographical assembly line capable of producing a standardised product at a minimal cost for mass consumption'. The Goncourt brothers, in their *Journal*, were not so kind, describing Migne as a 'brewer of Catholic books' and the Ateliers as 'a print shop full of proscribed priests, like him, of defrocked rogues, of death cheaters who have been cast out of grace and who, upon the very sight of a police inspector jump for the doors'.[4] Yet, by bringing together thousands of texts from hundreds of sources, together with commentaries and notes, he created a source for medievalists that has still not been surpassed.

By 1990 the large Belgian publisher Brepols had begun to publish an entirely new updated and corrected digital edition of many of the texts in the *Patrologia* called the *CETEDOC Library of Christian Latin Texts*, which included their own previously published *Corpus Christianorum Series Latina*. Goldman was in touch with medieval scholars, as Chadwyck-Healey France had published on microfiche the card catalogues of the IRHT, and he and I visited Brepols in Turnhout, Belgium. We were first taken into a large factory building, inside which was another building the size of a house and through its windows we could see a vast printing machine, used to print millions of Bibles, missals and prayer books for those of the Catholic faith. It made the same impression on us as the steam presses of the Ateliers catholiques must have made on Migne's visitors. We suggested to the publishers of *CETEDOC* that we work together to publish electronic editions of their new texts. They listened politely but told us that they were not interested. We were now at an impasse that went on for some months. I was reluctant to invest over £1 million in a project to convert Migne's apparently flawed texts into machine-readable form when new, better editions were in the process of being published. Hall and Everitt were more convinced and Calaluca enlisted the help of his old professor Mark Jordan to persuade me. He explained that not only would it take Brepols years to publish new editions of so many works but that the *Patrologia* had been the standard source for scholars for over 130 years, which meant that several generations of citations in books and journal articles referred to its texts. For that reason alone, it would remain the pre-eminent source for years to come. He also pointed out that while there were many errors in the *Patrologia*, they were often minor and made little difference to the interpretation of the texts. He also told us that the most complete text of Augustine is in the *Patrologia*, not in any more modern edition.[5] I had been annoyed by the patronizing attitude of Brepols and began to look again, more seriously, at the prospect of publishing an electronic edition. There was the siren call of publishing an 'improved' *Patrologia* where we would correct obvious mistakes and introduce known improved editions and commentaries but, to his credit, Jordan resisted this and we decided that we would not even correct spelling errors; the only changes we would make were those that were necessary to enable the text to be displayed correctly in digital form. As part of my personal market research I discussed the project with an elderly scholar in the Manuscripts Division at the Library of Congress who I did not think would be sympathetic to or even understand the reasons for publishing an electronic edition. He simply stated that it would be invaluable, and his only regret was that because of its expense his colleagues in Eastern Europe would not have access to it.

Production

The *Patrologia Latina Database*, or *PLD*, was an even larger project than *English Poetry* and had a production budget of $3 million. It was a Chadwyck-Healey Inc. publication and they were responsible for its production. In early 1991 I let them get on with it, even though colleagues in Cambridge thought it should be done there. Severtson involved Jordan not only as the chairman of a small editorial board but to manage a group of twelve research students at Notre Dame to carry out the 'mapping' of the volumes and the SGML coding, since to do it correctly required an intimate understanding of the Latin, Greek and Hebrew texts. A large part of the preparation of the texts for keying was therefore done under the aegis of a university department headed by a professor who had many other demands on his time, and by students who were only working on it part time. In other ways *PLD* followed the course of *English Poetry*. Mike Sperberg-McQueen, the editor of TEI, was on both editorial boards, the search and display software was DynaText and initially the keying was done by Computership, and later by Innodata.

The mapping carried out by Jordan's team required an analysis of the structure of each volume to identify prefaces, text, commentaries and indexes as separate elements to enable the user to restrict searches to particular elements and to know in what elements of the volume the hits from a search occurred. But there were problems arising from errors in the text. Sometimes there would be a number in the text referring to a note that was not there, or a note with no corresponding number in the text. These had to be resolved and it meant that the volumes had to be proofread as part of the SGML markup process, which was not made easier by the small nineteenth-century typeface set out in two long columns on each page (which Migne had designed to be easier to read than a single block of text). We also had to be careful to use the right edition of the *Patrologia*. In 1865 Migne had sold the rights to Garnier, a publisher in Paris who began to reprint the volumes. In 1868 a fire destroyed the original plates and type had to be reset. It was done carelessly, and the Garnier edition is inferior to the original. It is partly due to the Garnier edition that the *Patrologia* has a reputation for having such error-ridden texts. Unfortunately, this was not understood in Notre Dame and early on they marked up several volumes from the Garnier edition.

Chadwyck-Healey Inc. sent out their first sales brochure in June 1991, promising sample data on a CD-ROM that summer. The first order came shortly afterwards from Fordham University in New York. James McCabe, the University Librarian, wrote, 'We here in the Bronx are very advanced when it comes to new technology.'[6] Orders continued to come in, usually followed by payment in full to achieve the pre-publication price of $60,000, which required payment by the end of 1992. But after many months there were still no texts on CD-ROM, and it was not until 1992 that the first sample disk was produced. As soon as we received it, we saw that the text did not display correctly and that there were many other errors. We were faced with the most serious situation that we had ever experienced: we had accepted orders and taken money from libraries for over a year and now, in spite of our promises, we had nothing to offer them.

In November 1992 Pocock, who was the acknowledged expert on SGML encoding through his success with *English Poetry*, examined the *PLD* coding structure and considered it to be too complicated. A user would have to have an intimate knowledge of the organization of texts and other materials in *PLD* to be able to search it successfully. In December he wrote a nine-page discussion document setting out how the mapping and coding might be done,[7] and in early 1993 Severtson and her senior editor Ann Savers came over for a crisis meeting in Cambridge. By then, Calaluca, who had persuaded us to take on this huge project, had left the company.[8] It was a difficult meeting for Severtson, as Everitt, Moss and Pocock advised that to salvage *PLD* it had to be brought back to Cambridge, where it would be restarted from scratch. By now we had increasingly impatient customers who were asking when they were going to receive their first CD-ROM. One of our sternest critics was David Luscombe, who had been professor of medieval history at the University of Sheffield since 1972 and had made Sheffield a centre for medieval studies. Sheffield ordered it but Luscombe had always been doubtful about our ability to publish an acceptable electronic edition. The defective sample disk that we had mistakenly sent out to customers confirmed his worst fears. We knew that his opinion would have a strong influence on others, and Hall and I went to see him in Sheffield to explain to him and to Michael Hannon, the University Librarian, that we were going to start again. We asked him to wait for six months when, we assured him, we would be able to send him the first complete disk. Until then Sheffield's order was suspended. We expected other libraries to cancel their orders and ask for their money back when we told them that we were starting again. Total refunds could have been over £500,000, money that we were already using as working capital, not only for *PLD* but for other projects as well. Only one library cancelled but it did not ask for its money back. We kept the money on account hoping that it would re-order, which it did about a year later.

The disappointing sales and product development performance of Chadwyck-Healey Inc. over the previous two years, together with the *PLD* crisis, meant that a change of leadership was needed and Severtson left at the end of May. She was replaced by Doug Roesemann who had joined us as sales vice-president a few months earlier; he was an experienced professional who had worked for several competitors, including Research Publications. I put him in charge of Chadwyck-Healey Inc. but retained the title of president for myself. In the USA we had declining microfilm sales revenues and only a few home-grown electronic titles ready for sale, while in France microfilm had also declined, and though we had more electronic publications they were not sufficiently profitable to make the company viable.

It was a time of complete change at the top because the following month an equally demoralized Goldman left Chadwyck-Healey France, and in late July *The Bookseller* reported that Everitt had retired in what we had described as 'the most successful year in the company's 21 year history'.[9] It did not know that what it called 'one of Europe's leading electronic publishers' was facing the most serious production setback it had ever had. But during the summer I appointed new chief executives in France and the USA and after Everitt left, Hall took over as managing director of Chadwyck-Healey Ltd. During this very testing time I was ably supported by my PA, Renata Dallaway, whose role was to coordinate things and keep both me and other people informed during a time when I was away from Cambridge so much, since there was no email to enable us to easily stay in touch.

The month after Severtson left, Chadwyck-Healey Inc. did announce two new CD-ROM publications: *The Music Index*, which we had bought from a small Canadian publisher, and a series of government and business directories published by Washington-based Leadership Directories. Both sold well once they were published. The first disk of an important new database, *Periodicals Contents Index*, had also been published in March but technical problems had delayed its publication by more than a year and its production too had to be brought back to Cambridge (see Chapter 19).

At the start of the *PLD* project Computership had keyed five volumes, but when these were examined in the UK, it was realized that the error rate and mistakes in the coding made them unusable. Every day a teenager had come into the Chadwyck-Healey Inc. office after school to photocopy pages of the volumes, which were then sent to Notre Dame for marking up. Two large boxes of marked-up copies were shipped to Cambridge from Notre Dame. It was found that letters like 'e's and 'o's were breaking up because the photocopies were too light;[10] no one in Alexandria had thought to check this. The sheets, which had travelled so expensively by Fedex from Alexandria to Notre Dame and then to Cambridge, had to be thrown out. The photocopying of the pages of the *Patrologia* was started again at our microfilm production company in Bassingbourn. We also turned to Innodata to help us rescue the project and they did everything they could to get it back on track. A different keying company that had not had the experience of keying *English Poetry* might have been less able to help solve our keying and SGML problems, and the helpful attitude of Solomon, the owner, was also important.

Reception and sales

By April 1993 we had thirty-two orders even though we had nothing to deliver. In June we sent out a CD-ROM with four volumes to show our customers how it would look and work and were able to publish the first substantial part, containing forty-two volumes, in October. Although it was generally found to be satisfactory, even by Professor Luscombe, we knew that there was still work to be done on the software and that, inevitably, such a complex, divisive but important project would attract critical comment, though we hoped it would be constructive. The first helpful critique came from Professor Ivan Boserup of the Royal Library in Copenhagen, who had applied to the Danish Ministry of Culture to buy both *English Poetry* and *PLD*. After a visit to Cambridge in May 1993 he sent us his 'first impressions'. He pointed out a flaw in the search process that meant that some hits went unrecorded, and also complained that hits that might be single words were 'lost' in large pieces of text: a paragraph, which was our smallest search unit, could run to more than one page. In September Dr Norbert Martin, a senior librarian involved in the publication of the *Monumenta Germanica Historica* in Munich, commented on the sample disk and had some of the same criticisms as Boserup but also pointed out that a Boolean search of two words could result in hits in which the two words were a hundred pages apart, which was clearly unacceptable. He also looked forward to faster searches and simpler printing. He pointed out that *CETEDOC* on CD-ROM was faster, even though at the time it was a larger body of text. He wrote to us in German, calling these faults 'childhood illnesses'. In late 1993, after the October release, at a meeting at the IRHT in Paris, at which Hall spent six hours demonstrating *PLD* to French academics and librarians, an academic was heard to say gloomily, 'If my institution does not get this I will have to retire.'

In February 1994 Roesemann and I attended 'A Discussion' on 'Electronic Text Development in Theology' with a small group of librarians at the Princeton Theological Seminary. I described the history of the project and the difficulties we had had and, in response, Charles Willard from Harvard suggested that libraries would have responded differently both to cost and purchase if there had been a co-owner relationship rather than a vendor–purchaser relationship. Roesemann pointed out that to date only one-third of the sales were to US libraries. The discussion ranged over a series of full-text databases and did not concern itself with criticisms of *PLD*'s functionality, but the point was made again that any future project of this importance should be done in cooperation with the library community. I listened but knew that *PLD* would never have happened if we had tried to involve libraries in some kind of cooperative project. It had too many unknowns and difficulties to have ever convinced a wide group of librarians and scholars to support it. It could only be done as a risky entrepreneurial project by someone willing to invest $3 million in it. I remembered how my proposal in 1983 to microfilm the Sanborn Maps as a cooperative project was greeted with complete incomprehension by US libraries (see Chapter 8). At that time the vendor–purchaser relationship was the only one that they understood or wanted.

By June 1994 we had published more than half the 221 volumes and had two more releases to come. Another aspect of the complexity of converting the *Patrologia* into digital form was the need to insert images into the text; these included symbols, Hebrew characters, decorative capitals and other devices that Migne had reproduced from the documents he had published. By then 4,500 images had been copied at Bassingbourn and inserted into the digital text in Cambridge. The *Patrologia* also contained a substantial amount of Greek text. DynaText resolved the handling of accents on Greek characters in one of their many software upgrades and later we licensed a coded font program, SymbolGreek, which was modified for *PLD* and integrated into the software. In return we paid the owners, the Payne Loving Trust in Edmonds, Washington State, a licence fee of $50 per customer.

We were able to report in our September 1994 newsletter that we had sold almost one hundred sets in eighteen countries, and in some countries such as the Netherlands, Sweden and Austria, every institution that supported teaching and research in medieval studies had now bought it. This was equivalent to around $4.5 million of sales, most of which had been paid at the time of ordering. But we knew that there were many sales that would only come when the database was complete and scholars found it satisfactory. Opposition to the project still persisted and we had to respond to it. The loss of a single order because of adverse comment was financially significant. *CETEDOC*'s own sales material made clear that it was in competition with us, stating, 'Part of these not-yet-published texts will be taken from the *Patrologia Latina* of Migne', and, 'the CD-ROM updates will gradually replace the Migne editions by the Corpus editions as they become available'. But it did not say how many years this would take. Most of the texts were still only to be found in *PLD* and we knew that researchers needed them now.

Our most serious critic, Professor Paul Tombeur, the director of CETEDOC, published an article in the *Bulletin de SIEPM* in 1992 in which he described *PLD* as a 'sorte de photocopie électromagnétique' (a kind of electromagnetic photocopy) and went on to criticize some of the limitations in the search process.[11] He had only seen the early defective version of *PLD*, and Jordan and I were anxious to refute his comments. We even hired a Belgian lawyer to advise us on how we might respond to his potentially damaging statements that he had first posted on an electronic bulletin board. My letter in response was published in the next bulletin, almost a year later,[12] and he both replied to it and followed it with a six-page article laying out in detail why the *Patrologia* was so misleading for uninformed researchers. He emphasized the difficulties with which students and researchers coming to Migne for the first time were faced, in not being aware of the many errors and misattributions in the *Patrologia*, stating, 'Comme, je pense, Sir Charles Chadwyck-Healey a dû être trompé lui-même' (As, I think, Sir Charles Chadwyck-Healey, himself, must have been misled). He agreed that if no other edition was available, it was still necessary to go to the *Patrologia*, but stated that for him *PLD* was a commercial product that could only impoverish patrologists and medievalists.

We recognized Tombeur's main point that our electronic edition of the *Patrologia* did not reflect the enormous advances in the study of these texts since the mid-nineteenth century. Jordan suggested that we should add headnotes to the texts in *PLD* indicating where the user might go for information on ascription and for more recent editions. This had been suggested at the first advisory board meeting but had been set aside as we grappled with the difficulties of converting the text itself. I was interested in this for another reason. By 1994 I was increasingly concerned about the copyright protection afforded to electronic editions of works that in print were out of copyright. The European Union was about to bring in a new copyright directive for databases that would offer no protection for *PLD* as it would not be deemed to be copyrightable because of the lack of anything new or original that we had added to it. If it was not in copyright it would only be afforded a rather weak protection for fifteen years which, from our experience, was not long enough. In the case of *English Poetry*, I believed that the selection of poets and editions would make it sufficiently original to be copyrightable, but in *PLD* there was no selection and no additions other than the SGML coding, which we did not think would be enough. This concern was not resolved until our literary databases were collected together in a website (see Chapter 20), while for *PLD* it was never resolved. Pocock felt strongly that it was not practical, as it would require a huge amount of research work and we might still be criticized by Tombeur and others for our selections, and such bibliographic references could go out of date very quickly. Remembering my own rule from my Cornmarket Press experience with *The English Revolution* (see Chapter 1) that publishers should never commission and pay for original research, we deferred to Pocock and added nothing to *PLD*.[13]

Not all comments were critical. Paul Meyvaert, an eminent scholar from Harvard who had been a Benedictine monk and was self-taught, was reviewing *PLD* for the journal *Speculum*, and wrote to Everitt in March 1994. He had several suggestions and made comparisons with *CETEDOC* but went on to state:

> The advantage to me of the Chadwyck-Healey CD is that, even if it works more slowly, it puts immediately at my disposal all those texts of Migne which I have been combing through tediously all my scholarly life.... I find myself so happy that I have lived long enough to see both [*PLD* and *CETEDOC*] appear and to discover that their appearance had added a new zest to my scholarly work.

In June 1994, at the time of the third release, Hall reported that it was proving difficult to get *PLD* accepted in Italy. He estimated that there were thirty institutions who should have it but there was what amounted to a boycott. He thought that it was not only Tombeur who was talking it down. *PLD* was also perceived as being very expensive because the Italian lira had lost value against sterling in the last year. He recommended producing a sales brochure in Italian (which was done), a sample disk containing the works of an important author not in *CETEDOC*, and more demonstrations. Hall himself spoke Italian and found that his demonstrations had been well received. By the time *PLD* was completed in 1995, orders were coming in from universities and research centres in Italy but we never achieved the penetration that Chadwyck-Healey España achieved in Spain (see Chapter 11).

From a marketing point of view, we could not have chosen two more well-matched projects than *English Poetry* and *PLD*. Both were central to the research interests of all large university libraries in the English-speaking world, but *PLD* appealed to the Catholic universities in southern and eastern Europe, which had less interest in *English Poetry*, and so our overall world market for these two expensive databases was much increased by our choice of such contrasting subject matter. *PLD* also sold well to both

Protestant and Catholic universities in Germany, and libraries in Eastern Europe were able to afford it because they had been given money by the Soros Foundation to buy such research material. The electronic edition of the *Patrologia* was one of our most important contributions to scholarship. Latin was the common language of Europe for many centuries and the texts that Migne had collected together covered every aspect of life and beliefs in Europe. Theology, history, linguistics, philosophy, medicine and law were just some of the subjects covered.

We were advised that Migne's *Patrologia Graeca* was not worth republishing and we were happy not to have to incur the extra costs of converting texts entirely in Greek. Unlike *English Poetry*, which was followed by other full-text databases of English and American literature, we only published one other title to accompany *PLD*, *Acta Sanctorum*, a collection of sixty-eight volumes of texts published over 300 years by the Société des Bollandistes on every aspect of life in medieval Europe.

By now it was 1996 and libraries wanted to access databases online. They could not purchase the data outright as they had with the CD-ROM edition, as the data was on our server not theirs. Unlike our other online databases, to which we added new information each year, *PLD* and *Acta Sanctorum* remained unchanged. Libraries were willing to pay an annual access fee of several thousand pounds if new material was being added, but were more reluctant to pay such a fee for databases that never changed and that they would never be able to own outright. This dilemma is described more fully in Chapter 20. In an ideal world, *PLD* and *CETEDOC* should have been available on one integrated website with the new *CETEDOC* texts able to be searched alongside the old ones in *PLD*. But the world of publishing is not ideal, and after *PLD* was completed neither we nor Brepols made any effort to collaborate.

19

Periodicals Contents Index

Origins

Some of the most heavily used reference works in libraries are indexes to periodicals and in 1989 Severtson had suggested taking some of the best-known indexes of nineteenth-century periodicals, such as *Poole's Index* and *Readers' Guide*,[1] and merging them into a new database of such indexes. By then we knew through our experience with NUCMC (see Chapter 9) how difficult it was to merge indexes. Laborious manual editing and checking were required to iron out the small differences between entries from different publications for the same item and we were wary of embarking on such a potentially complicated project.

In the spring of 1990 Alston and I were having lunch outside in the yard of a pub near the British Museum. Sarah Tyacke passed by and stopped at our table. She was Keeper of Manuscripts at the British Library (which was still in the British Museum). She had previously been the youngest keeper ever appointed at the British Library, in charge of the philately collections and maps, the latter being her professional speciality. After chatting for a few minutes, she said to me that she thought we ought to consider creating a database of contents pages of journals to provide access to the millions of articles published in Europe and America before the British Library amongst others had begun to index current journal articles. It was a fresh approach to indexing journal articles, but I did not think it would be liked by librarians, who preferred indexes that used controlled subject terms that accorded with international standards such as Library of Congress Subject Headings. The database would contain the full titles of articles in the contents page of each issue of a journal. But users could not be sure that the term or name for which they were searching would be contained in the title of an article, and there might also be false hits through misleading terms used in titles. In the nineteenth century journal articles were given long, discursive titles, often with outdated terms and phraseologies that would not be familiar to a modern reader.

In August, when we were exhibiting at the IFLA annual conference in Stockholm, I visited the booth of Engineering Index, a New York publisher that I already knew. Their main index, the leader in its field, used a controlled vocabulary of names and subject terms, but they had now published another electronic index covering secondary journals, which consisted of the information from their contents pages. If Engineering Index and its customers thought this was acceptable, we could do the same for the journals in the humanities and social sciences in English and in all other European languages.

Severtson had commissioned Marlene Hurst, a librarian, to create a business plan and do market research for a Comprehensive Index to Eighteenth and Nineteenth Century Periodical Literature, which would include *Poole's Index* and 141 other cumulative indexes. But she reported that the response had not been encouraging. I wrote, 'It seems that in the US the Index could easily become just another second-rank CD-ROM publication, awaiting its turn until the libraries have bought all their first-rank titles. We have not had a single successful CD-ROM publication in the US so far.'[2]

I described to the senior managers the contents page database that I had seen at IFLA a few weeks before. The keying of the contents pages of journals should be a more straightforward project, and it was exciting because of its potential scale. Everitt and Hall were more cautious because, having embarked on two large full-text databases, *English Poetry* and *PLD*, they thought we were becoming overstretched, and at the time they were less interested in publishing a large bibliographic as opposed to a full-text database. Severtson, who had trained as a librarian, immediately understood the point of it and she offered to take it on.

Current Contents Index, as it was first called, should have been a straightforward project and yet we found it difficult to establish the principles on how the journals should be selected to create a reference publication that would be attractive to libraries in both the USA and the rest of the world. In December 1990 we held a conference on journals contents pages at a hotel in Cambridge with directors and senior managers, joined by Goldman from Paris and Severtson and Calaluca from Alexandria.[3] We thought that there was limited use of pre-1900 journals

Figure 13 Cambridge. Conference on journal contents pages. Left to right: Donald Goldman, Eric Calaluca, Alastair Everitt, Alison Moss, Stephen Pocock, Linda Burgess, Susan Severtson. December 1990.

and we should restrict ourselves to journal issues published between 1900 and 1960. There were also the journals that had already been indexed, which we decided would be included.

Production and sales

Severtson was in touch with Richard 'Dick' De Gennaro, the newly appointed Harvard College Librarian, and knew that Harvard was moving 25,000 journals (300,000 volumes) into store and wanted contents page information to appease readers. In June 1991 we signed an agreement with Harvard to supply the journals for copying in return for a royalty ranging from 2.5 per cent to 7.5 per cent, which, later, seemed far too generous. Severtson also hired two Harvard librarians to design the format in which the contents page information on each article would appear. In a press release announcing the project in late June there was a puff from De Gennaro: 'This is one of the most useful and interesting databases currently under development.' In a business plan we stated:[4]

> The current trend in library automation is to create a unified approach to information which allows the user to carry out research on one system.... By selling tapes of tables of contents information for those periodicals which are held by a library, the library may enhance their automation capacity to include even early periodical titles.... Because it will be seen as an automation product as well as a reference tool, technical services librarians should be as important a target market as our traditional reference and collection development people.

We estimated that the cost of producing a CD-ROM containing five hundred journal titles with an average of forty years per title, and with contents page information totalling just under two hundred million characters, would be $284,000. Each CD-ROM would sell for $5,000 and we expected sales by 30 June 1992 of $497,000. Chadwyck-Healey Inc., working with Harvard, arranged for the journal contents pages to be copied. They were then marked up and sent for keying by Apex, which had an office in Virginia but did their keying in India. The data was then sent to Chadwyck-Healey France where the Caravan software, which we had developed and were using for publishing *Hansard* on CD-ROM, could be used for what was now called *Periodicals Contents Index* (*PCI*). This meant that we did not have to buy in software or pay a royalty to a third-party provider. Inevitably the *Patrologia Latina*, to which we were committing $3 million, took precedence but unfortunately the production team at Chadwyck-Healey Inc. could not achieve acceptable results with either project. In February 1992, a year later, the data for the first disk was still not ready for processing in France. Meanwhile *PCI* had begun to attract attention. In March 1992 David Russon, director general of the British Library at Boston Spa, suggested that we link *PCI* with Boston Spa's document delivery service and that we build into our software a routine to order documents from the British Library.[5] This was an attractive idea, and in the same month Michael Keller, head of collection development at Yale, talked to Severtson about acquiring *PCI* and scanning the journals included in it. They were planning to carry out an experimental programme with the British Library to scan journals and Keller wondered if our microfilming company at Bassingbourn might take on the work for the British Library.

In the same month Hall met with Derek Law who was a member of ISC, the Information Sub-Committee (formerly the Computer Board), and was advising CHEST on the acquisition of datasets for the higher-education community. CHEST had already bought databases for the UK university library community from ISI (Institute for Scientific Information), the American publisher of online bibliographic databases such as *Current Contents Search* and *Scisearch*. Sixty members of CHEST were subscribing to the service, paying £5,000 to £6,000 a year just for the maintenance of the database and the online service. CHEST itself would have paid a very large sum to lease ISI's databases. Law thought that *PCI* was also a 'winner' and was ideal for CHEST because of the dearth of suitable databases in the humanities. But he warned Hall that they would need twenty users to make a national agreement possible. The next meeting did not take place until December 1992, when Hall proposed that it would cost CHEST £150,000 per segment or disk to lease the *PCI* database for the whole of UK higher education. This was equivalent to twenty-six orders at the price at that time, which had increased to £5,750 per disk. The libraries themselves would only pay £1,000 a year for database maintenance and online access. Hall thought that while it would be difficult to get subscribers to pay £11,500 a year for two segments or disks, there would be more than twenty libraries in the UK willing to pay CHEST £1,000 a year. But Hall knew that discussions could go no further until we had a product to demonstrate.

In April 1993 we were still testing the first disk, almost two and a half years after the project had started. There were searches that were too slow, due to the large number of hits on individual words such as 'review', and 'book' (362,725 and 211,379 hits respectively). Searches on these two words combined took even longer. A group of libraries in the Boston area wanted to trial *PCI* before deciding whether to purchase it and we sent them a 'gold disk', which was a single copy made in house. In April Carol Fleishauer at the library of the Massachusetts Institute of Technology (MIT) sent us their critique. They thought it was complex and inconsistent to use, that several important titles were not included, and that existing print indexes were faster. The Boston Consortium had judged *PCI* on the contents of the first disk, but it would be only when we had several million article records in the database that it would become a worthwhile resource for searching the journals of the past. While it was reassuring to have the approval and interest of Russon, Keller and Law, would that turn into orders? Hard-pressed libraries both sides of the Atlantic would be tempted to adopt a 'wait and see approach', particularly as at the same time we were asking them to spend £20,000 on *English Poetry* and £27,000 on the *Patrologia Latina*. We came up with various strategies to address this. The first disk contained only US journals from 1900 to 1960, and the second disk

European journals for the same period. We knew that there was more interest in twentieth-century journals, and on the advice of librarians we later extended the cut-off date from 1970 to 1990. At the same time, we undertook to include the complete backrun of every journal we included, whenever it had started.

The first disk was not published until May 1993 and the second was not completed until April 1994, by which time we had brought much of the work back to the UK. We measured ourselves against the Lending Division of the British Library at Boston Spa, who were producing a current contents pages publication on CD-ROM covering the many thousands of journals to which they subscribed. They employed two staff and a manager to generate 650MB of data a year. We planned for one member of staff and a part-time manager to generate 360MB a year. Our production costs in the USA and France had been well over budget but Moss now thought she could produce future disks for £185,000 each, £120,000 of which was the cost of keying by Apex.

During 1993 we were increasingly concerned that smaller university and college libraries both in the USA and in the UK could not afford to buy our new large, expensive publications – *English Poetry*, *PLD* and *PCI*. We asked Dick Harris, who had been the principal publisher at ISI and who was now doing consulting work, to advise us. At ISI he had established variable pricing dependent on the size of the library's budget and he suggested that we could do the same.[6] Hall did not think that it would work for these titles; they were too new and too different from anything else on the market and he believed that the market had changed since Harris had introduced variable pricing at ISI. He strongly disagreed with another of Harris's suggestions, that we reach an agreement with SilverPlatter to use their software with, in effect, *PCI* becoming a SilverPlatter product. Hall rightly saw that this would be the end of Chadwyck-Healey as an independent electronic publisher. A month later I circulated an action plan that listed a large number of points, from identifying the libraries who would most benefit by buying *PCI* (through the matching of their holdings of the journals to those that we were planning to include) to contacting library automation vendors like OCLC and GEAC to explore how *PCI* could be delivered through library automation systems.[7] The number of action points in my plan reflected my frustration: the project seemed so simple in concept and yet almost three years later we still could not see how to make it compelling for our customers. One of Hall's recommendations was to immediately reduce the price to £3,500 per disk and in December 1993 we saw a turnaround with twelve new orders in the month, increasing our sales to date by more than fifty per cent. Four customers paid in full for five or more disks, and six US customers ordered the first eight disks. We had thought that it should have a broader appeal than any of our other high-priced CD-ROM publications, but with only thirty-two orders for the first disk, we were a long way from our target of one hundred and were trailing behind where *English Poetry* and *PLD* had been at the same stage in their development. But as it grew, the librarians who initially had been wary of *PCI* because of its lack of standardized search terms began to realize what a powerful search tool it was. A librarian on the West Coast whose personal research interest was western Americana told us that he had found articles in *PCI* that he had not found anywhere else.

The Mellon Foundation

In 1994, as production settled down and sales began to accelerate, we were faced with the choice of cooperation or competition with one of the most powerful bodies in the library world. In January Roesemann had been phoned by Richard Ekman, the secretary of the Mellon Foundation, who had been told about *PCI* by De Gennaro, and on 23 March he and Savers were invited to a meeting in New York with William Bowen, president of the Andrew W. Mellon Foundation and past president of Princeton University. At it they were told that the Mellon Foundation wanted to buy from us contents page information of the journals of the past.

Founded in 1969 by Paul and Ailsa Mellon Bruce, the son and daughter of Andrew W. Mellon who had given the National Gallery of Art to the nation in 1941, its main mission was support for higher education, especially in the humanities, and it had become the major donor to academic libraries not only in the USA but in the UK and elsewhere in the world. With recent annual donations in the region of $300 million, Mellon grants have enabled hundreds of libraries to build extensions to house their ever-increasing collections of books and journals, as well as to improve their operations in many other ways. Through the late 1970s and 1980s ideas had been put forward to limit the need for new buildings by using interlibrary loan supported by electronic cataloguing.[8] The library consortia movement, which was about to become so important to us in the buying of our digital publications (see Chapter 23), had had its origins in the late 1980s in the alternative solution of sharing off-site warehouses for books. Now, in 1993, Bowen and his colleagues were thinking of ways in which Mellon could help libraries to store their material in digital media so that they would not have to invest in more buildings, which were so expensive to build and to maintain. Mellon had found that in a typical college library nearly a quarter of the total shelving was devoted to backruns of journals, growing at three per cent per year. While microfilm was the already established space-efficient way of storing backruns of journals, there was resistance to microfilm amongst readers and now that we were in the digital era, microfilm was no longer seen as an adequate solution. Bowen and others began to think about scanning journals and storing the images on CD-ROM. While the process itself would be expensive, copies could be made available to all libraries at a very low cost. At the end of 1993 Ekman had been advised by Buchanan, my friend and at that time occasional consultant, who gave them his view on the likely costs of scanning or digitizing fifty-year backfiles of twenty journals. Scanning would cost $0.08 per page, keying into searchable text would cost $2 per page. De Gennaro at Harvard also advised Ekman that the combination of the contents page information in *PCI* with the journals themselves being off-site was considered by the academic community to be an inadequate replacement for on-site access to journals and that Harvard itself was now considering digitizing thirty journals and linking the images to *PCI*. This, in spite of the adverse opinion of *PCI* by the Boston group of libraries of which Harvard had been a member.

Mellon knew that they needed metadata as a means of accessing the articles and that *PCI* could provide this. Reasonably, they thought that it would be less expensive to buy the data from us than create it themselves. In a 400-page book about the Mellon journal storage project (which came to be called JSTOR), published in 2003, Roger Schonfeld writes:

> The initial negotiations went remarkably well, in part because of Chadwyck-Healy's [sic] interest in the future of scholarly communications and tolerance of risk in looking to this future. We saw in chapter 1 that PCI had been built in conjunction with the Harvard library system. A for-profit concern, Chadwyck-Healy had become a partner with Harvard to meet the needs of scholarly institutions. It understood Mellon's scholarly purpose and was willing to alter its own plans somewhat to accommodate Mellon's needs.[9]

This was based on the author's interviews with Ekman of the Mellon Foundation and De Gennaro whom I knew well – I later contributed to his Festschrift. It is interesting to see how we were viewed by the library community, but the author did not interview anyone at Chadwyck-Healey so could not appreciate how different our approach was from that of Mellon. Schonfeld describes Chadwyck-Healey as 'the British bibliographic company' when only a minority of our publications were bibliographic. But in one way he was right: we had gone into the publishing of *PCI* with only the creation of a large bibliographic database in mind. We were aware that one day we might scan some of the journals and link their pages to *PCI*, but we would only consider it once *PCI* had proved to be a success. Mellon, on the other hand, saw *PCI* simply as a means of accessing the electronic journals that they wanted to scan. The author wonders why we were interested in participating in Mellon's project and goes on to say in a footnote, 'Perhaps Chadwyck-Healy [sic] representatives feared that the days of indexing services like PCI were numbered.'[10]

We had no fear of this because our interest was in the thousands of backruns of journals in every European language published before 1990, for which little or no metadata existed. I would have told him that we were flattered and intrigued by being approached by such a prestigious organization that wanted what we already had. We were sure that there was some way in which we could defray our costs if not make a lot of money by teaming up with Mellon. The fact that we could not immediately see how this could be done did not discourage us from exploring the possibilities.

I had written to Bowen in May with a proposal and in July he wrote to me with a progress report. He mentioned the copyright problems that he was having with publishers, which had led them to scale back their initial project to ten journals rather than sixteen. In response we agreed to include these in the next group of journals. Mellon had proposed paying us a flat fee for our data, but we soon realized that we would need a fee from Mellon equivalent to the net revenue we might expect from the worldwide sales of *PCI*, as we would be competing directly with Mellon who would also be able to offer the journals themselves. For the fee to equate to our expected revenues it would be in excess of anything that Mellon could consider paying us, and we began to discuss the payment to us of a fee relating to the number of institutions that JSTOR was sold to.

In July I made a proposal to Bowen for the supply of metadata for the first ten journals, for which Mellon would pay us a flat fee of $12,000 for use in five small private colleges, and for further sales we would charge $1,600 per sale for the first ten sales, on a sliding scale going down to $200 per sale for over 200 sales. Our intention was that our production costs would be covered once Mellon had paid us for around forty copies. Bowen described this proposal as 'fully acceptable'.[11] If Mellon had gone ahead on this basis, the cost to them for the 1,226 libraries who were subscribing to JSTOR by 2001 would have been over $300,000 plus the cost of tagging the articles with the *PCI* records. Mellon later found that it had only cost them twenty per cent of this price to do it themselves.[12] But in our pricing we had never envisaged the market of over 1,000 libraries that JSTOR later achieved. In July 1994 we still had fewer than fifty subscribers to *PCI*.

Mellon wanted to link the *PCI* records to the journal articles but Ira Fuchs,[13] who was advising Mellon, knew that to do it manually would be labour intensive and prone to error. Joe Fitzsimmons, chairman of UMI, had also warned Mellon that assembling the index would be the most difficult part of the project, and as Fuchs and his team examined *PCI* data throughout 1994, problems began to emerge. They found that some special issues and supplements were missing from journals in the Harvard collection and that, consequently, we had omitted them too. Our bibliographic control had not been good enough and neither we nor the Harvard librarians had known of these omissions. It taught us that we had to improve the way we accessioned journals. Often, when they were bound up into annual volumes, the covers of individual journal issues, on which were printed the contents of that issue, were torn off. Our information then came from whole-volume contents pages bound into each annual volume. But in the case of the *American Economic Review*, its 'Papers and Proceedings' were published as the second issue in each volume, but its contents were not included in the table of contents for the volume at the end of the year. Mellon wanted a more precise, more granular approach in order to match each *PCI* record to the article it referred to. They also wanted to include advertisements and readers' letters together with more information about books reviewed, and we were reluctant to modify our approach to include these. In *JSTOR* Schonfeld states that we were only including 'major articles' and did not fully understand what it was that Mellon was trying to do. This is not correct, in that we included every article entry recorded on the contents page and the book review information, which usually included the author and title of the books. But we did find it difficult to understand why Mellon wanted to include advertisements and letters. The author also makes the point that Mellon made several of their most important decisions without input from libraries. They had chosen *PCI* on the basis of a conversation with De Gennaro but had not discussed it with librarians at the University of Michigan, where much of the production work was going to be done and, similarly, they made the decision to drop *PCI* without any library input.

In spring 1995 Mellon informed us that they could not use our data and were now planning to create their own. We were not surprised, as by then we realized that it was unlikely we would be able to work together. While we were creating a standalone contents page reference work, Mellon had a broader vision that encompassed journals in their entirety. They had thought that they could buy scanned copies of articles from UMI and metadata from us, which would save them from having to create anything themselves. But neither worked, and an organization that had no publishing or production experience found that to fulfil its vision it had to undertake a very large-scale, complex publishing project in which it created the metadata and scanned the journals itself. It has done so with remarkable success. It was a setback for us but, to compensate, Hall's discussions with Law for the licensing of our databases to UK higher education came to fruition (see Chapter 17), and in the package of the three titles that they licensed, they paid £420,000 for *PCI* on CD-ROM to be made available to every higher-education institution in the UK.

PCI online

An equally transformative development was the delivery of *PCI* online rather than on CD-ROM, but it was not until 1996 that we launched an online version of *PCI* while still offering CD-ROM and magnetic tape alternatives. It made *PCI* seamless and easy to use, but we had to decide how to charge libraries for access to the database, which they were never going to own outright. We stated that we would add no fewer than one million article records each year to the database, and libraries could regard their access fee as payment for new information each year, similar to journal subscriptions in which new issues are bought each year to be added to an existing backfile. By the end of 1997 we had indexed more than 2,000 journals with 8.5 million articles, and we knew that an article record cost us £0.32 to produce so we needed annual sales of £320,000 to cover our production costs. The price that libraries paid to online vendors was conditional on the number of users who could access the database at the same time. While a single CD-ROM continued to sell outright for £3,500, a library could access the whole of *PCI* for an annual access fee of only £5,000 per year. But this was for one concurrent user – only one reader at a time. The fee rose to £12,500 for ten to fifteen concurrent users – enabling more than one reader to access the database at the same time was one of the advantages that online offered. While British university libraries could access *PCI* through CHEST, sales took off in the USA and in other countries. By May 1997 we had already gained twenty-seven new web customers, and ten of our twenty-eight CD-ROM customers in the USA had converted to the online version. Total sales of *PCI* on CD-ROM were £2,232,270 and to this could now be added a further £242,010 of web subscriptions. We needed this growth because in June 1997, the end of the 1996/7 financial year, almost seven years after we had started work on *PCI*, it was still showing a cumulative loss. By then, we had spent £2,558,067 building the database of around eight million records, and of this just over half was the cost of keying the data.[14]

In 1998 we began to plan the scanning of some journals but in 1999, in the business plan drawn up for the sale of the companies, we described *PCI* as the 'dominant gateway to retrospective periodical literature' and stated that 'as backruns of journals are digitized over the next 10–20 years, by commercial publishers, libraries and other bodies, the need for a comprehensive electronic index will grow'.[15] So even then, in contrast to Mellon, we still saw the index as the central product. While Mellon had hoped that UMI, with its huge resource of microfilmed journals, would be able to provide them with scanned images, it was to *PCI* that Bell & Howell Information and Learning (previously UMI), after it had bought Chadwyck-Healey, began to add scanned images of articles, later renaming it *Periodicals Archives Online*.

20

Publishing Online

Growth

By 1994 the growth of Chadwyck-Healey Ltd, and the volume of literary texts that we were now converting into digital form, required us to move from Cambridge Place (see Chapter 14) to much larger premises. Every person working in editorial and production had to have a networked PC on their desk. Before WiFi a network meant cabling beneath raised floors, which were only found in modern office buildings. But it was a good time to look for a new office as we were still in the property recession that had started in 1987. Vestey Estates had built a new office development called The Quorum, two miles from the centre of Cambridge, and it was almost

Figure 14 Cambridge. The Quorum, Barnwell Road. Our new fully networked office required miles of wiring under raised floors. Spring 1994.

empty. McCrae's keen negotiation enabled us to rent 13,000 square feet in three separate suites, each of which we could give up at any time without penalty. The rent averaged just over £7 per square foot, well down on the £10 we would have paid before the recession, and the landlord gave us £30,000 towards the cost of carpeting and floor sockets. Apart from a lack of air-conditioning it suited us well and we were able to plan the offices for text conversion on a large scale. By the time we moved in May 1994 we employed almost 100 people in Cambridge, and when by 1996 that figure had grown to 150 people, we took a fourth suite of offices. More than twenty-five years later ProQuest is still in The Quorum.

Literature databases

Work on *English Verse Drama*, 1,500 plays from the Middle Ages to the end of the nineteenth century, started before *English Poetry* was completed. At the same time, Chadwyck-Healey Inc. was publishing *American Poetry*, 35,000 poems by more than 200 poets, with the editorial work done in the USA and production in the UK. These were followed by two more specialized collections, *Editions and Adaptations of Shakespeare* and *The Bible in English*. The former, edited by the eminent Shakespeare scholars Anne Barton and John Kerrigan, included the most important editions, from the First Folio to the Cambridge edition of 1863–6. It also included the adaptations from after Shakespeare's death, and the editors found that the most complete listings were the sales brochures that I had produced at Cornmarket Press in 1968 and 1969 (see Chapter 1). They used these lists as their source, and my own copies of the reprints were used to convert the texts into digital form. I had now republished the same plays in two very different media – the wheel had turned full circle. *The Bible in English* contained twenty-one editions of the Bible from the tenth to the twentieth centuries that were selected to show the evolution of the English language through the centuries. Both titles were published on CD-ROM and sold for £2,500 and £1,250 respectively. I had hoped for much larger sales than the low hundreds we probably achieved, and we had hardly fulfilled Fellner's aphorism that 'Shakespeare, Dickens and the Bible always sell' (see Chapter 3).[1] We cautiously ventured into prose with *English Prose Drama*, a further 1,800 plays, and then embraced fiction even though the large number of characters to be keyed in novels meant much higher costs per title. We started with *Eighteenth-Century Fiction* in 1996, followed by *Early English Prose Fiction* in 1997, the latter developed in association with SCREEN (Salzburg Centre for Research on the Early English Novel). Together with *American Drama*, *Early American Fiction* and *African-American Poetry*, by the late 1990s we had published twelve separate literature collections on CD-ROM including *English Poetry Plus*, a schools edition containing 5,000 poems with biographies, images and recordings. It sold well at £250. But we were missing one outstandingly important component of English literature, twentieth-century English poetry. We acquired rights from Bloodaxe Books and Carcanet and most of the publishers of contemporary poetry, but we could not publish a comprehensive collection without an agreement with Faber & Faber, the publisher of so many of the most important twentieth-century poets – T. S. Eliot had been a director of the company and his widow Valerie still was.

I had written several times to Matthew Evans, then chief executive of Faber, to ask if we could meet and discuss it but had never had a response. In June 1995 Ed Victor, the literary agent, promised to arrange a meeting with Evans but at about the same time I was invited to join the new Library and Information Commission (LIC) set up by the minister Virginia Bottomley to advise the Department of National Heritage on matters relating to libraries and information. I would have declined as I had not found being a member of its predecessor, the Library and Information Services Council (LISC), very rewarding, but I agreed to join the LIC because it was chaired by Evans and it meant that he would have to meet me at least four times a year. The combination of the minister's patronage and Evans's style meant that the LIC was as different from LISC as the Orient Express was from the old British Rail. It had money, a secretariat and a determined and charismatic chairman. It was launched at a dinner in a private room at the Ivy, at the time one of the most fashionable restaurants in London, while the minister dropped in for a glass of champagne. Douglas Adams, author of *The Hitchhiker's Guide to the Galaxy*, was one of the members of the commission but he seemed to find library matters tedious and disappeared after a few meetings.

Evans was friendly and committed to making the LIC a body that really did something for UK public libraries. I could now talk to him about electronic editions of the Faber poets and eventually he invited us to make a presentation to the board. When Michael Healy, our editorial director, and I arrived to prepare for the presentation, the monitor that Faber had provided for displaying our presentation failed, a bad omen. Healy and I explained that access to electronic editions of not only the twentieth-century 'greats' but contemporary poets with relatively small readerships would be greatly increased by access via CD-ROM and the World Wide Web, and would earn the poets significant annual royalties. Valerie Eliot, the self-appointed guardian of the Eliot oeuvre, sat in the front row visibly unmoved and in the months that followed nothing happened. We had made our pitch and Faber were still not willing to take it further, but without Faber we could not move forward. It was stasis.

Then, in 1997, someone in the USA put T. S. Eliot's *The Wasteland* on the web, presumably for the convenience of their students. It was a direct infringement of the T. S. Eliot copyright and showed Faber how dangerous the 'free' web was. Faber came to us with a proposal that we should publish electronic editions of the Faber poets and in doing so become the guardian of Faber's poetry on the web. It would achieve three things: there would now be authorized rather than pirated editions of Faber poetry on the web, we would police the use of our editions online and would be made aware of the presence of other unauthorized editions through our relationships with the world's libraries, and the Faber poets would receive royalty income from the electronic editions. By this time, Evans was chairman and I negotiated both with him and with Toby Faber, the managing director. Faber may have been a grandson of the founder, but he had got the job through merit. He had been to INSEAD and brought a management expertise to Faber that few other publishers of a similar size enjoyed. We started to negotiate in early 1998 and signed an agreement on 22 May. One of their frequently stated concerns was that there was no financial benefit for Faber in this agreement because the royalties that we paid them would go straight to their authors. They accepted my suggestion that we pay them an administration fee of £5,000, as well as a royalty of fifty per cent of sales for the poets. Significantly, no advance against royalties was asked for, but we had to accept one important stipulation, that the Faber poets had to be published as a separate collection because, 'It would otherwise diminish the value of the Faber poetry brand especially if the database is as successful as we expect it to be.'[2] At the time of signing, Faber wrote to me to say that he was excited that it had come to fruition and, having sent us a list of fifty-three poets, from Rupert Brooke to Wendy Cope, agreed to have cleared rights with the first authors within a few weeks of the agreement being signed. The *Faber Poetry Library* was published on CD-ROM in 1998 but by then we were also able to include it in a new online database, which we called *LION* (see below).

Replacing the CD-ROM

At a dinner at ALA in early 1993 Severtson and I were warned that libraries no longer wanted our publications on CD-ROM. They wanted to access them online on networked PCs connected by phone line to our servers. Large libraries were now subscribing to so many publications on CD-ROM that they were overwhelmed by the number of disks they were receiving each month, with many different softwares, all of which had to be accessed through the PCs in the library. The most important limitation of the CD-ROM medium was that it could not be easily networked. While the information on a CD-ROM is digital, it is accessed by a head that moves mechanically across the spinning disk. The speed at which the head can move limits the access time and makes it difficult for more than one person to access the disk at the same time. Online access, on the other hand, allows simultaneous use of the same database. We were shocked but should not have been. In the early days of CD-ROM publishing we had been at a meeting at Yale University Library at which a librarian said that in her view the CD-ROM was an unsuitable medium for large libraries. At the time, in our excitement at the possibilities that the new medium offered, we discounted her views, but I remember feeling a slight unease at the logic of her argument, which proved to be entirely right. And so, in less than ten years, the CD-ROM revolution was over. These silver disks were a catalyst that brought about change but, like all catalysts, they were consumed in the process. We were now returning to what had been in place since the 1970s, online delivery by phone line from one computer to another, but it would not be the old un-user-friendly online culture of the past – CD-ROMs had changed all that. Users now did their own searches and expected them to be easy to do even if they were accessing a database or using an interface that they had not used before.

John Taylor, our very experienced head of technology, who reported to Moss and who had joined us from the software house Technologic in 1994, started to plan for the online delivery of all our databases. We started discussions with several software providers, knowing that we would be making an investment of several hundred thousand pounds to license what was called client–server software, in which software on our servers could communicate with software that our clients – the libraries – had installed on their terminals. We had employed a consultant from the international technology firm Capgemini to advise us, but on a visit to the US office I met with another consultant who said to me, 'I don't understand why you are not using the Internet.' I explained that our CD-ROM software was too sophisticated for the Internet, since it allowed users to do such things as displaying two texts on the screen and scrolling through both of them at the same time. He smiled and asked if we had any idea of how much Netscape and Yahoo (Google had not yet been invented) were spending on development. Were we suggesting that we could compete with them? I could immediately see the advantages. The Internet was free, we would not have to buy expensive software and, most important of all, our clients would not have to install our software on their terminals, a huge administrative headache for every publisher because every software upgrade depended on the upgrade also being installed by every client. When I reported this to the technical group in Cambridge, I expected some resistance. To my surprise they immediately agreed. I was later told that when the Capgemini consultant returned to his office after his first day with us, he had been asked by a colleague, 'Why don't they use the Internet?' His reply was that we had already decided not to. It made me realize how misleading advice from consultants can be if they start with their own unwarranted assumptions. Most of our competitors went through the same exercise, adapting new client–server software and then abandoning it and using the Internet instead.

At the time, in 1995, only two years after the Internet had been made public, my own understanding of it was very limited. I saw it solely as a means of transmitting data from one computer to another, although I understood that people would use it to sell things. But when the web browser Netscape went public on 9 August 1995, valuing the company at $2.9 billion, I could not understand how a company that was offering a free service and seemed to have no income could be worth so much. In my world information had to be paid for. There was a current catch phrase, 'surfing the web', but why would I want to surf the web? What concerned me more was how much libraries should pay for the information we were about to deliver to them via the Internet.

Access not ownership

Libraries would be paying us for access to a database that they could no longer buy outright because it was on our server. Paying for access without being able to own the database was an alien idea to most librarians. For us, too; our business model was based on one-time sales. We thought that an annual access fee for *English Poetry* should be £5,000 per annum – we would get back the full price of the publication in five years. It would hit our cashflow, but we thought we could manage it. Librarians were thinking in terms of an annual access fee of around £500 to £1,000, which, financially, was impossible for us – it would take between twenty-five and fifty years to get back the equivalent of one outright sale. It appeared to be an insoluble impasse, particularly as our customers were as confused about it as we were. Fortunately, the transition from CD-ROMs to online, between 1994 and 1998, was gradual so we had time to adjust even though in 1997 it led to a financial crisis for us. We were also having to adjust to the new way in which US libraries were beginning to buy electronic publications – through large buying consortia. This proved to be our salvation and enabled us to survive and begin to grow again. It is described in Chapter 23.

Literature Online (LION)

As soon as we had published the first CD-ROM of *English Poetry*, I had begun to worry about the long-term security of a database that was costing us £1 million to create. While librarians are punctilious about observing copyright, some academics are not. My concern was that an English professor would borrow a set of *English Poetry* from the library and spend the weekend making copies to give to his/her students. I was also concerned about copyright protection (see Chapter 18).

In April 1995 Angela and I flew to Australia for a three-week holiday, during which we also visited Hong Kong and the Philippines. Buchanan had sent me an article from a computer magazine that I read on the plane. It described how pieces of text in a database on the web could be connected through hypertext links. The links were created by indexing the data so that a name or subject could be searched for across all the texts on the website. The article also pointed out that if a user downloaded a text from such a website, its value was immediately reduced through being cut off from all its links. It immediately made me see what we should do with our twelve English literature databases. They should be part of what would be a very large website devoted to English literature. I spent the rest of the long flight to Singapore working out what this website would look like. I envisaged it as a vertical spine. Coming off on one side of the spine in a series of branches were the full-text databases. These alone were a substantial body of English and American literature, and would immediately make it the largest English literature website. On the other side of the spine we would add reference material: biographies of writers, bibliographies of which there were many, criticism and commentaries. There was so much material out there that we should be able to license.

Piracy would be solved because even if a user downloaded some texts, they would only be a small part of a much larger whole that was enriched by the myriad links in this combination of reference works and literary texts, and by downloading them they would lose those links. We would also know if there was unusual activity on the website, as we were able to monitor the usage of the data on our servers. It would also bring together all our databases into a coherent whole, and we could add new material each year that we licensed or created, thus making the annual subscription to the website more attractive to our customers. This could be the future of web publishing – not simply to publish separate databases, but to build websites devoted to a particular subject by populating them with all the key texts and references in that subject, all related to each other by hypertext links. I thought it was a tremendously exciting concept, and on my return I gave a presentation to the directors and senior managers, telling them that this was where our future lay. They listened with interest but not with the overwhelming enthusiasm that I had expected. Nothing happened. Every month or so I would mention it to Hall or Moss or Pocock, and they would agree that it was something that we should do, but still nothing happened. I raised it again at a monthly board meeting and was about to lose my temper when Hall, who was sitting next to me, said quietly, 'Leave it to me, we will get it started.' Within a few weeks the 'Electronic Home of the Humanities', as it was first called, was in the production schedule and was being worked on. I had thought that an idea as exciting as an English literature website would be welcomed by everyone, but no one wants the future when it is so hard to keep up with the present. It needed Hall, the managing director, not the chairman, to persuade his colleagues that it had to be done and to get it into the production schedule.

Our first public announcement of our move to the web was in time for Valentine's Day in 1996, when we put 1,000 love poems on the web for free. It was widely reported in the UK newspapers, including the *Sunday Times* of 9 February 1996: 'This site is worth a visit if only to see how slushy the whole thing can get.' *Literature Online*, abbreviated to *LION*, was launched at the Online Conference in London in December 1996. There were six literary databases on one side of the spine, with others still in preparation. The first release of *Modern Poetry*, twentieth-century English poetry, came a year later though we were still without the all-important poets published by Faber & Faber (see above). But the other side of the spine – reference – was almost empty. We had licensed the *Bibliography of American Literature*,[3] but we needed two much more important bibliographical databases – the *Annual Bibliography of English Language and Literature* (*ABELL*) and the Modern Language Association's (MLA) *International Bibliography*. We had reached a publishing agreement with the Modern Humanities Research Association (MHRA), the UK publisher of *ABELL*, and had started converting their annual volumes, which had begun in 1920, into digital form with the first release in June 1997. The *MLA International Bibliography* was more important to US libraries but in spite of many visits by Roesemann and me, and later by Rhind-Tutt, MLA would not license it to us, even though rights had been granted to other publishers, such as SilverPlatter. Only after the companies were sold to Bell & Howell was the MLA bibliography added to *LION*. We created a master index, which tied the databases together and also indexed other resources on the web from discussion groups to sites on particular authors or works. We ran weekly automated checks on these sites and had an editor who worked full time on reviewing what had already been indexed.

We moved from Electronic Book Technology's DynaText software to OpenText's Latitude Web server software and developed the first version of *LION* for Netscape 1.2 rather than 2.0 or 3.0 because we knew that many libraries would still have networked computers running on the older version and that they would not upgrade just to access our new website. The web software did not have the functionality we had developed so expensively for the CD-ROMs, but we had no complaints from users, which suggested that the extra functionality was not being missed. We were learning that it was more important to make the interface easy and attractive to use and enable readers to find things quickly. Don Fowler, the Oxford classicist who wrote one of the first reviews, was critical of the interface:

too many screens had to be gone through to complete a search. He thought that we should offer the master index with its access to other web resources as a free service to attract users. He concludes, 'there is no denying that LION is impressive in what it provides and will be even more so when ABELL is fully online.'[4] While Andrew Brown in the *Telegraph* wrote, 'But in its unglamorous way the Lion Web site is a new medium, just as much as the games Quake or Myst. Lion is a library with all the traditional virtues of a library, not often found on the Web: everything is indexed; everything is where and what it claims to be.'[5]

By the time *LION* was launched we were in discussions to license the Cambridge Encyclopedias and the American Novel Critical Essays series from CUP, Oxford Companions from OUP, the index to the *Times Literary Supplement* and Gale's 375-volume *Dictionary of Literary Biography*. But in the middle of 1997, Hall summed up some of the problems:

- not enough subscribers;
- prices too high;
- too large discounts offered to libraries that had bought the CD-ROMs;
- too difficult for undergraduates to use;
- weak in biography, criticism and twentieth-century literature.[6]

The initial price of online access to *English Poetry*, £3,000 for one to four users, was soon brought down to £2,000, but if the library already owned it on CD-ROM, they received a ninety per cent discount, later reduced to seventy-five per cent. In 1998 the complete *LION* for one to four simultaneous users was £8,457, increasing to £11,840 for five to eight users. But libraries could also buy packages – the 'English Corpus', which excluded American literature, the 'Starter Package', which was mainly poetry, and packages 'with or without *ABELL*', the bibliographic database. This gave libraries flexibility in how much they wanted to spend, but by 1999 eighty per cent of US sales were for the complete *LION*.

Improving the interface and adding more critical and biographical material were the overriding requirements, but there were also other more technical improvements that were gradually introduced, such as libraries being able to see their own usage statistics. In 1997 we also added a writer-in-residence, the first one being the Irish poet Matthew Sweeney. This was a free section of *LION* with an audio version of the poem of the week, a masterclass and a poetry surgery in which would-be poets could ask advice of the writer-in-residence. It consumed much editorial time, which would have been better spent improving the areas in which we were weak.

Our most serious problem in mid-1997 was that falling sales of literature CD-ROMs were not yet being compensated for by sales of *LION*. In the *LION* launch year, 1996/7, sales of literary databases on CD-ROM were £1,112,000 for the whole group compared to £1,660,000 the year before and just under £2 million in 1994/5 – a fall of forty-four per cent over two years. But in its first year *LION* revenues were only £202,000. The difference was that this was revenue that renewed each year, while sales of CD-ROMs did not. In 1997/8 sales began to climb again. CHEST licensed the 'English Corpus' in *LION* on behalf of higher-education establishments in the UK, paying a minimum of £80,000 a year for thirty-two institutions with £2,500 for every additional institution. CAUL in Australia also entered into a three-year agreement. We gradually strengthened the areas in which *LION* was weak. We improved the interface, and once we had reached agreement with Faber & Faber in 1998, we were able to add the Faber poets alongside *Modern Poetry*. *LION* went through further reviews by us in 1998 and 1999. An overview by Rhind-Tutt of *LION* in the USA, written in August 1999, two months before the companies were sold, showed that sales of literary databases had climbed steadily over the last two years and in 1998/9, which had just ended, sales to North American libraries had been $1,581,000 (£952,000), slightly ahead of forecast. Infrastructure costs had been higher than expected, but this was compensated for by royalties that had been estimated at 20 per cent of sales revenue coming in at only 11.2 per cent. Across the group, sales of CD-ROMs had also grown, and it seemed that online and outright sales encouraged each other. It also appeared that in the USA four-year colleges had a budget of $5,000 to $10,000 to be spent annually on English literature, and *LION* prices needed to be at this level to achieve maximum penetration. The average annual spend on *LION* was $7,061 but for two- and four-year schools it was below $4,000.

Our main competition came from the publishers of reference material. There was anecdotal evidence that Gale Research, a Thomson-owned company, had achieved over $2 million in the first twelve months of the launch of their *Literature Resources Center*, while the *MLA International Bibliography*, which we had been unable to license, was selling $3 million per annum to over 1,000 subscribers in North America alone. Our traditional market had always been ARLs, members of the Association of Research Libraries, the 125 largest research libraries in North America. By mid-1999, fifty-one per cent subscribed to *LION*. But only eighty-seven four-year schools were subscribers, a far cry from the thousand we were aiming for. We had also licensed to our competitor UMI a version of *LION* to sell to US schools. They liked the new interface, but their main complaint was the absence of contemporary criticism. The security of the databases, in which we had invested so many millions of pounds and which had so concerned me, was now improved by them being held on servers that we controlled. We monitored our customers' usage patterns and on one occasion Taylor reported unusual activity overnight from OUP, which was a subscriber. We wondered if they were downloading individual texts that they planned to republish in print, but it turned out that it was the *Oxford English Dictionary* team carrying out a global search for the earliest use of a large selection of words. At the time the companies were sold, the full potential of *LION* still lay in the future. With its comprehensive collection of texts it was already 'the electronic home of English literature' and with further investment in reference material it would eventually become the dominant resource for teaching and research in English literature, providing the student with everything he or she needed to complete that important essay.

21

German Literature

By 1992 *English Poetry* was well under way and we were now planning to publish a separate collection of editions of Shakespeare's plays and poetry (see Chapter 20). It was time to look at foreign literature, and French literature published by Chadwyck-Healey France was the obvious choice. But discouraged by the lack of financial success of most of our French electronic publications, we were reluctant to invest in a large database of French poetry and it was only in 1997 that we published our electronic edition of the works of Voltaire (see Chapter 11).

It was said that Goethe was one of a small band of super-geniuses, the others being Shakespeare, Rembrandt and Beethoven, men who transcended mere genius. At the end of 1991 Nicholas Boyle, a Cambridge professor, published the first volume of his important new biography of Goethe,[1] and Hall and I went to see him. He explained that the source we should consider digitizing was the Weimar edition, known as the 'Sophien-Ausgabe', a huge edition in 143 volumes. Even allowing for Goethe's remarkably large output, its size was mainly due to its extensive notes and commentaries. It had been published between 1887 and 1919 by Hermann Böhlau, with six editors and seventy contributors, and was itself an outstanding work of scholarship. Goethe's own writings were out of copyright, and I hoped that an edition published before 1919 might also be, but with the German copyright term being seventy years after the author's death, it was likely that some of the editors of the edition would have still been alive in the 1920s and their work would therefore still be protected. Boyle warned us that an electronic edition published without properly clearing rights would be unacceptable in Germany.

After the end of the German Democratic Republic (GDR) in 1989, a young entrepreneur from West Germany had acquired several newspapers and with them the intellectual property of Hermann Böhlaus Nachfolger, which owned the rights to the Weimar edition and which itself had been owned jointly by the GDR and a Swiss foundation. We approached him but there was no response. He was more interested in his newspapers and appeared to regard the titles owned by Böhlau as a distraction. When Tony O'Rourke, our sales manager, who travelled extensively in Germany, advised me that Goethe's works had now been published on an inexpensive CD-ROM, I lost interest. Then Boyle wrote to ask what progress we were making and told me that we should ignore the cheap CD-ROM and persevere with an electronic Weimar edition. Encouraged by his advice, we hired a top copyright lawyer in Munich, reopened discussions with Böhlau and signed an agreement in October 1994 in which we agreed to pay a royalty of 7.5 per cent rising to 12.5 per cent on sales over £300,000, with an advance of £5,000. It was now just over two years since our first meeting with Boyle.

For a British publisher to publish the definitive electronic edition of Goethe was like a German publisher publishing the definitive edition of Shakespeare. We knew that if we did it, we had to do it well. A team of Germanists led by our in-house editor Matt Hillyard marked up the texts with SGML coding, and for the first time we used SGML to identify different categories of text – poems, essays, scientific writings, letters and diaries. It meant that a user could restrict a search to a selection of these categories. We also made use of the meticulous detailing of the Weimar edition in which variants crossed out by Goethe were printed in a different typeface and the editors also distinguished between the different writing materials that Goethe had used; all of this was captured in the coding. We included *Goethes Gespräche*, a late nineteenth-century record of Goethe's spoken word, and a modern edition of his letters discovered since the completion of the Weimar edition.[2]

The text was double keyed by Innodata in the Philippines and they also carried out 100 per cent proofreading of the most important texts. Angela and I visited Innodata in May 1995 and saw the keyers proofreading the original text in the traditional Fraktur typeface against the transcribed text in a Roman typeface – particularly demanding when German is not your native language. We carried out further detailed proofreading in Cambridge and published the CD-ROM edition in October 1995.

The edition was well received in Germany and sold widely at a price of £3,950. The Goethe-Institut, the German equivalent of the British Council ordered fourteen copies. Hall was invited to give a paper about it at a conference in Weimar, which he gave in German. The Deutsches

Figure 15 Manila. Staff at Innodata keying newspapers and books including the Weimar edition of Goethe. May 1995.

Literaturarchiv in Marbach emailed us: (in translation) 'It's crazy what you can search for. Astonishing how such a medium makes you formulate new questions. An equally astonishing side-effect: one starts to read Goethe again'.[3] I was never aware of any serious criticism, but there were not many formal reviews in German journals and newspapers. The most substantial was by Fotis Jannidis in *Arbitrium*, a journal of reviews of German literary studies.[4] He states that, 'The English producers have not quite managed to pinpoint and meet all the specifically German language challenges' – the only acknowledgement in a long review that the publisher is English – and also goes on to analyze the value and potential of electronic editions in general. Publication came shortly before we had been awarded our second Queen's Award for Export Achievement in April 1996. An article about the company in the *Financial Times* began, 'It's not quite selling coals to Newcastle but selling Goethe to Germany is one of the reasons why Cambridge-based information specialist Chadwyck-Healey has won its second award for export achievement.'[5] The *Sunday Telegraph*, in an article reviewing the 107 Queen's Award winners, declared that 'the biggest coup has come from the publisher Chadwyck-Healey' in publishing 'the first electronic database' of the complete works of Goethe.[6] In a review in the

American library journal *Choice* in June 1998, J. Hardin of the University of South Carolina, who had been wary of the electronic edition, concluded that 'the anonymous creators did an outstanding job. The transcription appears to be accurate and complete ... this electronic resource offers incalculable benefits to a close and rapid study of the works in a manner previously unimaginable.' The most widespread response came in August 1999 when we offered temporary free access to the Goethe database online providing that users registered with us.[7] It was accessed by users from Hawaii to Croatia, including the German ambassador to the Sudan. It was reported in all the main German newspapers and weekly magazines.

Böhlau also owned rights to both Friedrich Schiller's works in a series from 1940 called the *Nationalausgabe*, in fifty-five volumes (with a further seven in preparation), and to the Weimar edition of the works of Martin Luther. Our first release of *Schillers Werke* was in late 1998 on both CD-ROM and online. This was followed by the works of Martin Luther in the edition that had been started in 1883 on his 400th anniversary. It was in more than 117 quarto volumes and the digitization would not be completed until 2009. The first release of *Luthers Werke* was in October 1999, the month the company was sold.

We also published *Die Deutsche Lyrik*, a database of three centuries of German lyric poetry. It was a cautious approach compared to *English Poetry*, as it was issued in a series of small releases, each containing the works of about ten poets, the first being in March 1998. This was later extended to '600 years of German poetry online' including all the volumes of German poetry that had been published in the series Reclams Universalbibliothek. By 1999 we had ventured into the twentieth century with the works of Bertolt Brecht, published by permission of Suhrkamp, and the fifteen-volume edition of Franz Kafka's works and diaries published with S. Fischer. By the time we published these databases we were offering them simultaneously on CD-ROM and online – outright ownership and online access. In 1997 online access to *Die Deutsche Lyrik* cost £1,250 a year for one user. The first release on CD-ROM cost £3,000 to buy outright with further releases still to come. Such pricing was complicated and was usually settled by negotiation with the library, depending on the entirety of what it was ordering.

My belief, shared by Hall, was that the doors to German literature would not remain open for long. German publishers were conservative and unwilling to take the risk of going into electronic publishing. They were content for a British publisher who had the resources to both create and sell electronic publications not only in Germany but throughout the world to publish electronic editions of the works that they controlled. The royalties they received would show them how successful we were and if they could see that we were doing well, they would then begin to publish their own electronic editions.

Being the leading publisher of electronic editions of German literature was not only profitable but greatly enhanced my experience of the Frankfurt Book Fair. Each year more German publishers and librarians visited our stand. Arend Kuester was one of our two German employees in Cambridge and several others, such as Hall, Hillyard and O'Rourke, spoke fluent German. I was invited to the exclusive lunch given each year at the book fair by the Holtzbrinck Publishing Group who owned S. Fischer with whom we were publishing Kafka. After the barren years of the 1970s, without a base at Frankfurt, I enjoyed our new status, apparently part of a publishing establishment with which, in reality, we had little in common.

22

Red Archives

Red Archive I: Radio Free Europe/Radio Liberty

In June 1984 Angela and I had dinner with Charles and Miriam Palm while we were at the ALA Summer conference in Dallas. Charles was librarian and archivist of the Hoover Institution, situated on the Stanford University campus, and Miriam was a senior serials librarian in the university library. The Hoover Institution on War, Revolution, and Peace is one of the most influential research centres in the USA. In the tradition of its founder Herbert Hoover, later president of the United States, its library and archives are dedicated to documenting war, revolution and peace in the twentieth and twenty-first centuries. Hoover, one of the first graduates of Stanford University, had been in Europe during the First World War helping Belgium's civilians when, after invasion by Germany, they were facing starvation. He knew that Andrew White, a diplomat, historian and first president of Cornell University, had regretted not collecting documents relating to the French Revolution at the time of the revolution itself when they would have been easily available, and Hoover realized that this was now the time to collect documents about the First World War. In 1919 he pledged $50,000 to Stanford University to support the Hoover War Collection, later writing, 'Therein lay the origins of the Library on War, Revolution and Peace at Stanford University', which became the world's largest private repository of documents on twentieth-century political history.

The day after our dinner, Palm asked me if we might be able to help him secure an important collection of biographical information on Russian politicians and functionaries created by Radio Free Europe/Radio Liberty (RFE/RL) in Munich, known as the Red Archive. It was in daily use as a reference source for the journalists who compiled and broadcast programmes to audiences throughout the USSR and the Eastern Bloc. It was unfeasible to have a single copy made of this very large database solely for Hoover, and I thought that it could be a commercially viable microform publication. We discussed a deal whereby Hoover would help us negotiate a publishing agreement with RFE/RL and would receive a free microform copy in return.

RL had been set up in 1953 to broadcast into the USSR along the lines of RFE, which was already broadcasting to the Soviet satellite countries. It was listened to by millions of Russians for news about events in their own country, which were not reported on their own radio and TV channels. The creator of the Red Archive was Victor Zorza, a Polish expert on Soviet affairs. His staff at RL combed Soviet newspapers and magazines and wrote abstracts of much of what they found. They filed and cross-filed both the newspaper and magazine clippings and the abstracts into an index that Zorza had devised, with 8,000 subject categories.[1] There were separate copies for each person mentioned, for each *oblast* (province) and for each subject category. In this pre-computer era, a single abstract could require thirty to forty copies for filing. A former British army officer, Keith Bush, had taken over from Zorza and continued to develop the research service into one of RL's major assets. In the archive there would be the whole history of a new deputy of the Supreme Soviet tracked by the archive from when he had first been reported as an obscure official in some distant *oblast*. When in the 1960s and 1970s there was a move to close down both RL and RFE as 'relics of the Cold War', there was support for RL from Sovietologists who recognized the importance of this database with its unique insight into the closed world of the Soviet Union.

Palm and I visited RFE/RL in Munich in April 1985 and met Ted Curran, the chief executive, who later came to the UK and had dinner with us at home. After we reached an agreement, Goldman and I went to RFE/RL in Munich to plan the microfilming, which was done on their premises by a young German whom we had hired.

We announced *The Soviet Biographic Archive, 1954–1985* in January 1986 with publication in September. It contained over 1 million clippings on over 50,000 people on 2,812 microfiche and sold for £7,000/$10,000. Sales were good, particularly in Europe. The Hoover Institution received its free copy and RFE/RL earned some useful royalties. By 1987 RL had compiled a computerized biographic index from 1984 of all party and state officials together with many other categories including the children of prominent personalities. We published it as *Public Figures in the Soviet*

Union on computer-output microfiche (COM) in early 1988 even though by then we were beginning to publish such databases on CD-ROM. (We did not have the software or the expertise to publish an electronic edition of a Cyrillic text database.) The Base File was £325 and there were two updates a year.

The Palms became good friends and I stayed with them whenever I was on the West Coast. I also regarded Stanford, with its Californian climate and Spanish-style architecture, as my favourite university campus, while the university library was one of our most important customers.

Red Archive II: The Archives of the Central Committee of the Communist Party

Jana Howlett is a lecturer in Russian history at Cambridge University and had been our neighbour when we first moved to Cambridge in 1976. Her mother was English, her father was Czech. In the 1960s she moved with her mother and stepfather to Beijing where she attended Chinese and Russian secondary schools. As a postgraduate student and later lecturer she had spent many months working in Russian archives. In May 1990 she was invited to a medieval history conference in Sverdlovsk in the Urals organized by the then head of the history faculty, Rudolf Pikhoia. She took some reels of our microfilm to Sverdlovsk and brought back some Russian microfilm and a list of illuminated manuscripts that might be published in facsimile.

Shortly after, I was approached by a library automation company that wished to sell a library management system to the Russian Academy of Sciences Library (BAN) in Leningrad. BAN did not have the foreign exchange to pay for it, and the company asked me if I would visit the library at their expense and advise on how it could earn foreign currency by publishing facsimiles of their most important books and manuscripts, and microfilms or CD-ROMs of collections in the library. I asked Fellner to come with me, as I needed his expertise in identifying the most important rare books and illuminated manuscripts. With his demanding workload, compiling sales catalogues in the book department at Christie's, for him to come to the USSR for a week was a substantial commitment. We flew to Leningrad in February 1991 and spent several days in BAN, one of the largest libraries in the USSR, looking at their finest books and manuscripts, but we could not find anything suitable for republishing in facsimile for a Western market. Nor was there anything obvious for publishing on microfilm or on CD-ROM. We did agree to market and sell copies of their *Catalogue of Foreign Language Books and Periodicals to 1930*, which was already on microfiche. During our few days in Leningrad we were taken to two operas by the teenage daughter of the director of BAN, and found that the Russians could share their love of music with us but little else. One of the barriers was the currency, and when we were taken to a shop selling luxury goods and souvenirs for dollars, which Russians could not enter, it was humiliating for them and an embarrassment for us.

We took the overnight train to Moscow and through an introduction by Howlett I was able to meet Pikhoia, the historian with whom she had discussed potential microfilming in Sverdlovsk. He was now the head of the Committee on Archival Affairs in the government of the RSFSR (Russian Soviet Federative Socialist Republic).

Howlett had also arranged for a friend, Natalia Volkova, to act as interpreter and guide while we were in Moscow and for a driver to chauffeur us in his small battered Lada. Pikhoia was friendly and quite different from how I expected a senior Russian official to be. He proposed that we should microfilm archives and books on several themes, including the industrialization of Russia from Peter the Great to the 1930s, and the development of Siberia and the Far East from the sixteenth century. Before we left Moscow we were able to do some sightseeing, but it was not a good trip for Fellner who suffered from the cold and was quite ill after it, for which I felt responsible. Nor was there any benefit for the company who had paid for our trip.

We signed a letter of intent with Pikhoia in May 1991 but in August 1991 came the coup that attempted to depose Mikhail Gorbachev. The coup failed thanks to opposition organized by Yeltsin. Gorbachev resigned as president of the USSR on 25 December 1991 and the next day the USSR ceased to exist, with its constituent republics gaining independence. The former RSFSR was the largest of these and Yeltsin became the head of the new Russian government.

Pikhoia became a junior minister, with responsibility for all the state and party archives on Russian territory, with the exception of the KGB archive. In the autumn he came to Cambridge and we met again with Howlett. He suggested that we publish on microfilm the personal papers of the leaders of the Russian Revolution, most of whom were members of the first Soviet.

These included Trotsky, Molotov and seven others. The archives would carry out the microfilming for us but, unusually for manuscript material, they would be published on microfiche.[2] This may have been because there were microfiche cameras available in the archives that could be put to use for this project. I sent Pikhoia a draft agreement and once again a Russian version and English translation came back quickly, with few changes, and we signed on 17 December 1991.

Our press release went out to the wire services on 21 January 1992 and the next day I found myself experiencing Andy Warhol's 'fifteen minutes of fame'. If I had read our press release more carefully, I should have realized that it implied that we had signed an agreement with the Russian government in which everything, including secret material, was going to be microfilmed, on an exclusive basis. 'All', 'secret' and 'exclusive' are trigger words for journalists. The phone rang all day as news agencies and broadcasting services like CNN wanted interviews and quotes. The next day there were articles in all the broadsheets and foreign newspapers. The London *Times* published articles two days running, while *The New York Times* stated:

> the company said it had reached an agreement with the Russian government to microfilm the entire archives, which some have estimated include more than 70 million documents. . . . In winning the contract Chadwyck-Healey has gained the publishing rights to the scholarly equivalent of a runaway best seller.[3]

I flew to New York the next day and visited Edward Kasinec at NYPL. Chief of the Slavic and Baltic Division, he was one of the most respected Slavonic librarians in the USA. As we walked though one of the reading rooms, he pointed at the hundreds of books on the Soviet Union, telling me that they were now all out of date because their authors had not had access to the archives.

A few days later I was staying with the Palms in Palo Alto. Palm, who was now deputy director of the Hoover Institution, congratulated me on our project but said that he was planning something much bigger. Pikhoia had visited him at Hoover in May 1991 and they had met again in Moscow in November. He had proposed to Pikhoia that Hoover and the Russian government enter into an agreement to microfilm 25 million pages of the archives of the Central Committee of the Communist Party, with Hoover providing money, equipment and materials and the Russians providing the facilities, the labour and the archives themselves. He asked me if we would be interested in being the third partner, the enabler who would ensure that the microfilm was produced to international standards and who would make the microfilm copies for both the participants and any other libraries in Russia entitled to them. We would also be the sales agent, selling the microfilms to libraries throughout the world to help fund the project. It was an extraordinarily ambitious project that depended on full cooperation by the Russians and the provision of several million dollars of investment by Hoover, and I was immediately excited by it. Pikhoia had also met with James Billington, the Librarian of Congress, in London on 17 December 1991, the day that he signed our agreement. Billington was a noted Sovietologist and had been director of the Woodrow Wilson International Center for Scholars where he had founded the Kennan Institute for Advanced Russian Studies. He regarded himself as a central figure in the opening up of the Soviet archives, and had invited Pikhoia and his colleagues to meet in London for a private conference entitled 'Archival Project: Discussion', attended by twelve people including Howlett.

The discussion was characteristic of the approach of librarians and academics to any new project. All aspects were explored in theoretical and abstract ways. There were discussions on the organization of the archives and technical questions on preservation and access. There were the broad priorities of world scholarship, and the prioritization of sixteen projects for rapid publication, with proposals for three archival projects and for nine longer-term projects. Billington himself proposed seven subjects including Soviet high politics, Soviet foreign policy, 1939–56, the demography of twentieth-century Russia, and the Terror system, which came to be known as 'The Seven Sisters'. There was a list of the institutions that already had agreements or were in discussions with Pikhoia. They included the American Enterprise Institute; the Hoover Institution; a project from the University of California, Riverside, headed by J. Arch Getty, who later was so critical of the Hoover project; the British Academic Committee for Liaison with Soviet Archives headed by John Barber and Tony Cross at the University of Cambridge; the Fondazione Giangiacomo Feltrinelli in Italy; and the Institute for Social History, Amsterdam. Our agreement was also listed but described as only including *opisi* (in this case, finding aids). In Russia archives are divided into *fondy* or, to use the US term, record groups, and are further divided into *opisi*, which contain from one to several thousand *dela* or files. The average number of *dela* in an *opis* is 150. Confusingly, *opisi* is also the term for finding aids (see also Chapter 9). Such *opisi* often contain enough information to satisfy a researcher's enquiry. Finally, there were three Jewish projects relating to the Holocaust and Jewish genealogy. But there was no mention in the minutes of the meeting as to how this huge mass of material would be published.

In contrast to Billington's, Palm's approach was urgent and direct. The doors to the Central Committee archives were being opened for the first time; Hoover, whose mission has always been to collect the archives of left-wing and communist regimes, wanted to bring out as much material as possible before the doors were closed again. John A. Armstrong, in a memo that was part of the papers of the Billington meeting, pointed out that in the Khrushchev era, Russian dissertations had been available to foreign researchers, but then access to them had suddenly been curtailed. Palm did not think that this unpredictability would change. The editorial decisions about what records to select, which so preoccupied Billington and his colleagues, could be made later once we had a binding agreement and a plan for the infrastructure that would allow large-scale microfilming to take place.

On the morning of Monday 24 February 1992 we meet in the Rosarkhiv office in the old headquarters of the Central Committee, a building which had been a bank before the revolution and still had elegant high-ceilinged halls on the ground floor that housed part of the Central Committee's archives. Palm is accompanied by Joseph Dwyer, Robert Shanks (from a prominent Californian law firm) and Richard Kahn. Howlett is there to advise and Volkova, who had shown us round Moscow a year earlier, is our translator. I am accompanied by Edward Lee-Smith, a lawyer from Norton Rose whom I have hired to advise us. Rosarkhiv, the ministry headed by Pikhoia, presides, among others, over three physically and organizationally separate archives, generally known by challenging acronyms because of their long names. They are RTsKhIDNI (now RGASPI), the former Central Party Archive in Pushkin Square; TsKhSD (now RGANI), the former CPSU Secretariat Archive in Old Square; and GARF, formerly TsGAOR, Archive of the October Revolution. Each has its own director: Kirill Anderson at RTsKhIDNI, Vladimir Kozlov at TsKhSD, and Sergei Mironenko at GARF. Pikhoia's relationship with them is a delicate one in that although he has overall authority, they have considerable independence within their own archives.

Pikhoia hands round a draft agreement, saying that he would like to see a general definition of the material we are going to microfilm and wants the agreement to state that creating a microfilm copy will enhance the security of the documents. Kozlov then says that he wishes to make a personal statement:

> I look on this proposal as one of many proposals and it needs very careful analysis. The public reaction to the Chadwyck-Healey announcement [the press coverage that we got in response to our press release] makes me feel that I must be much more careful. I would prefer to see a gradual, stage by stage approach: first, filming of secondary material aimed at making the world understand the kind of life that the Communist Party was trying to make and to include material from local party archives. But I recognise that there is disagreement with this amongst my colleagues.

After further discussion Kozlov continues:

> There will be enormous technical problems, particularly in disbinding, and material that is being filmed being out of use for long periods of time. It could take one and a half years to find out if this exercise has value for Russians. I agree that it is important for the rest of the world.

V. P. Tarasov, whom I had met with Pikhoia the year before and who is head of the Department of International Relations, asks why a target of 25 million pages has been chosen. Palm explains that it relates to the $2.5 million Hoover is investing in the project. It could be more if the project is successful, less if it is not. There is a further discussion on the supply of free copies of the microfilm to Russian libraries. We break for a typical Russian lunch with salads, fish and meats, wine, beer and coffee, and in the afternoon in the falling snow we look at a building that might be suitable to house the project, a gaunt concrete shell called the Centre for Cosmic Documentation. I can see that it will not be ready for at least a year, but we are later told that there will be space for microfilm cameras and for processing film in the three principal archives themselves.

Our meetings with Pikhoia are scheduled for Monday and Tuesday but he has a meeting with the deputy prime minister on Tuesday morning and a press conference for the public opening of the archives in the afternoon. So, at 6.15pm on the same day, we start a new meeting to put together a letter of intent. Pikhoia proposes that the material to be microfilmed will be the archives of the most recent period, including the papers of the Central Committee of the Communist Party and the papers of the central, local and party organs, chosen by a committee of American and Russian scholars.

Pikhoia then tells us that he has a fax from Billington requesting that the 'Seven Sisters' be passed on to Research Publications. For the first time I become aware that Billington and our old rival Research Publications are working together. Palm suggests that he will offer Billington an invitation to join our group and drop Research Publications. Tarasov observes that the chief problem is the accusation that they are giving it all away. Palm replies that Hoover and the committee are both making a large commitment, while the sale and distribution of the film by Chadwyck-Healey is very much a secondary part. Both Pikhoia and Kozlov agree that they need to prepare for the response to what is being proposed, from the 'Russian Billingtons'. As a further contribution, Palm offers to give Rosarkhiv all Russian materials at the Hoover Institution that have already been microfilmed, including the diplomatic files from embassies in Paris and the Okhrana files of the Czarist State Security organization. Kozlov asks if the embassy files at Hoover are stolen property. Palm answers, 'Possibly'. Palm has already suggested that Chadwyck-Healey should pay a royalty of forty per cent on the sale of microfilm copies and Pikhoia thought that twenty-seven per cent should go to Rosarkhiv to emphasize that it was being properly compensated for making its archives available, while thirteen per cent would go to Hoover. Palm points out that 'Hoover's contributions are really very substantial. . . . It is [the] expression of our desire to do something important for you.' Kozlov replies, 'The desire for a positive relationship is mutual but Hoover will become the owner of the most valuable collection in Russian history. The increase that this will give to the moral authority and reputation of Hoover is a much greater gain than money.'

Kozlov knows that we have published on microfiche Foreign Office Registers on Russia and Persia from the PRO and I offer to donate a set. As the meeting ends, Kozlov states, 'It is very important that this agreement is seen as adding to our national pride which has been so damaged in this past two years. In ten to twenty years, Russian scholars will be able to use these materials.' We go back to our hotel to draft a two-page protocol. After Pikhoia returns from his meeting with the deputy prime minister the next day, the meeting continues. Rosarkhiv's letter of intent states that a separate agreement will be signed within a month. They will be paid a royalty of twenty-seven per cent and Palm offers to pay an advance against royalties of $50,000 on signature of the agreement.

The opening of the archives in the afternoon is a symbolic event of extraordinary importance and I feel privileged to be there. The archives of the Central Committee have been amongst the most inaccessible archives on earth, available only to a few trusted members of the elite and even they would be dependent on the archivists since they had no direct access to them. The archives were for the day-to-day running of the Communist Party. When action had to be taken against an individual, the record of some past error or miscalculation was there in the archives to be used against him. Now these archives were being thrown open to the world, and the hope in the faces of the young people present in the hall, with many smartly dressed men and women in army and navy uniforms, was very moving. There was such expectation in the air, which events of the next twenty-five years have so signally failed to fulfil.

After the press conference we return to the letter of intent. For every change that is made, Pikhoia's secretaries have to retype the complete page on their electric typewriters. Eventually a much reduced and somewhat general two-page letter of intent in Russian is signed by all three of us. The last hurdle is the farewell dinner. Even though Kozlov advises me to not mix beer and vodka, the endless toasts extract a heavy price and the last day of each visit to Moscow is always marred by a hangover that simply has to be endured.

Figure 16 Moscow. Young Russians at the official opening of the archives of the Soviet Communist Party and the Soviet State. 25 February 1992.

A press release was issued in March announcing the forthcoming agreement and we met again in Moscow on 14 April. Before the meeting I had been told by Palm that Research Publications had been in Moscow to discuss the publication of an electronic edition of the catalogues of the Central Committee archives. He also told me that for some time Billington had been 'bad mouthing' Chadwyck-Healey both in Washington and in Moscow. Research Publications had also been running down Chadwyck-Healey in Moscow by saying that the company was just me and a few helpers (at the time we had over 100 employees in Cambridge). Palm also told me that when the Hoover agreement had been announced he had a call from someone he knew at Research Publications to say how astonished they had been when they went to Moscow in February and had been refused a meeting with Pikhoia.

In the afternoon, Pikhoia, who has shown remarkable good will towards us, now seems distracted by the momentous events happening in Congress at that time and by the possibility of an end to Yeltsin's government. Howlett is on vacation in Morocco and is due to arrive two days later, and Palm has brought with him Dena Schoen, a Slavic cataloguer and a fluent Russian speaker. We discuss Palm's original proposal that Hoover would provide all the equipment and materials and the Russians would provide the labour and facilities, and we realize that it is not going to work because the Russian archives have so little money. Hoover is going to have to pay for all the labour costs as well.

The next day we spend the morning drafting changes in English and then in Russian. Schoen incorporates the clauses on her laptop, but every time she tries to charge it, it blows the fuses leaving the public areas of the hotel in semi-darkness. Fortunately, I have the same model, a Toshiba CX2200, and am able to lend her a battery and recharge hers. We do not have a printer for the Cyrillic version, and Volkova and Schoen write out the Russian draft incorporating the changes. We arrive late for the meeting but find Pikhoia in a better mood and anxious to get on with it. He is expecting a party of US Congressmen and Senators, including Senator Bill Bradley, a basketball star and future presidential candidate. I ask Kozlov if I can see the microfilming they are doing in his archive for the *Leaders* project. He replies that he is no longer the archivist of TsKhSD as he has been promoted to vice-chairman of Rosarkhiv. He is clearly so unhappy about this that I change my congratulations to condolences. There is a look of surprise and consternation on Bradley's face when he meets Palm. We know that Bradley is a supporter of Billington, but as a Senator in a foreign country, he cannot show support for one American institution against another. Colin Kyte, who is the manager of Research Publications in the UK, is also in the group but we do not speak. Pikhoia's assistant takes us in search of a printer. As we go through a door down a wood-panelled corridor with an embroidered carpet, she says, 'You are now entering the archives of the Central Committee. You will realize by the change of atmosphere that you are now entering a "holy place". We do not find a printer and Schoen and Volkova start typing the Russian draft so that it can be ready to print the next morning. At 10.30pm I leave them exhausted but still working. The next day, 17 April, we print out both versions at the Norton Rose office.

That afternoon when we are all tired and dispirited Howlett arrives from Morocco. She is wearing a white tunic and with her deep tan she brings the exoticism of the desert into the drab Moscow meeting room. The atmosphere improves. She acts as both mediator and translator, breaking her own rule that you cannot do both, and we finally sign the agreement. The main changes are that Hoover's investment is increased from $2.5 million to $3 million, to cover the salaries of the Russian staff, as well as paying for all the microfilming equipment and materials. The advance against royalties is

Figure 17 Moscow. Left to right: Charles Palm, Rudolf Pikhoia, the author signing the first agreement, 17 April 1992.

doubled to $100,000, of which we are to pay half. Repayments of advances against royalties will not start until 31 March 1994. Our position has been strengthened in several ways. One of my fears had been that we would pay out money and then find that the project did not get under way because of arguments about what to microfilm. But now we will only pay our share of the advance when the list of *fondy* to be filmed is agreed.

After the signing of the agreement on 17 April there was immediate criticism of both the *Leaders* and the Hoover projects. Although the details were kept confidential, it was known that Hoover were promising large amounts of money, and suspicions ranged from it being too much, with some going into certain pockets, to that it was not enough, and the soul of Russia was being sold for a pittance. The criticism came from Russia, the USA and the UK. A journalist, Natalya Davydova, published articles on 'the sale of the "Party's Paper Gold"'[4] about the *Leaders* project, and 'The "party cause" for sale'[5] in response to the Hoover project, writing that 'the top-secret venture is arousing serious opposition even... amongst Roskomarkhiv [Rosarkhiv] personnel'. She suggests that Chadwyck-Healey's involvement is an important part of the arrangement:

> Wasn't a merchant required for the project precisely because it could peter out in the near future due to a shortage of money? And who will vouch that while Chadwyck-Healey is pocketing net earnings from the sale of our archives we will not be repaying our debt with interest from the sales?

A more serious criticism came from Yuri N. Afanasyev who wrote an article in *Izvestia* calling into question both projects.[6] He had left the Communist Party in 1990 and helped found the Democratic Russia political movement. He was a liberal reformer and should have welcomed the dissemination of information in the archives but asked if such agreements, 'would serve to benefit individual researchers or a private company' and whether 'such a transfer of copied materials' would 'move the centre for the study of Russian history to the USA – the Hoover Institution', when it might be better 'to establish a similar international center here'. He thought that documents transferred to Hoover might be accessible abroad even before they were accessible in Russia and that Russian historians were being given a raw deal. Pikhoia responded with an article in *Izvestia*[7] and also addressed the Russian Academy with Afanasyev present.[8] He was relieved when the agreement was applauded by all. In the English translation of an interview with Pikhoia entitled 'Shameless Trade Goes on Around Archives' he is reported as saying:

> We had been conducting the most complicated negotiations with the firm 'Research Publications' but we didn't sign the agreement. And do you know, how it was interpreted by our western partners? 'That you don't sign the agreement with us', a representative of the firm said to me, 'it contradicts democratic principles!' So I'm often seen as a non-democrat in the eyes of my foreign colleagues just because I try to defend Russian interests.

A distinguished historian at Stanford, Terry Emmons, in an article in *Izvestia*, wrote, 'I don't quite understand you gentlemen; compare this to "the bad old days" when foreign researchers in Soviet archives were systematically refused access to materials that had not been previously used by Soviet researchers.'[9]

In the USA, Billington, who on the announcement of our project in January 1992 had said that 'these archives are perhaps the most important, single untapped resource for understanding the history of the 20th century anywhere',[10] by July was saying that 'the bulk of it [the archives] is "banal" bureaucratic paper work. Besides, the archives have been purged several times by Soviet leaders over the years.'[11]

Patricia Kennedy 'Pat' Grimsted, an expert on Soviet archives at Harvard, sent Palm and me a forty-eight-page pre-publication review copy of an article, 'More *Glasnost* than *Perestroika*: Russian Archives in a New World Setting'. She approved the Library of Congress's exhibition of 300 documents from Rosarkhiv but was critical of the Hoover project. She recited Afanasyev's criticisms in full and went on to list the direct benefits to Russian archives that 'large Western supported archival filming projects' ought to provide, without pointing out that that was exactly what the Hoover project provided. She also stated that Pikhoia had turned down a project with Research Publications, which meant that 'a major Western microform publisher ... was turned away at the negotiating table in May with no adequate explanation'. Palm responded to her draft with a five-page letter. Towards the end he writes:

> Your reference to Hoover as 'a traditionally conservative, private research institute', and your lament at the absence of projects by 'more neutral Western academic institutions' leaves the unmistakable suggestion that our motives are crassly ideological and political. You clearly defame our scholarly integrity. In my own 20-year career as an archivist, you are the first person ever to question my professional integrity. Indeed, to my knowledge, you are the only person, either in Russia or in the United States,

to question the appropriateness of the Hoover Institution as a sponsor of the sort of project we have undertaken with Roskomarkhiv [Rosarkhiv].

Grimsted duly amended her article but Palm's indignation was entirely justified; that year *The Economist* had rated the Hoover Institution as the world's number one think-tank. Soviet historians in the USA tended to have left-wing leanings and saw Hoover as a right-wing Republican institution. They were infuriated that the Hoover Institution had brought off the largest and most important project to obtain copies of Soviet archives, overlooking the fact that the Hoover library and archives were resources for scholarship and had no political bias.

In spite of her initially hostile attitude we developed a good relationship with Grimsted. In January 1993 she sent us a preprint of an article entitled 'Russian Archives 1992: Amidst the Politics and Economics of Transition'. It made the point that Russian public opposition to large-scale Western microfilming was hard for foreigners to understand and had not been limited to the Hoover project alone. She told us that we could use her article as a 'menu' to select any topics that we might want her to highlight in her talk at the ALA Midwinter conference in Denver in January 1993. In the *Guardian* David Hearst wrote in his 'Moscow Diary', 'Not a day seems to pass without another former Soviet institution succumbing to the predations of the free market. The *Moscow Times* recently gave a chilling account of how the body in charge of most of the state and federal historical archives in Russia, was selling off publication rights to Western publishers.'[12] He goes on to mention Hoover and Chadwyck-Healey and other projects in other countries, adding, 'Apart from the fact that none of these countries or institutions would allow the same thing to happen to their archives.' This was not correct: the National Archives in the USA and the PRO in the UK had had microfilming agreements with commercial publishers since the 1960s, and at the time we had cameras in the Archives nationales in Paris. As sometimes happens in the *Guardian*, righteous indignation is undermined by a failure to check facts.

Another critique came from an acquaintance in Cambridge, the Russian dissident Vladimir Bukovsky. In a long letter to Christopher DeMuth, president of the American Enterprise Institute, Bukovsky wrote, 'I have returned from Moscow a week ago from what may be described as a [sic] most useless trip in my life, only to discover a copy of the letter you received from the Hoover Institution.' (This was a letter of 9 March

1992 from John Raisian, director of the Hoover Institution, to DeMuth.) He continued:

> I am convinced that Hoover is making a monumental mistake in signing their agreement with Pikhoia at this moment and in the form they indicated. This agreement will simply be used as a smokescreen by the KGB in the Russian leadership, as a result of which we might never see the true picture.

I admired Bukovsky, whom I had met in Cambridge through a mutual friend. His strong views about the Soviet Union and the inadequacies of its successor governments were hardly surprising since he had spent twelve years in prisons, labour camps and psychiatric prison hospitals, and had been tortured before being expelled from the Soviet Union in 1976. Bukovsky's 'true picture' was different from ours. He was interested in the most recent archives because in 1992 he was called as an expert witness at the trial at the Constitutional Court where the Communist Party (CPSU) was suing Yeltsin for banning the party and seizing its assets. Bukovsky had gone back to Russia to help Yeltsin prove that the CPSU was an unconstitutional organization and he was given access to documents from the Central Committee archives at TsKhSD. He secretly scanned many documents and smuggled them out to the West. Our approach was more historical although *fond 89*, the collection of 3,500 documents assembled from a wide range of archives for the trial, was later microfilmed and sold by us (see below). While it did include many of the key documents that excited Bukovsky, because it was selective it did not give the true insight into life under communism that was given by the *fondy* that we were microfilming in their entirety.

In May three Russians responsible for microfilm production came to Cambridge and were entertained by Everitt at his home, which Valeri Abramov, their chief, said, 'sealed the relationship'. We took them to the photographic department of Cambridge University Library to show them that the Kodak MRD microfilm cameras that Hoover was about to give them were widely used. But, on their way home, they made a detour through Germany to look at another make of microfilm camera, as a way of asserting their independence by going through the motions of selecting a more 'modern' design.

Meanwhile the *Leaders* project was quietly making progress. Rosarkhiv had started by microfilming the personal papers of Julius Martov. Though Jewish and middle class, Martov had been a close colleague of Lenin.

He was one of the outstanding Menshevik leaders but was politically marginalized when the Bolsheviks came to power and he died in exile in 1923. I received a letter in English from a Mrs Tamara Popova who said that she was Martov's granddaughter. She explained that his papers had been stolen from her family or had gone astray when Martov's brothers had been arrested. She was writing a book about her family and was trying to establish her rights of inheritance and complained that the authorities had negotiated with us without any reference to her family. She raised no objection to the microfiche project but hoped that it would not affect the sales of her book. I replied sympathetically without promising anything. We finally signed the English-language version of the agreement in mid-May. Its schedule forecast production between May 1992 and July 1996 of 540 reels a month or 6,480 reels per year, with equipment to be installed by 1 August. None of this was achieved.

The first editorial board meeting took place in Moscow in June 1992 with Palm, Emmons and John B. Dunlop, a leading Sovietologist, from Hoover and Pikhoia and Howlett. Dmitri Volkogonov was also at the meeting. He was a Russian general who had headed the political and propaganda sections of the Soviet Army, but resigned from the Communist Party in 1991, becoming a supporter of Yeltsin. Volkogonov supported Pikhoia in the opening of the archives. At the meeting it was agreed to start microfilming the *opisi* of materials in the Central State Archive of the October Revolution. A second editorial board meeting was held in Washington in September. I did not attend these meetings as we had no direct responsibility for editorial decisions. They decided that they would microfilm

> Materials from the archives of the Communist Party of the Soviet Union, and also from state archives, pertaining in the first place to the mechanisms of power, including documentation of political decision making of the central organs of the CPSU and of the most important political figures of the CPSU.

Led by Emmons, the board began to refine these to:

- Party congresses, conferences, protocols (to the 18th Congress)
- Central Committee plenums (to 1941)
- Politburo: protocols, transcripts, decisions, materials (to 1941)
- Secretariat CC CPSU
- CC CPSU Apparat
- NKVD RSFSR 1917–1930.

We had chosen the microfilm medium because it was reliable and was a technology that was familiar to the Russians. Hoover agreed to ship fifteen microfilm cameras costing $10,000 each, and other equipment including microfilm processors, a PC, a printer, a microfilm reader and a fax machine. The project divided into four parallel streams. The first was the high-level policy and editorial discussions between Rosarkhiv and Hoover, interspersed by board meetings in Moscow, Cambridge and Washington that, at the beginning, took place every six months. The second was the day-to-day issues of microfilm production – the filming of the correct documents, the quality of the microfilm, and the rate at which it was being produced. These were well managed by Judith Fortson at Hoover, Everitt in Cambridge, and Chapman in Bassingbourn, and their staff. The third was the contractual and practical relationship between Hoover and Chadwyck-Healey and to a lesser extent between Rosarkhiv and Chadwyck-Healey. The fourth, which came later, was the sale of microfilm copies, handled by our sales staff in the UK and USA. In a letter to Palm on 24 February 1993 I wrote, 'It is almost a year since we signed the agreement with Roskomarkhiv [Rosarkhiv] and five months since the three cameras were delivered to Moscow, and all we have to show for it today is six reels of film brought back last week.' We arranged for Volkova to go to the archives every week, collect whatever film had been produced and ship it to us and, by May, film began to come through regularly. But because the shipments were so small transport was costing us $5 per reel, which was more than Hoover had agreed to pay us.

In May Hoover delivered a further eight cameras together with film developers, splicers, densitometers, microfilm readers, water-mixing valves and all the accessories needed for a fully functioning microfilm bureau. Chapman and one of his managers, Reuben Starling, spent two weeks in Moscow to help install the equipment and make sure that it was working. I wrote to Palm on 19 May 1993:[13]

> I believe that the project can be successful through us acting as an intermediary because of the very nature of our style of operation. You can liken us to a terrier, snapping at the heels of both parties, worrying away at each little issue until it is resolved. As Judith [Fortson] knows well, microfilming is not rocket science, it is not very creative and it is not very complicated but to do it well does need enormous attention to detail by pragmatic down-to-earth people who do not mind spending time on small mundane items of management to make sure that the whole operation is

carried out properly. This has been the philosophy in this company for twenty years and on the whole we are very good at it.

Hoover and Chadwyck-Healey were able to resolve issues quite quickly, knowing that we had to present a united front to the Russians to get their cooperation. When Emmons at Hoover received the first sales brochure on the *Leaders of the Russian Revolution*, he wrote to congratulate us: 'I predict this series will be in use by scholars long after the Yale project will have been totally forgotten.'[14] The 'Yale project' was to publish a series of books containing selected documents with commentaries. The price for the *Leaders* project was £28,900 but it sold well, as libraries were able to buy separately the papers of each of the nine individuals from as little as £270. The papers differed from much of the material in the Hoover project because they were so personal: diaries, family letters, photographs and other ephemera. The core of the collection had come from the archives of ISTPART, the Department for the History of the Party, formed in 1918 by the Bolsheviks. It was supplemented by personal papers, given, or seized as in the case of Martov.

The next editorial board meeting, held in Cambridge in January 1993, was hosted by us and was held at Jesus College, where Howlett was a Fellow. Over the next few years we held several meetings at Jesus, always in the Prioress's Room, which opens out on to the cloisters. The intimacy of those ancient spaces seemed to suit our meetings and the atmosphere was always better tempered than in Moscow. In the evening a dinner was held in the college attended by the Master, Colin Renfrew, and by several Soviet historians including Orlando Figes and Robert Conquest. Dinners for subsequent Russian delegations were held in pubs around Cambridge. At the meeting, which included a visit to the microfilming bureau in Bassingbourn, the subjects chosen for microfilming ranged from agriculture, heavy industry and schools to the NKVD administration of prisons and camps.

A further amendment made to the agreement on 18 August 1993 required Hoover to pay $60,000 to Rosarkhiv. This was to be the first of five similar payments, each one of which would only be made when a further 5,000 reels of film had been delivered. One of the reasons for the constant demands for more money was because of the deteriorating economic situation in Russia. In January 1992, just as we had our first meeting in Moscow, Yeltsin had brought in sweeping economic reforms that created enormous hardship, with a dramatic fall in GDP matched by runaway inflation. In the first half of 1992 a citizen's average income dropped by half. In September Yeltsin tried to dissolve the legislature, which in turn declared his decision null and void. In early October 1993 demonstrators took over the mayor of Moscow's offices. The army stormed the Supreme Soviet building and arrested the leaders of the resistance. The ten-day conflict resulted in 187 people being killed – the unofficial figure was 2,000 – with the deadliest street fighting in Moscow since the revolution. In December Yeltsin pushed through his new constitution, giving the president sweeping powers. The result was that while Russia was now ruled by a dual presidential–parliamentary system, substantial power now lay in the president's hands, which Yeltsin and his successor, Vladimir Putin, have used to the full.

The positions of Rosarkhiv and Pikhoia were strengthened by the crisis. From February 1994 Rosarkhiv was made part of a formal structure of government, reporting directly to the Office of the President, along with defence, foreign affairs and internal security, and Pikhoia himself had more direct control. This new status was surprising, as Howlett had once said that because archives were so unimportant compared to defence, security and transport, they were a useful political football to be kicked around by politicians to score points off each other, knowing that none of it would do any real harm. At the editorial board meeting in Washington that took place in the same month, Pikhoia reported that papers now being transferred from the Kremlin Archives to RTsKhIDNI included Politburo protocols for 1919–21, and 1941–52, two periods of particular importance. Other papers transferred to TsKhSD included Politburo protocols 1952–90 and other material from the 1980s and the Gorbachev era. But all archives that we filmed had to be declassified by archivists, who read through the files looking out for sensitive and confidential material, which they would remove or flag up as not to be filmed.

We were still concerned about the amount of film being sent through – by then about 200 reels a month, which was still not enough. Many of the *fondy* we wanted to microfilm had already been filmed by the Russians and copies of their film were available. But the quality was too variable and too much time was spent checking it and ordering refilms, which also had to be checked. In the end, the only existing microfilm we used had been produced at GARF on a German microfilm stock that was superior to Russian film. At an editorial board meeting in Moscow at the end of September 1994 we now noted that 1,837 reels of film had been produced by the three archives.

But, once again, the discussion was dominated by money. Between 1992 and 1994 the cost of living in US dollars had increased 16.2 times but the monthly salary of a camera operator was still only $100 plus a further fifty per cent for benefits. According to Pikhoia, electricity had increased in price from 30 kopeks per kWh in 1992 to 98 rubles in 1994, an increase of over 300 times, which directly affected the cost of production in the archives. In response, Palm agreed to increase payments to the Russians and persuaded me to increase the royalty we paid to Hoover from thirteen per cent to fifteen per cent. At the end of the visit, Pikhoia and his wife entertained us and some of his friends in his large dacha outside Moscow in a fashionable neighbourhood containing the dachas of other ministers and senior functionaries. The long journey back to our hotel gave us time to partially recover from the many vodka toasts.

In May 1994 IDC announced the publication on microfiche of the archives of Comintern, the international communist organization. The agreement was made with RTsKhIDNI and its director Kirill Anderson, not with Rosarkhiv. We now understood the limitations of Pikhoia's authority in respect of agreements made by the individual archives. After the elections of December 1993 the Communist Party had won a big majority, and this made Pikhoia's position as a Yeltsin appointment quite vulnerable even though his official position had given him more authority. In December 1994 he warned that he might be sacked and wanted an annex to the agreement to strengthen his position. But he also confirmed that we would be given the documents in *fond* 89 (see above), and all *opisi* at RTsKhIDNI except the Trophy and Comintern *opisi*, and the American Communist Party *opisi* and *fondy*. The Trophy Archive was primarily German archives removed from Germany at the end of the war.

The year 1995 passed quietly. A meeting took place in Cambridge in June when a 'Third Annex to the Agreement of April 17 1992' was signed. In it there is a definition of the limits of the agreement and the circumstances by which it might be renewed or ended. Howlett kept us aware of how precarious our agreement was in the face of continuing hostility within the three archives and hostility to Rosarkhiv and Pikhoia from outside. It was like living with a frail relative who you know may die at any time but when he does it still comes as a shock. The shock came on 28 December 1995 when we received a faxed letter in Russian signed by Pikhoia, followed by an English translation. It was headed, 'Notification regarding extraordinary circumstances (conditions of "force-majeur")'. It started by praising what we had achieved but went on to note several shortcomings, including the absence of joint team-work by Russian and foreign scholars and archivists and 'insufficient financial incentives for the Russian archives'. It also noted that

> the agreement contradicts current Russian laws ... which forbid government institutions including Rosarkhiv, to conclude agreements involving the receipt of non-government funds, especially from non-government sources. It also contradicts a Federal law of the Russian Federation regarding 'participation in international information exchange' passed by the Duma on Dec 8 1995 and now under consideration by the Council of the Federal Assembly of the Russian Federation.... Rosarkhiv must inform you of its decision to abrogate the Agreement of April 17th 1992 citing extraordinary (force-majeur) circumstances.

The letter invited us to meet in Moscow 'to discuss new principles for the organization of collaborative scholarly work on the archival collections as well as the microfilming of documents'. Immediately on receiving this, Pikhoia, Palm and Howlett met in Prague, a meeting of which I was unaware until some time later, and there was then a meeting in Moscow on 11–12 January. Palm and Schoen were joined by Herbert 'Pete' Hoover, the grandson of the founder of the Hoover Institution and chairman of the Hoover Board of Overseers. His family foundation was a substantial donor to the project. Howlett and I were also present. Pikhoia, now main state archivist of Rosarkhiv, was accompanied by ten Russians including the archivists of the three main archives, Vladimir A. Tiuneev, Pikhoia's first deputy, and Kozlov, who was now his second deputy. Pikhoia explained that there was a new civil code that prevented Rosarkhiv from participating in commercial activity, while the new law on international informational exchange, still to be adopted, limited the export of archival *fondy*. This was understood, but Palm objected to the use of clause 23, 'force-majeur', as the reason for termination of the original agreement because it would mean that the Hoover Institution had entered into an agreement that was unlawful according to Russian law, which Palm regarded as harmful to Hoover's reputation.

He suggested that the agreement should be ended without cause as set out in clause 6c by one or both parties giving each other six months' notice of termination. To encourage Rosarkhiv to agree, Hoover offered to donate to the archives two-thirds of the equipment and half of the supplies and materials for $135,000. Hoover also offered to give to Rosarkhiv the same number of microfilm reels of archives in the USA as had been filmed in the Russian archives. Palm suggested that they reduce the number of reels to be filmed from the previously agreed 25,000 to 13,500 while agreeing to increase the amount paid for a reel of film from $27 to $40. This was a generous offer considering that all materials and equipment were also being paid for by Hoover, and Palm hoped that it would encourage the Russians to continue the project. By the end of the second day a Memorandum of Mutual Understanding had been drafted. Shortly after, Pikhoia resigned as head of Rosarkhiv.

The termination of the agreement and Pikhoia's resignation were reported in the *Sunday Telegraph* as a 'double blow', describing Pikhoia as 'one of the many middle-ranking Kremlin officials hit by a purge of liberals by Mr Yeltsin's administration'.[15] *The Economist* published a long article, 'The Battle for the Moscow Archives', stating that 'access to the archives has been miraculously transformed since 1988. They are not yet as open as the British Public Record Office.... But Russian archives are now more fully open than those of Turkey or the Vatican – roughly comparable with those of France.'[16] It goes on to say, 'A vast private contract to microfilm the former party archives seems sound to Western historians, despite its cost. But it was bitterly resented by many Russian historians and archivists.' The article ends, 'To save the archivists from poverty and protect tens of millions of files for the 21st century requires a substantial injection of money from private charities or international agencies', which was exactly what Hoover had done, and for which it was being so widely criticized.

In the May/June issue of *Perspectives*, the newsletter of the prestigious American Historical Association, the Soviet historian J. Arch Getty, who had his own publishing agreement with Rosarkhiv, published an article, 'Russian Archives: Is the Door Half Open or Half Closed?' with a well-informed description of the state of archives in Russia and this statement: 'On its face, the Hoover Project(s) seemed to be good for everyone.' It is followed by extraordinary mud-slinging against Pikhoia:

> Pikhoia's reputation and a cloudy financial atmosphere surrounding the Hoover Project also led to trouble in Moscow. One archive official told me in December that his archive had received 'not one kopek' from Pikhoia, Hoover or Chadwyck-Healey. Meanwhile, the Americans were busy photographing his entire archive .... an archive official said at one point

last year 'Pikhoia and Company are touring Europe and America in high style, but the city is about to shut off our electricity because we cannot pay our bills.'

On the day we had paid over $40,000 of royalties into the RTsKhIDNI's bank account in Moscow, the bank was closed by the government and its assets frozen. The archivists told us that they were sure that they would get their money eventually, but perhaps not in time to pay their electricity bills. Palm wrote a letter to the editor of *Perspectives*, which was published in the December 1996 issue. They also published Getty's reply, in which he asked whether there were, 'valid questions to be raised here about the privatisation and commercialisation of archives? (Hoover is not a public organization and Chadwyck-Healey is a private firm)'. I had also written to the editor and she replied to say that their lawyer did not regard the quotation regarding 'the archives not receiving one kopek from Pikhoia, Hoover or Chadwyck-Healey' as libellous, but that 'we are exploring whether our policy regarding quotations may need to be sharpened'. It was an admission that the article was unreliable, and she also offered to publish my letter, but Palm and I decided that this would give more air to Getty and it was best to let the issue die.

While these articles were creating background noise, Palm was trying to reach a new agreement with either all three of the archives or whichever archive was prepared to cooperate. In a letter to me of 1 May 1996 he wrote, 'Dealing with people who lack the capacity to know their own self-interest is the most difficult part of our relationship with the Russians. If we are going to continue this project, we will have to try to do a better job of educating them.'

In a letter signed by Tiuneev, who was now acting chairman, and Mironenko, the director of GARF, they agreed to continue the microfilming of archives at GARF while they finished work on the draft of the new agreement, which they admitted was taking a long time. Mironenko understood how important it was to get as much of the archives microfilmed as possible, both for security and to generate revenues to help keep GARF, his large archive, going at a time when he was getting no financial support from the government. The new agreement consisted of a detailed agreement with GARF supported by a 'Framework Agreement' with Rosarkhiv. The other two archives did not wish to make new agreements with Hoover. GARF, on the other hand, agreed to microfilm:

- the remaining parts of *fond* r-393: the NKVD in the 1920s
- *fond* r-9401: the NKVD-USSR c.1930–46
- the most important *opisi* relating to the gulags.

Palm doubted if there would be enough interest in the gulags. Tiuneev, on the other hand, was nervous about filming complete sets of *opisi* on sensitive subjects such as the NKVD. There was no longer a need for an editorial board because the selection of material for filming was incorporated into the agreement. The agreement with GARF finally came through in December 1996 in the form of an order from Hoover listing the *opisi* and *dela* from *fond* r-393 to be filmed: 600,000 frames, equivalent to 660 nominal reels. The film was declared to be for scholarly research, not for resale (by Chadwyck-Healey), to avoid having to pay substantial export duty. Palm regarded this as a stopgap until a further agreement could be negotiated with GARF.

In the summer of 1997 Hoover ended its consultancy agreement with Howlett and its employment of Volkova. By now there was only one archive to deal with and Hoover was employing another agent in Moscow to work on other projects. I was deeply concerned. Without Howlett the Hoover project would never have got off the ground. Her fluent Russian and her personality, which was so Russian, enabled her to fit in at all levels of Russian society. She had a good relationship with Pikhoia – as fellow historians they shared many of the same interests. She got on well with the archivists, even the difficult ones, and she knew by name all the camera operators, the doormen and the security staff in each of the archives; when one of the camera operators lost her husband, Howlett knew that it was customary to give her some money towards the funeral and did so. We were now trying to organize a large-scale microfilming project in Moscow without anyone there to represent our interests and with no one in the office in Cambridge who spoke Russian. But Hoover had no objection to us employing Howlett, which we did.

It had now become GARF's responsibility to ship film back to the UK. Palm sent GARF a new longer-term proposal in January 1997. This included an agreement to co-publish a documentary work on the gulags with Hoover.[17] Hoover also wanted a five-year exclusive agreement with Rosarkhiv and GARF to microfilm the remaining records in *fond* r-393 so that Palm could raise the money to pay for it. In September Palm asked for some minor changes to a new draft agreement submitted by Mironenko, and at a meeting in Cambridge in October we confirmed that we were due to pay Rosarkhiv

£140,000 in royalties, some of which would go to GARF. Clearance by customs in Russia was becoming increasingly difficult. Some camera operators had been laid off because replacement parts for cameras were held up in customs, and one of our staff, Inga Markan, went to Moscow to bring out as much film as possible as excess baggage. Yet a few weeks later Palm complained that GARF had exceeded Hoover's order of December 1996 and had filmed more than the five million pages in *fondy* r-393 and r-9414.[18]

By the end of 1997 Tiuneev, the acting chairman, had been replaced by Kozlov. We were sorry to see him go. He was quite different from Kozlov, who was angular in every way. Both men were typical ex-communist functionaries: very cautious, concerned about having support from above but determined to see the project continue, if only because it was such an important source of funds for the archives. We paid Rosarkhiv royalties of $333,949 for the year 1996/97.

In March 1998 Dr Gordon Hahn, who had been appointed 'coordinator of Russian archival special research programs' at the Hoover Institution, met with Mironenko in Moscow to discuss the signing of the new agreement, which had kept on being delayed. Mironenko wrote to Palm on 27 May 1998, 'The situation with our contract is so complicated that making any changes to the draft Agreement approved by Rosarkhiv will take considerable time.... I suggest ... we sign a Letter of Understanding and include all amendments in it.'

The agreement and the letter of understanding were both signed on 11 June, two and a half years after the last agreement had been terminated. The new agreement included the microfilming of 1.5 million frames, and the productivity at GARF was now creating a large volume of film duplication work for CHMPS in Bassingbourn (renamed International Imaging (II)). The processed camera film, which was the original master negative, was sent to II for checking and for duplication. Second-generation printing master negatives were made, and we also made two positive copies, for Rosarkhiv and the Novosibirsk Regional Archives. This was a political gesture to demonstrate that archives outside Moscow were benefitting from the project. Two further positive copies were made, for Hoover and the Library of Congress (though the latter only received the first 5,000 reels as a donation from Hoover and did not buy any more). Five of the negative and positive copies that were made were paid for by Hoover and the sixth, our own printing master, was part of the cost of making copies for customers. We made a profit on every reel we duplicated. While in the first three years only 5,000 reels were produced in total, in later years the annual output was around 5,000 and II was producing 30,000 reels of film a year just for the partners, excluding the additional copies made to fulfil sales. By the mid-1990s, when microfilm publishing using archival silver film was in decline, this made II the largest producer of silver microfilm copies outside the USA and was one of the key selling points when I sold II to Micromedia in 1997 (see Chapter 23 and Appendix 2).

Under Mironenko's management GARF had become a highly efficient producer of quality microfilm and there was a good relationship between it and Rosarkhiv. A memorandum from E. L. Lunacharskii, acting director of GARF, to Kozlov sets out in positive terms the work that has been done since the agreement was signed in June 1998 and that the addition of further *fondy* will 'raise the quality of the editions'.[19] In his programme of microfilming for 1999 he suggested:

- MVD: main administration of camps for the metal-mining industry 1941–53.
- MVD USSR: camps for railway construction 1934–53.
- NKVD: child and labour educative colonies 1943–56.

He proposed to film documents from *fond* r-1055, the VTsIK[20] supreme revolutionary tribunal of 1921–2, 'because in preparing a documentary history of the Gulags we must look at directives on the development of the camp system from the supreme organs of power'. He ended by stating that the net income of the last two years ($141,000 in 1997 and $100,000 expected in 1998) 'will allow us to resolve the hugely acute economic problem of the archival establishment in 1999–2000 on B. Pirogovskaia Street [at GARF], at least in part'.

Problems between Hoover and GARF did not entirely disappear. After Chadwyck-Healey was sold in October 1999 the project continued for another few years. In a letter to Mironenko of 11 August 2000 Palm expressed surprise that GARF had produced 1.3 million frames of microfilm (about 1,200 reels) in anticipation of a third agreement. He was concerned that this pre-emption limited his ability to choose material for filming under the third agreement. In a letter to Hall, who was now chief executive of Bell & Howell Information and Learning in the UK, Palm observed, 'You will note that GARF has continued to produce a substantial amount of microfilm beyond what has been authorized. After seven years of partnership, the Russians still do not follow basic business practices!'[21]

For Palm, GARF's over-production was a headache because he was responsible for raising the money to pay for the film and was directly responsible to his board if Hoover's liabilities exceeded allotted funds. Somehow, for over ten years, he raised the money, kept his donors onside, tried to control both the Russians and his British partner, and in the end completed what was one of the largest and most important microfilm publications ever undertaken. But he could not have done it without Pikhoia's remarkable vision and straight-dealing pragmatism.

The sale of microfilm copies

The fourth strand of the Hoover project was sales. There were few libraries in the world that could consider an open-ended commitment to buy around 12,000 reels of microfilm at a price (in 1995) of £60 per reel. This would be an outlay of £720,000 plus shipping costs, plus VAT at fifteen per cent in the case of UK libraries. But the first indications of a sale came as early as November 1992 when I was in Japan and was told by Kinokuniya that the National Diet Library, Japan's national library, was likely to buy. In January 1993 the British Library was the first library to place an order, for $160,000 of microfilm. In the same month at the ALA Midwinter meeting in Denver I introduced a short film, *The Russia House*, that had been made by a British film-maker, John Quick, on behalf of the UK Foreign and Commonwealth Office, followed by presentations by Dwyer from Hoover and by Grimsted who was now our ally. A few days later, Howlett, Cheryl Crosby, one of our best sales-people, and I made a presentation at Yale University to twenty-one historians and librarians who were in the East Coast Consortium of Slavic Collections. We expected to make a sale to the consortium, but it was not until 1999 that Harvard ordered the complete collection, the first library in the USA to do so. As an example of the extent of our sales activity, in one week in 1995 we were exhibiting the Hoover and the *Leaders* projects at events in Birmingham in the UK, Gottingen, Pretoria and Montreal, and in August at the World Congress of Slavists. In November, the Bayerische Staatsbibliothek in Munich ordered a further 2,991 reels and sales for 1995 totalled $945,054. Hall was concerned by how difficult we were finding it to make sales because the material being filmed was so extensive and so difficult to describe. But in 1996 sales increased slightly to $1,120,762.

We marketed separately from the rest of the archives *fond* 89, the 3,500 selected documents assembled for the trial of the Communist Party, and it sold well on its own. The documents ranged from Politburo agendas recording the setting up of labour camps in the first years of the party to the money paid to foreign Communist parties known as 'Moscow gold'. The twenty-five reels of microfilm cost $3,500, a price that was affordable even to smaller libraries.

In late October, after the sale of Chadwyck-Healey to Bell & Howell, I returned to the USA at the invitation of the Harvard College Library to speak at a celebration of the acquisition of 10,000 reels of microfilm of the *Archives of the Central Committee of the Soviet Communist Party* through a gift by Harvard alumnus George O'Neill and his wife Abby. I enjoyed the occasion and the sale, worth $600,000, which had been made before Chadwyck-Healey Inc. was sold, was a valuable contribution to our turnover in such an important year. But the ceremony was marred by ill-informed press comment made earlier that month. The *Boston Globe*, reporting on the 'Harvard archives deal', stated that the Davis Center for Russian Studies at Harvard had responded to our offer to reduce the price from $1 million if ordered before 15 April 1999, thinking that they would be the only library in the USA to have a set of the microfilms.[22] Presumably, the donors had also been told this. Harvard had now discovered that there was a set at the Hoover Institution, leading the *Globe* to describe the microfilm as 'old' rather than 'new'. Palm was unhappy, not only through the disclosure of the price, which concerned us too, but because the Harvard press release suggested that I had negotiated the microfilming of the archives and Hoover's only role had been to finance the project. I shared Palm's annoyance and in my address at the ceremony I gave a full account of the Hoover project.

It remains the only large-scale project to make important archives of the Soviet state available to scholars outside Russia, but it has been constantly misreported by the world's press and misunderstood by many of the scholars who would most benefit from it. Much of what has been written about it is little more than speculation, and in 1998 the British bestselling author Robert Harris published *Archangel*,[23] a 'fast-paced thriller' in which the hero, an American academic, attends a conference in Moscow to discuss a large-scale microfilming project by Rosarkhiv. At the conference Adelman, a delegate from Yale, exclaims, 'He's talking about how the Hoover Institution tried to buy the Party archive for five million bucks.' This time it does not pretend to be fact. But, in the end, the only facts that matter are those recorded on the almost 12,000 reels of microfilm that the three partners have made available to scholars throughout the world.

My last meeting in Moscow was in April 1999 with Mironenko, Kozlov and Howlett but without Palm. I could not tell them about the sale of Chadwyck-Healey, but it was almost as if Mironenko knew that it was my last visit. In GARF he took me to a room where inside a box on a table there was a square Perspex box purportedly containing Hitler's skull, pierced by a jagged hole where the bullet had entered. It was only shown to important visitors, and I felt that it was a gesture of appreciation for all that we had done together in the previous seven years. We met once more, in 2003, when I was passing through Moscow on my way back from a bird-watching trip in Eastern Siberia. We had lunch and talked about the old days and he told me of the dinner held to celebrate the end of the project where there were many toasts, including one to me. I thought then that it was better to be toasted than to toast.

23

Towards the End

Consortia

The impact on our sales revenue of the change of publishing media from CD-ROM to online was accompanied by another fundamental change in the way that libraries bought electronic publications. Initially we regarded it as a threat, but later it became our salvation. In the early 1990s US libraries began to form 'buying consortia' with names like OHIOLink, GALILEO and CIC, which were ad hoc buying clubs including libraries from all over the USA, large and small. A typical consortium might range from ten to over two hundred libraries, a mixture of large research libraries, four-year college libraries, smaller college libraries, junior college libraries and public libraries. The consortium would be represented by an experienced negotiator who was not necessarily a librarian. We could be asked for a price for a collection of publications for all its members that might include *English Poetry*, *PCI* and some other smaller CD-ROM publications. In an early approach, in the spring of 1994, one buyer discovered that our year-end was 30 June and that both the company and the sales staff were keen to close the sale by then. The buyer simply delayed its decision, finally securing a deal at a much lower price a few days before the end of June. Roesemann and I agreed that we should never let this happen again. I was concerned that consortium deals would disrupt the smooth flow of individual orders that we were used to. If one or two large deals either did not happen or slipped into the next year this could have a major impact on the results of that year. In 1996 I appointed an experienced electronic publisher, Stephen Rhind-Tutt, as president of Chadwyck-Healey Inc. and he joined us in June. He had been director of product management at Information Access Company, owned by Thomson, with annual sales of about $110 million. Before that he had been at SilverPlatter in its formative years. Both he and the sales team knew how to negotiate consortium deals, which by then had become central to the way we sold to libraries.

The concept of consortium buying had been brought about by the cheapness of the publishing medium. It could not be done so easily with books, journals or microforms, where the physical copy and its shipping had a significant cost for the publisher. When online began to replace CD-ROMs consortium buying became even more important, as the only additional cost was the need to maintain an electronic pipeline large enough to support additional access to the databases. When calculating the price, we would apportion the full price to the largest libraries, who we knew would have bought the publication, a lower price for the next category and all the way down to zero or near zero for junior college libraries and small public libraries. But even with very low prices for the smaller libraries the total amount was usually substantial, often running into hundreds of thousands of dollars. For online sales, while we were still faced with the problem of persuading libraries to pay adequately for online access, our cash flow was improved by these deals because we were asked to quote for a three-year term and were then paid in advance at the time the order was placed. We benefitted more than any of our larger US competitors from selling to consortia. Most of our sales were still to the 125 ARLs where we had a seventy per cent penetration, but for the 3,000 four-year colleges we only had a five per cent penetration, and less than one per cent for all other college and junior college libraries. This contrasted with competitors such as UMI, who were selling microfilm publications like *The New York Times* to almost every college library in the USA. Now a consortium sale meant that publications like *English Poetry* were in libraries that had never bought from us before, and although they might not be paying much, it was revenue we would not have got in any other way. The CHEST deal in the UK for *English Poetry* in 1995 and the CAUL deal in Australia had both been consortium deals but on a national scale, and the very last large sale that we made before the companies were sold was to a Danish consortium of university and public libraries (see Chapter 24). By the end of the century, the buying of electronic publications by library consortia had spread throughout the world.

Financial crisis

In the autumn of 1993 a new manager at Coutts in the branch where we banked in the City of London looked at what we were publishing and advised us to talk to their media department at their headquarters in the

Strand. Once again, a manager at Coutts had given us unsolicited advice that changed the course of our business (see also Chapter 4). No longer were their loans limited by the security I could offer them, which were the family home and the office building in Cambridge Place, which I owned; they now began to treat us as they would a company making films and lent us money against individual publishing projects. McCrae had predicted that under the old arrangement we would run out of money by 1996. Now he was able to negotiate loans against our large publishing projects totalling £3 million. Each new database like *Periodicals Contents Index* had its own business plan against which a loan would be granted, to be repaid over several years from its revenues. Each project had its own monthly report and it needed a sophisticated accounting system, much of which McCrae had written himself, to enable so many reports to be issued each month together with the accounts and balance sheet for each of the companies. Coutts also gave us a loan to buy PCs and other hardware, and an overdraft facility. Because of McCrae's detailed and timely reporting, Coutts had confidence in us, even when in 1996 our sales began to fall.

At a board meeting in November 1997 McCrae reminded us that over the last three years group sales had gone down from £10 million to under £8 million and then told us that within a few months our sales revenue would be less than our costs. It was clear to me that we had to slash costs, which would mean, inevitably, reducing the number of employees. There were software engineers and other agency staff whose employment could be ended at short notice, but Hall and I decided that we would have to make a further ten people redundant, some of them employees in the microform area who had worked for us for years and were at the top of their salary range. Our human resources manager organized the redundancy process, helped by her young assistant who knew that the process also applied to her. Michael Healy, the commissioning and editorial director, was also made redundant as Hall and I felt that I could take on some of his responsibilities. We reduced our office space by vacating one of the suites that we occupied at The Quorum and were able to do this immediately because of the favourable leases that McCrae had negotiated.

On a visit to New York I discussed our situation with Sufrin, my close confidant and advisor. In 1997 we had received over $2.3 million from the MicroPatent sale (see Chapter 16) and I had also sold International Imaging to Micromedia for £1 million, but Sufrin told me that we were still undercapitalized. The move to the Internet was not only resulting in lower sales but was incurring costs that we had not properly budgeted for. These were the significant costs of having our databases mounted on servers and the cost of connections to them. We now had no cushion to fall back on and were too dependent on the vagaries of month-to-month sales revenues. In Sufrin's opinion, we needed an additional $6 million of capital. The next day we visited John Suhler, the founder of Veronis, Suhler & Associates, a New York investment company that specialized in media and publishing. Suhler, tall and imposing, was the epitome of an investment banker. He told me that he and his colleagues had looked at our accounts and valued our business at $12 million. When I questioned such a low valuation Suhler explained that we had not yet proved that the online delivery of databases would be profitable. He said, 'It is as if you are crossing a river and have one foot on the bank and the other in the water.' To raise $6 million I would have to sell fifty per cent of the companies. After twenty-five years of owning one hundred per cent I could not consider such a dilution and decided that we would have to go on as we were.

We delayed the redundancy process until January where, unhappily, it coincided with our twenty-fifth anniversary. The employees, most of whom I had known for years, left with dignity and a complete absence of bitterness. Some said that they had expected it. The staff that remained were more disturbed and there was an unhappy atmosphere in the office for several months, as it was thought that there were bound to be more redundancies. But we still believed that the business had a potential that we had not begun to realize, and in mid-January we held a seminar for senior staff in a hotel outside Cambridge, 'to begin the process of agreeing on the strategies needed to create a quantum leap in the value of the business'.[1]

We were being buffeted by the changes in technology that were also affecting many other publishers, some of which had already gone out of business. SilverPlatter had laid off thirty people the previous November and the British book publisher Dorling Kindersley had laid off eighty people from its multimedia division. At the seminar we discussed a paper by Tim Miller, the principal of a San Francisco consulting firm, New Media Resources. In 'Paradigms Lost: The Information Industry in 1997' he writes, 'The real story of 1997 is the story of how information distribution models blew up in our faces.' He describes the implosion of *Encyclopedia Britannica* in the face of low-cost CD-ROM and online competitors such as *Encarta*, and the acquisition of Dialog, the once imperious online pioneer, by MAID, a tiny British start-up.[2] He warned us to not underestimate the immensity of the changes that were taking place. 'The web enjoyed an investment of $600 million of venture funding in the second quarter of 1997 alone ... while our industry has simply been unprepared to adapt our crusty old models to the new distribution order.' This is what we now had to do, adjust our entire business model to the delivery of information online in a climate in which online information had a much lower perceived value than information in print or even on microfilm and CD-ROM.

In 1998 sales did begin to improve and two other events, small in themselves, helped restore morale within the company. One was the arrival of new staff. Newcomers are unsentimental, they have no interest in the past, their only interest is in the present and their future. The other was a visit by the Duke of Kent on 6 November 1998. Our mainly young staff were not excited by the prospect of a royal visit, but when the day came and local dignitaries lined up outside the office to welcome the Duke, followed by a buffet lunch for everyone, they realized that it was a special occasion. The Duke was genuinely interested in what we were doing and his visit helped to settle us all. Chadwyck-Healey Inc. under Rhind-Tutt was also doing well; we were working on some large new projects, and by the second half of 1998 there was a more positive atmosphere throughout the group.

The indexes to *The Times*

The London *Times* is one of the most heavily used sources for British history for the period from its inception as the *Daily Universal Register* in 1785 to the present day. We wanted to publish digital versions of the two indexes that give access to it. The first was produced by the London bookseller Samuel Palmer and his family, who, starting in 1868, indexed the period from 1790 to 1841. The second is *The Times*'s own official index from 1906. Our electronic edition of Palmer's index ends in 1905.

We started work on *Palmer's Index to the Times* only a year after the beginning of *English Poetry* and estimated that it contained 170 million characters and that it would cost £173,190 to produce the CD-ROM edition, of which seventy per cent was the cost of keying the data. The electronic edition made *Palmer's* much easier to use because we expanded the highly abbreviated date and page references, which were difficult for the occasional user to remember. For example, in the volume for the Winter Quarter of 1860 under the heading 'Accidents', an entry which reads:

—Accident at Goodalor, to a Horsekeeper, Shot by his Master, under the Impression it was a Tiger 20 j 6 b

had its references in the electronic edition expanded to:

Date: 20 January 1860 Day: Friday Reference: page 6 column 2.

It was launched in July 1992 with a pre-publication price of £4,000, and the two-disk edition was completed in October 1993. Hall was disappointed that by August 1994 we had only sold thirty-eight copies, but we could see from the wide range of libraries that had bought it, including several British public libraries, that there should be many more orders still to come. Over the next few years *Palmer's* did sell steadily and was included in the big CHEST deal for institutions of higher education that Hall negotiated in 1995 (see Chapter 17).

At the Frankfurt Book Fair in 1997 I was approached by Henry Pordes, an old-time antiquarian and second-hand bookseller with a shop in the Charing Cross Road, who had published a microfilm edition of *Palmer's*. He told me that he had an interest in the copyright of *Palmer's* and was looking for a consideration. We agreed to meet but he became ill and died and I never discovered the grounds for his claim. We were faced with a more serious copyright problem when we wanted to create a digital edition of *The Official Index to the Times* published by Times Newspapers.

We had first approached Richard Withey, the director of new media, at News International plc, the owner of *The Times*, in 1991 when we reached agreement to sell their CD-ROM edition of the current *Times*. We asked him for rights to produce a digital version of *The Official Index to The Times* from its start in 1906 to 1980. We knew that the *Times* newspaper would eventually be scanned but at that time Optical Character Recognition (OCR) was not sufficiently developed to be able to recognize characters in nineteenth- and twentieth-century newsprint, and I assumed that the digital indexes would be the only way of accessing what was one of the most heavily used historical resources in the world. Withey prevaricated for several years. We could not understand why it took him so long to draw up an agreement but we eventually signed it in 1996. I regarded the index as one of the most important and potentially profitable projects that we would undertake in the mid-1990s. It comprised 297 volumes containing 12 million entries and, with *English Poetry* and *PLD* now completed, it was the large project that we needed. But on the announcement of its publication

I received a letter from Mark Holland, publisher and general manager in the UK of Primary Source Media (PSM; the new name of Research Publications, our old rival), which informed us that PSM, not Times Newspapers or their parent News International, owned the rights to the index. It was extraordinary that Withey and his lawyers had not discovered this over the many months they spent preparing our agreement, but Withey confirmed that it was true. It appeared that when Thomson had sold *The Times* and the *Sunday Times* to Rupert Murdoch's News International, the buyer and its lawyers had not discovered that before the sale Thomson had granted Research Publications (a company they owned) microfilm rights to the newspapers and all rights to the index. One imagines that in the excitement of acquiring the newspapers neither of these rights seemed important, and the agreements were simply overlooked or were not seen at all. Contractually we were in a strong position. News International had granted us rights that they did not own. In English law the compensation to the injured party can be equivalent to all the profits that might be earned from that property, which in the case of the index would be substantial. But I was less sanguine than McCrae about a legal battle with a Murdoch-owned company, and it soon became clear that Withey had been told to find a solution. He persuaded PSM to grant us rights, which they did in an agreement signed the following July.

Although we had lost a year, we had already done much to prepare for production and we published the first release in April 1998 with completion in December 1999. For the index on CD-ROM the pre-publication price was £16,000 and the full price £20,000. An eighteenth-month introductory subscription to the version on the web was £1,600, or £1,950 with *Palmer's Index*, for four concurrent users. Our relationship with News International continued to be amicable and when they pulled out of publishing their newspapers on CD-ROM because of disappointing sales,[3] Withey asked us to take over production as well as the marketing of the current *Times* and *Sunday Times* on CD-ROM for both their and our subscribers. We did so but knew that by now we were nearing the end of the CD-ROM era.

By the time the index was under way we had realized that a scanned image edition of *The Times* was the obvious companion. We thought that the nineteenth-century *Times* would be out of copyright and that we could publish it without an agreement with Times Newspapers. We estimated the cost of production to be £700,000 and informed Withey in October 1997 that we would start production in 1998 and complete it in three years.

Initially he was receptive but warned us of the potential infringement of their trademark, the title, *The Times*. We took legal advice from our solicitors and from counsel, and while we could resolve the trademark issue by careful wording, we were warned that there was almost certainly material in the last years of the nineteenth century that would still be in copyright. Forty librarians attended a meeting in February 1998 in which we demonstrated a sample of the scanned *Times* and also showed the Index on the web. In the same month, Hall and I had dinner with Sir Edward Pickering at the Times Newspapers plant in Wapping. Pickering had been vice-chairman and, even at eighty-five, was an important figure in News International because he was so highly regarded by Murdoch whom he had befriended and mentored when Murdoch first entered journalism in Fleet Street. At dinner we discussed rights to publish a scanned image edition of both the nineteenth- and twentieth-century *Times*, and Pickering seemed receptive to the idea. PSM had expressed interest in publishing an electronic edition but were reluctant to commit to the investment that it would require. In April Holland and I had lunch and we discussed a joint venture. He wrote afterwards, 'Your proposal clearly deserves careful consideration.' But in May he wrote again, 'Our Thomson parent has recently made special development funds available to us for this task, and enthusiasm for this and other projects at main Board level makes us confident that we have available to us the financial support and technical skills necessary for a project of this size.'

Even scanning would be a big undertaking: a single issue of *The Times* in the nineteenth century contained more words than a 400-page novel, and PSM, unlike us, had not yet carried out a large full-text digital project. That should have been the end of it, as we were already making a substantial investment in the index, which was being manually double keyed, not scanned. But throughout the summer we continued to explore the possibility of publishing a nineteenth-century scanned *Times*, carefully avoiding trademark infringement of the name of the paper and stopping in 1870 to avoid any copyright infringement. In July the News International lawyers wrote to us demanding that we cease marketing and abandon production of a scanned version of the *Times*.[4] We ignored this and produced a lavish eight-page sales brochure entitled *Palmer's Full Text Online, 1785–1870* (avoiding the use of the word 'Times' in the title) and continued to consult with our lawyers who warned us that if we went ahead, we could expect a response from News International. We did go ahead, starting with 1860 to 1870, the period of the American Civil War, and planned the final release for September 2000. On 10 December 1998 at the Online Conference in London PSM announced their 'facsimile' of *The Times* for 1785 to 1985 on the web and we were now competing with them with our limited, unofficial edition. Yet, by June 1999 Chadwyck-Healey Inc. alone had invoiced orders worth $344,105.

I wrote to Pickering telling him what we had done and that we had heard that they had not yet reached an agreement with Thomson. A month later he replied that they now had a contract with another party.[5] By this time the sale of Chadwyck-Healey was well advanced, and it is unclear what we could have achieved by reaching such an agreement. It might have added to the perceived value of the company but for me it was more a bone that I could not let go of. In the meantime, the success of the Index led Chadwyck-Healey Inc. to start publishing the *Historical Index of the New York Times, 1851–1922* on CD-ROM and online, carefully restricting it to the out-of-copyright period.

Scanning replaces keying

When we had started to produce *English Poetry* in 1991, we assumed that our larger competitors, UMI and PSM, would follow us with competing projects but neither did. It seemed that the risks attached to making such large investments were seen as being too great, and it also depended on having a production team with the necessary skills. But they were more willing to embrace scanning, which was much less expensive and was similar to microfilming. We, in our turn, were so committed to the creation of SGML databases, which required keying that, in the very late 1990s, we were slow to recognize that the accelerated development of OCR meant that it was now possible for older scanned texts to be searchable. It became increasingly clear that scanning would replace the much more expensive SGML-coded double keying. The cross-over between scanned and SGML-coded texts is reflected in the founding in 2000 of the not-for-profit Text Creation Partnership based in the library of the University of Michigan to produce large-scale SGML-coded fully searchable texts from scanned images, often taken from microfilm. The first project was Bell & Howell's *Early English Books* microfilm publication, for which the scanned images became available online in the early 2000s.

Information for All

Apart from their own survival in the face of continuing budget cuts and closures, one of the greatest challenges that faced public libraries in the UK in the 1990s was how they were to engage in the explosion of information being delivered via the Internet when they had no money and very little in-house expertise. In the summer of 1996 Matthew Evans, the chairman of the LIC, asked me if I would take on a special project to apply to the Millennium Commission for funding to install Internet-connected computers in public libraries throughout the UK. The Millennium Commission had been set up in 1993 by the National Lottery and we would be applying to it for £50 million, which would have to be matched by another £70 million from other sources to install networked computers in 4,000 public libraries. There had been an earlier unsuccessful bid, but it was thought that it would be worth trying again with a much more ambitious, better-funded bid. It would be supported by the LIC, the Library Association (LA) and its equivalent bodies in Scotland and Northern Ireland, to bring about connection to the 'information superhighway', in other words, the Internet. It had to be submitted by 11 November, so I only had a few months to set up an organization, appoint a board, get support for the bid not only from librarians but from business leaders, MPs and others, and compile a fully worked-out proposal. The two supporting organizations provided £130,000 of funding and I had to find further funding to meet our budget. Some of it went to the consulting company Logica who drew up the business case and technology model and a detailed financial plan, and we also employed the advertising agency Charles Barker to provide publicity and public relations. I set up a company limited by guarantee and named it 'Information for All', with a very striking orange sun logo. Martin Dudley, a semi-retired librarian, worked with me on the project from an office lent to us by the LA in their headquarters in London. Leading librarians agreed to join the board but when on 20 August I discussed the project with Iain Sproat, the junior minister at the Department of National Heritage (DNH), he told me that I needed more influential people on my board, not just librarians. After we left his office, Duncan Wilson, head of the Libraries Division of DNH, informed us that the minister had said, 'By 11 November? You haven't got a hope in hell.' Nonetheless I did take his advice and invited Rabbi Julia Neuberger, who was another member of the LIC, and Lady Cooksey, who was a friend, to also join the board.

Evans and I had a clear idea of what we were proposing but it needed Logica to formalize it, and we worked with their consultant David Iron to put together the proposal with the technical and financial information and a schedule. My job was to elicit as much public support as possible. Dudley visited library authorities all over the country to understand what they needed and to get their backing, and there were eighty-eight articles about our bid in national newspapers and magazines, and in local newspapers from the Orkneys to the Isle of Wight. I wrote to captains of industry, organizations, and even officials I knew at the EU. I sent a personally signed letter to every MP asking for their support, and ninety-five MPs and members of the House of Lords responded positively. On 11 November 1996, the closing date of the application, a cross-party group of seven MPs published a letter in *The Times* supporting the bid. We knew that our initiative was very much in keeping with official thinking. The DTI was about to launch 'IT For All' to 'break down the barriers for people to join the Information Society', and there was also a sub-committee of the House of Lords that had conducted an enquiry, *Information Society: Agenda for Action in the UK*.

But there was one area in which there was disagreement. There were those who felt that the bright new future of the Internet should be accessed in new purpose-built information centres and not in shabby old public libraries with their limited opening hours. The LIC and the LA strongly opposed this, believing that public libraries were seen by the public to be safe and familiar and were the ideal places for people to be able to access information via the Internet.

In early October Wilson warned me that the Millennium Commission were expecting bids totalling £3 billion but only had £500 million to offer. Officials would make the decisions and five out of six bids would be rejected. In spite of this I was still optimistic that our bid would at least go for what was called 'long listing', until I had lunch with Margaret Haines, the experienced civil servant who ran the LIC secretariat. She listened in silence as I talked optimistically about our bid going through to the next stage, but I could tell from her expression and from what she did not say that she thought otherwise. For the first time I realized that there was another plan afoot of which she and others were aware, but I was not.

A few weeks after the bids had gone in, Sir Simon Jenkins, one of the four Millennium Commissioners who would be judging the bids, published an article in *The Times*, 'No Plug, No Wires, No Rivals',[6] extolling books at the expense of electronic media: 'Had the book come after, not before, the screen, I lay money the pundits would have declared the Internet a passing and costly fad.' He ends, 'If we want to splash public money on culture splash it on books.' I wrote to Jenkins to protest, and Ian Taylor, Minister of Science, also responded with a letter to *The Times* in which he said of Jenkins, 'his praise for print could have been credible without the need to attack electronic communications'.[7] Taylor wrote to me that he would draw my concerns about Jenkins's article to the attention of the Secretary for State for National Heritage who was chairman of the commission. I should not have been surprised, knowing Jenkins's views on non-print media that he had stated so clearly in the British Library Chadwyck-Healey lecture in 1995 (see below).

In early February we were informed that our bid would not be long listed because it did not have as distinctive an input as others, and that the commissioners were not interested in general infrastructure projects, which did not have much visibility and were not related to particular locations. It was not until November that the final list of seventy-one successful projects was announced, and one of them, not unexpectedly, was a grant of £4 million to the publisher of the Everyman Library to give sets of 250 hardbound volumes of the classics to 4,500 secondary schools. MPs in particular were sympathetic. Robert Maclennan, who at the time was President of the Liberal Democrats, wrote to Ross Shimmon, chief executive of the Library Association and on our board, 'I am flabbergasted by the comment that this project is "not as distinctive as others".'[8] The library community was disappointed and when I delivered a report at an LA conference there was little applause for this admission of failure.[9] But Evans then told me in confidence that he was working on another much larger scheme that would be supported by the renamed Department for Culture, Media and Sport (DCMS),[10] which soon had a new minister, Chris Smith, after the Labour victory of May 1997. I was left with the impression that Evans had never expected Information for All to succeed and that it was simply a 'warmup act' for a much larger scheme funded directly by government.

The new scheme was headed by Evans with John Dolan, head of the Birmingham Central Library (formerly Birmingham Reference Library) as the project leader. Advance information about it was released to a few in August 1997 in a volume entitled *New Library: The People's Network*, published in a 'consultative edition ... of only 50 copies'. The scheme was set out in detail; there was a statement by Tony Blair, and in true Evans style, a specially commissioned poem, 'Hear it Again' by Ted Hughes that he had only completed in July and which, sadly, was not included in the 'consultative edition'. There were also estimated costs for a project that would be spread over six years. The public launch, which came in October 1997, was reported by *The Times* on its front page, with the headline, 'Libraries Will Put Grannies on the Net'.[11] But it was not until early 1999 that DCMS confirmed that £200 million would be made available to fund a network of 1,000 IT-based learning centres in public libraries under the 'Community Access to Lifelong Learning' (CALL) project. The timing was perfect for the launch of *KnowUK*.

KnowUK

At a dinner in the autumn of 1996 Healy, our editorial director, explained to us that the central reference library in every public library authority had what was called the 'core collection' of reference books with protected funds to buy them. He suggested that we should acquire digital rights to such books and bring them together in one large online reference website. He also pointed out that, as there was no one dominant publisher, each of the many publishers could be negotiated with individually. I told him that it was the best idea that we had had for a long time and that we should go ahead with it, even though at the time there were few public libraries in the UK that had public terminals connected to the Internet. Because of the work I was already doing for Information for All I knew that this would change within a few years.

There were three reference books that we had to have to make the project viable: *Who's Who*, *People of Today* and *The Local Authority Yearbook*. We also needed a directory of libraries, which we decided to compile ourselves. After several months we had still not approached the three publishers on which the project depended, and I eventually took over the negotiations myself. I visited Charles Black, the chairman of A. & C. Black, the publishers of *Who's Who* and *Who Was Who*, and a gentlemanly publisher of the old school, who was surprisingly open to the idea of an electronic edition. As the publisher of two of the most important reference books, we offered him a fixed 0.5 per cent royalty on all revenues rather than a share of the royalty, which would be divided between the other publishers on a pro-rata basis depending on the number of other titles and their individual prices. We estimated that sales revenue could be as high as £4 million, in which case Black's royalty would be £20,000. But we also offered him the opportunity to sell *Who's Who* and *Who Was Who* as single titles via our website, on which we would pay Black a thirty per cent royalty on their cover price or a transaction fee of £0.30 for single searches. He agreed and we now had our first and most important title. In our negotiation for Debrett's *People of Today* we differentiated between the 'Standard Price', which was the cover price of the print edition, and what we called 'Usage Income', extra revenue from the higher charges we made for multiple simultaneous users. They received forty per cent of both. The Hemming Group were the publishers of *The Local Authority Yearbook*, which was the most comprehensive source on every aspect of the world of local authorities, from the number of parks and public lavatories to the names of council members. I had known the chairman, John Hemming, when he was director of the Royal Geographical Society, and he ran his family firm alongside his other interests as a writer and explorer. He agreed to the inclusion of the *Yearbook*, and we now had the three leading titles and could sign up others confident that the project would go ahead.

KnowUK, as it came to be called, with its alliterative web address 'knowuk.co.uk', was entirely new in two ways. It was only available online and it could only be licensed by a public library authority, not by individual libraries. A library authority divides its libraries into three or four tiers and the number and the currency of the reference books in each library depends on what tier it is in. Many libraries had to make do with last year's edition of the standard reference books, or even older, while the smallest had none at all. *KnowUK* enabled every library in the authority to have the same range of up-to-date reference books, fundamentally changing the long-established practice of public libraries in the UK. If a library authority had twenty libraries connected to the Internet, we would expect them to pay ten or fifteen full subscriptions at a rate of £2,400 for a single site and a single user. An authority might therefore pay from £24,000 to £36,000 a year but in return would have the most up-to-date editions of all the important reference books in every one of their libraries. University and other libraries could buy *KnowUK* individually.

Libraries could subscribe to a central module and then add other modules including health, law, sport and religion. We added other reference books and directories with a good coverage of education and government, together with gazetteers and maps. It was a very varied selection of books – from *Crockford's Clerical Directory* and the *Police and Constabulary Almanac* to the *British Music Yearbook* and *Whitaker's Almanac*. But the full potential of *KnowUK* lay in being able to search across all titles or selections of titles. The bringing together of so many widely differing reference works into one coherent whole created a resource for libraries that they had never had before. We planned to include fifty-four titles and incur a production cost of over £200,000. But we still had to wait until enough public libraries had terminals connected to the Internet. While some public library authorities had already invested in Internet connectivity, we now knew that funding from government would accelerate this process.

We announced *KnowUK* in late 1998 and launched it in March 1999 at the Library Association. The first order came from the Cambridgeshire Library Authority, with whom we had closely consulted. We had also announced that we would add the sixty volumes of Nikolaus Pevsner's *The Buildings of England, Ireland, Scotland and Wales*. We reached an agreement with Penguin, their publisher, and with the trust that controlled the series, which was chaired by Simon Jenkins. Pevsner's style of imparting information in small, self-contained chunks perfectly suited online dissemination. Robert McCrum, literary editor of the *Observer* and previously editorial director at Faber & Faber, commenting on our announcement that the series would be included in *KnowUK*, wrote, 'It is not possible to overemphasise the momentous nature of this news. At a stroke, every single printed copy ... will be rendered commercially redundant ... the new information technology would be the death of reference-book publishing.'[12] But after the sale of Chadwyck-Healey to Bell & Howell, the addition of Pevsner was abandoned.

By the end of 1999 there was also a schools version of *KnowUK* with a selection of twenty-seven reference books aimed at teachers and administrators rather than at pupils. The cost of unlimited online access for a school was £495 a year. Although I sold the companies before *KnowUK* could realize its potential, it was one of my favourite projects. It quickly retrieved its development and production costs and became a valuable subscription title for the new owner, until it too was overtaken by the power of the web and the free availability of information, and after about sixteen years became, in McCrum's words, 'commercially redundant' and ceased to be published.

The British Library

Early in 1997 the British Library and their advisor KPMG had taken market-soundings on a proposed 'Digital Library Programme Private Finance Initiative' (PFI), in which consortia would be invited to bid for the rights to create digital copies of material in the British Library in London and to create another digital library at its Lending Division in Boston Spa in Yorkshire. In London they wanted digitized texts and images to be deliverable to every reader and in Boston Spa they hoped that digital document delivery of patent information and journal articles would generate substantial revenue for both the PFI partner and the British Library itself.

We were interested and immediately started talking to potential partners, most of them companies very much larger than us. We held a meeting in London in July, which was attended by thirteen companies including BT, Gestetner and Unisys as well as other publishers such as B H Blackwell and Dawson UK. It was chaired by Dr John Green, who was a Cambridge academic turned businessman who had been recommended to me by Haines to manage Information for All. At a later meeting, Geoff Fermor-Dunman, commercial director of Gestetner, told us that he could not understand the business case for what the British Library was asking us to do and thought that public tendering would be a disaster. We continued to talk to other publishers like Blackwell's, but no one could see how we could make money from it. By the end of the year both the project itself and our interest in it had petered out, but it had one important outcome. I had been impressed by Green and I invited him to be our first non-executive director; he joined us in early 1998 as a consultant rather than director (see below).

Our relationship with the British Library was also fostered by the annual Chadwyck-Healey lecture. Skip Gates had given the first in 1994 (see Chapter 12) and was followed by Simon Jenkins in 1995 who spoke on the 'Death of the Written Word', making negative comments about both microfilm and CD-ROMs, for which, afterwards, he apologized. From then on, I made sure that I briefed every speaker beforehand. Father Leonard Boyle, the Librarian of the Vatican Library, whom I had got to know through a project in his library and whom I considered to be one of the few truly good people I have ever met, spoke in 1996, and was followed by Anthony Giddens, Gillian Beer and Lord Puttnam. By 1997 we were able to hold the lecture in the British Library's own lecture theatre, but the opening of the theatre meant that our lecture soon became one of many and lost some of its distinction. The last lecture was given by Matthew, now Lord, Evans in 2000. He talked about the installation of networked computers in public libraries and acknowledged the role that Information for All had played in helping it to happen.

Late 1998

In late 1998 we had an important departure and an important visitor. Moss told me that she had worked for me for twenty years, for the whole of her career, and she wanted to leave to do other things. I knew her well enough not to try to dissuade her but also knew that her husband David Worthington would leave with her so we would lose two good people. I had no doubt that we would manage without them but she was amongst the one or two best people that had ever worked for me, and much of the success that we had enjoyed was due to her considerable intellect, her remarkable organizational abilities and the fact that she was always calm, always considerate to the people around her, and was consequently liked and respected by everyone who worked for and with her. There may have been other reasons for her wishing to leave. There was still considerable tension at board level and Hall and Green wanted to make some organizational changes that Moss may not have agreed with.

Worthington left a few weeks after Moss and asked me in his usual direct way, 'Charles, I don't understand, what makes you go on?' I found that I had no answer. Green was improving the functionality of the management team by getting me to step back. The directors were all in their forties, highly experienced men and until then, a woman, and Green had explained to them that they worked for the Chadwyck-Healey shareholders, and not just for me, and they could not expect to keep their jobs if the company went on losing money. In turn, he told me to back off and let the directors run the companies. The only meeting that I now chaired was the monthly group board meeting for which Rhind-Tutt came over from the USA. I did have some external roles to fill my time. Apart from being a member of the LIC, I had resigned as a member of the British Library's Advisory Committee for Bibliographic Services and became chairman of the Publishers Association (PA) Electronic Publishing Committee. This meant that I was now on the Council of the PA, which brought me into contact with senior executives in trade and academic publishing, almost for the first time. My slot at the end of the morning was always squeezed because the chairman was anxious that we broke for lunch punctually at 1pm. But it did not matter because I had little to say of interest to the others. No one else wanted to build large online databases. Their interests were the electronic delivery of journals, and the electronic or e-book, which was in its infancy and of which I knew very little. I had also strengthened my relationship with Cambridge University Library, first with Fred Ratcliffe, and then with Peter Fox when he became University Librarian. Fox and Peter Swinnerton-Dyer, the distinguished Cambridge mathematician who also had a strong interest in libraries, and I would discuss over dinner the most pressing issues facing libraries, which almost always included the ever-increasing price of journals and what, if anything, libraries could do about it.

When Moss left, we appointed John Taylor to the board. He had started as head of software development but was now responsible for the technical side of all our electronic publishing including the maintenance and delivery of our online databases. He was an outstanding manager and technically brilliant and his promotion was long overdue.

We also had an important visitor, Joe Reynolds, the new president and CEO of Bell & Howell Information and Learning, a division of the Chicago-based conglomerate Bell & Howell, a billion-dollar company quoted on the New York Stock Exchange. The origin of Information and Learning had been University Microfilms that was still the world's largest microfilm publisher. Reynolds had come to the UK to visit Micromedia, another company Bell & Howell owned, which in turn had bought our microfilm production company II in 1997. Ronaldson, the managing director of Micromedia, never allowed customers who were competitors of other customers to enter their premises and he would not allow Reynolds to visit Micromedia's plant where work was being done for Chadwyck-Healey. Instead he brought Reynolds to Cambridge to meet me. I showed him around the office and he was impressed. He was a large, genial man and I liked him, and he made clear that he liked us. As he left, he said to me that if I ever considered selling, he would be interested as they were increasingly aware of the importance of overseas markets and he wanted to strengthen Bell & Howell's presence outside the USA.

In late November I went on a bird-watching trip in the Danube delta. The short, grey winter days meant long evenings and plenty of time to think. While I was away, I decided that I would sell the three publishing companies and that Bell & Howell would be high on our list of preferred buyers. The other most likely buyer was the Thomson Organisation, the owner of our old rival Research Publications, now PMS. On several occasions I had been invited by Michael Brown to a small dinner at the Frankfurt Book Fair. Brown had built up the Thomson publishing empire, excluding newspapers, from nothing to a very substantial group of highly profitable academic and professional publishing companies, and, with his red bow tie and blue striped shirt, he was a colourful figure in this rather prosaic sector of the publishing world. But I knew that I was only invited to be appraised and to strengthen a relationship that could be useful to them if an opportunity to buy us did arise.

24

The End

At the end of 1998, before the office closed for the Christmas holiday, I told the directors that I wanted to sell the companies and that the process would start in the New Year. McCrae said that he had expected this for some time, but he thought that my decision was premature as we should spend a year preparing the group for sale. Having made up my mind, I could not contemplate waiting another year. We were also now in what came to be known as the 'dotcom bubble' in which exceptionally high values were being given to businesses connected with the Internet (a bubble that burst a year later). I also knew that both Bell & Howell and PSM wanted to strengthen their position outside the USA by having a stronger European base and, if we delayed, they might find someone else to buy.

When we returned in the New Year McCrae told me that he and Rhind-Tutt wished to buy the group. He told me how much they would offer and gave me a document that went into detail over the terms. So much detail so early was a tactical error and the sum offered was low, but I told McCrae that I would consider it. In the afternoon of the same day, 4 January 1999, I flew to Amsterdam to meet Sufrin who was there for the audit of his most important client, the magazine publishing group VNU. Over dinner we planned the sale of Chadwyck-Healey. He agreed that we did not need a year; with his help we would create a pro-forma business plan alongside our existing business plan and sales forecast. The pro-forma plan would strip out all the costs associated with the existing companies including my salary and benefits and the cost of the office in Alexandria, which would be closed if we sold to a US-based company as we expected. The net revenue and thus the potential value of the business was greatly enhanced by removing these costs.

I already knew two intermediaries who could help us sell the companies. In 1991 Tim Rix, the retired chairman of Longman (see Chapter 3), had introduced me to Munroe Pofcher and his younger colleague Kit van Tulleken. The Pofcher Company acted for both buyers and sellers of publishing companies in the USA and Europe, but Pofcher had died in 1995 and van Tulleken, whom I liked and respected, took over his business. The other contender was the New York bank Veronis, Suhler, which I had visited in late 1997. I chose the latter because Sufrin, whose advice I would be relying on, was closer to them. A few weeks later the directors and Green flew to New York to meet with Suhler and his colleagues. He told us that he was confident that there would be several prospective buyers. We discussed the purchase price and he suggested that we should not accept less than £20 million. This was a far cry from the $12 million valuation he had put on the group only just over a year earlier, but that is the nature of banking – buy low, sell high. Sellers of small businesses are at a disadvantage when they sell to companies who are regularly buying other companies. The seller will only sell his life's work once; the buyer is buying companies all the time. But Hal Greenberg, the Veronis, Suhler executive who was advising us, explained that they would follow a well-defined process that every buyer understood. Rather than being full of uncertainty, it would proceed like a stately dance, in a series of clearly defined stages. Greenberg even knew when it would be completed, in September 1999.

We were selling the three companies in the UK, USA and Spain. Hall, McCrae and Rhind-Tutt prepared a Black Book that described every aspect of the companies and their growth with a five-year projection of sales and costs. Apart from the directors and senior managers, such as Pocock and O'Rourke in the UK, our sales vice-president in the USA, Eileen Lawrence, and my PA, Jackie Hyland, no one else in the group knew that we were planning to sell the companies. Each of the directors and senior managers had share options and Deloitte, our accountants, set up a trust that owned shares in the three companies to be distributed to employees. If the sale value equalled or exceeded £30 million, the proceeds of a maximum of twenty-eight per cent of the shares in each of the companies would be distributed to them.

The Black Book took over two months of very hard work to complete. Its production brought home to us facts about the group that we had not, until then, fully realized. We knew we were the largest electronic publisher in the UK but perhaps not that we were the fourth largest microfilm publisher in the world. By now we had over 400,000 electronic texts, more than fifty per cent of the world's total. But our most important message was that we were a 'super-premium brand' representing the highest standards in scholarship and quality.

Greenberg then contacted the list of potential buyers, which was more than the usual list of names because at the end of 1990s there were new players in the electronic library publishing field, such as NetLibrary and Questa Media, each with funding of over $100 million who had announced that they would be scanning every book that a college library might need and would deliver them via the Internet. It was the same business that we were in but omitted the most important aspect of our business, that of selection. These new companies had an arrogant confidence in their strategy. In June 1999, at the ALA Summer conference in Detroit, Rhind-Tutt and I had dinner with a young manager from one of the new companies. Together we had almost fifty years of experience in publishing for the library market, but all he wanted was to tell us what his company was doing and he did not ask us a single question.

Other potential buyers were the Bertelsmann group; Macmillan, the majority now owned by the Holtzbrinck Publishing Group; Elsevier, through their US company CIS (see Chapters 5 and 14); Bell & Howell; and Thomson. Most of the companies responded by saying that they were not interested. This included all the newcomers, which was fortunate because NetLibrary was bankrupt within a few years and all the others failed. Bertelsmann and Hachette were not interested but Macmillan was, as were CIS, PSM and Bell & Howell. It was a shorter list than we had hoped for, but I was not disappointed. What was remarkable was the professionalism of all the companies that had been approached. Even those who were not interested treated the fact that we were 'in play' in complete confidence. No one in the library or publishing communities knew that we were for sale until it was publicly announced eight months later.

We had to create a data room in which all the legal and financial documents, including our many hundreds of publishing agreements, were assembled. Representatives of the potential buyers were allowed to examine the documents and make notes, but nothing could be removed from the room or be photocopied. Because we were selling both a UK and a US company and the buyer was likely to be from the USA there were two data rooms, one in London in the Portman Hotel, where by coincidence Angela and I had signed the papers that set up the company in January 1973. The other was in Burt Rubin's offices in the Rockefeller Center in New York. We went as a group to make presentations to each of the prospective buyers, first in London and then in New York.

McCrae was still among the potential buyers, wearing two hats: as the finance director presenting our finances to enhance the value of the companies and as a potential buyer hoping to buy the companies for as low a sum as possible. I could not see how McCrae and I could maintain a satisfactory relationship, but Green told me that it was quite a common situation and that he would handle all negotiations with McCrae and would then report them to me. This would leave McCrae and me free to work together on presenting the group to the outside world.

Veronis, Suhler asked those who were interested for an indication of the price they might offer subject to further discussions and due diligence. The only potential buyer I met with at this stage was Richard Charkin, the CEO of Macmillan. Charkin had been brought in to run Macmillan by Holtzbrinck, which now owned seventy per cent of one of the UK's best-known publishers. Holtzbrinck was interested in Chadwyck-Healey because we had published electronic editions of German authors licensed from companies that they also owned (see Chapter 21). Charkin and I had talked about some exciting ideas of his, including moving the publishing of the Grove Dictionaries to Cambridge and possibly rebranding them. But when I asked him how much he would offer, 'Twelve million' came the answer. I reminded Charkin that the bank had asked for all offers in dollars not pounds and he answered, 'Yes, twelve million dollars.' There was no further discussion.

CIS prevaricated, as their parent, Elsevier, were waiting for a new chief executive and until he or she arrived the board could not make a decision. Thomson suggested about $38 million and then Bell & Howell came in with their offer, $52 million. This was considerably more than we had been expecting from any buyer, even the West Coast newcomers. It was exciting for us all but sobering for McCrae who now knew that he could not compete. He had the backing of the large venture capital company in the UK, the 3i Group. His revised offer would have been in the region of a very respectable $34 million. I took it as a compliment that a professional investor was prepared to underwrite McCrae's offer to that extent.

I found Reynolds from Bell & Howell good to deal with, and it seemed fitting that the business would become part of the company that was the founder of microfilm publishing but, like us, had now moved decisively into electronic publishing. They, in turn, told us that they wanted to buy us for content, technology and distribution. While no other buyers would be excluded until the deal was done, we now started an increasingly anxious six weeks through August and early September while preparations were made, and discussions continued for the final meeting in Cambridge to negotiate terms in detail and sign a sale agreement. Before this could take place, Bell & Howell asked for a meeting in New York to discuss some outstanding items. We had exceeded the forecast for the 1998/9 financial year in the Black Book. This had been helped by the $600,000 order for the Russian microfilm from Harvard and an order of several hundred thousand pounds for online databases from a national consortium of Danish libraries that came in a few days before the end of our financial year. By now Bell & Howell knew that they were a 'finalist' but did not know, or so we thought, that Thomson had come in with a lower offer. Although Thomson had refused to increase their offer, I thought that we could persuade Bell & Howell to pay more in view of our improved results.

On Monday 30 August Rhind-Tutt, Greenberg and I met in Rubin's office in New York with two Bell & Howell vice-presidents, Dwight Mater and Jim Barcelona. They had an agenda with ten points. One of them was the sale of II in 1997 to Bell & Howell. The price of £1 million was based on an ambitious forecast of how much microfilm the publishing companies would order over the next five years. If we did not meet the forecast, I would have to give back some of the money. They agreed that if they bought Chadwyck-Healey there would be no clawback from the II sale. They were concerned about the publishing agreements that could be terminated if our companies changed ownership. The most important of these were our agreements with the Financial Times, Faber & Faber and Thomson for the *Official Index to the Times*.

We, in turn, explained that we expected them to pay a higher price in view of the fact that we had exceeded our forecast for the financial year that had just ended. They replied that if they were to move on price, they would need more ammunition in terms of hidden value, which at present they could not see. While they were in another room talking to head office in Chicago, I spoke to Green and McCrae (the latter was at a family barbecue because it was a Bank Holiday). Both pleaded with me not to push Bell & Howell too far. They were concerned that if they went back to Chicago without an agreement, people against the deal would have their say and the whole deal could quickly fall apart. Sufrin, on the other hand, felt that it was time to 'play hardball'.

After lunch Bell & Howell asked to talk to Greenberg on his own. They wanted to know the price that we wanted, and he told them it was $53 million. They said that they would accept it but could not shake on it as it had to be cleared at a meeting in Ann Arbor the next day. We also said that we could not accept any adjustment to the price if any of the conditional publishing agreements were terminated due to change of ownership. To my surprise, they agreed but could not confirm that either. After they left, I felt very flat. If they agreed, a one-day trip to New York had gained us $1 million, but we would now have an anxious wait. A few days later the agreement was confirmed but Reynolds then told me that shortly before our meeting in New York one of his colleagues had been playing golf with a Thomson executive who mentioned Chadwyck-Healey, saying, 'Congratulations. I presume you outbid us.' If I had known this, I would have been more cautious. I would have been even more nervous if I had known, as I was told later, that no one on the main board of Bell & Howell was much interested in the Chadwyck-Healey acquisition. Reynolds was the new CEO and they were simply letting him have his head.

There was a workmanlike atmosphere at the meeting to tie up the agreement, which took place on 27 September in the offices of Hewitsons, our lawyer in Cambridge. We had an agreement in principle, and we now had to work through the legal documents, haggling over them point by point. The team from Bell & Howell with their lawyer from Chicago had flown into London that morning. Also present were their UK lawyer, Helen Cleaveland from Wilde Sapte in London, and our US lawyer, Bob Zimmerman, Rubin's colleague. Bridget Kerle, a Hewitsons partner, welcomed them and managed the meetings superbly.

They went on for three days as we slogged through the details, working late into each night. There were some delays because Hewitsons still used WordPerfect word processing software while Bell & Howell's lawyers used Word. Converting between the two was clumsy. On the second day I had to go to a family dinner in London and it enabled me to create an interim deadline, in that they would not have access to me for twelve hours. Barcelona told me that it was the most important acquisition they had made in the last five years. The Thomson lawyers and executives would have been very different to deal with and at times I could sense Cleaveland's frustration as she had to defer to the Chicago lawyer who set out the Bell & Howell strategy. We had employed a Deloitte partner in Cambridge, Chris Maton, an outstanding tax expert, to design the whole shape of the deal for the best possible tax position in the UK and the USA, but by the end it was so complicated that no one, including me, knew in advance exactly how the proceeds of the sale would be divided amongst the three parties: the family, the directors and senior managers, and the employees.

On the morning of the third day I announced to the staff in Cambridge that I was selling the company and that we expected to complete the deal later that day. I explained that Bell & Howell would use the UK business as the base for their non-US operations and there would probably be an expansion of activities rather than a reduction. I also promised that everyone would benefit financially from the sale. It was clear that the news was a complete surprise to everyone. The silence was broken by a question from the back of the room: 'Will this mean that we can now have new shelving in the comms room?'

By now Rodriguez had come from Madrid to meet with me and learn about the sale, and Rhind-Tutt had informed his staff in Alexandria. From late afternoon on the third day, Angela and our three children, who were all shareholders, waited in the office to sign papers. Mater and Barcelona were

Figure 18 New York. Completion of the sale of Chadwyck-Healey to Bell & Howell Information and Learning. At the far left: Dwight Mater and Jim Barcelona (partially hidden). Others include: Bob Zimmerman holding agreement; Joe Reynolds, with glasses; Angela, seated; Hal Greenberg behind her. 7 October 1999.

still talking to head office in Chicago, trying to get agreement on the final points. At 8pm I went into their meeting room, reminded them how long we had been waiting and urged them to hurry up. Soon after we signed. Angela, the children and I had dinner in Cambridge, not quite believing that it had happened. The Bell & Howell press release was out by midnight, but the full price was not stated. The price agreed was somewhat more than we had negotiated in New York as it included some extras such as the office building in Alexandria, which had been given to me. Angela and I had to take part in a second signing in New York on 7 October, after which the money would be paid to us. We first flew to Vancouver where I had been asked to give one of the addresses at a memorial gathering for our friend Dick Fredeman who had died after a long illness. We then flew to Washington, DC to say goodbye to the staff of Chadwyck-Healey Inc. in Alexandria, knowing that it would be the last time I would see most of them. All the papers from the UK had been shipped by Fedex to Rubin's office in New York but then in error they had been shipped back to Belgium, so we had nothing to sign. The next morning the papers arrived and by the afternoon there were smiles, champagne and confirmation that the money was in our bank account. Angela and I flew back to London that night – first class.

In the late 1990s *The Bookseller* had developed an unfortunate habit of devoting a large amount of space on its financial page to the reporting of our losses as shown in our annual accounts. I wondered if, subconsciously, they wanted to demonstrate to the publishing and bookselling industries that electronic publishing was not yet a financially viable alternative to print. I thought that they might devote an equal amount of space to news of the sale of the largest electronic publisher in the UK. But it was not to be. Under the heading 'Chadwyck-Healey Sold', a small piece mentioned our global turnover in 1998/9 of £15 million but also emphasized the operating loss of the UK company of £223,982 in 1997/8 and stated that, 'It has been hit more recently by the constraints imposed on library spending and the shift from publishing on CD-ROM to the Internet.'[1] On the contrary, it was the worldwide growth in library spending on electronic publications, at the expense of print, that had enabled us to recover as well as we had. The *Financial Times* was more generous, both in space and attitude,[2] and an article in the *Times Higher* quoted Daniel Greenstein of the Arts and Humanities Data Service who said, 'Chadwyck-Healey has been easily the most innovative of electronic publishers' and 'was one of the first to take the risk and go online in a big way, moving away from CD-ROMs'.[3]

After the sale I went to my last Frankfurt Book Fair, where we had a large stand, and to Harvard to celebrate the gift of the Russian archives microfilm by a donor (see Chapter 22). Bell & Howell had given me a generous consultancy contract, which only required a few days' work each month. Hall had been appointed as senior vice-president and head of the UK operation, and he and I found it difficult to find things for me to do so I soon ended the arrangement. I was surprised when I learned that Bell & Howell were going to use 'Chadwyck-Healey' as a brand-name for high-level research collections including the rebranding of some of their own publications. Among these were the *Gerritsen Collection for Women's Studies* and *Early English Books* (now *EEBO* or *Early English Books Online*). This seemed to me to be the final irony, as I had once dreamed of publishing a collection like the *Gerritsen Collection*, and *Early English Books* had been conceived by Eugene Power before I was even born. Now my dream had come true but, as in many dreams, there was a twist. From time to time I would meet scholars who thanked me for these electronic publications, now being marketed in my name, and I would have to explain that they were not really mine. But nor, any longer, was the rest of the business that Fellner and I had set out to create twenty-seven years earlier.

Appendix 1

History of Microfilm Publishing[1]

The reproduction of miniaturized images of documents by photography is almost as old as photography itself. In 1839 John Benjamin Dancer, the son of a Liverpool microscope manufacturer, put a microscope lens in a camera and photographed a document twenty inches long reducing it to an image 0.125 inches long, which was legible under a microscope with 100x magnification. In 1858 René Patrice Dagron patented the first microfilm viewer and in 1870 sent pigeons with messages on microfilm from Paris under siege. In 1906 two Belgians, Paul Otlet and Robert Goldschmidt, gave a paper at a conference entitled 'Sur une forme nouvelle du livre: le livre photographique' (A new form of book: the photographic book), which describes the microfiche, only differing from the modern one by its size and the number of images. They did design a reader for their microfiche but received little support and by 1911 they had abandoned their project, although they returned to it in 1925, again without success.

The first commercial use of microphotography came through the invention of the Check-O-Graph microfilm camera in 1926 by an American bank manager, George L. McCarthy, which could film cheques at a high speed since the cheques moved on a belt at the same speed as the film so the camera did not require a shutter. For the first time banks could keep records of the cheques they had cleared without laborious copying by hand. As more banks adopted the system the microfilm industry was born. McCarthy's invention was taken over by Eastman Kodak in what became its Recordak subsidiary and in 1929 Remington Rand followed Kodak into the micrographics industry with a microfilm camera that could photograph both sides of documents. Again, the first users were banks and other businesses.

The use of microphotography for scholarly publishing took longer to evolve. Dr Robert C. Binkley, who had been a librarian at the Hoover Institution at Stanford University, directed the Joint Committee on Materials

Research set up by the Social Science Research Council and the American Council of Learned Societies to explore ways in which hard-to-obtain research material could be made more easily available for students. In his report in 1931 Binkley described 'a device which is independent of book manufacturing and which will put before the scholars' eyes an image of a text projected on a screen, rather than the tangible pages of a book'. He called it 'filmslides' and predicted 'the most sweeping changes in the cost level at which research material can be produced'.[2] Binkley was one of the first to understand that the increasing specialization of academic research meant that there was a greater demand for documents, either printed or manuscript, which the book publishing industry would never find it economical to publish. There had to be another way of disseminating such information and Binkley was convinced that microfilm was the answer. He understood that the main benefits of the microfilm medium were not just that of space saving but that it was an economical way of producing a limited number of copies, since creating the original microfilm by photographing the document was not expensive, and copies could be made to order. He put it well in an article in 1935:

> When many, if not all scholars wanted the same things, the printing press served them. In the twentieth century, when the number who want the same thing has fallen in some cases below the practical publishing point (American Indian language specialists are an illustration), the printing press leaves them in the lurch.[3]

In the same year, Binkley's committee sponsored the microfilming of 315,000 pages of the code hearings of two US government agencies, the National Recovery and Agricultural Adjustment administrations. To have published these in print would have cost $500,000, equivalent today to $8.7 million. The first ten microfilm copies were produced for $413.50 each. From the mid-1930s, thanks to Binkley's enthusiasm, scholarly microfilming began to gather pace. His committee considered an ambitious project to microfilm all the books printed in England before 1640 listed in Pollard and Redgrave's *Short Title Catalogue (STC)*,[4] which totalled over 2 million pages. In 1936 John D. Rockefeller donated $490,000 to 'Project A', the microfilming of 2.5 million pages of material in Europe, Canada and Mexico relating to the USA, with the microfilms being deposited in the Library of Congress. The Rockefeller Foundation also underwrote a microfilm exhibit at the 1937 Paris Exposition; the primary aim of the exhibit, which included a complete laboratory, was to encourage European libraries towards microfilm and away from making full-size paper copies.

In 1938 Eugene Power set up the first commercial micropublishing company, University Microfilms. He had been a manager at a large book printer, Edwards Brothers in Ann Arbor, the home of the University of Michigan. He was familiar with the problems of publishing scholarly books for very small markets and had been exploring alternatives such as photo-offset, photostat, multigraph (the latter enabled typesetting on a typewriter-style keyboard, which stamped characters on strips of aluminium) and microfilm. The secretary of Binkley's committee, Dr T. S. Shellenburg from the National Archives, convinced Power of the advantages of the microfilm medium through the cost savings that had been achieved in the filming of the code hearings. Power persuaded Edwards Brothers to let him microfilm the early English books in *STC* that had been suggested to the committee in 1935 and in the same year he took a specially converted cine camera to England and photographed all available books printed before 1550. Eleven libraries agreed to buy microfilm copies of these books, for $500 a year, and it took him four years to complete delivery at a rate of 100,000 pages annually. But his employer decided that its future lay in book production and in 1938 Power acquired Edwards Brothers' microfilm business, including the name University Microfilms, and set up on his own. His new company made a profit in the first year and did so every year in which he ran the company. By 1939 he had demonstrated that publishing research materials on microfilm for the library market was a viable concern.

There was another, very different, visionary also searching for the ideal publishing medium for specialized material. Albert Boni had been a successful trade book publisher, starting his own bookshop and publishing house in 1912 and creating the bestselling 'Little Leather Library' of pocket editions of the classics – Woolworths sold one million copies in twelve months in 1913–14. In 1917 he went into partnership with Horace Liveright to found the publishing house Boni & Liveright, which published the *Modern Library of the World's Best Classics*. Boni sold his share of the company in 1919 and in 1923 with his brother Charles purchased another publishing company, renaming it A. & C. Boni. It published Boni Paper Books, offering one soft-cover book per month for an annual subscription of $5, but it failed during the Depression. In 1932 Boni became interested in using photography to reduce images in order that information could be stored and disseminated at lower cost and would occupy less space.

Seemingly unaware of the rapid developments in microfilm technology, he envisaged the images being printed on paper. One hundred images were printed on each 6 × 9-inch card, which were called 'microprints' and required a special reader to read them. He reasoned that for editions of more than twenty-five copies microprint was more economical than microfilm because the unit cost went down as more copies were printed, while for microfilm the unit price stayed the same. Boni called his company Readex. He struggled for a long time with the quality of the miniaturized printed images, which depended on the quality of the paper on which they were printed. Only in 1949, seventeen years after he started experimenting, was he able to find a paper that was entirely satisfactory, a new high-gloss paper called Kromekote, which was also archivally permanent.

A third pioneer who experimented with new micro formats was Fremont Rider, a librarian at Wesleyan University in Connecticut. He had seen his own library filled with books within ten years of being opened and calculated that the holdings of a research library would double every sixteen years. His solution set out in his book[5] was the 'microcard', a sheet of high-contrast photographic paper, measuring 3 × 5 inches, the same size as a library catalogue card, on which there were thirty to fifty page images. He suggested that these microcards, because they were the same size, might be combined with the catalogue card for that book to make a single entity. Rider wrote:

> for the first time in over two thousand years, libraries were being offered the chance to begin all over again ... in a brand-new form, an utterly, completely, basically different form, a form that demanded and that, if we could only see it, would require an utterly and completely and basically different library treatment.

In 1948 Rider and Charles Gelatt, a businessman and regent of the University of Wisconsin, formed the Microcard Corporation, which designed, built and sold microcard readers and equipment for making microcards. They also established the Microcard Foundation, a non-profit organization to select and acquire materials to be reproduced on microcards and to provide advice to publishers who wanted to use this format.

The Second World War held up the publishing plans of Power and Boni but stimulated the use of microfilm for other purposes. After the attack on Pearl Harbor in 1941, the plans on microfilm of the damaged warships were sent to Honolulu by plane. It would have needed a fleet of planes to transport the hundreds of thousands of blueprints on paper. The National Archives responded to Pearl Harbor by immediately ordering the microfilming of historically important documents, and by 1943 had microfilmed over 400,000 pages. After America entered the war, microfilm was used for V Mail, a correspondence service for soldiers based on the British 'Airgraph' system in which their letters on special forms were microfilmed on 16mm film and sent by air to a central point. Each reel contained 4,000 letters, which were printed, put in envelopes and mailed to the addressees; over 150 million Airgraphs were sent worldwide between 1941 and 1945.[6] Use of microfilm during the war helped its acceptance and increased awareness of its advantages.

By the 1950s librarians had a fourth format from which to choose. This was the microfiche, a 105 × 148mm sheet of film on which are reproduced ninety-eight A4 pages at a reduction of twenty-four times. Along the top of the microfiche is an eye-legible strip containing bibliographic information including the title and page numbers. In the Netherlands Dr L. J. van der Wolk of the Delft Technology University and Dr Joseph Goebel, the German developer of the microfiche, formed an association to explore the microfiche medium, and in 1954 proposed an English name, the Microcard Foundation, the same name as Rider's. Fortunately, a colleague at the British Museum objected to the name on the grounds that a card cannot be transparent and suggested that they borrow the French word 'microfiche'.

The microfilm image was superior to that of the microprint or the microcard because it was projected by transmitted light through the film onto a translucent screen, which made it much brighter than the printed cards, which were projected on to the screen by light reflected off the opaque surface of the card. To read microprints and microcards libraries had to buy specialized readers, a further capital investment in equipment, which also took up space in the library. Unlike microfilm few other publishers adopted microprint, and the reason why Readex was initially so successful was that Boni had an unerring eye for the most important materials that needed to be republished in an economical, space-saving format, such as the British Parliamentary or Sessional Papers for the nineteenth century, which he published after the war. They totalled 4.2 million pages but were later selectively reprinted in full size by IUP (see Chapter 1) and published in their entirety on microfiche by Chadwyck-Healey in 1980–82 (see Chapter 5). Readex also pioneered the 'compact edition' in which they reprinted books with nine original pages reproduced on one page of the reprint. Their most important compact edition was *The British Museum General Catalogue of Printed Books to 1955*, published in 1967 in twenty-seven volumes. These miniaturized pages were just readable without a magnifying glass and we used this method for our reduced reprints (see Chapters 3 and 5).

Microfilm and microprint were the ideal media for preserving backfiles of fragile and voluminous newspapers with their large page sizes (though the microfilming of important American newspapers and the consequent destruction of the originals became a controversial issue in the late 1990s as it led to some irretrievable losses; see Chapter 17). In the late 1930s Recordak began filming backfiles of *The New York Times* and in 1938 Keyes D. Metcalf, who had advised Recordak and who was now director of libraries at Harvard University, started a large-scale project to microfilm foreign newspapers, including two UK dailies. In 1946 Samuel Freedman, who had worked for Remington Rand, set up his own microfilm publishing company, Micro Photo, and realized that there was a huge untapped field in the backfiles of American local newspapers. By 1950 Micro Photo had acquired the microfilm rights for eighty per cent of the most significant newspapers in the USA. In the meantime, Rider's Microcard Corporation continued to make progress, supported by some powerful institutions; in 1953 the Atomic Energy Commission (AEC) contracted with the corporation to publish all its reports on microcards and during the next twelve years, twenty million microcards were distributed. But by 1965 the AEC had abandoned microcards in favour of microfiche and soon after Rider's microcards disappeared from use.

Power made University Microfilms (UM) the leading microfilm publisher by monopolizing individual publishing sectors. One was PhD dissertations from American universities. Theses from British universities and from a limited number of other foreign universities were added later. The dissertations were published on microfilm, but Power also published a comprehensive printed bibliography, *Dissertations Abstracts*, which provided abstracts of the dissertations that were on microfilm. This was well received by libraries, for whom unpublished dissertations had always been difficult to obtain. Vernon D. Tate, director of libraries at MIT and one of the early proponents of microfilm publishing, described it as 'defrosting a frozen asset'.[7] Another sector was the backruns of journals and magazines, and UM signed microfilm publishing agreements with hundreds of publishers. The advantage for the libraries was that they did not have to bind their backruns or find shelf space for them. The savings on binding could be set against the cost of the microfilm, and the microfilm reels occupied relatively little space. In 1956 the Xerox Corporation introduced an early paper copier called 'copyflo', which UM used to make single copies of paperbound books from microfilms. Many of the libraries that lent UM original copies of books in the Pollard and Redgrave catalogue received paperbound copies in return, as well as free copies on microfilm. The Xerox Corporation bought UM in 1962 for $8 million. They had thought it was a logical add-on to their reprographics business, but publishing and engineering did not mix and after several attempts Xerox eventually sold what had now become a very much larger company to Bell & Howell in 1985 for $100 million.

Scholarly micropublishing was a small world when set against the widespread use of microfilm for copying business records, and architectural and engineering drawings – 35mm microfilm for architectural and engineering drawings, 16mm microfilm for business records, and microfiche for parts catalogues. Most people's memory of microfiche is going into an auto or electric store and watching the store assistant look up a part on a microfiche reader. The huge commercial use of the medium throughout the world should have led to the production of high-quality readers but this never happened. Some early readers were housed in wooden cases like the radios and televisions of the time, but even as they were modernized, they remained strictly functional, made from sheet steel and plastic, with none of the aesthetic quality of a personal computer. Winding through a thirty-metre reel of microfilm to find a page could be tedious, and though more and more readers were motorized, too often the image was upside down because the user had put the reel in the wrong way round. Most users preferred microfiche. With its eye-legible title-strip it was easy to pick the relevant microfiche. Once in the reader the glass platen holding the microfiche could be moved around quickly to bring up the right page. Because microfiche readers did not have to have winders or a motor to wind the film, they were also smaller and neater.

One of the other weaknesses of microfilm publications was in their presentation. Thirty metres of film wound onto a plastic reel in a cardboard box with the title typed on a label does not have the presence or distinction of a book in a colourful, well-designed jacket. Until the 1970s publishers made little effort to make their microfilms or microfiche look like professional publications. The captions that guided the reader through the sequence of pages on the reel were usually typed, sometimes even handwritten. They were often grubby and dog-eared because they had been used so many times. Microfiche tended to be a little better, though the first frame was usually typed, and not much care went into the typography of the eye-legible strip along the top. Yet in 1973 the price of a reel of microfilm was £20 (reproducing 800–1,000 pages), equivalent to an expensive hardbound book, while microfiche, each with 98 pages, were more competitive at £0.85 each.

In spite of its far from perfect interface with the user, and the uninspired presentation of most microfilm publications, microforms were accepted because of their obvious advantages – they made available material that was otherwise unavailable, they were less expensive than print, they were used to make preservation copies, and they offered libraries enormous savings in space. They were also a new media in which text had to be read on the screen of a machine rather than on a sheet of paper, which brought the first major change in the transmission of the printed word since the invention of printing. Analogue microfilm prepared the way for digital media by making librarians and library users accustomed to reading text on a screen.

But there had been one visionary who as early as 1930 conceived a machine that used microfilm to store information with automated methods of retrieving information, which anticipated digital search techniques. Emanuel Goldberg had had to leave Russia for Germany to complete his education because he was a Jew, and he was awarded his PhD in 1906 by the University of Leipzig, in the same city and the same year that Johnson's father had started his scientific publishing firm (see Chapter 2). Goldberg specialized in photographic technology and had designed the Zeiss Contax 35mm camera. His 'knowledge machine', conceived around 1930, held microfilmed documents accompanied by previously assigned retrieval codes printed along the edge of the film, which were read by a photocell. The user entered his search request and the film halted when the request and the document code matched. Goldberg patented it in both Germany and the USA, and IBM acquired US rights to his patent. But an American librarian, Ralph Shaw, devised a similar machine called 'Shaw's Rapid Selector' without being aware of Goldberg's patent, and in 1945 the scientist Vannevar Bush published an article in *Atlantic Monthly*, 'As We May Think', in which he described a similar machine which he called the 'Memex'.[8] At the time, Bush was director of the Office of Scientific Research and Development and in overall charge of the Manhattan Project and was probably the most influential scientist in America after Albert Einstein. He had seen how the war had led to a huge increase in the amount of scientific publishing and realized that traditional publishing methods could not handle the growth in the volume of data. It needed the application of new technology and Bush saw the Memex as the scientists' workstation from which they could call up on their screens the pre-indexed data – books, journals and research notes – stored on microfilm. The Memex never came into being, but Bush's thinking expressed in that one article strongly influenced the early computer scientists.[9] By the beginning of the 1970s there were new readers that could recognize codes printed along the edge of microfilm.[10] Exactly as Goldberg had envisaged, the user entered a search term on a keyboard and the film, which had been indexed, was advanced to that frame. These were closed systems used to handle specific bodies of data. It was a technology that was soon overtaken by digital storage on CD-ROM.

In 1962, the same year that the Xerox Corporation bought UM, Bell & Howell bought Freedman's Micro Photo, while four years later Freedman started Research Publications, which was then bought by the Thomson Organisation and for twenty-seven years was our most formidable competitor. Until the 1970s there were few micropublishers outside the USA. In the UK there was Micro Methods, later E. P. Microform, founded in 1956. It was one of their directors, N. A. Brampton, who was employed by Johnson as a consultant to advise me on the microfilming of *The Builder* (see Chapter 2). In 1968 Harvester Press had been set up by John Spiers, a young academic at the University of Sussex, who established an interesting list of academic monographs, reprints and microfilm collections. In the Netherlands Henri deMink, an engineer and one of van der Wolk's former students, set up the Inter Documentation Company (IDC) and built up a large, eclectic list of publications on microfiche in the humanities and social sciences including the *Patrologia Latina*, which became so important to Chadwyck-Healey in the 1990s (see Chapter 18). Both UM, now UMI (University Microfilms International), and Research Publications had a presence in the UK and when we started in 1973 these five were our main competitors. I knew deMink, who built his own cameras and processing equipment, and I also met Eugene Power, whom I regarded as the father of microfilm publishing. By the time I met him and his wife in Ann Arbor in the early 1980s he was not in good health. He died in 1993 aged eighty-eight.

By 1975 there were 123 micropublishers in the USA alone,[11] though many were institutions or publishers who were primarily printed book or journal publishers. Readex was bought by Newsbank, a small microform publisher, in 1984 and continues to publish microforms and electronic publications. One of the most important non-US book publishers that also published microforms was the Munich-based publisher K. G. Saur, with a list of monographs, collections of papers and journals on library science. Its head, Klaus Saur, successfully grew the publishing company his father had started after the war, publishing a series of national biographical dictionaries on microfiche, and the last multi-volume printed edition of the catalogue of the British Library (see Chapter 15). Bell & Howell bought the microform production company Micromedia in 1979, and Peter Ashby, one of its founders, started his own microform publishing company, Oxford Microform Publications, which he sold in 1982 to Robert Maxwell's Pergamon Press. The last micropublisher to be established in the UK was Adam Matthew in 1990. Since 2012 it has been part of SAGE Publishing.

But for us there were never more than five or so significant competitors publishing for the worldwide academic library market. There was also an important division between these micropublishers. Some, like UMI, Research Publications, MCA (owned by The New York Times Company), Kraus Reprint (which did some microfilm publishing) and Johnson, were owned by large corporations, while others, such as Harvester, IDC, Saur and Chadwyck-Healey, were owned by their founders and had been started with very little capital. Yet having the financial and organizational resources of a large corporation did not seem to provide a significant advantage; what was important was the ability to choose the right materials to publish, and much of this book has been about finding and publishing those materials.

Postscript

Bell & Howell, the Chicago-based group of companies that included Bell & Howell Information and Learning, which bought Chadwyck-Healey, changed its name to the ProQuest Company in 2001. Publicly quoted on the New York Stock Exchange, ProQuest later admitted to overstating its profits for several years, and in 2006 was bought by the privately held Cambridge Information Group. Since then CIG has acquired other publishing companies in this sector including CIS, and in 2016 Alexander Street Press, which was founded by Stephen Rhind-Tutt, the last president of Chadwyck-Healey Inc.

Appendix 2
Microfilm Technology

Microfilm formats

Microfilm

A reel of microfilm contains 30.5 metres of 35mm-wide silver halide film. This is the same width as is used in the film industry and in 35mm cameras. Cine and camera film have perforations down each side to ensure the accurate advance of each frame, but microfilm has no perforations so that the full width of the film can be used in the reproduction of the image, giving a usable width of 30mm, as opposed to the width of 24mm on perforated film.

A typical reduction ratio is 1:15. On microfilm at this reduction the image of an A4 page has a height of 19.8mm. Images are arranged on the film in either cine mode, in which the lines of text on the page are at right angles to the edge of the film, or comic mode, in which the lines of text are parallel with the edges of the film. 'Broadsheet' newspaper pages are often microfilmed singly in cine mode, while the two facing pages of an open book are generally filmed in comic mode.

The width of the standard microfilm used for preserving records in business and industry is 16mm, similar to a cine film of that width. But it was used much less in libraries. The images are less than half the size of those on 35mm film and most libraries preferred the larger format.

The most widely used microfilm camera was the Kodak MRD-2 roll film camera (see Figure 8 on p. 142). The detachable camera head holds a 30.5-metre roll of negative film and sits on a mounting that contains the lens and is attached to the column. The operator moves the camera head up and down the column according to the size of the document being microfilmed and the focus is automatically adjusted by a series of levers. The camera lenses are small and vary in quality; we used our best lenses for microfiche, which required a higher magnification. The table on which the document to be filmed is laid is illuminated by four flood lamps. The operator makes the exposure either through a foot switch or through a switch on the table. There were other more modern and better-made cameras but the MRDs were ubiquitous and these were the cameras that in the early 1990s the Hoover Institution supplied to the Russians to microfilm their archives (see Chapter 22).

Microfiche

Microfiche are sheets of film 105mm high and 148mm wide with ninety-eight frames (fourteen columns and seven rows) at a reduction of 1:24. If books are being microfilmed the preferred format is forty-nine frames (seven columns and seven rows) in which the two pages of an open book can be reproduced in one frame. In both formats the first frame is occupied by a caption containing bibliographic information about the publication (see below), so the maximum number of pages that can be reproduced on a microfiche is ninety-seven, or ninety-six in the 49-frame format.

The COSATI[1] format was an earlier format with sixty frames (twelve columns and five rows) at a reduction of 1:20. We used this for publishing microfiche editions of photographs, since we were using a film that had a lower resolution than microfilm (see below). We also used a 30-frame format (six columns and five rows) for filming oversize artwork (see Chapter 6).

Along the top of each microfiche is a title-strip, 15mm deep, which carries the title, page range, publisher's name and logo, and often a microfiche number to make it easier to refile the microfiche in the right order.

Computer-output microfiche (COM) were widely used both in libraries and in commerce, and contain from 270 to 420 frames at a reduction ratio of 1:48. A COM recorder converts data on computer tape into images that are shone directly on to moving, unexposed 105mm-wide film, creating high-quality images at a high speed of 250 frames a minute. It was a technology that was important in the period through the 1970s and 1980s when data was increasingly being stored in digital form, but most organizations had few terminals on which they could view the data because they were so expensive. Microfiche offered a much less expensive alternative. Our microfilm production company, CHMPS, created COM both for indexes to publications that were frequently updated, such as the *National*

Inventory of Documentary Sources (see Chapter 9), and for commercial customers like Sainsbury's, the supermarket chain, who in the evening delivered tapes to us containing the day's sales data, which we would process overnight to produce COM copies ready for collection at 6am the next morning. This was the business that we sold to Microgen (see Chapter 4).

The most efficient microfiche cameras were those such as the Bell & Howell Diplomat camera that made each exposure on to a roll of 105mm negative film. The drawback of these cameras is that if there is an error, the whole microfiche has to be refilmed. The alternative is a less elegant, quite labour-intensive method of production that was used very widely and that we used because it was easier to refilm pages that needed correction.

To make a 49-frame microfiche, consisting of seven rows of seven frames, the original material is filmed at a 24x reduction on a Kodak MRD camera fitted with a platen with the frame size for that format. During filming, two or more blank frames are added after every seven frames. The operator uses an electronic counter to know when to add the blank frames and when the seven rows have been completed (see Figure 8 on p. 142). The 35mm film is processed and is cut down to a 12.5mm width in a special cutter. It is then cut up into seven strips, which are laid down in order with the title-strip at the top (making eight strips in all). Each strip is attached with pins through the blank film at each end to a piece of polystyrene. When the make-up of the microfiche is completed, the pins are removed and adhesive tape is run down each side of the strips to keep them in position. If any refilming is necessary, the strip that is being replaced can be cut out of the master and the new strip put in its place. This flimsy and difficult-to-handle 'master' microfiche is then used, often only once, to make a printing master by copying it on to 105mm-wide negative film. The 105mm-wide printing master will consist of a roll of film carrying as many as 1,000 microfiche and is used, in a high-speed duplicator, to make positive copies.

Film types

Silver halide microfilm

This film is required by libraries because it is considered to be archivally permanent. The film base until the 1980s was cellulose acetate. This was replaced by a tougher polyester 'Estar' base. It is coated with a thin layer of silver halide emulsion. Because the emulsion contains silver the film is more expensive than the alternatives below. The image on the positive copy is usually black text on a transparent background. To achieve this the silver halide emulsion in the unexposed background areas is dissolved by the developer and is washed off during film processing. The waste solution is trapped in a tank in the film processor and the silver in the solution attaches itself to anodes. We sold the clumps of almost pure silver to Johnson Matthey, the largest precious metals processor in the UK, which, conveniently, was only two miles from Bassingbourn, and this recouped some of the cost of the film.

Archival permanence of silver halide film may be as long as 200 years. Properly processed silver emulsions do appear to be chemically stable providing they are kept in the right conditions. High temperatures and humidity can lead to staining and even fungus on the emulsion. But microfilm is most vulnerable to scratching through careless handling and storage, and this can quickly degrade the image.

Microfilm has a high-contrast emulsion to achieve the most effective reproduction of black and white text. With limited shades of grey between full black and the transparent film background, microfilm is unsuitable for reproducing photographs or prints, which require a continuous tone film. In the 1970s we used a slow, fine-grain Kodak camera film, Panatomic X, for microfiche publications containing images (see Chapter 6). It did not have as high a resolution as microfilm, so we used the 60-frame format at the lower reduction of 1:20. In the early 1980s Pibworth, the manager at Kodak in the UK who was always so helpful to us, told us about an 'unofficial' method of achieving continuous tone reproduction using standard microfilm. This does not appear to have been formally documented by Kodak. It introduces a bleach bath of the type used for colour film processing, after development of the microfilm and before it goes through the fixing bath. Our manager Chapman used it very effectively in the microfilming of the hundreds of thousands of images in the New York Public Library *Artists File* and *Print File* (see Chapter 10), and we also used it in the production in the USA of the *Artists Files* and *Artists Scrapbooks* of the Museum of Modern Art, New York.

Colour microfilm

A slow, fine-grain colour film. It does not have such high resolution as black and white film and is not archivally permanent.

Diazo film

Diazo film has several advantages over silver film. It is much less expensive, and the image is locked inside the plastic film, so it is not as vulnerable to scratching. But it is not archivally permanent in that it fades after a few years. It is used in libraries for library catalogues and by publishers for indexes that are regularly replaced. It is used almost universally in commerce, where archival permanence is not required. It is processed in an atmosphere of ammonia and its acrid smell is a characteristic part of diazo film processing.

Vesicular film

This is another tough, inexpensive film in which the image is in vesicles or microscopic bubbles inside the film itself and is processed by heat. It is used commercially but only rarely for library publications.

Presentation and storage of microform publications

On a roll-microfilm publication, to meet official standards, the publisher is required to include additional frames with information about the material that is reproduced on the reel. There will be a 'title page' caption including all the necessary bibliographic information about the publication, the publisher, and the copyright notice as one would find in a book. There is a resolution chart and a ruler to enable the user to check the original size of the image on film. A blank frame is left for a 'hypo' test so that the buyer of the microfilm can check that the residual level of hypo, the chemical used to 'fix' the film, is below the minimum allowed. Otherwise the film will be rejected, as it will eventually discolour. Not many libraries carried out this test.

Every 100 frames there is a caption consisting of an enlarged eye-legible number to enable the reader to more easily find the page he is searching for while the film is being wound on. The final caption is 'End' and 'Please rewind'. At the beginning and the end of each reel is a length of blank film for threading the film into the storage and take-up spools.

The roll-film copies are on plastic spools secured with straps of thin card in boxes made from acid-free cardboard. The publisher uses printed boxes with its name and logo, to which is added a label to identify the publication and the page range on that reel of film.

Microfiche are stored in protective envelopes.

Microfilm and microfiche readers

Microfilm readers divide into two groups: those in which the reel of film has to be wound by hand and those in which the film is wound by a motor controlled by the user. Some readers have dual lenses to allow the images on film to be enlarged at different magnifications.

Microfiche readers are smaller and more portable. Agfa, Canon, Minolta and Bell & Howell all made readers. They are precision instruments with light sources, cooling fans, lenses and focussing systems, but all lack the satisfying look and feel of a personal computer.

The most important advance in the late 1970s was the reader printer. This was a microfilm or microfiche reader attached to a photocopier. In the early days they did not work well and needed a high level of maintenance, which in many libraries they rarely got. But as plain-paper photocopiers became more reliable so did reader printers and they improved the experience of using microforms, as the user could print out the pages being viewed. Now there are microfilm reader scanners, which can send scanned images directly to a PC.

The material being microfilmed

The condition and legibility of the material being microfilmed is one of the most important factors in the legibility and general acceptability of the microform publication itself. While this may seem obvious, it is often overlooked, as it is assumed that in some way the microform publication is able to overcome problems with the legibility of the originals. It is not always a question of age. When we microfilmed the *Husting Rolls of Deeds and Wills, 1252–1485,* transcripts of deeds and wills from the principal court of medieval London, including the deeds of William Caxton's house, the parchment rolls were so tough that we were allowed to use metal weights to keep them flat. The handwriting in oak gall ink was as black as when it was first written. At the same time, we were microfilming *The*

Historical Records of the High Authority of the European Coal and Steel Community, 1952–1956, which were documents only around forty years old. The paper was thin and fragile, the typewritten texts were fading, and it was almost impossible to produce an acceptable microfiche publication. It seems that the longevity of textual material is in inverse proportion to the quantity produced, and even more so now with emails. Perhaps this is to protect us from being overwhelmed by the sheer quantity of material we are now producing, most of which, fortunately, will quickly disappear.

The state of a book's binding is another important factor in its microfilming. To be filmed it has to be able to be opened flat. Sometimes, in order not to damage the binding, only single pages can be filmed, and the camera operator holds the other half of the book at an angle while making the exposure. There are also adjustable book cradles, which hold the book with the two sides slightly angled. The depth of field is sufficient for the text on both pages to be sharp and readable. Alston designed a device with a very large prism positioned above the book, which compensated for the angle of the pages and made them appear to be flat and fully legible.

Bindings have to be taken into account when planning a microfilming project. In the case of the Sanborn Maps (see Chapter 8) we spent $20,000 disbinding and boxing maps so they could be microfilmed; the Burney Collection at the British Library was only microfilmed after it had been disbound; and the volumes of the Parliamentary Papers from the library of the DTI could only be filmed satisfactorily because their bindings were loose from years of heavy use (see Chapter 5).

The business model

Microform publishing was an example of an almost perfect business model. We bought the raw materials, film and chemicals from Kodak, added intellectual property and sold the final output directly to the user without any intermediaries and often with little or no royalties to be paid. There was only a modest upfront investment in making the master negatives and there was very little capital tied up in stock. All microfilm copies were made to order because there was no saving in making several copies at a time. With microfiche it was more efficient to make more than one copy at a time, but we rarely made more than five to ten copies for stock. The production of sets of microfiche was labour intensive. Five sets of the *Nineteenth-Century Parliamentary Papers*, totalling 232,500 microfiche, after duplication and film processing, had to be cut up, put into envelopes and organized into sets of 46,500 microfiche each. This required hours of manual work, yet there was very little change in our working methods in the seventeen years we produced our own microforms.

Quality control

Every reel of microfilm and every microfiche when first produced were looked at by checkers who usually worked at home or in the office in Cambridge. They looked for missing pages, illegible text and filming errors where pages were out of focus or the film was too light or too dark. Jane Coston, who worked for us for seventeen years checking film, combined this apparently monotonous job with her role as a prominent local councillor, and there is now a bridge in Cambridge named after her. What was more difficult to manage was the quality control of copies, which depended on spot checks and the expertise of the staff making the copies who could see after the film had been processed whether it was too light or too dark, normally the most common fault.

Conclusion

This is a short summary of the production of microforms, which are now so little used that these processes have only a historical interest. But many of the disciplines required in the handling of large quantities of material apply equally to the scanning of printed material, which is the method now used to convert the printed materials of the past into digital media.

Notes

Preface

1 Eugene B. Power with Robert Anderson, *Edition of One: The Autobiography of Eugene B. Power. Founder of University Microfilms* (Ann Arbor, MI: University Microfilms International, 1990).
2 *Independent*, 24 July 1996.

1 Beginning

1 Roger L. Geiger, 'What Happened after Sputnik? Shaping University Research in the United States', *Minerva* 35 (1997): 349–67.
2 Yong Zhao, *Catching Up or Leading the Way: American Education in the Age of Globalization* (Alexandria, Virginia: ASCD, 2009).
3 *Time*, 16 October 1960.
4 Committee on Higher Education, *Higher Education: Report of the Committee . . . under the Chairmanship of Lord Robbins 1961–1963*, Cmnd. 2154 (London: HMSO, 23 September 1963).
5 A description by Michael Beloff for his book *The Plateglass Universities* (London: Secker & Warburg, 1968).
6 *Troilus and Cressida Or, Truth Found too Late. A Tragedy As it is Acted at the Dukes Theatre. To which is Prefix'd A Preface Containing the Grounds of Criticism in Tragedy, Written By John Dryden, Servant to his Majesty* (London, Printed for Abel Swall, 1679).
7 *Romeo and Juliet. By Shakespear. With Alterations, and an additional Scene* [by David Garrick]. *As it is performed at the Theatre-Royal in Drury-Lane.* (London: Printed for J. and R. Tonson and S. Draper. MDCCL [1750]).
8 Alastair Jamieson, 'The Prince of Wales on Architecture: His 10 "Monstrous Carbuncles"', *Daily Telegraph*, 13 May 1979.
9 The principal publication in the collection of books by G. F. Waagen is, *Treasures of Art in Great Britain: Being an Account of the Chief Collections of Paintings, Drawings, Sculptures . . . Translated from the German by Lady Eastlake*, 3 volumes (London: John Murray, 1854).

10 Michael Adams, 'The World of Irish University Press', in *The Irish Book in the Twentieth Century*, ed. Claire Hutton (Dublin: Irish Academic Press, 2004), 157–77.
11 Interview with Seamus Cashman, January 2017.
12 Cashman introduced me to Farmar who kindly gave me a proof of part of his forthcoming book, *The History of Irish Book Publishing* (Stroud: The History Press, 2018). Sadly, Farmar died in November 2017 before his book was published.
13 Reagan was responding to an audit of the libraries of the University of California, as reported in the *Los Angeles Times*, 29 February 1972.
14 Farmar, *Irish Book Publishing*.

2 Johnson Reprint Corporation

1 Edwin Beschler, 'Academic Press: Walter J. Johnson and Kurt Jacoby', *Logos* 18:3 (2007): 153–66.
2 Albert Henderson, 'Walter J. Johnson and the Scholarly Reprint', *Logos* 17:1 (2006): 42–7.
3 Beschler, 'Academic Press'.
4 William Prynne, *Histrio-Mastix. The Players Scovrge: or, Actors Tragaedie. Divided into Two Parts* . . . (London: Printed by E. A. and W. I. for Michael Sparke, 1633).
5 Henry Chettle, *Kind-harts dreame. Conteining fiue apparitions, vvith their inuectiues against abuses raigning.* . . . (London: Imprinted . . . for William Wright, 1593).
6 This was a new technical development in short-run offset litho printing. Plastic plates were cheap but had to be discarded after a relatively short print-run. It meant that printers could produce editions in runs as few as 100 copies and still keep unit prices in line with the prices of larger editions.
7 J. Mordaunt Crook, *Victorian Architecture. A Visual Anthology* (London: Johnson Reprint Company Ltd, 1971).

3 Chadwyck-Healey

1 W. E. Fredeman, 'The Bibliographical Significance of a Publisher's Archive', *Studies in Bibliography* 23 (1970): 183–91.
2 Letter from Walter J. Johnson to Charles Chadwyck-Healey, 19 September 1973.
3 Letter from Walter J. Johnson to Charles Chadwyck-Healey, 21 March 1974.
4 E. L. C. Mullins, *Texts and Calendars: An Analytical Guide to Serial Publications* (London: Royal Historical Society, 1958).
5 The genesis of the British Library is described in detail in P. R. Harris, *A History of the British Museum Library 1753–1973* (London: The British Library, 1998). Harris himself was fully involved in the difficult transition.

6 Royal Gettman, *A Victorian Publisher* (Cambridge: Cambridge University Press, 1960).
7 Letter from J. H. Plumb to Charles Chadwyck-Healey, 28 September 1978, giving advice on the choice of editors for a series of books containing satirical prints (see Chapter 6).
8 Beatrice Webb, Diary, 7 July 1891.
9 Curiously her near namesake Beatrix Potter died the same year.
10 Ian Bradley, 'Putting the Webbs in Their Right Place?', *The Times*, 15 May 1978. Review of the microfiche edition and interview with Norman Mackenzie.
11 *Index to the Diary of Beatrice Webb 1873–1943*, with preface by Matthew Anderson, 'The Text of the Diary' by Geoffrey Allen, 'Historical Introduction' by Dame Margaret Cole, 'The Diary as Literature' by Norman Mackenzie, 'Chronology' (Cambridge: Chadwyck-Healey, 1978).
12 Norman Mackenzie (ed.), *The Letters of Sidney and Beatrice Webb*, 3 volumes (Cambridge: Cambridge University Press for the London School of Economics and Political Science, 1978).
13 Letter from P. D. C. Davis to Charles Chadwyck-Healey, 23 November 1982.
14 Letter from P. D. C. Davis to Charles Chadwyck-Healey, 14 December 1982.

4 Cambridge and Our Own Production

1 *Choice*, September 1981.

5 Official Publications

1 B. R. Mitchell and H. G. Jones, *Second Abstract of British Historical Statistics* (Cambridge: Cambridge University Press, 1971).
2 Later editions were edited by Eugene Sheehy, so the title numbers we quoted were referred to as 'Sheehy'.
3 K. Mallaber, 'The Sale Catalogues of British Government Publications 1836–1965', *Journal of Librarianship*, 5:2 (April 1973).
4 Letter from Charles Chadwyck-Healey to Kenneth A. Mallaber, 21 January 1975.
5 R. G. Surridge, *Library Association Record*, 77:11 (November 1975), in the Liaison Section.
6 Taking into account US inflation since 1940 and the exchange rate between the dollar and the pound in 1979.
7 K. A. C. Parsons, *A Checklist of the British Parliamentary Papers (Bound Set) 1801–1950*, privately printed for the University Library, 1958, and reprinted, 1971, by Cambridge University Press.

8   One of a number of anecdotes and references sent to me by Peter Ashby in November 2018.
9   Mallaber had retired in the summer of 1976 and died suddenly three months later.
10 Jack Grove, 'Thatcher had "immense impact" on higher education', *THE*, 8 April 2013. https://www.timeshighereducation.com/news/thatcher-had-immense-impact-on-higher-education/2003059.article#survey-answer. Accessed 29 May 2019.
11 Peter Cockton, *House of Commons Parliamentary Papers, 1800–1900: Guide to the Chadwyck-Healey Microfiche Edition* (Cambridge: Chadwyck-Healey, 1991).
12 Peter Cockton, *Subject Catalogue of the House of Commons Parliamentary Papers 1801–1900*, 5 volumes (Cambridge: Chadwyck-Healey, 1988).
13 Suzanne Dodson, *Microform Review*, 11:4 (Fall 1982). Review of Chadwyck-Healey's microfiche edition of the 1980–1 Sessional Papers.
14 Home Office, Joint Fire Prevention Committee of the Central Fire Brigades Advisory Council, *Report of the Planning/Legislation Sub-Committee on the Fire at Woolworth's, Piccadilly, Manchester on 8 May 1979*.
15 Diana Marshallsay, *Official Publications: A Survey of the Current Situation* (Southampton: Southampton University Library, 1972).
16 John E. Pemberton, *British Official Publications,* 2nd ed. (Oxford: Pergamon, 1973).
17 Charles Rogers, 'Government and Colleagues', *Library Association Record*, 82 (6 June 1980).
18 Alan Macfarlane et al., *Records of an English Village. Earls Colne 1400–1750* (Cambridge: Chadwyck-Healey, 1980–1).
19 Library Association EC&R and RSI Groups, Open Government Seminar, University of Technology, Loughborough, 21 April 1982.
20 Memo from Mark Barragry to Julie Carroll-Davis and others, reporting on a meeting with TSO about *UKOP*, 24 February 1999.
21 Mr David Shaw to Mr MacGregor, Lord President of the Council, 12 and 14 December 1990.
22 Memo from Paul Holroyd to Alison Moss, 16 March 1992.
23 The censuses that used Supermap software ran on Windows 3.0 (see Chapter 15).
24 Letter from Carol Tullo to A. J. Hastings, Copyright Officer, House of Commons, 16 December 1997.

6 Visual Images on Microfilm

1   British Museum, Department of Prints and Drawings, *Catalogue of Political and Personal Satires Preserved in the Department of Prints and Drawings in the British Museum*, by F. G. Stephens and M. D. George (London, 1870–1954).
2   Letter from Charles Chadwyck-Healey to Michael Hoare, 3 October 1975.
3   *Times Higher Education Supplement*, 4 December 1981.

4   Memo from Peter Miller to Charles Chadwyck-Healey, 5 July 1988.
5   *Guardian,* 13 February 1986; *Daily Telegraph,* 21 February 1986; *Financial Times,* 1 March 1986; *London Review of Books,* 20 March 1986. BBC *Timewatch* was transmitted on 6 March 1986.
6   Vladimir Markov, *Russian Futurism: A History* (Berkeley, University of California Press, 1968).
7   Recent exhibitions include 'Malevich: Revolutionary of Russian Art', Tate Modern, London 2014; 'Kazimir Malevich and the Russian Avant-Garde', Stedelijk Museum, Amsterdam, 2013/14, described as the 'largest survey for 20 years'; and 'Revolution: Russian Art 1917–1932', Royal Academy of Arts, London, 2017.
8   Stuart Levine, 'Visual Arts in Microfiche', *American Studies Journal,* 19:2 (1978): 93–9.
9   Van Wyck Brooks, 'On Creating a Usable Past', *The Dial,* 11 April 1918, 337–41.
10 Clarence Hornung, *Treasury of American Design: A Survey of Popular Folk Arts Based upon Watercolor Renderings in the Index of American Design, at the National Gallery of Art* (New York: H. N. Abrams, 1972).
11 Kodak internegative film 5271.
12 National Gallery of Art, Washington, DC, Gallery Archives. Interview with Lina Steele conducted by Anne Ritchie, 20 November 1996, 15–16.
13 Ibid.
14 Letter, 5 October 1978.
15 Part 1 to 1980, 1,567 microfiche; part 2, 1980–8, 2,720 microfiche.
16 *Camera* 10 (October 1962). Rothstein photographed the skull against two different backgrounds, a manipulation that the FSA strongly disapproved of. See William Stott, *Documentary Expression and Thirties America* (New York: Oxford University Press, 1973), 61.
17 Jerald C. Maddox, *Walker Evans Photographs for the Farm Security Administration 1935–1938* (New York: Da Capo Press, 1973).
18 Carl Fleischhauer and Beverly W. Brannan (eds.), *Documenting America, 1935–1943* (Berkeley: University of California Press, 1988).

7 Carving up the Centuries

1   Early books tended to have very long titles, and Pollard and Redgrave had devised a system in which the book could be clearly identified by a much-shortened title; hence the term 'short title catalogue' or 'STC'.
2   Donald Goddard Wing, *Short-title Catalogue of Books Printed in England, Scotland, Ireland, Wales and British America, and of English Books Printed in Other Countries, 1641–1700, Compiled by Donald Wing* (New York: Index Society, 1945–51).

3   Library of Congress, MARC Development Office, *Subscriber's Guide to the MARC Distribution Office* (Washington, DC: Library of Congress, 1968).
4   British Library, *First Annual Report 1973–1974* (London, 1974).
5   Willison made this point to me in a conversation in May 2017.
6   In 2008 Alston left a colourful account on the web of how it came into being: *The History of ESTC to 1989*. Available at: http://archive.li/9WSur. Accessed 25 July 2019.
7   *Early English Books 1475–1640: Selected from Pollard and Redgrave's Short-title Catalogue*. Ann Arbor, University Microfilms International, 195?–.
8   Paul Korshin, 'The ESTC and Eighteenth-Century Literary Scholarship', in Henry L. Snyder and Michael S. Smith (eds.), *The English Short-Title Catalogue: Past, Present, Future. Papers Delivered at a Conference at the New York Public Library on 21 January 1998* (New York: AMS Press Inc., 2003), 169–89.
9   The eight libraries are: the British Library, National Library of Scotland, Library of Congress, Bodleian Library, Cambridge University Library, Trinity College, Dublin, Harvard University Library, University of Newcastle Library.
10 *The Journal*, 6 September 1986. In 2010 Miller was released from a ten-year prison term for financial fraud in a maximum-security prison in the Philippines. He moved back to Gosforth near Newcastle and has been implicated in a billion-dollar misappropriation of Malaysian government funds through his company Ladylaw Securities Pte. Ltd. See http://www.sarawakreport.org/2018/03/najib-pushed-malaysias-savings-funds-to-invest-more-billions-with-another-convicted-foreign-fraudster/. Accessed 30 May 2019.
11 D. H. Stam, *National Preservation Planning in the United Kingdom* (London: British Library Research and Development Department, 1983).
12 Cambridge University Library, British Library Conservation Project, Dissemination Seminar, 21–22 September 1983.
13 R. C. Alston, *The Arrangement of Books in the British Museum Library 1843–1973 Compiled from Manuscript and Printed Sources* (Cambridge: Chadwyck-Healey in association with the British Library and Avero Publications, 1986).
14 UMI's *Early English Books* and Research Publication's 61,000 books on economics from the London School of Economics and the Kress Collection of economic literature at the Baker Library, Harvard. See also Martin D. Joachim, 'Cooperative Cataloging of Microform Sets', *Cataloging & Classification Quarterly* 17:3–4 (February 1994): 105–26.
15 *The Times*, 27 February 1987.
16 *Times Literary Supplement*, 27 February 1987.
17 Memo from Steven Hall to directors and managers of Chadwyck-Healey Ltd, 4 January 1991.
18 *The English Poetry Full-Text Database* and Migne's *Patrologia Latina*.

8 The Sanborn Fire Insurance Maps

1. Wolter retired in 1991 and was succeeded as chief by Ehrenberg, who retired in 1998.
2. Andrew M. Modelski, *Railroad Maps of North America. The First Hundred Years*, (Washington, DC: Library of Congress, 1984).
3. Library of Congress. Geography and Map Division, *Fire Insurance Maps in the Library of Congress: Plans of North American Cities and Towns Produced by the Sanborn Map Company. A Checklist Compiled by the Reference and Bibliography Section, Geography and Map Division* (Washington DC, Library of Congress, 1981). The introduction gives useful information on the history of fire insurance maps in the USA, as does Diane L. Oswald, *Fire Insurance Maps. Their History and Applications* (College Station, Texas: Lacewing Press, 1997), which also describes the Chadwyck-Healey microfilm edition.
4. Mrs Madel Morgan, Department of Archives and History, State of Mississippi, to Charles Chadwyck-Healey, 13 September 1983.

9 Finding the Archives

1. Letter from Dr Frank G. Burke to Charles Chadwyck-Healey, 20 April 1982.
2. Reported in the Chadwyck-Healey Inc. *NIDS Newsletter*, 1:1 (June 1985).
3. Chadwyck-Healey Inc. sales brochure, *The National Inventory of Documentary Sources in the United States,* R17 January 1986.
4. *American Archivist,* 'Reviews', Summer 1987, p. 420.
5. Review by Anne Bristow in *American Historical Review*, February 1988.
6. Letter from Kenneth Silverman to Charles Chadwyck-Healey, 12 February 1988.
7. The score and lyrics of the song were published in the SAA Newsletter, November 1983.
8. *Microform Review,* 16:4 (Fall 1987).
9. Ibid.
10. Letter from Charles Chadwyck-Healey to A. Wilson, 26 September 1983.
11. Letter from Hugh Cobbe to Charles Chadwyck-Healey confirming acceptance of our submission to tender for the publication of the printed index.

10 The New York Times

1. With a letter from William Kerr to Charles Chadwyck-Healey, 10 November 1982.
2. The second most valuable newspaper microfilm publication was the *Wall Street Journal* with only 1,300 subscriptions according to MCA.

3 Susan E. Tifft and Alex S. Jones, *The Trust. The Private and Powerful Family Behind The New York Times* (Boston: Little Brown, 1999): 540–1.
4 Letter from Willa Baum, University of California, Berkeley, 20 July 1983.
5 Letter from Roberta Waddell, the New York Public Library, 13 December 1988.
6 Letter from Donald Anderle, the New York Public Library, to Alison Moss, 4 April 1988.

11 France and Spain

1 *Pareil à des enfants* (Paris: Gallimard, 1942).
2 I wrote for myself a detailed note about this dinner.
3 Mercier Composition Photogravures Industries.
4 Memorandum to Charles Chadwyck-Healey, 'État des projets proposés par CHF', 19 December 1985.
5 Annick Bernard, *Guide de l'utilisateur des catalogues des livres imprimés de la Bibliothèque nationale* (Paris: Chadwyck-Healey France, 1986).
6 The exchange rate between the French franc and the pound sterling changed very little from 1985 to 1998, from 1 franc=£0.09 to £0.13. For most years it was close to 1 franc=£0.1.
7 The highest rate of TVA in France at the time was 33.3 per cent.
8 Isabelle Carbonnel and Ghislain Brunel, *Guide de l'utilisateur des inventaires des Archives nationales* (Paris: Chadwyck-Healey France, 1990).
9 Great Britain, House of Commons, *Appendices to the Votes and Proceedings, 1817–1890*; *Reports of the Select Committee on Public Petitions, 1833–1890*; *Division Lists, 1836–1909*.
10 *Microform Review,* 17:3 (August 1988).
11 La Banque d'information politique et d'actualité de la Documenation française.
12 Such as *Hansard* on CD-ROM (see Chapter 5).
13 In a memo to Everitt, Hall and Moss, 12 March 1993, 'CHF Accounts to 31 Jan 1993'.
14 PDG. Président directeur general is equivalent to managing director or CEO.
15 30 June 1995.
16 Including seventy-two orders for *DocThèses*, a catalogue of French doctoral theses on CD-ROM, at an annual subscription of 5,500 francs (£700).
17 Email from Charles Chadwyck-Healey to Jean-Pierre Sakoun, 19 June 1995.
18 Email from Jean-Pierre Sakoun to Charles Chadwyck-Healey and Don McCrae, 15 March 1996.
19 Confidential memo from McCrae to the board of Chadwyck-Healey Ltd, 16 November 1996.

20 The standard microfiche reduction is 24x. See Appendix 2.
21 18 October 1997.

12 Black Studies

1 Reader printers are a combined microfiche reader and photocopier, enabling photocopies to be made from the microfiche.
2 Introduction by Henry Louis Gates Jr, in *Black Literature 1827-1940*, Chadwyck-Healey Inc., sales brochure L68, February 1988.
3 Review by Henry Louis Gates Jr of Rayford W. Logan and Michael R. Winston, *Dictionary of American Negro Biography*, in the *New York Times Book Review*, 1 May 1983, 13.
4 Cyprian Glamorgan, *The Colored Aristocracy of St. Louis* (St. Louis, 1858).
5 A neighbourhood in Brooklyn with many immigrant communities. In 1989 a black teenager had been shot dead by a gang of white youths. In 1994, just ten weeks before the lecture, a Dr Benjamin Goldstein, who had lived in Bensonhurst for many years but had emigrated to Israel, opened fire in a West Bank mosque, killing forty Muslims.

13 The National Security Archive

1 Quoted in Chadwyck-Healey Inc. sales brochure, *'It'll scare the hell out of you'*, AH01, November 1990.
2 Boutros Boutros-Ghali, *From Madness to Hope: The 12-year War in El Salvador* (United Nations: Commission on the Truth for El Salvador; United Nations. Security Council, [New York], United Nations, [1993]).
3 Canonized by Pope Francis on 14 October 2018.
4 Tom Blanton, 'Where George Was. What North's Diaries Tell Us about Bush's Iran-Contra Role', *Washington Post*, 10 June 1990.
5 Memo from Tom Blanton to Doug Roesemann, vice-president, Chadwyck-Healey Inc., 5 November 1993.
6 Email from Tom Blanton to Charles Chadwyck-Healey, 7 March 2018.

14 The Last Years of Microform

1 Letter from Tim Rix to Charles Chadwyck-Healey, 20 February 1986.
2 Letter from James C. Bradford to Mark Hamilton, 25 January 1985.

3   *Annotation,* the newsletter of the NHPRC, 14:2 (August 1986).
4   Quoted in Alice Wexler, *Emma Goldman: An Intimate Life* (New York: Pantheon Books, 1984), 94.
5   *Mother Earth,* September 1907.
6   Emma Goldman, *Living My Life* (New York: Alfred A. Knopf, 1928).
7   Emma Goldman and Alix Kates Shulman, *Red Emma Speaks* (New York: Random House, 1972).
8   She died on 14 May 1940.
9   Volume 1. *Made for America*; Volume 2. *Making Speech Free, 1902–1909* (Oakland, CA: University of California Press, 2003 and 2005); Volume 3. *Light and Shadow, 1910–1916* (Urbana: University of Illinois Press, 2012).
10 *Publishing History Occasional Series,* edited by Robin Myers and Michael Harris.
11 Statement by Robin Myers for the sales brochure.
12 *Sir Isaac Newton: Manuscripts and Papers* (Cambridge: Chadwyck-Healey, 1991). Microfilm with printed guide.
13 *Microform Review,* 19:1 (1990).
14 *Wilson Library Bulletin,* 58:4 (December 1983).

15 The Silver Catalyst

1   Article in *The Australian*, 31 March 1987.
2   Memo from Charles Chadwyck-Healey to Susan Severtson and Mark Hamilton, three-page report on STR, undated but probably March 1987.
3   *Programmatic Engineering & Remote Sensing,* vol. 54 (1988): 406.
4   Letter from Fred W. Grupp, Central Intelligence Agency (CIA), Washington, DC, to Alan Fox, 24 August 1988.
5   *Mapping Awareness,* 4:8 (October 1990).
6   Review by Jack Kenny, *Times Educational Supplement,* 20 March 1992.
7   A full description is given in A. H. Chaplin, *GK: 150 Years of the General Catalogue of Printed Books in the British Museum* (Aldershot: Scolar Press, 1987).
8   Saztec Europe Ltd, *Bulletin* (press release), 26 September 1988.
9   Eric Korn, 'A Dazzling Glimpse of the Private Case', *Times Literary Supplement,* 22 February 1991.
10 Count Ernest von Heltzendorff, *The Secrets of Potsdam ... chronicled by William Le Queux,* (London, London Mail, 1917).
11 John Davitt, 'A Horn of Plenty for the Schools', *Guardian,* 28 February 1991.
12 Alison Moss, 'Producing the *Guardian* on CD-ROM', *Aslib Information,* 19:6. ASCII (American Standard Code for Information Interchange) is a character encoding standard.

13 Dr Frank Ryan, 'Searching *The Times, The Guardian* and *The Independent* on CD-ROM', *Program*, 25:4 (October 1991).

16 Other Digital Ventures

1 Memo in French and English, 27 May 1993.
2 Memo from Don McCrae to Charles Chadwyck-Healey, 8 May 1990.
3 Comprehensive Environmental Response, Compensation and Liability Act, 1980.
4 Superfund Amendments and Reauthorization Act, 1986.
5 *The New York Times,* 28 April 1991.
6 20 January 1993.
7 We met again in London in 2015.
8 There was a large US educational organization called ERIC and there was concern about us having the same name if we were to float.

17 *English Poetry*

1 In 2019 *Philosopher's Index* is available from Ovid, EBSCO and ProQuest.
2 Frederick Wilse Bateson (ed.), *New Cambridge Bibliography of English Literature* (Cambridge: Cambridge University Press, 1969–77). We had used *NCBEL* in the 1970s when we published *Literary Taste, Culture and Mass Communication* (see Chapter 4).
3 TEI was an international project funded by the NEH, the European Community (DGXIII) and the Andrew W. Mellon Foundation.
4 *The English Poetry Full-Text Database Newsletter,* 1 (December 1991).
5 *English Poetry. A Bibliography of The English Poetry Full-Text Database* (Cambridge: Chadwyck-Healey, 1995).
6 My filofax notes of the meeting, 10 November 1990.
7 This was described by Law in 'Game, Dataset and Match', *Times Higher*, 14 July 1995, iii (supplement).
8 *The English Poetry Full-Text Database Newsletter,* 3 (September 1993).
9 *The Times,* 5 July 1991.
10 *Guardian*, 20 January 1993.
11 *Times Higher Education Supplement,* 10 June 1994.
12 *Times Literary Supplement,* 30 April 1993.
13 For some reason Potts thought that the ultimate price of *English Poetry* was going to be £30,000 with a pre-paid price of £23,500.
14 *New Library World*, 95:1111.
15 *Wall Street Journal,* 25 March 1993.

16 *The New Yorker*, 20 & 27 February 1995.
17 In Nicholson Baker, *The Size of Thoughts* (London: Chatto & Windus, 1996).
18 Which we lent to him so that he could review it for the *New York Review of Books*.
19 'How Prologues into Prefaces decay, And these to Notes are fritter'd quite away: How Index-learning turns no student pale, Yet holds the eel of science by the tail.' In the *Dunciad: an heroic poem. In three books,* by Alexander Pope (London: printed for A. Dodd, 1728). Pope complains about the modern practice of including prefaces, notes and indexes in books. Baker presumably thinks that he would have found an electronic edition equally reprehensible.
20 *London Review of Books,* 16:11 (9 June 1994).
21 Nicholson Baker, *Double Fold. Libraries and the Assault on Paper* (New York: Random House, 2001).
22 *Times Literary Supplement,* 5 April, 26 April, 17 May 1996.
23 James Gleick, *The Information. A History. A Theory. A Flood* (London: Fourth Estate, 2011).
24 *The Times,* 5 July 1991.

18 *Patrologia Latina*

1 The full title is *Series Latina* of the *Patrologiae Cursus Completus* (Paris, Adalbert G. Hamman, 1844–55).
2 This draws on the entertaining biography of Migne by R. Howard Bloch: *God's Plagiarist: Being an Account of the Fabulous Industry and Irregular Commerce of the Abbé Migne* (Chicago, IL: University of Chicago Press, 1994).
3 Montrouge is a Paris suburb in which there were many printers, notably Draeger, one of the most important printers in France in the twentieth century.
4 Edmond and Jules de Goncourt, *Journal: mémoires de la vie littéraire ... texte intégral établi et annoté par Robert Ricatte* (Monaco: Imprimerie nationale, 1956-8). Translation by Bloch.
5 This was later disputed by Professor Tombeur; see below.
6 In the *Patrologia Latina Database Newsletter,* 1 (June 1992).
7 Memo from Pocock, 'The Coding and Structure of *PLD*. Adapting *PLD* to Run with a Poetry-Type Interface', 21 December 1992.
8 In 1993 Calaluca started his own digital publishing company, Paratext.
9 *The Bookseller,* 22 July 1994.
10 We had experienced the same problem when photographing catalogue cards for the printed edition of the *British Library Index of Manuscripts* in 1984 (see Chapter 9).
11 *Bulletin de SIEPM*, no. 34 (1992). SIEPM is the Société Internationale pour l'Étude de la Philosophie Médiévale.
12 *Bulletin de SIEPM*, no. 35 (1993).

13 Both sides of the argument are contained in a letter from Charles Chadwyck-Healey to Mark Jordan, 1 November 1994.

19 *Periodicals Contents Index*

1 A digital edition of *Poole's Index to Periodical Literature* (W. F. Poole, 1882) has now been published by ProQuest under the Chadwyck-Healey brand-name. A digital edition of the *Readers' Guide to Periodical Literature* (H. W. Wilson, 1901) is published by EBSCO. There has been no attempt to amalgamate them.
2 Memo from Charles Chadwyck-Healey to Severtson, Asleson, and Chadwyck-Healey Ltd directors, 5 September 1990.
3 Minutes of the meeting (on 13 December) by Stephen Pocock, 28 December 1990.
4 Susan Severtson, Chadwyck-Healey Inc, 'Cumulative Contents Index: Business/Publication Plan,' revised 15 November 1991.
5 Letter from David Russon to Charles Chadwyck-Healey, 6 March 1992.
6 Memo from Steven Hall to Charles Chadwyck-Healey, Doug Roesemann, Alastair Everitt and others: 'PCI: Assessment by Dick Harris', 22 June 1993.
7 Memo from Charles Chadwyck-Healey to directors and managers: 'Proposed Action Plan on *PCI* in Response to Dick Harris's Report', 13 July 1993.
8 One of the earliest was Daniel Gore (ed.), *Farewell to Alexandria: Solutions to Space, Growth, and Performance Problems of Libraries* (Westport, CT: Greenwood Press, 1976).
9 Roger C. Schonfeld, *JSTOR: A History* (Princeton, NJ: Princeton University Press, 2003).
10 Schonfeld, *JSTOR*, 78.
11 Letter from William G. Bowen to Charles Chadwyck-Healey, 21 July 1994.
12 Schonfeld, *JSTOR*, 81–2.
13 Fuchs was an important figure in the development of JSTOR. In 1985 he had been appointed by Bowen as vice-president for computing and information technology at Princeton University. He had also been one of the founders of BITNET, a forerunner of the Internet.
14 Nic Sinclair (Marketing Manager, Chadwyck-Healey Ltd), 'PCI Review. Executive Summary', 13 June 1997.
15 Don McCrae, 'The Chadwyck-Healey Publishing Group', 23 March 1999.

20 Publishing Online

1 Our *Charles Dickens Research Collection* had also been an exception. While Sylvère Monod, the well-known author, Dickens scholar, and member of the editorial board

described it in the Chadwyck-Healey Ltd sales brochure (L69, September 1988) as 'an unprecedented service to scholarship', much of it was only of interest to Dickens specialists. The 102 reels of microfilm initially cost £4,800 and sales were disappointing.

2 Letter from Toby Faber to Charles Chadwyck-Healey, 2 March 1998.
3 *Bibliography of American Literature* (Yale University Press for the Bibliographical Society of America, 1955–91), 9 volumes.
4 Don Fowler, 'Literature Online. The Home of English and American Literature on the World Wide Web', *Computers & Texts*, 14 (April 1997).
5 Andrew Brown, 'Open Up Your Reading Room', *Daily Telegraph*, 6 May 1997.
6 Steven Hall, memo, 'Plan for Literature Online', 12 August 1997.

21 German Literature

1 Nicholas Boyle, *Goethe: The Poet and the Age, Volume 1. The Poetry of Desire (1749–1790)* (Oxford: Clarendon Press, 1991).
2 Woldemar Freiherr von Biedermann, *Goethes Gespräche* (Leipzig, 1889–96); Paul Raabe (ed.), *Nachträge zur Weimarer Ausgabe* (Munich, 1990).
3 Reported in the Chadwyck-Healey Newsletter, Christmas 1996.
4 Fotis Jannidis, 'Goethe, Johann Wolfgang von: Goethes Werke auf CD-ROM' [Rezension], *Arbitrium* (Berlin: de Gruyter, 1998), H.2, 192/201.
5 *Financial Times*, 22 April 1996.
6 *Sunday Telegraph*, 21 April 1996.
7 Memo, 'Goethe Goes Global' from Arend Kuester to all staff in Cambridge and in Alexandria, 26 August 1999.

22 Red Archives

1 There is a description of the creation of the archive in an entertaining book by James Critchlow, *Radio Hole-in-the-Head. Radio Liberty. An Insider's Story of Cold War Broadcasting* (Washington, DC: The American University Press, 1995).
2 When produced over the next few years some of the nine archives were on microfiche and the others were on microfilm.
3 *The New York Times*, 22 January 1992.
4 Natalya Davydova, 'Bumazhnoe zoloto partii', *Moskovsii novosti*, no. 8 (23 February 1992).
5 *Moscow News*, no. 19 (1992).

6   *Izvestia*, 10 March 1992.
7   *Izvestia*, 17 March 1992.
8   30 April 1992.
9   *Izvestia*, 26 June 1992.
10 *Financial Times*, 22 January 1992, but widely quoted elsewhere including *Library Journal*, 1 March 1992.
11 *Wall Street Journal*, 7 July 1992, in a front-page article, 'Information Flow is Freer in Russia, But It Is Not Free', commenting on Afanasyev's criticism.
12 David Hearst, 'A Heritage in Hock to Keep the Lights on', Moscow Diary, *Guardian*, 27 July 1992.
13 Letter from Charles Chadwyck-Healey to Charles Palm, 19 May 1993.
14 Letter from Professor Terence Emmons to Charles Chadwyck-Healey, 26 May 1993.
15 *Sunday Telegraph*, 4 February 1996.
16 *The Economist*, 2 March 1996.
17 *The History of the Gulag, 1918–1953* (Moscow: Russian Encyclopedia Publishing House, 2004 and 2005), 7 vols.
18 Letter from Palm to Mironenko, 9 December 1997.
19 16 March 1999.
20 VTsIK is the All-Russian Central Executive Committee, which was the highest legislative and administrative body from 1917 to 1937.
21 11 August 2000.
22 *Boston Globe*, 6 October 1999.
23 Robert Harris, *Archangel* (London: Hutchinson, 1998).

23   Towards the End

1   Chadwyck-Healey Group. 'Corporate Strategy and Planning Seminar 15–16 January 1998'.
2   Dan Wagner's MAID failed, and Dialog was then bought by Thomson. They could do nothing with it, and it was eventually bought by ProQuest.
3   Fiona Harvey, 'Murdoch Firm Axes CD-ROMs', *PC World*, 4 February 1997.
4   Letter from Bruce McWilliam, General Counsel, News International plc to Charles Chadwyck-Healey, 27 July 1998.
5   Letter from Sir Edward Pickering to Charles Chadwyck-Healey, 8 July 1999.
6   *The Times*, 4 January 1997.
7   *The Times*, 11 January 1997.
8   Letter from Robert Maclennan MP to Ross Shimmon, 17 February 1997.
9   Technology in Libraries Conference, 23 April 1997.
10 From 2017, the Department for Digital, Culture, Media and Sport.

11 *The Times*, 11 October 1997.
12 *Observer*, 14 February 1999.

24 The End

1 *The Bookseller*, 8 October 1999.
2 *Financial Times*, 4 November 1999.
3 *Times Higher*, 15 October 1999.

Appendix 1 History of Microfilm Publishing

1 Much of the information in this appendix has been taken from Alan Meckler's excellent book *Micropublishing: A History of Scholarly Micropublishing in America 1938–1980* (Westport, CT: Greenwood Press, 1982).
2 Robert C. Binkley, Joint Committee on Materials for Research, *Methods of Reproducing Research Materials: A Survey Made for the Joint Committee on Materials for Research of the Social Science Research Council and the American Council of Learned Societies* (Ann Arbor, MI: Edwards Bros., 1931).
3 Robert C. Binkley, 'New Tools for Men of Letters', *Yale Review*, November 1935, 523.
4 A. W. Pollard and G. R. Redgrave, *A Short Title Catalogue of Books Printed in England, Scotland and Ireland and of English Books Printed Abroad, 1475–1640* (London: The Bibliographical Society for B. Quaritch, 1926). See also Chapter 7.
5 Fremont Rider, *The Scholar and the Future of the Research Library: A Problem and Its Solution* (New York: Hadham Press, 1944).
6 Peter Bower, 'The Airgraph and Other Photographic Means of Communication', *The Quarterly: The Journal of the British Association of Paper Historians* 100 (September 2016), 1.
7 Vernon D. Tate, 'Defrosting a Frozen Asset: The Publication of Doctoral Dissertations', *College and Research Libraries*, January 1953, 35–8, 45.
8 *Atlantic Monthly*, July 1945.
9 I wrote about this in Simon Eliot and Jonathan Rose (eds.), *A Companion to the History of the Book* (Oxford: Blackwell Publishing Ltd, 2007), ch. 33, 'The New Textual Technologies', but at the time I did not know that Goldberg had preceded Bush. Little was known about Goldberg's work until an account of his life and work was published by Michael Buckland in *Emanuel Goldberg and His Knowledge Machine: Information, Invention, and Political Forces* (Westport, CT: Libraries Unlimited, 2006).

10 There were three code systems: Miracode, Image Control Code and Kodamatic Line Scale. Microfilm editions of *Chemical Abstracts* were available with each of these codes.
11 *Guide to Microforms in Print 1975* (Englewood, CO: Microcard Editions Books, 1975).

Appendix 2 Microfilm Technology

1 The US Committee on Scientific and Technical Information of the Federal Council for Science and Technology.

Index

Page numbers in *italics* refer to illustrations.

A. & C. Black, 315–16
A. & C. Boni, 333
ABELL see Annual Bibliography of English Language and Literature
Abramov, Valeri, 288
Academic Press, 3, 14–17, 25
Acta Sanctorum, 243
Adam, Robert and James, 73
Adam Matthew, 340
Adams, Douglas, 258
Adams, Michael, 29
Adler, Esthy, 46
Adler, James B. 'Jim', 46–7, 51, 68
AEC *see* Atomic Energy Commission
Afanasyev, Yuri N., 285, 286
AFP-Doc, 144
African-American Biographical Database, 159–60
African-American Poetry, 1760–1900, 258
African Official Statistical Serials, 1867–1982, 50
Agence France Presse, 144
agents *see* dealers
Air Liquide, 204
airgraphs, 335
Aitken, Jonathan, 167
ALA *see* American Library Association
alchemy, 181
Alexander Street Press, 340
Allardyce, Alex, 66
Allen & Unwin, 22
almanacs, 317
Alston, Robin, *103*; background, 27; device for filming tightly bound books, *347*; and *ESTC*, 93–6, 100; lunch with author, 244; and *The Nineteenth Century*, 100–6; and Scolar Press, 27
America, 1935–1946, 83–6, 110, *111*

American Drama, 1714–1915, 258; *see also Literature Online*
American Enterprise Institute, 278
American Library Association (ALA) conferences, 6–8, *7*, *103*
American Novel Critical Essays series, 265
American Poetry, 1600–1900, 257; *see also Literature Online*
American Revolution (1775–83), 129
American Statistics Index, 46, 47
AMS, 16
Anamorphic Art, 26
anarchism, 177–9
Anderson, Robin, 67
Anderson, Kirill, 279, 293
Annual Bibliography of English Language and Literature (*ABELL*), 264, 265
Apex, 247
Appiah, Anthony, 156, 159
Apple, 189
APS *see* Automated Patent Searching
architectural drawings, microfilming of commercial, 337
architecture, 19–20, 73, 83, 101–2, 317
Archives nationales, 136–7, 141–3, *142*
The Archives of British Publishers, 20, 22–4, 29, 30–3, 88
Archives of the Central Committee of the Soviet Communist Party: censorship, 292; editorial board meetings, 289–90, 291, 292–3; filming, 290–1, 292, 298–9; negotiations and business arrangements, 277–85, 291, 293–8; overview, 277–302; partners, 277–8; reception, 285–8; sales, 300–1
ARL *see* Association of Research Libraries
Armistead, William, 159
Armitt, David, 21
Armstrong, John A., 279

Armstrong, Scott, 163–4, 167
Arnold, Matthew, 8
art and art history, 6, 26, 73–90, 101–2, 130–4
art exhibition catalogues, 79, 135, 136
Artists File (NYPL), 130–4, 344
Artists Files (MoMA), 344
Artists Scrapbooks, 344
Ashby, Peter, 39, 340
Asleson, Bob, *183*, 206, 216
ASLIB, 69–70
Association of Research Libraries (ARL), 102
Ateliers catholiques, 233, 234
Atlantic City, 6–8, *7*
Atomic Energy Commission (AEC), 336
Australia: censuses, 189; as Chadwyck-Healey market, 33; libraries, 186; library consortia, 225, 266
Automated Patent Searching (*APS*), 207
Averley, Gwen, 97, 100, 103
Avero Publications, 96–101
Avram, Henriette, 198, 203
Aylmer, Gerald, 11

Babbage, Charles, 8
Bacon, Mildred, 41–2, 170
Baillieu Library, 186–7
Baker, John, 50
Baker, Nicholson, 229–30
Baltrušaitis, Jurgis, 26
BAN *see* Russian Academy of Sciences Library
Bancroft, R. F. L., 17
La Banque d'information politique et d'actualité de la Documentation française (BIPA), 144
Barber, John, 278
Barcelona, Jim, 326–7, 328–9, *328*
Barker, Nicolas, xvi
Barnard, John, 219, 220
Barr, John, 101
Barragry, Mark, 70
Barrie, J. M., 22
Barton, Anne, 257
Bartrum, Giulia, 74
Bassingbourn, 43–4, 132–4
Bayerische Staatsbibliothek, 300
Baylor University, 104

BBC, 90
Bedfordshire County Library, 58
Beer, Gillian, 318
Bélaval, Philippe, 147–8, 150
Bell, Alan, 22
Bell & Howell Information and Learning (later ProQuest), *328*, 337, 339; buys Chadwyck-Healey, 320–2, 324, 325–30; buys Micromedia, 44, 340; *Early English Books*, 311, 330; later history as ProQuest, 340; overview, 320
Bennett, Arnold, 32
Bennett, Scott, 31–2, 32–3
Bentley, Michael, 103
Bentley archives *see* Richard Bentley archives
Berger, Alec 'Al', 211–12
Berger-Levrault, 223
Berkman, Alexander, 177–8
Berlin, Isaiah, 77
The Berlin Crisis, 1958–1962, 166
Bernard, Jacqueline, 136
Bernard, Marc, 136
Bertelsmann Group, 324
Bettencourt, Liliane, 140
The Bible in English, 257
Bibliographie d'éditions originales et rares d'auteurs français, 26
bibliographies: on CD-ROM, 191–4, 196; English, 91–101, 191–4, 332, 333, 336, 337, 340; French, 26–7, 91, 135–6, 137–9, 140–1, 143, 144, 149; and *LION*, 264, 265; online searching, 216; poetry, 217; REMARC, 137, 173, 185, 198–203; software as CD-ROM selling point, 216; Spanish, 150–2; *see also Periodicals Contents Index*
Bibliography of American Literature, 264
Bibliopolis, 150
Biblioteca Nacional de España, 150–3, 154
Bibliotecas sin Fronteras, 152–3
Bibliothèque nationale de France (BnF): art exhibition catalogues, 136; CHF's relationship with, 144, 147–8, 150; French National Bibliography, 143, 144; library catalogue, 91, 136, 137–9, 140, 143, 149; other catalogues, 135–6, 140–1; and REMARC, 201

Billington, James, 278, 281, 283–4, 286
Binkley, Robert C., 331–2
biographies and biographical dictionaries: black, 159–60; in *KnowUK*, 315–17; and *LION*, 265; Saur editions, 340; Soviet, 273–5
BIPA *see* La Banque d'information politique et d'actualité de la Documentation française
Birmingham, Library of (formerly Birmingham Reference Library, Birmingham Central Library), 1, 4–5, 58, 220, 314
Black, Charles, 315–16
Black Biographical Dictionaries, 1790–1950, 159–60
Black Literature, 1827–1940, 155–8
Black Studies: *Black Biographical Dictionaries*, 159–60; *Black Literature*, 155–8; civil rights, 176, 178; Gates lecture, 160–1; *Hampton University Newspaper Clipping File*, 155; *Joe Louis Scrapbooks*, 155; *Papers of the Congress of Racial Equality*, 133; *Schomburg Clipping File*, 130–2, 133, 155
Blackwell's, 39, 63, 318
Blackwood's Magazine, 22
Blair, Tony, 315
Blanton, Tom, 167, 168
Blaser, Linda, 110
Blassingame, John W., 155–6
Bloodaxe Books, 258
Bloomsbury Group, 181–2
Blum, Claude, 149
BnF *see* Bibliothèque nationale de France
Bodleian Library: book loans to Chadwyck-Healey, 77; and *English Poetry*, 225; finding aids, 119, 120; library catalogues, 91, 99, 194; and *Nineteenth-Century Parliamentary Papers*, 55, 56; and Non-HMSO Catalogue, 66; and Oxford's departmental libraries, 225
Böhlau *see* Herman Böhlaus Nachfolger
Bond, Cynthia, 158
Boni, Albert, 55–6, 333–4, 335–6
Boni, Charles, 333
Boni & Liveright, 333

Bonnell, Bertie, *103*; background and character, 89; and CHF publications, 139; leaves Chadwyck-Healey, 176; and the NSA, 164, 165; and *NSTC*, 99; and sales trips, 38; and Sanborn Maps, 112, 113
Bonner, Raymond, 162
book cradles, 347
book reprint industry: article and extract anthologies, 40–1; author's experiences, 4–20; decline, xi, 19; function, form and market, 1–3; history, 3–4; reduced reprints, 26, 50–3, 335–6
The Bookseller, 237, 329
Boone, Daniel, 129
Boothroyd, Betty, 71
BOPCAS *see* British Official Publications Current Awareness Service
Boserup, Ivan, 239
Bottomley, Virginia, 258
Bourke, Thomas A., 182, 184
Bourne, Charles 'Charlie', 68
Bowen, William, 250, 251, 252
Boyle, Father Leonard, 318
Boyle, Nicholas, 268, 269
Bradford, James C., 177
Bradley, Bill, 283–4
Brampton, N. A., 19–20, 339
Brando, Marlon, 87
Brandt, Carl D., 156–7
Brecht, Bertolt, 271
Brepols, 234–5, 243
Brewer, Derek, 219, 226, 230
Brewer, John, 75
Briggs, Asa, 33
Bristol, University of, 56
British Academic Committee for Liaison with Soviet Archives, 278
British Columbia, University of, 64
British Government Publications Containing Statistics, 1801–1977, 47
British Library: Advisory Committee for Bibliographic Services, 319; and Bentley archives, 30–1, 32; book loans to Chadwyck-Healey, 52; Burney Collection, 48–9, 347; and Chadwyck-Healey annual lecture, 160, 314, 318–19; Chadwyck-Healey

publications bought by, 58, 142, 300; collections filmed by Chadwyck-Healey, 74–5; and CURL, 200; Digital Library Programme PFI, 318; establishment, 30–1; and *ESTC*, 93–6; *Index to Manuscripts in the British Library*, 121–3; Lending Division, Boston Spa, 58, 247, 249, 316; library catalogue on CD-ROM, 191–4; library catalogue's physical form, 91; microfilming for Chadwyck-Healey, 48, 49, 50; newspaper holdings, 229; and *The Nineteenth Century*, 99–106; nineteenth-century Parliamentary Papers set, 55; Readex edition of catalogue, 336; Russian Futurism collection bought by, 77; Saur edition of catalogue, 340

British Library Newspaper Library, 106

British Museum, 74–5

The British Museum General Catalogue of Printed Books to 1955, 336

British Music Yearbook, 317

British Official Publications Current Awareness Service (BOPCAS), 70

brochures, 6, 32, 37–8

Brontë, Anne, 229

Brontë, Charlotte, 229

Brontë, Emily, 220, 229

Brooks, Van Wyck, 78

Brown, Andrew, 265

Brown, J. Carter, 81

Brown, Karen, 70

Brown, Michael, 321

Browning, Robert, 104

Bruce, Paul and Ailsa Mellon, 250

Bruguière, Francis, 87, 88

Brunel, Isambard Kingdom, 8

BT, 318

Buchanan, Bill, *201*; CD-ROMs introduced to author by, 185; consultancy work for Chadwyck-Healey, 203, 262; and Goldman, 137; and JSTOR, 251; and REMARC, 198–9, 201, 203

Buchler, Pavel, 123

Buffett, Warren, 109

The Builder, 19–20, 339

Bukovsky, Vladimir, 287–8

Bunker, Nat, 117–18

Bureau Marcel van Dijk, 147

Burgess, Linda, *246*

Burke, Frank, 116–17

Burkett, Nancy Hall, 159–60

Burkett, Randall K., 159–60

Burliuk, David, 77

Burnard, Lou, 219

Burney Collection, 48–9, 347

Bush, George H. W., 167

Bush, Keith, 274

Bush, Vannevar, 338–9

Business and Government, 70

business and marketing models: advance payments, 59–60, 183–4; book reprint industry, 6; brochures, 6, 32, 37–8; library consortia, 225–6, 247–8, 250–4, 262, 266, 303–4, 308; microform publications, 347–8; online publications, xii–xiii, 243, 254–5, 262, 304–7; partner subscriptions, 54–6, 62, 112; subscriptions vs high-ticket one-offs, 144; timing of subscription invoices, 174; variable pricing, 249

business records, microfilming of, 330, 337

Cain, Julien, 137–8

Calaluca, Eric, *183*, 232–3, 234, 236–7, 245, *246*

California, University of, 10, 202; Berkeley, 177–9; Irvine, 218; Los Angeles, 30, 33; Riverside, 93–4, 278

Callil, Carmen, 37

Cambridge, University of, 278; *see also* Jesus College; King's College

Cambridge Encyclopedias series, 265

Cambridge Information Group (CIG), 340

Cambridge University Library: author's relationship with, 320; and Chadwyck-Healey archive, xiv, xvi; library catalogue automation, 200; library catalogue's physical form, 91; and *Nineteenth-Century Parliamentary Papers*, 54–5, 56; photographic department, 288

Cambridge University Press (CUP), 22, 36, 265

Cambridgeshire Library Authority, 317

cameras *see* microform: cameras

Camus, Albert, 136
Capgemini, 261
CAPP *see* Central American Papers Project
Caravan software, 147, 148, 247
Carcanet, 258
Carlyle, Thomas, 23
Carnegie Foundation, 164–5
Carpenter, Ken, 123
Carr, Jane, 101
Carr, Reg, 200
Carroll-Davis, Julie, 105
Carrolton Press: and HMSO catalogues, 51–2, 53; and the NSA, 164; REMARC, 137, 173, 185, 198–203
Carter, Jimmy, 59
Carter, Rosalynn, 82
cartography *see* maps
cartoons and satirical prints, 74–6
Cashman, Seamus, 9
Cass, Frank, 8, 18, 29
Catálogo de Autores de la Biblioteca Nacional de España, 150–2
Catalogue de la Troisième République, 140
Catalogue de l'histoire de France, 140
Catalogue général des livres imprimés, 136, 137–9, 140, 143, 149
Catalogue général des périodiques des origines à 1959, 140
Catalogue of British Official Publications Not Published by HMSO, 65–9
Catalogue of Manuscripts in the Houghton Library, Harvard University, 123
Catalogue of United Kingdom Official Publications (UKOP), 69–70
catalogues and cataloguing: English, 91, 99, 191–4, 336, 340; French, 135–6, 137–9, 140–1, 143, 144, 149; history of, 91; library automation projects, 198–206; manuscript indexes, 121–4; MARC cataloguing, 92, 95–6, 102, 198; REMARC, 137, 173, 185, 198–203; Russian, 276; Spanish, 150–2, 152–3; union catalogues, 91–101, 105, 152–3, 193–4, 202, 332, 333, 337
Catalogues du Département de la Musique, 140

CAUL *see* Committee of Australian University Librarians
Caxton, William, 346
CD-Actualité, 144
CD-ROM publications: label positioning, 208–9; MS-DOS vs Windows, 71; and networking, 223–4, 260; origins, 185–6; pros and cons, xi–xii, 185–6, 215–16, 223–4, 260; software, 143, 147, 148, 189, 192, 197, 206, 207, 247; software as selling point, 216
censuses, 187–9, 190–1
Center for Research Libraries (CRL), 113–14
Central American Papers Project (CAPP), 162–3
Central Intelligence Agency (CIA), 165, 166, 168, 189
CERCLA law (1980), 209
CETEDOC Library of Christian Latin Texts, 234, 239, 240–1, 242, 243
Chadwyck-Healey, Angela, *328*; Australia visit, 262; awards, 133–4; and Chadwyck-Healey sale, 328–9; and foundation of Chadwyck-Healey Ltd, 21; Innodata visit, 269; USA visits, 79, 81, 104, 273
Chadwyck-Healey, Charles (author), *111*, *284*; awards, 133–4; baronetcy, xv; early career, 1–20, 84; family background, 2; homes, 98; liveryman of Stationers' Company, 180; work on library and publishing committees, 258, 312–15, 319–20
Chadwyck-Healey, Sir Charles (author's father), 20, 174
Chadwyck-Healey, Sir Charles (author's great-grandfather), xv, 28
Chadwyck-Healey, Nicholas, 1
Chadwyck-Healey annual lecture, 160–1, 314, 318–19
Chadwyck-Healey group: archives, xiv, xvi; competitor overview, 215, 339–40; Elsevier consider buying, 170–4; finances and plans, 176, 182–4; financial crisis, 304–7; inter-company relations, 143, 232; orders and despatches process, 41–2, 53; sale, 320–30, *328*

CHADWYCK-HEALEY ESPAÑA (CHE), 150–4, 328
CHADWYCK-HEALEY FRANCE (CHF): Caravan software, 147, 148, 247; CD-ROM production for the group, 71, 143, 145, 247; finances, 144–6, 147–8; foundation, 137; and MultiLIS, 203, 205; overview, 135–50; premises, 139, 145, 147; sale, 149–50; and Spanish projects, 151; staff and management, 137, 139, 146; tax issues, 139
CHADWYCK-HEALEY INC. (FORMERLY SOMERSET HOUSE): annual revenues, 170, 182–3; cashflow, 183–4; foundation and early days, 27, 33, 81; name change, 81; premises, 27, 89, 118, 173–4; sales penetration, 266–7, 304; staff and management, 27, 81, 89, 118–19, 172–3, 176, *183*, 237, 302
CHADWYCK-HEALEY LTD: annual revenues, 30, 170, 182–3; awards, 173, 270; cashflow, 183–4; foundation, 20–2, 29–30; name choice, 21; premises, 21, 40, 41, 170, *221*, 256–7, *256*, 305; staff and management, 21–2, 40, 41, 174–6, 237–8, 257, 305, 306, 319–20
Chadwyck-Healey Microform Publishing Services (CHMPS; later International Imaging): and *Artists File*, 132–4; awards, 133–4; and *Catalogue général des livres imprimés*, 143; and COM fiche, 342–3; and *English Poetry*, 221; foundation and premises, 42–5, 59, 60; and *The Nineteenth Century*, 102; and *PLD*, 238, 240; and *Print File*, 132–4; and Russian publications, 290, 291, 298–9; sale, 44, 305, 326; staff and management, 44, 126; work for other customers, 44, 106, 342–3
Chahuneau, François, 223
Champion, 148–9
Chang, Laurence, 166
Chapman, Dave, 44, 133, 290, 344
Charkin, Richard, 325
Charles, Prince of Wales, 5, 134

Charles Barker, 312
CHE *see* Chadwyck-Healey group: Chadwyck-Healey España
CHEST *see* Combined Higher Education Software Team
Chevalier, Mme, 141
CHF *see* Chadwyck-Healey group: Chadwyck-Healey France
Chicago University Press, 77–8, 82
CHMPS *see* Chadwyck-Healey Microform Publishing Services
Christelow, Duncan, *196*
Church of England, 317
CIA *see* Central Intelligence Agency
CIG *see* Cambridge Information Group
CIS *see* Congressional Information Service
CIS Index, 46, 47
civil rights, 176, 178
Clarinet software, 189, 197
Claudel, Paul, 138
Claughton, Stephen, 21–2
Clearview software, 189, 197
Cleaveland, Helen, 327
climate, 191
Clinton, Bill, 166, 167, 212
Clive Bingley, 192
Cobbe, Hugh, 32, 49, 95, 121, 122
Cockton, Peter, 61–2
Cohen, Elaine Lustig, 77
Columbia Granger's Index to Poetry, 217
Columbia Granger's World of Poetry, 228
Columbia University, 33, 88, 113
Combat, 136
Combined Higher Education Software Team (CHEST), 225–6, 247–8, 254, 266, 308
Comintern, 293
Committee of Australian University Librarians (CAUL), 225, 266
Compton, Susan, 77
computer-output microfiche (COM), 97, 117, 274–5, 342–3
computers: and Non-HMSO Catalogue, 66–7; *see also* CD-ROM publications; Internet; online publications; software
Computership, 222, 235, 238
Conduitt, John, 180
Congress of Racial Equality, 133

Congressional Information Service (CIS): as Chadwyck-Healey competitor, 164, 165, 215; Chadwyck-Healey represents in UK and Europe, 46–7, 51; and Chadwyck-Healey sale, 324, 325; and Chadwyck-Healey's attempted sale to Elsevier, 172; CIG buys, 340; and the NSA, 164, 165; online access to databases, 68; publisher acquisitions, 173
Connolly, Jim, 174
Conquest, Robert, 291
conservation and preservation, 53, 54–5, 101, 110
Consortium of University Research Libraries (CURL), 200
Cooksey, Lady, 312
Cooper, Peter, 10, 12
copyflo copier, 337
copyright: and collection deposits, 88; and electronic editions of texts, 241, 262–3; Keynes Papers, 181–2; manuscripts, 30; US, 26–7
Cornell, Katharine, 87
Cornmarket Press, 1–13, 29
Coston, Jane, 348
Council for Small Industries in Rural Areas (CoSIRA): Rural Employment Award, 133–4
Coutts bank: and CHF, 146; finance for Chadwyck-Healey Ltd, 29–30, 42–3, 60, 170, 213, 304–5; finance for MultiLIS, 204
Coward, Richard, 199, 200–1, *201*
Cox, Jacqueline, 182
CRL *see* Center for Research Libraries
Crockford's Clerical Directory, 317
Crosby, Cheryl, *183*, 300
Cross, Robert, 180
Cross, Tony, 278
The Cuban Missile Crisis, 165–6
Culture, Media and Sport, Department for (DCMS; formerly Department of National Heritage), 312–15
CUP *see* Cambridge University Press
CURL *see* Consortium of University Research Libraries
Curran, Ted, 274
current awareness services, 70

Dagron, René Patrice, 331
Daily Mail on CD-ROM, 195
Dainton, Sir Fred, 200
Dallaway, Renata, 238
Dancer, John Benjamin, 331
data conversion: British Library Catalogue, 191; *English Poetry*, 218–19, 222–3; *PCI*, 247; *PLD*, 235–6, 238; scanning and OCR, 308, 309, 311
David, R. W., 22
Davies, H. Neville, 5
Davies, Mike, 39
Davis, Charles T., 156
Davis, Julie, 44
Davis, P. D. C., 36–7
Davison, Peter, 18–19, 40
Davydova, Natalya, 283
Dawson, 3, 93, 318
DCMS *see* Culture, Media and Sport, Department for
De Gennaro, Richard 'Dick', 246, 250, 251, 252
dealers, relationship with, 27, 57
Debrett's, 316
Deloitte, 323, 327–8
deMink, Henri, 339
Dennett, Daniel, 230
Derwent Publications, 207
Deutsche Bibliothek, Bonn, 199, 201
Die Deutsche Lyrik, 271
Deutsches Literaturarchiv, Marbach, 269–70
Dialog, 68–9, 215, 306
The Diary of Beatrice Webb, 35–7
diazo film *see* microform: film
Dickens, Charles, 229
Dickinson, Harry, 75, 103
Dictionary of Literary Biography, 265
Diefendorf, Elizabeth, 224
Digital National Security Archive, 168–9
Directory of Opportunities for Graduates, 1
Dissertations Abstracts, 336
DNH *see* Culture, Media and Sport, Department for (formerly Department of National Heritage)
Dodson, Suzanne, 64
Dolan, John, 314
Dorling Kindersley, 306
Draper Manuscripts, 129

Drawings of Robert and James Adam, 73
Druce, Robert, 227
Dryden, John, 4
DTI *see* Trade and Industry, Department of
Dudley, Martin, 312, 313
Duffy, Michael, 75
Duke University, 230
Dunlop, John B., 289
Dwyer, Joseph, 279, 300
DynaText software, 223, 227, 235, 240

E. P. Microform (formerly Micro Methods), 20, 339
Earls Colne, 67
Early American Fiction, 1789–1875, 258; *see also* Literature Online
Early English Books, 311
Early English Books Online (*EEBO*), 330
Early English Prose Fiction, 1500–1700, 257–8; *see also* Literature Online
East Anglia, University of, 191
Eccles, David, 93
economics, 181–2
The Economist on CD-ROM, 195–6
Edelstein, Jerome 'Mel', 78
Edinburgh, University of, 58, 199, 200, 202
Editions and Adaptations of Shakespeare, 257
EDR *see* Environmental Data Resources
Edwards Brothers, 333
EEBO *see* Early English Books Online
EGPP *see* Emma Goldman Papers Project
Ehrenberg, Ralph, 107, 110, 112
Eighteenth-Century Fiction, 257–8; *see also* Literature Online
Eighteenth Century Short Title Catalogue (*ESTC*), 92–6, 221
Ekman, Richard, 250, 251, 252–3
El Salvador: The Making of U.S. Policy, 1977–1984, 165
El Salvador: War, Peace and Human Rights, 1890–1994, 166
Electronic Book Technologies, 223; *see also* DynaText software
Eliot, Simon, 35
Eliot, T. S., 258, 259
Eliot, Valerie, 258, 259
Elkin Mathews archives, 22

Elsevier, 47, 170–4, 211, 212, 324, 325; *see also* Reed Elsevier
Emma Goldman Papers, 177–9
Emma Goldman Papers Project (EGPP), 177–9
Emmett, Jim, 121
Emmons, Terry, 286, 289, 291
Encarta, 306
Encylopedia Britannica, 306
The Engineer, 20
Engineering Index, 245
English Cartoons and Satirical Prints, 1320–1832, 74–5, 76
English literature, 181–2, 257–60, 264, 311, 330
English Poetry Full-Text Database: editorial decisions, 219–20; and LION, 262–3; online access fees, 262, 265; origins, 215–20; overview, 215–31; production, 220–3, *221*; reception, 226–31; sales, 223–6; scoping, 218
English Poetry Plus, 258
English Prose Drama, 257; *see also* Literature Online
English Record Society publications, 28
The English Revolution, 11–13, 29
The English Satirical Print, 1600–1832, 75–6
English Verse Drama, 257; *see also* Literature Online
environment, 177, 209–14
Environmental Data Resources (EDR), 213–14
Environmental Protection Agency (EPA), 209
Environmental Risk Information Center (ERIC; later ERIIS, Geosure), 209–14
EPA *see* Environmental Protection Agency
EPO *see* European Patent Office
equipment sales, 82, 143, 204
ERIC *see* Environmental Risk Information Center
Erickson, Edgar L., 54
Ernst & Young, 205
Erskine-Hill, Howard, 219, 226
Espace, 207
Essex County Library, 52
ESTC *see* Eighteenth Century Short Title Catalogue

European Coal and Steel Community, 346-7
European Court of Justice Library, 204
European Official Statistical Serials, 1841-1984, 39-40, 47-8, 50
European Patent Office (EPO), 207
European Patent Searching, 207
European Union Library, 204, 205
Evans, Matthew, Lord, 258-9, 312, 313, 314-15, 319
Evans, Walker, 84
Everitt, Alastair, *246*; background, 175; and *English Poetry*, 217, 218, 219, 224; at Harvester, 36, 175; joins Chadwyck-Healey, 175-6; microform publications produced by, 180-2; and *PCI*, 245; and *PLD*, 234, 237, 242; retirement, 237; and Russian publications, 288, 290
Everyman Library, 314
Ex Libris, 77
Exeter, University of, 56

Faber, Toby, 259
Faber Poetry Library, 258-60, 264
Falk, Candace, 177-9
Family Planning Association Archives, 119
Faraday, Michael, 8
Farm Security Administration (FSA), 83-6, 110, *111*
Farmar, Tony, 9, 10-11
Farrand, Roger, 12
Fawcett, Trevor, 101
Fawcus, Arnold, 1
Feller, Siegfried, 7
Fellner, Hans, *34*; aphorisms, 18, 48, 257; appearance and background, 17-18; artwork importation plan, 135; author meets, 17-18; bought out by author, 96; and *ESTC*, 94; family, 136; and foundation of Chadwyck-Healey Ltd, 20; and French projects, 135-6; friends and contacts, 76, 93, 135; on Kraus Reprint catalogue, 37; and *The Nineteenth Century*, 101; obituaries, xvi; publications suggested by, 24, 26, 28, 35; regular meetings with author, 34-5; Russia visit, 275-6

Ferguson, John, 175, 199, 200-1, *201*, 202
Fermor-Dunman, Geoff, 318
Fern, Alan, 110, *111*
fiction, 101, 152, 155-8, 257-8, 268-71
Fidelity National Information Solutions, 214
Figes, Orlando, 291
film *see* microform: film
Financial Times on CD-ROM, 195-6
finding aids, 115-20, 141-3, 278-302
fire insurance, 107-14
Fischer *see* S. Fischer
Fitzsimmons, Joe, 253
Fleishauer, Carol, 248
Flesch, Juliet, 186-7
floods and flooding, 213
Fonda, Henry, 87
Fondazione Giangiacomo Feltrinelli, 278
fondy, 278
Foot, M. R. D., 103
Ford, Percy and Grace, 8-9
Ford Collection, 9, 69-70
Ford Foundation, 164-5, 179
Fordham University, 236
Foreign Office Registers and Indexes of Correspondence, 1793-1919, 136
Foreman, Lewis, 58-9
Forjett, Charles, 102
Forster, E. M., 181
Fortson, Judith, 290
Foskett, Douglas J., 56-7, 200
Fowler, Don, 264-5
Fox, Linda, 89
Fox, Peter, xiv, 320
Frankfurt Book Fair, 272
Franklin, Norman, 22
Fredeman, W. E. 'Dick', 23-4, 27, 329
Freedman, Samuel 'Sam', 194, 336, 339
freedom of information, 162-9
Freeman, Tom, 228
French National Bibliography, 143, 144
French publications, 26-7, 137-44, 148-9
Freud, Sigmund, 181
Frost, Thomas, 102
FSA *see* Farm Security Administration
Fuchs, Ira, 253
Fund for Peace, 162, 163
Fusi, Juan Pablo, 152
Futurism, 76-7

G. K. Hall, 91
Gale Research, 265, 266
GARF (formerly TsGAOR), 279, 292, 294, 296–300, 302
Garland Publishing, 40
Garnier, 236
Garrick, David, 4
Gaskell, Eric, 205
Gates, Henry Louis Jr, 'Skip', 155–61
Gauvin, Jean-Louis, 205
Gay, Tom, 213
GEAC, 205
Gelatt, Charles, 334
gender issues *see* Women's Studies
George, Dorothy, 74
George Allen archives, 22, 30
George Routledge archives, 22
Geosure *see* Environmental Risk Information Center
Germany: literature, 268–72; publishing industry from 1906 to 1941, 14; university library funding, 3
Gerritsen Collection for Women's Studies, 330
Gestetner, 318
Gettman, Royal, 31, 32
Getty, J. Arch, 278, 295–6
Giddens, Anthony, 318
Gide, André, 136
Girón, Alicia, 152
Giroud, Gérard, 207
Gleick, James, 230
Gloucester, Richard, Duke of, 133–4
Goebel, Joseph, 335
Goethe, Johann Wolfgang von, 268–71
Goethe-Institut, 269
Goldberg, Emanuel, 338–9
Goldman, Donald, *142, 246*; background and character, 137; Brepols visit, 234; at Cambridge conference, 245; and CHE, 150–1, 152; and CHF, 137–46, 150, 237; and MultiLIS, 203–5; and *The Soviet Biographic Archive*, 274
Goldman, Emma, 177–9
Goldman, Monique, 137, 150
Goldschmidt, Robert, 331
Goldsmith, Oliver, 229
Gompers, Samuel, 129
Goncharova, Natalia, 77

Goncourt brothers, 234
Gorbachev, Mikhail, 276, 292
Grant Richards archives, 32
Graves Educational Resources, 185
Greek fonts, 240
Green, John, 318, 319, 322, 325, 326
Greenberg, Hal, 323, 324, 326–7, *328*
Greengrass, Paul, 42
Greenstein, Daniel, 329
Gregg, Pauline, 11
Gregoire, Henri, 159
Grimsted, Patricia Kennedy 'Pat', 286–7, 300
Gruson, Sydney, 125–6
guard-books, 91
Guardian on CD-ROM, 195–7, *196*
Guide to Reference Books (Winchell), 48, 51
gulags, 297, 299, 301
Gustav Fock, 14

H. W. Wilson, 215
HABS *see* Historic American Buildings Survey
Hachette, 324
Hahn, Gordon, 298
Haines, Margaret, 313, 318
Hakim, Albert, 166–7
Hall, Steven: background, 175; and British Library Catalogue, 192; and Chadwyck-Healey sale, 323; and CHEST, 226, 247–8, 254, 308; and *English Poetry*, 217, 218, 224, 225–6; and German publications, 268, 269, 271; joins Chadwyck-Healey, 175; languages spoken by, 175, 272; and *LION*, 263, 265; and *MicroPatent*, 207; and newspapers on CD-ROM, 197; and *The Nineteenth Century*, 105; and organizational changes, 319; and *PCI*, 245, 247–8, 249, 254; and phone sales, 38; and *PLD*, 234, 237, 239, 242; positions held by, 175, 238, 299, 330; and redundancies, 305; and Russian publications, 299, 300; and *Times* indexes, 308, 310
Hambro Grantham bank, 187
Hamilton, Mark, 118–19, 130, 131, 170, 176, 178

Hampton University Newspaper Clipping File, 155
Handelman, Benjamin, 125–6
Hannon, Michael, 237
Hansard, 70–2
Harcourt Brace Jovanovich, 17, 25
Hardin, J., 271
Harlem Renaissance, 155
Harper & Brothers archives, 33, 88
Harris, Dick, 249
Harris, Michael, 49
Harris, Robert, 301
Harvard University: and *Black Biographical Dictionaries*, 159; Chadwyck-Healey publications bought by, 117–18, 300, 301; Houghton Library Catalogue, 123; materials loaned to Chadwyck-Healey, 159, 246–7, 253; and *PCI*, 246–7, 251, 253; relationship with Chadwyck-Healey, 38
Harvester Press, 22, 36, 175, 180, 339, 340
Hatvany, Bela, 216
Hayes, Ted, 187
Hayhoe, Barney, 68
Haymarket Press, 1
Healy, Michael, 258–9, 305, 315
Heaney, Henry, 160
Hearle, Elizabeth, 207, 208
Hearst, David, 287
Hemming, John, 316
The Hemming Group, 316
Henderson, Albert, 16
Her Majesty's Stationery Office (HMSO): and current Parliamentary Papers, 63–4; *Hansard*, 70–2; HMSO catalogues, 50–3; and Non-HMSO Catalogue, 67–8; responsibility for official publications, 63–4, 65; split into HMSO and TSO, 69; *UKOP*, 69–70
Hermann Böhlaus Nachfolger, 268–9, 271
Heseltine, Michael, 1
Hewitsons, 327
Hill, Christopher, 11
Hill, Lamar M., 120
Hillyard, Matt, 269, 272
Historic American Buildings Survey (HABS), 83, 85, 110, *111*

The Historical Records of the High Authority of the European Coal and Steel Community, 1952–1956, 346–7
Hitler, Adolf, 302
HMSO *see* Her Majesty's Stationery Office
Hoare, Michael, 31, 32, 74
Holland, Mark, 308–9, 310
Holroyd, Paul, 71, 189, 190
Holtzbrinck Publishing Group, 272, 324, 325
Home, Roderick, 187
Hookway, Harry, 93
Hooley, Frank, 67–8
Hoover, Herbert, 273
Hoover, Herbert 'Pete' (grandson of above), 294
Hoover Institution on War, Revolution, and Peace: and *Archives of the Central Committee of the Soviet Communist Party*, 277–302; and Emma Goldman, 179; overview, 273; Palm's positions at, 178–9, 273, 277; and *The Soviet Biographic Archive*, 273–4; Soviet historians' attitude to, 286–7
Hoover Presidential Library, 117
Hornstein, Gabriel 'Gabe', 16
Horwitz, Carl, 125, 127, 128, 129, 130, 131
House of Commons Library, 58, 63
House of Lords Record Office, 179
Housman, A. E., 32
Howard, Leslie, 87
Howard, Philip, 226, 231
Howard University, 159
Howlett, Jana: background, 275; on importance of archives to Russian government, 292; and Russian publications, 276, 279, 283, 284, 289, 291, 293, 294, 297, 300
Hughes, Ted, 315
Hull, University of, 58
Hunt, Herbert, 60–1
Hunt, Nelson Bunker, 60–1
Hurst, Marlene, 245
Husting Rolls of Deeds and Wills, 1252–1485, 346
Hutt, Charles, 15, 16–17, 25
Hyland, Jackie, 323
hypertext links, 262–3

IBM, 91
IDC *see* Inter-Documentation Company
IDIOM *see* In-Depth Indexing of Monographs
IFLA conferences, 200–1, *201*
Illinois in Urbana-Champaign, University of, 30, 31–3
Imperial War Museum, 119–20
In-Depth Indexing of Monographs (IDIOM), 203
Independent on CD-ROM, 195, 197
The Index of American Design, 77–82
Index to Manuscripts in the British Library, 121–3
Information Access Company, 302
Information for All, 312–15
Information Sub-Committee (ISC), 247–8
Innodata, 222–3, 235, 238, 269, *270*
INSEAD, 204
Institut de recherche et d'histoire des textes (IRHT), 141
Institute for Scientific Information (ISI), 247–8, 249
Institute for the Study of Social Change, 177–9
Institute of Directors, 103
insurance, 107–14, 213
Inter-Documentation Company (IDC), 232, 293, 339, 340
International Imaging (II) *see* Chadwyck-Healey Microform Publishing Services
International Institute of Social History, Amsterdam, 179, 278
Internet: Chadwyck-Healey move to Internet delivery, 261–7; funding to install in public libraries, 312–15
Inventaire des instruments de recherche: manuscrits occidentaux, 140
The Iran-Contra Affair: The Making of a Scandal, 1983–1988, 166–7
IRHT *see* Institut de recherche et d'histoire des textes
Irish Academic Press, 29
Irish University Press: at ALA, 7–8, *7*; history, 8, 10–11; influence on author, 10–12; *Nineteenth-Century British Parliamentary Papers*, xi, 8–10, 29, 54
Iron, David, 313
Irvine, Betty Jo, 82

ISC *see* Information Sub-Committee
ISI *see* Institute for Scientific Information
Israel, Nico, 7–8
ISTPART, 291

Jackson, Ian, 230
Jacoby, Kurt, 14–15, 16–17
Jamieson, Peter, 210
Jannidis, Fotis, 270
Japan: library agent practices, 57; Yushodo, 57–8, 97–9, 182–3, 193
Javitz, Romana, 78
Jeffs, Maia, 11, 13
Jeffs, Robin, 11, 12, 13
Jenkins, Nick, 5, 11
Jenkins, Sir Simon, 313–14, 317, 318
Jensen, Oliver, *111*
Jesus College, Cambridge, 291
Jewish National and University Library, 181
Jewish Studies, 279
JISC *see* Joint Information Systems Committee
Jobs, Steve, 189
Joe Louis Scrapbooks, 1935–1944, 155
Johansson, Eve, 55, 65
John F. Kennedy Presidential Library, 117
The John Maynard Keynes Papers in King's College, Cambridge, 181–2
John Murray archives, 20, 22
Johnson, Samuel, 229
Johnson, Thekla, 25
Johnson, Walter J., 3, 14–17, 20, 25, 29
Johnson Matthey, 344
Johnson Presidential Library, 117
Johnson Reprint Corporation, 3, 14–20, 25, 340
Joint Committee on Materials Research, 331–2
Joint Information Systems Committee (JISC), 225–6
Jolliffe, John, 99
Jolowicz, Leo, 14
Jones, Hywel, 47
Jones, John Paul, 176–7
Jones, Peter, 181
Jordan, Mark, 232, 234–5, 241
journals *see* periodicals and journals; *Periodicals Contents Index*

Jouve, 147, 205
Jouve software, 206, 207
Jovanovich, William, 17
JSTOR, 250–4

K. G. Saur, 147, 192, 340
Kafka, Franz, 271
Kahn, Richard, 279
Kansas, University of, 224
Karlin, Daniel 'Danny', 219, 220, 227
Karpel, Bernard, 79
Kasinec, Edward, 277
Kegan Paul, Trench, Trübner & Henry S. King archives, 22
Keillor, Garrison, 119
Keller, Michael, 247
Kelley, Augustus M., 18
Kelsall, Malcolm, 220
Kennedy Presidential Library, 117
Kent, Edward, Duke of, 307
Kent, University of, 202
Kent State Massacre (1970), 12
Kerle, Bridget, 327
Kerr, Clark, 2
Kerr, William T. 'Bill', 125, 127–8
Kerrigan, John, 257
keying *see* data conversion
Keynes, John Maynard, 180–2
Keynes, Lydia, 181
Kilgour, Frederick G., 92
King's College, Cambridge, 180–1
Kinokuniya, 57, 193, 300
Klasse, Alvaro, 153
Knight, Gerald, 195
KnowUK, 315–17
Kodak: and colour microfiche, 76–7, 79–80, 83; and early days of microfilm, 331; microfilming for Chadwyck-Healey, 39; microfilming for Johnson Reprint Corporation, 20; and tonal reproduction, 344
Kogan, Philip, 12
Kogan Page, 12
Korn, Eric, 193, 229–30
Korshin, Paul, 92–3, 94, 95–6
Kozlov, Vladimir, 279–83, 294, 298, 299, 302
Kraus, Hans P., 3
Kraus Reprint Corporation, 3, 29, 37, 340

Kruchenykh, Aleksei, 77
Kuester, Arend, 272
Kurz, Peter, *26*; background, 19; and *Index of American Design*, 79; at Johnson Reprint Corporation, 19, 25; at Somerset House, 27, 33
Kyte, Colin, 284

LA *see* Library Association
Labour Party Archives, 119
Labovitch, Clive, 1, 10, 13
Laker, Freddie, 33–4
land-use data, 209–14
Landry, Harold, 76–7
Lane, Anthony, 228–9, 230
Lange, Dorothea, 84
Larkin, Philip, 58
Latin American and Caribbean Statistical Serials, 1821–1982, 48, 49–50
Law, Derek, 200, 202, 225–6, 247–8, 254
Lawrence, Eileen, 323
layout sheets, 61
Leaders of the Russian Revolution, 276–7, 283, 285, 288–9, 291, 300
Leadership Directories, 238
Lealand, Conrad, 191–4
Lee-Smith, Edward, 279
Leeds, University of, 220
Leslie, Michael, 227
Levine, Mary, 75
Levine, Stuart, 77–8
La Librairie Honoré Champion, 148–9
Library Association (LA), 312, 313, 314
Library and Information Commission (LIC; formerly Library and Information Services Committee), 258, 312–15
library automation, 198–206
library catalogues *see* catalogues and cataloguing
library consortia, 225–6, 247–8, 250–4, 262, 266, 303–4, 308
Library Microfilm conferences, 115
Library of Congress, *111*; and *Archives of the Central Committee of the Soviet Communist Party*, 298; and *Black Literature*, 157–8; FSA collection, 83–6; HABS collection, 83, 85; Manuscript Division finding aids,

116, 117; and REMARC, 137, 173, 185, 198–203; Sanborn Maps collection, 107–14, 209–13, 214, 347; *see also* National Union Catalog of Manuscript Collections (*NUCMC*)
LIC *see* Library and Information Commission
Lietart, Frederic, *142*, 151
Lightbown, Ronald, 6
linguistics, 101
LION see Literature Online
Literary Taste, Culture and Mass Communication, 40–1
Literatura Femenina Española, 1500–1900, 152
literature: American, 257, 258, 264; black, 155–8; children's, 101; English, 181–2, 257–60, 264, 311, 330; French, 26–7, 148–9; German, 268–72; Spanish, 152, 153; women writers, 101; *see also English Poetry Full-Text Database*
Literature Online (*LION*), 154, 262–7
Little Leather Library, 333
Littlefield Adams, 29
Liveright, Horace, 333
Liverpool, University of, 56
Llewellyn, J. Bruce, 211, 214
The Local Authority Yearbook, 315, 316
Lockheed bribery scandals, 156
Lodge, Jean, 21
Logica, 312, 313
Lohf, Kenneth, 33
London: deeds and wills, 346; restaurants, 34, 258
London Library, 23, 220
London School of Economics (LSE), 35–6
Longman, 33, 171
L'Oréal, 140
Louis, Joe, 155
Louisiana, University of, 93, 129
Louisville, Kentucky, University of, 86
LSE *see* London School of Economics
Lunacharskii, E. L., 299
Luscombe, David, 237, 239
Luther, Martin, 271
Lymington, Viscount, 180
Lyndon Baines Johnson Presidential Library, 117

MacArthur Foundation, 164–5, 168
McCabe, James, 236
McCarthy, George L., 331
McCrae, Donald: background, 176; and Chadwyck-Healey sale, 322, 323, 325, 326; and CHF, 145–6, 150; and *English Poetry*, 231; and financial crisis, 305; and group finances and plans, 176; joins Chadwyck-Healey, 176; and MultiLIS, 204, 206; and The Quorum, 257; reporting systems, 305; and *Times* indexes, 309
McCrum, Robert, 317
MacDonald, Peter, 69–70
Macfarlane, Alan, 67
McFarlane, Robert, 166–7
McGinn, Howard, 129, 130
MacGregor, John, 71
McIlhenny, Ann, 21, 40
McIntyre, Bill, 70
Mackay, Charles, 227
Mackenzie, Norman, 35
Maclennan, Robert, 314
McMahon, James, 8
MacManus, Martin J., 8, 9, 10
Macmillan, 33, 324, 325
McNamara, Robert, 165–6
Maddox, Jerald 'Jerry' C., 85
MAID, 306
Maidment, Brian, 22
Maistre, Patrice de, 139–40
Malevich, Kazimir, 77
Mallaber, K. A. 'Ken', 51–3, 59, 63
Mallett, Robert, 102
Man About Town, 1
Management Today, 1
Manchester, University of, 58
Manuel de l'amateur de livres du XIXe siècle, 26
manuscript collections, indexes to, 121–4, 140
maps: cartographic publications on CD-ROM, 186–91; chloropleth, 187; and ERIC, 209–14; Sanborn, 107–14, 209–13, 214, 347
MARC cataloguing, 92, 95–6, 102, 198
maritime history, 6, 18
Markan, Inga, 298

marketing models *see* business and marketing models
Markov, Vladimir, 77
Marsh, Lynn, 153
Marshallsay, Diana, 53, 55, 57, 61, 65
Martin, Norbert, 239
Martov, Julius, 288–9
Maruzen, 14, 57, 193
Marx, Karl, 22
Mascorda, Carlos, 154
Massa, Paul, 172, 212
Massachusetts at Amherst, University of, 7
Massachusetts Institute of Technology (MIT), 248
Massey, Jack, 187–9, 190–1
Massey, Raymond, 87
Mater, Dwight, 326–7, 328–9, *328*
Maton, Chris, 327–8
Mattson, Walter, 128
Mayakovsky, Vladimir, 77
MCA *see* Microfilming Corporation of America
MCP Industries, 137
Mead Corporation, 128
Meckler, Alan, 28, 115, 125–6, 182
Medieval Studies, 67, 232–43
medicine, 185
Melbourne, University of, 114, 186–7
Mellon Foundation, 200, 203, 250–4
Memex, 338–9
Merritt, Sandy, 29, 40
Metcalf, Keyes D., 336
Meyersohn, Rolf, 40
Meyvaert, Paul, 242
MHRA *see* Modern Humanities Research Association
Michigan, University of, 254, 311
Michigan State University, 118
Micro Methods *see* E. P. Microform
Micro Photo, 336, 339
Microcard Corporation and Foundation, 334, 336
microcards, 334, 335, 336
Microfilming Corporation of America (MCA): and EGPP, 178; office and production facility, 125, 126, 128; ownership, 125, 340; sale, 125–34; and Sanborn Maps, 107–8

microform: citing microform publications, 86; decline in importance, 182; economics of microfilm vs microfiche production, 55; economics of publishing, 19; as forerunner of digital media, 338–9; original material's condition, 346–7; prejudice against microform editions, 177; presentation and storage of publications, 338–9, 345–6; pros and cons, xi, xii, 86, 337–9; publishing business model, 347–8; publishing history, 331–40; quality control, 348; reader printers, 346; readers, 78, 82, 337, 338–9, 346; technology, 341–8; use as alternative to book reprints, 3–4

CAMERAS: history of, 331, 331, 339; technology, 341–2, 343; used by Chadwyck-Healey, 77, 80, *142*, 151

FILM: colour, 80, 344; diazo, 42, 44, 345; for images, 344; silver halide, 42, 44, 60, 343–4; for tonal range, 85, 133; types, 42, 44, 343–5; vesicular, 345

MICROFICHE: colour, 76–7, 78–83; computer-output microfiche (COM), 97, 117, 274–5, 342–3; formats, 342–3; layout sheets, 61; origins and overview, 335; text fiche, 77–8; title-strips, 335, 337, 342

MICROFILM: captions, 338–9, 345; formats, 341–2; splicing, 75

MICROFILMING: card catalogues, 140, 151–2; colour, 73, 76–7, 78–83; lights, 80, 81, *142*, 342; page counts, 31–2; process, 31–2, 341–2, 343, 346–7; *see also* Chadwyck-Healey Microform Publishing Services

Microform Edition of the John Muir Papers, 177
Microform Review, 28
Microgen, 44, 343
Micromedia: Bell & Howell buys, 340; buys International Imaging, 44, 305, 326; and Parliamentary Papers, 54, 57; production for Chadwyck-Healey, 39–40, 42–5, 75; Reynolds visits, 320
MicroPatent, 144, 148, 206–9
microprints, 54, 334, 335

Migne, Abbé, 232–4, 236
Milburn, Matthew Marmaduke, 102
Mill, John Stuart, 8
Millennium Commission, 312–15
Miller, George, 97, 99–100
Miller, John, 187
Miller, Peter, 41–2, 76, 127, 172, 174–5, 176
Miller, Tim, 306–7
Milwaukee public library, 82
Mironenko, Sergei, 279, 296, 298, 299, 302
MIT *see* Massachusetts Institute of Technology
MLA International Bibliography, 264, 266
Modern English Poetry, 258, 264
Modern Library of the World's Best Classics, 333
Modern Humanities Research Association (MHRA), 264
Molotov, Vyacheslav, 277
MoMA *see* Museum of Modern Art, New York
Mondale, Joan, 82
Montaigne, Michel Eyquem de, 148–9
Moody, Jim, 162
Moon, Brenda, 199
Moore, James, 116
Mordaunt Crook, Joe, 19, 73
Morgan, Madel, 114
Morgan Grampian, 2, 20
mortgages, and pollution, 209–14
Moss (later Worthington), Alison, *246*; background, 67; and CD-ROMs, 186; and *English Poetry*, 217, 218, 222, 224, 231; and *Hansard*, 71; leaves Chadwyck-Healey, 319; and *LION*, 263; and Non-HMSO Catalogue, 67; and *PCI*, 249; and *PLD*, 237; and software development, 194, 260, 320
Mother Earth, 178
Muir, John, 177
Muller, Dieter, 46–7
Mullins, E. L. C., 28
MultiLIS, 145, 203–6
Mundocart, 189–90
Murdoch, Rupert, 310
Murray, John, 189–90, 210, 211
Museum of Modern Art, New York (MoMA), 344
music, 238, 317

The Music Index, 238
MVD, 299
Mydans, Carl, 84
Myers, Robin, 180

NADAL network, 204
Nagamouchi, Fayçal, 148
Nakov, A. B., 77
Nash, N. Frederick 'Fred', 31
National Archives, UK, 120; *see also* Public Record Office
National Archives, US, 116, 287, 335
National Art Library, 101–2, 133
National Defense Education Act (1958), 2
National Diet Library, 300
National Endowment for the Humanities (NEH), 92–3, 130, 156, 158, 177, 179
National Gallery of Art, Washington, DC, 78–9, 81, 82, 250
National Heritage, Department of (DNH) *see* Culture, Media and Sport, Department for
National Historical Publications and Records Commission (NHPRC), 176–7
National Inventory of Documentary Sources (*NIDS*), 115–20, 136
National Library of France *see* Bibliothèque nationale de France
National Library of New Zealand, 105
National Library of Scotland, 22, 142
National Library of Singapore, 202
National Library of Spain, 150–3, 154
National Library of Wales, 56, 199, 202
National Maritime Museum, 6
National Portrait Gallery, Washington, DC, 82–3
National Register of Archives (NRA), 115–16, 119, 120
National Research Center, 213
National Security Archive (NSA), 162–9
National Security Council, 165, 166
National Union Catalog of Manuscript Collections (*NUCMC*), 118; personal names index, 117, 123–4; subjects and corporate names index, 123–4
Naylor, Bernard, 55
NCBEL see New Cambridge Bibliography of English Literature

Neale, Ken, 170
Neato, 208–9
NEH *see* National Endowment for the Humanities
Nelson, Ronnie, 8
NetLibrary, 324
Netscape, 261
Neuberger, Rabbi Julia, 312
New Cambridge Bibliography of English Literature (NCBEL), 217
New Catalogue of UK Official Publications (NUKOP), 69–70
New South Wales, State Library of, 224
The New Statesman, 35
New York Public Library (NYPL): *Artists File*, 130–4, 344; book loans to Chadwyck-Healey, 49–50; and *English Poetry*, 224; holdings on the Soviet Union, 277; *Norman Thomas Papers*, 129; *Print File*, 130–4, 344; *Schomburg Clipping File*, 130–2, 133; Vandamm Collection, 87–8
New York restaurants, 212
New York Theater, 1919–1961, 87–8
The New York Times, 125–8, 311, 336
The New York Times Company, 125–8
New Zealand, 189
Newcastle-upon-Tyne, University of, 97
Newman, Francis William, 229
Newman, John Henry, Cardinal, 229
News International, 308, 309, 310–11
Newsbank, 340
newspapers: British Library holdings, 229; Burney Collection, 48–9, 347; on CD-ROM, 194–7, 309; microfilming, 336; *The New York Times*, 125–8, 311, 336; online, 197; *Times* indexes and scanned edition, 307–11
Newton, Sir Isaac, 180–1
NeXt, 189
NHPRC *see* National Historical Publications and Records Commission
NIDS *see* National Inventory of Documentary Sources
Nineteenth-Century British Parliamentary Papers (IUP) *see* Irish University Press: *Nineteenth-Century British Parliamentary Papers*

Nineteenth Century microfiche programme, 99–106
Nineteenth-Century Parliamentary Papers (Chadwyck-Healey): financing, 54–8, 59–60; genesis and overview, xi, 53–62; guide and subject catalogue, 61–2; libraries' original holdings, 10, 53; production, 43–4, 58–9, 347–8; source material, 8–9
Nineteenth Century Short Title Catalogue (NSTC), 96–101
Nitta, Hisaku, *98*
Nitta, Mitsuo, 57–8, 97–9, *98*, 193
NKVD, 289, 297, 299
Non-HMSO Catalogue *see* Catalogue of British Official Publications Not Published by HMSO
Norman Ross Publishing, 173
Norman Thomas Papers, 129, 131, 132
North, Oliver, 166–7
North East London Polytechnic, 58
Northwestern University, 32–3
Norton Rose, 279, 284
Notre Dame, University of, 232, 235–6
Nottinghamshire County Library, 58
novels *see* fiction
Novosibirsk Regional Archives, 298
Nowell-Smith, Simon, 23–4, 30
NRA *see* National Register of Archives
NRC Insurance Services, 213
NSA *see* National Security Archive
NSTC *see* Nineteenth Century Short Title Catalogue
NUCMC *see* National Union Catalog of Manuscript Collections
NUKOP *see* New Catalogue of UK Official Publications
Nutt, David, 18
NYPL *see* New York Public Library

Obama, Barack, 161
Observer on CD-ROM, 195, 197
Oceana Publications, 51, 53, 54
OCLC *see* Ohio College Library Center
OCR *see* Optical Character Recognition
Odier, Jeanne, 138
OECD *see* Organisation for Economic Co-operation and Development
The Official Index to the Times, 308–11

official publications: *Hansard*, 70–2; HMSO catalogues, 50–3; Non-HMSO Catalogue, 65–9; *Reports from Committees of the House of Commons*, 24; statistics, 39–40, 47–50; *UKOP*, 69–70; *see also* Nineteenth-Century Parliamentary Papers; Parliamentary Papers
official statistical serials, 39–40, 47–50
Ohio College Library Center (OCLC), 92, 105, 194, 202
oil crisis (1979–80), 59
O'Neal, Hank, 86
O'Neill, George and Abby, 301
O'Neill, T. P., 8
Online Computer Systems, 143, 192
Online conferences, London, 70, *196*, 197, 264, 311
online publications: business models, xii–xiii, 243, 254–5, 262, 304–7; Chadwyck-Healey's move to online delivery, 260–7; effect on revenues and business models, 304–7; monitoring data usage, 263, 267; traditional mainframe publications, 68–9, 215–16
Open Text Latitude Web server software, 264
Open University, 58
opisi: definition, 278–9
Optical Character Recognition (OCR), 308, 311
Organisation for Economic Co-operation and Development (OECD) Library, 204
O'Rourke, Tony, 269, 272, 323
Otlet, Paul, 331
OUP *see* Oxford University Press
Ovid, 196, 215, 216
Oxford, University of, 119, 201, 225; *see also* St Anthony's College
Oxford Companions series, 265
Oxford English Dictionary, 267
Oxford Microform Publications, 340
Oxford Text Archive, 219
Oxford University Press (OUP), 24, 192, 265, 267

Palm, Charles, *284*; and *Archives of the Central Committee of the Soviet Communist Party*, 277–87, 289–300, 301; background, 178–9; positions held by, 178–9, 273, 277; and *The Soviet Biographic Archive*, 273–4
Palm, Miriam, 178, 273, 275
Palmer, Beverly, 176
Palmer, Maria del Carmen Simón, 152
Palmer, Samuel, 307
Palmer's Full Text Online, 1785–1870, 309–11
Palmer's Index to the Times, 226, 307–8, 309
Papers of Charles Sumner, 176–7
Papers of John Paul Jones, 176–7
Papers of Martin Van Buren, 176–7
Papers of the Congress of Racial Equality, 1941–1967, 133
Paragon, 121–2
Paris Exposition (1937), 332–3
Parker, A. G., 54–5
Parker, Ralph, 92
Parks, Gordon, 84
Parliamentary Online Indexing System (POLIS), 63
Parliamentary Papers: 1900–75, 62; current, xi, 62–4; Readex edition, 10, 54, 335; *see also* Irish University Press: *Nineteenth-Century British Parliamentary Papers*; *Nineteenth-Century Parliamentary Papers*; *UK Parliamentary Papers*
Parsons, Kenneth A. C., 57
parts catalogues, 337
PatentImages, 207, 208
patents, 206–9
Patrologia Graeca, 243
Patrologia Latina Database (*PLD*): origins, 232–5; overview, 232–43; production, 235–8; reception and sales, 143, 154, 238–43
Patten, Jo, 42
Payne, Waveney, 5
Payne Loving Trust, 240
PCI see Periodicals Contents Index
Peatross, Ford, 83
Pei, I. M., 79
Pemberton, John, 65
Penguin, 317

People of Today, 315, 316
Percy, Thomas, 220
Pergamon Press, 340
periodicals and journals: contents page information, 144; microfilming backruns, 336–7; origins of reprint industry, 3
Periodicals Archives Online, 255
Periodicals Contents Index (PCI): and JSTOR, 250–4; online, 254–5; origins, 244–6; overview, 244–55; production, 238, 246–50; sales, 154, 226, 247–50, 254
Perris, William, 108
Personnel and Government, 70
Petroconsultants, 189–90
Pevsner, Nikolaus, 317
PFIs *see* Private Finance Initiatives
Phillips, Andrew, 49
Phillips, Rodney, 224
Philosopher's Index, 216
photography, 83–9, 130–4
Piala, Vanessa, 88
Pibworth, Andy, 80, 344
Pickering, Sir Edward, 310, 311
Pikhoia, Rudolf, *284*; and Chadwyck-Healey's and Hoover's Russian publications, 276–85, 289–96, 300; dacha, 293; meets Howlett, 275; positions held by, 276, 292, 293, 294; resigns as head of Rosarkhiv, 295
piracy, 262–3, 267
plays *see* theatre
PLD *see* Patrologia Latina Database
Plumb, J. H., 35
PMS Publications, 71
Pocock, Stephen, *246*; background, 221; and Chadwyck-Healey sale, 323; and *English Poetry*, 221, 224; and *LION*, 263; and *PLD*, 236, 241–2
poetry: *African-American Poetry*, 258; *American Poetry*, 257; *English Poetry Plus*, 258; *Faber Poetry Library*, 258–60, 264; French, 149; German, 271; *Modern English Poetry*, 258, 264; *see also English Poetry Full-Text Database; Literature Online*
Pofcher, Munroe, 322–3
Poindexter, John, 166–7

Police and Constabulary Almanac, 317
POLIS *see* Parliamentary Online Indexing System
Politburo, 289, 292, 301
Politique et Société, La France des années 80, 144
Politique et Société, La France des années Mitterand, 144
Pollard and Redgrave *see A Short Title Catalogue of Books Printed in England, Scotland and Ireland and of English Books Printed Abroad, 1475 to 1640*
pollution, 209–14
Poole's Index, 244, 245
Popova, Tamara, 289
Pordes, Henry, 308
Portraits of Americans, 82–3
Portsmouth Papers, 180–1
Potter, George, 11, 32, 115
Potts, Robert, 228
Power, Eugene, xiv, 330, 333, 336, 339
Poynter, John, 187
Pratt, Dana, 85, 107, *111*
Pratt, David, 40, 54
Pre-Raphaelites, 24
preservation *see* conservation and preservation
presidential libraries, US, 117
Prickett, Dan, 211–12, 213, 214
Primary Source Media (PSM; formerly Research Publications), 308–9, 310–11, 321, 322, 324
Princeton University, 38
Print File, 130–4, 344
printing: plastic plates, 19; unions, 29
Private Finance Initiatives (PFIs), 318
PRO *see* Public Record Office
ProQuest *see* Bell & Howell Information & Learning
PSM *see* Primary Source Media
Public Figures in the Soviet Union, 274–5
public libraries: and the Internet, 312–15; and *KnowUK*, 315–17
Public Record Office (PRO; later the National Archives), 120, 136, 287
publishers' archives *see The Archives of British Publishers*
Publishers Association Electronic Publishing Committee, 319–20

publishing history, 101, 180
Publishing History, 35
Puttnam, David, Lord, 318

quality control, 348
Quebec, University of, 206
Queen's Award for Export Achievement, 173, 270
Questa Media, 324
Quick, John, 300

race issues *see* Black Studies
Radford, Tim, 226–7
Radio Free Europe/Radio Liberty, 273–5
Raisian, John, 287–8
Rappaport, Fred, 16, 19
Ratcliffe, Fred, 200, 226, 320
Rawles, Jim, 44
Ray, Gordon N., 31
Readex, 10, 26, 54, 333–4, 335–6, 340
Reagan, Ronald, 10, 167
Reclams Universalbibliothek, 271
RECON project, 203
Recordak, 331, 336
Records of an English Village. Earls Colne, 67
Records of the Stationers' Company, 1554–1920, 180
Redgrave, Gilbert R. *see A Short Title Catalogue of Books Printed in England, Scotland and Ireland and of English Books Printed Abroad, 1475 to 1640*
Reed Elsevier (RTIS), 147
Reeves, Ruth, 78
Reichman, Else, 136
Reitman, Ben, 178
Reliques of Ancient English Poetry, 220
REMARC, 137, 173, 185, 198–203
Remington Rand, 331, 336
Renfrew, Colin, 291
Reports from Committees of the House of Commons, 1715–1801, 24
Research Libraries Group (RLG), 118
Research Publications (later Primary Source Media): and Burney Collection, 49; buys Harvester Press, 175; and CHF, 147; and *ESTC*, 94, 95, 100, 101, 221; foundation, 339; and MARC cataloguing, 102; and newspapers, 194; and the NSA, 164, 168; ownership, 340; and patents, 207; and sale of MCA, 128; and Soviet archives, 281, 283–4, 286; UK presence, 339; *see also* Primary Source Media
Reynolds, Joe, 320, 325, 327, *328*
RGANI *see* TsKhSD
RGASPI *see* RTsKhIDNI
Rhind-Tutt, Stephen: Alexander Street Press sold by, 340; background, 303; and board meetings, 149, 319; Chadwyck-Healey Inc. under, 307; and Chadwyck-Healey sale, 322, 323, 324, 326, 328; joins Chadwyck-Healey, 303; and *LION*, 264, 266; place in group reporting structure, 232
Richard, Stephen, 55, 65, 66
Richard Bentley archives, 30–3
Richards archives *see* Grant Richards archives
Richardson, Denis, 186–7
Richnell, D. T. 'Don', 32, 93, 103
Rider, Fremont, 334, 336
Rietdyk, Ron, 216
Ring, Richard, 224
Rix, Tim, 33, 171, 322–3
RLG *see* Research Libraries Group
RLIN, 118
Roberts, Julian, 48, 96
Robinson, Frank, 96–100
Robinson, Jennifer, 100
Rockefeller Foundation, 179, 332–3
Rodriguez, Mercedes, 151, 153, 328
Roesemann, Doug, 237, 239, 250, 264, 302
Rogers, Charles, 66
Romero, Archbishop Oscar, 166
Ronaldson, Chris, 39, 44, 320
Roncato, Janine, 136, 137, 201
Roots, Ivan, 11
Rosarkhiv, 279, 281, 283, 288, 291–2, 293–9
Rosskam, Edwin and Louise, 84
Rothstein, Arthur, 84
Routledge, Roberta, 36
Routledge & Kegan Paul, 22, *23*
Roy Stryker Papers, 1912–1972, 86, 129

Royal College of Physicians, 119
Royal Library, Copenhagen, 105, 239
Royal Statistical Society, 48
Rozkuszka, W. David, 10
RTIS *see* Reed Elsevier
RTsKhIDNI (later RGASPI), 279, 292, 294, 296
Rubin, Burt: author meets, 28; and Chadwyck-Healey sale, 324, 326, 327, 329; and Chadwyck-Healey's attempted sale to Elsevier, 172; and ERIC, 211–12
Ruskin, John, 22
Russell, Bertrand, 181
Russia: economy and Yeltsin government, 291–2, 293; *see also* Soviet Union
The Russia House, 300
Russian Academy of Sciences Library (BAN), 275–6
Russian publications: *Leaders of the Russian Revolution*, 276–7, 283, 285, 288–9, 291, 300; *Public Figures in the Soviet Union*, 274–5; *Russian Futurism*, 76–7; *The Soviet Biographic Archive*, 273–4; *see also* Archives of the Central Committee of the Soviet Communist Party
Russon, David, 247
Ryan, Mike, 127
Rykwert, Joseph, 25

S. Fischer, 271, 272
SAA *see* Society of American Archivists
SAGE Publishing, 340
St Andrews, University of, 202, 221
St Anthony's College, Oxford, 77
Saint Martin's Press, 86
St Paul's Bibliographies, 180
Sakoun, Aline, 146
Sakoun, Jean-Pierre, 146–50, 205
Salzburg Centre for Research on the Early English Novel (SCREEN), 258
Samuel Gompers and the American Federation of Labor, 129
Sanborn, D. A., 108
Sanborn Fire Insurance Maps, 107–14, 209–13, 214, 347
Sanderson, Michael, 6, 18
SARA law (1986), 209

Sarkozy, Nicolas, 140
satirical prints *see* cartoons and satirical prints
Saur *see* K. G. Saur
Saur, Klaus, 340
Savers, Ann, 237, 250
Saztec, 191–4, 222
scanning, 308, 309–11
Schiller, Friedrich, 271
Schoen, Dena, 283, 284
Scholefield, Stephen, 189
Schomburg Clipping File, 130–2, 133, 155
Schonfeld, Roger, 251–2, 253–4
schools editions: *English Poetry Plus*, 258; *KnowUK*, 317; *LION*, 267; newspapers on CD-ROM, 195; UK Censuses, 190; *World Climate Disc*, 191
Scialom, Nane, 135, 136
Scolar Press, 27, 51
Scott, Lloyd M., 15, 16
SCREEN *see* Salzburg Centre for Research on the Early English Novel
searching: full-text, 196–7; hypertext links, 262–3; proximity, 196–7; relevancy, 197
Second World War (1939–45), 334–5
Secord, Richard, 166–7
selling: brochures, 6, 32, 37–8; phone sales, 38; sales tours, 38; timing, 38; *see also* business and marketing models
Senate House Library, 225
Severtson, Susan, *183*, *246*; background, 173; and *Black Biographical Dictionaries*, 159; blue-sky thinking conference organized by, 215–17; and *Emma Goldman Papers*, 179; and ERIC, 210; and IDIOM, 203; joins Chadwyck-Healey, 173, 176; leaves Chadwyck-Healey, 237; and MicroPatent, 206; and *Mundocart*, 189; and *PCI*, 244, 245, 246; place in group reporting structure, 232; and *PLD*, 232, 235, 236–7; and REMARC, 200; and Supermap, 188
SGML *see* Standard Generalized Markup Language
Shaffer, Norman J., 110
Shahn, Ben, 84

Shakespeare, William, 4–5, 7, 257
Shanks, Robert, 279
Shaw, George Bernard, 22, 32
Shaw, Ralph, 338
Sheffield, University of, 237
Shellenberg, T. S., 333
Sherren, Graham, 20
Shils, Edward, 40
Shimmon, Ross, 314
A Short Title Catalogue of Books Printed in England, Scotland and Ireland and of English Books Printed Abroad, 1475 to 1640 (STC), 91, 332, 333, 337
Shulman, Alix Kates, 178
silver halide film *see* microform: film
Silverman, Kenneth, 118
SilverPlatter, 144, 196, 215, 216, 249, 264, 306
Sir Isaac Newton: Manuscripts and Papers, 180–1
Sir John Soane's Museum, 73
Skyrme, Pat, 21, 30
Slaine, Mason, 208
Sloan, Tony, 118–19
Slutzky, David, 209–12
Smethurst, Michael, 104, 160
Smith, Chris, 314
Smithsonian Institution Archives, 116
Snoeker, Rudolph 'Rud', 170, 172, 173
Snyder, Henry L., 93–4, 95
Soane Museum *see* Sir John Soane's Museum
Sobeco, 203, 204, 205, 206
Société des Bollandistes, 243
Society of American Archivists (SAA) conferences, 119
software: Chadwyck-Healey's own software for CD-ROM publications, 147, 148, 247; client–server, 260–1; hiring of developers, 194; for Internet delivery, 264; MS-DOS vs Windows, 71, 197; as selling point for CD-ROMs, 216; for SGML texts, 219, 223, 227, 235, 240; third-party suppliers for CD-ROM publications, 143, 189, 192, 197, 206, 207
Solomon, Todd, 222–3, 238
Somerset House *see* Chadwyck-Healey group: Chadwyck-Healey Inc.

Southampton, University of, 8, 9, 53, 55, 69–70
The Soviet Biographic Archive, 1954–1985, 273–4
Soviet Union: collapse, 276; public opening of archives, 280, 281–2, *282*; *see also* Russia; Russian publications
space race, 1, 2
Space Time Research (STR), 187–9, 190–1
Spanish National Bibliography, 152
Spanish Theatre of the Golden Age, 153–4
Spanish Women Writers, 1500–1900, 152
Sparks, Peter, 110
Sperberg-McQueen, Michael, 219, 223, 235
Spiers, John, 175, 339
SPINDEX, 116–17
splicing, 75
Sproat, Iain, 312
Sputnik, 1, 2
Stam, David H., 101
Standard Generalized Markup Language (SGML): and *English Poetry*, 218, 219, 221–3; and *Goethe*, 269; and *PLD*, 235–6; and scanned texts, 311; Text Encoding Initiative, 219
Stanford University, 10, 39–40, 273, 275
Starling, Reuben, 290
State Historical Society of Wisconsin, 129
Stationers' Company, 180
The Stationery Office (TSO), 69; *see also* Her Majesty's Stationery Office
statistics *see* official statistical serials
STC *see A Short Title Catalogue of Books Printed in England, Scotland and Ireland and of English Books Printed Abroad, 1475 to 1640*
Steele, Lina, 79, 81
Stephens, Frederic, 74
Stern, Josianne, 139, 146
Stern, Laurence, 162–3
Stern, Philippe, 139, 146
Stern, William, 10
Stewart, Ruth Ann, 131–2
STR *see* Space Time Research
Strachey, Lytton, 181–2
Streisand, Barbra, 168
Strong, Roy, 6
Stroud, Dorothy, 73

Stryker, Roy, 84–5, 86, 129
subscriptions: partner subscriptions, 54–6, 62, 112; timing of invoices, 174
Sufrin, Les: advice re undercapitalization, 305–6; author meets, 28; and *Black Literature*, 157; and Chadwyck-Healey sale, 322–3, 326; and Chadwyck-Healey's attempted sale to Elsevier, 170–1, 172; and ERIC, 211; role as advisor, 41; and sale of MCA, 125, 127
Suhler, John, 306
Sulzberger, Punch, 125, 128
Summerson, Sir John, 73
Summit, Roger, 68
Sumner, Charles, 176–7
Sunday Times, 196, 309
Supermap, 187–9, 190–1
Surridge, R. G., 53
Sutherland, John, 101, 229
Swan Sonnenschein archives, 22
Sweeney, Matthew, 265
Swinnerton-Dyer, Sir Peter, 59, 320
Sydney, University of, 186
SymbolGreek, 240

Tarasov, V. P., 280, 281
Tate, Vernon D., 336
Taylor, Bill, 4–5
Taylor, Ian, 314
Taylor, John, 260, 267, 320
Taylor, Miles, 62
Tchemerzine, Avenir, 26
Teatro Español del Siglo de Oro, 153–4
Telegraph on CD-ROM, 195
Telford, Thomas, 8
Texas at Austin, University of, 117
Text Creation Partnership, 311
Thatcher, Margaret, 59
theatre, 18–19, 87–8, 153–4, 257, 258, 271; *see also* Shakespeare, William
Theatrum Redivivum, 18–19
theology, 232–43, 271
Thesaurus Linguae Graecae, 218
theses, 336
Thomas, George R., 87
Thomas, Norman, 129, 131, 132
Thomas Nelson, 8
Thomson Organisation: and Chadwyck-Healey sale, 321, 324, 325, 326, 327; companies owned by, 8, 202–3, 207; and REMARC, 202; and sale of *The Times*, 309
'Three Day Week', 28–9
3i Group, 325
Tiger Files, 210, 212
The Times: on CD-ROM, 195, 196, 197, 309; indexes to, 226, 307–11; scanned edition, 309–11
Times Literary Supplement index, 265
Times Newspapers, 308, 309
Tinkham, Sandy Shaffer, *183*; and *Index of American Design*, 81; joins Chadwyck-Healey, 81; and *NIDS*, 116; overview of Chadwyck-Healey work, 33, 89; reduced role taken by, 118–19; and Sanborn, 107–8, 113
Tiuneev, Vladimir A., 294, 296, 297, 298
Tombeur, Paul, 240–1, 242
Toronto, University of, 224
Torrington, F. W. 'Bill', 54, 57
Tracy, Peter, 206–9
Trade and Industry, Department of (DTI): Library, 51–2, 58–9, 63
Trickey, Kevin V., 228
Trollope, Anthony, 8
Trotsky, Leon, 277
TRW, 211, 212
Tryon, Roy H., 118
TsGAOR *see* GARF
TsKhSD (later RGANI), 279, 283, 288, 292, 294, 296
TSO *see* The Stationery Office
Tulleken, Kit van, 323
Tullo, Carol, 72
Turner, Michael, 35
Tyacke, Sarah, 244

UCLA *see* California, University of: Los Angeles
UK: attitude to entrepreneurs, 52–3; censuses, 190–1; public libraries and the Internet, 312–15; university funding, 3, 59
The UK National Medical Slide Bank, 185
UK Parliamentary Papers, xi, 62–4
UKOP *see* Catalogue of United Kingdom Official Publications

UMI *see* University Microfilms International
Unisys, 318
universities: funding, 2-3, 12, 59, 182; library acquisition methods, 3
University College, London, 225
University Microfilms International (UMI; formerly University Microfilms): ambitions for eighteenth-century STC, 93; as Chadwyck-Healey competitor, 215, 339; and digitization, 311; and *ESTC*, 94, 95; foundation and history, 333, 336-7; and JSTOR, 253, 254; and MARC cataloguing, 102; and *The New York Times*, 128; ownership, 320, 340; and sale of MCA titles, 129; sales penetration, 304; schools version of *LION* sold by, 267; UK presence, 339
University Publications of America (UPA), 164, 165, 173
Unsworth, Mike, 118
Unterberg, Tommy, 212
Unterberg Towbin, 212-13
Unwin, Rayner, 22
UPA *see* University Publications of America
US Army in Europe, 202
US Patent Office (USPTO), 206-7
USA: censuses, 187-9; as Chadwyck-Healey market, 38; Great Depression, 83-6; library budgets, 2-3, 12, 182; oil crisis, 59; Westward expansion, 129
USSR *see* Russia; Russian publications; Soviet Union
UTLAS, 202-3

V Mail, 335
Vachon, John, 84
Vaisey, David, 120, 160
Value Added Tax (VAT), 24-5
Van Buren, Martin, 176-7
Van Damm, Vivian, 87
van Dijk *see* Bureau Marcel van Dijk
Vandamm, Florence, 87-8
Vandamm Collection, 87-8
Veronis, Suhler & Associates, 306, 323, 324, 325, 326-7
vesicular film *see* microform: film

Vicaire, Georges, 26
Victor, Ed, 258
Victoria and Albert Museum, 101-2, 133
videodisks, 182, 185
Vietnam War (1955-75), 12
Virago, 36-7
VISTA Information Solutions, 213-14
Volkogonov, Dmitri, 289
Volkova, Natalia, 276, 279, 283, 284, 290, 297
Voltaire, 128, 150, 268

Waagen, Gustav Friedrich, 6
Wales, University of, 56
Waley, Daniel, 31, 32, 121, 122
Wallis, Peter, 93, 96-7
Walter J. Johnson, 14, 17, 25
Wardroper, John, 103-4
Warner, Robert, 99
Watson, Thomas J. Jr, 92
Watt, James, 30
Webb, Beatrice: diaries, 35-7
Webb, Sidney, 35
Weinberger, Caspar, 166-7
Welbourn, Roy, 200
Wells, S. Greeley, 111
Wesleyan University, 334
West, Lucy Fisher, 176-7
wet letter books, 30
Wheatley, Phillis, 155
Wheeler, Barbara, 15
Whitaker's Almanac, 317
White, Andrew, 273
Who's Who, 315-16
Who Was Who, 315-16
Wilde Sapte, 327
Willard, Charles, 239
William Blackwood archives, 22
Willison, Ian, 23, 93
Wilson, Alex, 122
Wilson, Duncan, 312, 313
Wilstar Securities, 10
Winchell, Constance, 48, 51
Wing, Donald, 91
Wisconsin Progressives, 129
Withey, Richard, 308-10
Woerner Report, 166
Wolcott, Marion Post, 84
Wolf, Leo, 135

Wolfson Foundation, 200
Wolk, L. J. van der, 335, 339
Wollongong, University of, 224–5
Wolter, John, 107–8, 112
Women's Studies: black women writers, 155, 158; *Emma Goldman Papers*, 177–9; *Gerritsen Collection*, 330; women writers, 101, 152
Wood, Thor, 88
Woolf, Virginia, 181
Works Projects Administration (WPA), 78–83
World Climate Disc, 191
Worthington, Alison *see* Moss, Alison
Worthington, David, 67, 319

Woudhuysen, H. R., 104
Wright, Hazel, 67

Xerox Corporation, 337

Yahuda, Abraham, 181
Yale University, 38, 247
Yeltsin, Boris, 276, 283, 288, 291–2
Yushodo, 57–8, 97–9, 182–3, 193

Zayas, Maria de, 152
Zboray, Ron, 178
Zimmerman, Bob, 327, *328*
Zola, Émile, 138
Zorza, Victor, 274